LATIN AMERICA'S COLD WAR

LATIN AMERICA'S COLD WAR

HAL BRANDS

HARVARD UNIVERSITY PRESS

Cambridge, Massachusetts, and London, England

2010

Library of Congress Cataloging-in-Publication Data

Brands, Hal, 1983–
    Latin America's Cold War / Hal Brands.
      p. cm.
    Includes bibliographical references and index.
    ISBN 978-0-674-05528-5
      1. Latin America—History—1948–1980. 2. Latin America—
History—1980– 3. Latin America—Politics and government—1948–1980.
4. Latin America—Politics and government—1980– 5. Latin America—Foreign
relations—1948–1980. 6. Latin America—Foreign relations—1980– 7. Cold
War—Influence. 8. World politics—1945–1989. I. Title.
    F1414.2B693   2010
    980.03—dc22   2010006742

Contents

Introduction

At the level of superpower relations, the Cold War was remarkable for its stability. Although the United States and the Soviet Union were locked in ideological and geopolitical struggle for more than four decades, they never directly engaged each other in armed conflict. The massive nuclear stockpiles accumulated for this eventuality went unused, and when the Cold War came to a close, it did so not in an apocalyptic spasm of violence, but in a transition less bloody or disruptive than nearly anyone had thought possible. Viewed from this angle, the Cold War was indeed a "long peace."[1]

In the Third World, by contrast, it was more like a "long war." The Cold War was an era of febrile volatility in the developing countries, as East–West struggles mixed with unstable local politics to promote polarization and bloodshed. An essential stasis governed relations between Moscow and Washington during the Cold War, but violence, conflict, and upheaval prevailed in the global south.[2]

Latin America was in some respects a Third-World outlier—most of the region had been independent for more than a century before the end of World War II touched off decolonization in Asia and Africa—but it nonetheless fit squarely within this pattern. The postwar period, and especially the three decades following the Cuban revolution in 1959, saw internal and external turmoil become near-permanent features of Latin American affairs. Superpower rivalry, foreign intervention, and inter-American diplomatic strife dominated Latin America's external relations; ideological polarization, rapid swings between dictatorship and democracy, and acute internal violence constituted the essential features of its domestic politics. Conflict unfolded on multiple levels; crises came rapidly in succession. In Latin America as throughout the Third World, the Cold War was a period of intense and often bloody upheaval.[3]

Trauma and carnage attract attention, and there is no shortage of scholarship on Latin America during the Cold War. Historians have produced an immense corpus of literature on U.S. policy and Latin American politics, culture, and society.[4] A smaller number of writers have explored the Soviet and Cuban presence in the region, while others have pursued a fuller understanding of the interaction between global currents and local events.[5]

These studies are quite valuable as far as they go. Yet if the literature is vast, it is also fragmentary. Most scholarship by U.S. diplomatic historians focuses on the view from Washington, as is the case with even the best accounts of U.S.–Latin American affairs. There are studies that bring a multiarchival, international perspective to various aspects of the Cold War in Latin America—works by Jonathan Haslam, Greg Grandin, Tanya Harmer, William Robinson, and John Dinges rank among the most important—but such an approach has yet to be applied to this period as a whole.[6]

Fortunately, the time is ripe for such an undertaking. The past fifteen years have witnessed a profusion of new sources on Latin America and the Cold War. Archives have opened throughout the region, as well as in the United States, Europe, and the former Soviet bloc. These repositories contain documents that shed light on a broad range of issues: Latin American governance and statecraft; U.S., Cuban, and Soviet policies; right- and left-wing violence; and the texture of regional politics, society, and economy. The archives remain shuttered in some countries, and we still lack detailed information on many aspects of this period. Yet the material that has emerged is of immense value. In conjunction with the existing literature, these records make it possible to tell a fuller, better-integrated story of Latin America's Cold War than has heretofore been possible.

That is the purpose of this study. Drawing on archival and documentary sources from more than a dozen countries, as well as the relevant scholarship, I seek to reconstruct the history of Latin America's Cold War in a way that is both multinational and multilayered: multinational in that it deals seriously with all sides of the diplomatic and transnational struggles that occurred during this period; multilayered in that it integrates perspectives from several diverse realms—from the highest echelons of superpower diplomacy to the everyday negotiation of social and political relationships—into an understanding of how the global, the regional, and the local interacted in shaping Latin America's Cold War.

That conflict—or rather that collection of conflicts—began with the introduction of Cold War tensions into Latin America following World War II, but would take on peak intensity only after the Cuban revolution in 1959. During the fifteen years prior to Fidel Castro's triumphant march into Havana, Latin America became the focus of several convergent crises: intensifying internal strife, characterized by a seesawing of political arrangements in the 1940s and 1950s; inter-American diplomatic discord, heightened by Washington's policies during the early Cold War; the ideological ferment occasioned by decolonization and the emergence of the Third World; and the escalating U.S.–Soviet competition for mastery in the global south. These dynamics flowed together during the late 1950s, creating a fluid, volatile situation.

Castro's revolt reverberated strongly within this context. The Cuban revolution exacerbated anti-Americanism and *tercermundismo* ("Third-Worldism") within Latin America, led to a precipitous escalation of superpower competition in the region, and magnified the militancy of both Left and Right. Perhaps most important, it gave these crises a single nexus, fusing them together in the policies and ideological influence of revolutionary Cuba. Over the next three decades, the interaction between these issues ensured the relentless intensity of Latin America's Cold War.

This effect was clearly evident in the 1960s. Insurgencies informed by domestic grievances and energized by the Cuban example waged destructive campaigns throughout Central and South America. Internal instability fostered external meddling: Cuba, the United States, and the Soviet Union competed fiercely to manage or exploit this turmoil and guide the evolution of Latin American society. Havana and Moscow forged a military alliance and aided the region's various guerrilla groups, while Washington unveiled a vast economic program—the Alliance for Progress—and deployed counterinsurgency, covert action, and direct military intervention to thwart the radical Left.

These initiatives had profound effects on regional affairs—effects that were often much different than their creators had intended. Castro, Ernesto "Che" Guevara, and Soviet premier Nikita Khrushchev failed parlously to stir revolution in Latin America, or even to make Cuba an attractive example of socialist development. U.S. officials claimed these outcomes as victories, but

Washington's policies were little more successful than those of its rivals. The ideological contradictions inherent in the Alliance for Progress frustrated that initiative, as did Latin American resistance to the reforms that program entailed. Counterinsurgency, covert action, and military intervention seemed to compile a better record, but caused a severe ideological and diplomatic backlash. During the early 1960s superpower and Cuban officials had dreamed of transforming Latin America; by the close of that decade, they were left to contain the fallout from their own ambitions.

That blowback was a key factor in ensuring that Latin America did not achieve stability through the demise of the guerrilla challenge, but merely moved from one crisis to another. During the 1960s a mix of ideological, social, and political influences propelled Latin America toward even greater upheaval. A collection of concepts known as National Security Doctrine underlay a spree of coups and foretold the ascendancy of the assertive, ideologically driven military regime; liberation theology and urban unrest informed a widespread growth of popular protest; and the emergence of dependency theory augured heightened North–South conflict in hemispheric diplomacy. These diverse currents forged the various resentments and anxieties at play in the region into more potent, ideological form, and from the late 1960s onward they grated against one another in increasingly incendiary fashion.

The tensions of the 1960s drove the diplomatic upheaval and rising body counts of the decade that followed. During the early 1970s dueling Left and Right extremisms collided in the Southern Cone. An urban guerrilla movement, guided by theorists like Abraham Guillén and Carlos Marighella, launched a serious challenge to internal order in Argentina and Uruguay, using violence and sabotage to erode the social, political, and economic fabric of those countries. When added to the rise of a socialist government under Salvador Allende in Chile, the insurgents' successes raised the possibility that revolutionary change might be the order of the day.

This was not to be; advances by the Left set the stage for a devastating response by the Right. The guerrillas were destroyed amid the popular disillusion, economic chaos, and military radicalization that their rise occasioned, while Allende's administration fell as a result of its own errors, an inability to restrain the most radical sectors of the governing coalition, and the not-so-covert machinations of the Nixon administration. Radical change came to South America, not as the result of revolutionary triumphs, but as an outcome of military coups and counterrevolutionary "dirty wars."

The course of the urban guerrilla movement mirrored the trajectory of a concurrent, though less bloody, attack on the status quo: the Latin American diplomatic challenge of the early 1970s. The global shifts of this period—the emergence of détente, the U.S. defeat in Vietnam, the breakdown of the Bretton Woods system of international finance, and the oil shocks of 1973–1974—promoted a pronounced feeling of empowerment among many Latin American officials. The West and the United States were in decline, they calculated; the Third World was on the rise. This optimism, combined with the leftover resentment from the U.S. interventions of the 1960s and the need to channel intensifying domestic strains outward, led a broad group of Latin American statesmen to mount a sustained challenge to existing patterns of regional affairs. Diplomats in Brazil, Mexico, Venezuela, and elsewhere sought to expand their countries' geopolitical sway into the vacuums created by U.S. retrenchment, while leaders in Peru, Cuba, and Chile aimed at a more thoroughgoing assault on Washington's hegemony. By 1973–1974 the combined effect of these efforts was to raise the prospect of a major departure in hemispheric relations.

Certain Latin American statesmen did manage to ride this wave, but for the most part, the United States escaped the first half of the 1970s with its regional preeminence intact. U.S. opposition and unexpectedly adverse economic conditions limited the flexibility of Latin American diplomats, while ideological cleavages and the contradictions of rising nationalism corroded regional unity. As had been the case for generations, Latin American solidarity was evanescent, and the diplomatic challenge lost momentum as a result.

By the late 1970s it had been two decades since revolutionary forces had swept to power in Latin America. The insurgents' losing streak came to an end in 1979 with the Sandinista revolution in Nicaragua. Why did the Sandinistas succeed where other post-Castro rebels had failed? This revolution was not, as is sometimes asserted, the "inevitable" outcome of poverty, authoritarianism, and exploitation. If revolutions flowed solely from such factors, nearly all of Latin America would long before have fallen to the insurgents.[7] The Sandinista revolution, rather, drew on a peculiar confluence of forces that, together, cancelled out the factors that had frustrated insurgent dreams since Castro's triumph. Building social and economic pressures; the cross-class resistance provoked by Anastasio Somoza's toxic personality and dynastic ambitions; and the Sandinistas' ability to learn from the travails of previous revolutionary movements created the conditions for radical upheaval within Nicaragua.

A hospitable international environment, characterized by the intrigues of a broad foreign coalition of anti-*somocistas* and Jimmy Carter's inability to reconcile the contradictions of his Latin America policy, encouraged and hastened this outcome. Somoza was forced from power in mid-1979, giving Latin America its first truly revolutionary triumph since Castro's.

This episode augured intense violence throughout much of Central America. The spiraling ideological extremism so characteristic of Latin America's Cold War mixed with long-running domestic and ethnic disputes to produce massive bloodletting in Guatemala and El Salvador, and the consolidation of Sandinista hegemony in Nicaragua revived civil violence in that country as well. Intervention by the United States, Cuba, the Soviet Union, and their respective allies only intensified these conflagrations, and life in Central America became indisputably nightmarish during the 1980s.

The forces of the Left looked strong during the early part of the decade, but dreams of radical social revolution were once again disappointed. Extremely bloody counterinsurgency strategies—epitomized by the killing of roughly 100,000 Guatemalans in the space of only two years—debilitated the guerrillas, while U.S. intervention took a toll on the Sandinista government. Just as important, the Left failed to maintain the popular sympathy that had been so crucial to its recent successes. The Guatemalan and Salvadoran governments embraced just enough reform to separate the guerrillas from the mainstream, while the authoritarianism and errors of the Central American left resulted in grave, self-inflicted wounds. In Nicaragua the incompetence, brutality, and missteps of the Sandinistas undermined their popularity and left that government increasingly isolated as the decade went on. Across Central America, the civil wars came to a close via negotiated settlements that rejected revolutionary change in favor of a limited—and in many ways superficial— evolution toward democracy.

The limited transitions in Central America indicated broader structural changes occurring across Latin America. During the 1980s factors ranging from economic difficulty to foreign pressure weakened the dictatorships that had seized power during the 1960s and 1970s and caused a regionwide return to electoral democracy. At the same time, the massive debt crisis that struck the region allowed opponents of the venerable import-substitution model to reorient Latin American economies along neoliberal lines.

When added to the failure of the Central American revolutions, these changes were widely hailed as evidence that the United States and its allies had won a decisive victory in Latin America's Cold War. That victory was hardly as sweeping as it initially appeared. The limits of Latin American democracy and the uneven effects of neoliberal reforms ensured that sociopolitical conflict remained ubiquitous, while radical populism, drug shipments, and illegal immigration emerged as new bogeys in inter-American affairs. The close of the Cold War did not end conflict in Latin America; it simply shifted long-running conflicts onto different ground.

There are multiple themes that run through this book; two are of principal importance. The first is that the intensity of Latin America's Cold War was a product of its complexity. As alluded to earlier, Latin America's Cold War was not a single conflict; it was a series of overlapping conflicts. It fused together long-running clashes over social, political, and economic arrangements; the persistent tension between U.S. power and Latin American nationalism; the ideological ramifications of decolonization and the rise of the Third World; and the influence of the bipolar struggle for preeminence in the developing countries.

By itself, any of these conflicts would have had a strong impact on Latin American affairs; together, they gave Latin America's Cold War its pervasiveness and fury. Throughout the decades after World War II, and especially during the 1960s, 1970s, and 1980s, these issues interacted dynamically, reinforcing one another and exacerbating each other's effects. In Latin America the Cold War drew together local, regional, and global conflicts, and the result was to lend the struggles that occurred during that period their intense and seemingly intractable nature.

The second theme is that prevailing interpretations of this subject need revision. Conservative pundits and American officials have described Latin America's Cold War as proof of the good that can come from U.S. intervention and democracy-promotion programs.[8] Many scholars, on the other hand, interpret the Cold War as a "savage crusade," conducted by the United States and local reactionaries, that broke popular movements, ravaged the Left, and eviscerated Latin American democracy.[9]

Both of these characterizations oversimplify a more tangled, complicated affair. Latin America's Cold War was undoubtedly a tragedy for many who experienced it. The profound polarization, the bloodshed of the "dirty wars" in Central America and the Southern Cone, and the stifling of democracy that occurred in most of the region reveal the superficiality of triumphalist assessments. Yet that tragedy cannot be reduced to a story dominated by Right repression and U.S. complicity. The upheaval that afflicted Latin America during the postwar period was the result not simply of the malignity of a single group of actors, but rather of the multisided and mutually reinforcing nature of the conflicts that comprised Latin America's Cold War. Foreign intervention, internal instability, and ideological extremism on both Left and Right: these influences fed on and fueled one another during the Cold War, and the outcome was often ruinous for the region's population. The history of Latin America's Cold War is rich and nuanced, if indeed tragic. To lose sight of this complexity is to obscure fundamental aspects of that story.

1

Convergent Conflicts

Latin America's Cold War consisted not of a single conflict, but of several convergent conflicts in the region's internal and external affairs. At the deepest level was the continuing struggle over political and social arrangements in Latin America, a theme that dated to the colonial period but played out with escalating intensity in the mid-twentieth century and after. The long-running tension between U.S. power and Latin American anti-imperialism, also growing stronger during the postwar period, constituted a second layer of conflict. These issues, neither peculiar to the Cold War, formed a foundation on which world events of the late 1940s and 1950s laid two newer sources of instability. Decolonization and the rise of the Third World heightened tensions both domestically and externally in Latin America, while the changing nature of the Cold War tightly linked superpower competition to the contested internal politics of the developing countries. These emerging trends exacerbated existing issues in Latin American politics, adding new dimensions to older struggles and providing the combustible mix that accounted for the particular intensity and, often, bloodiness of regional affairs during the 1960s, 1970s, and 1980s.

The issues that informed Latin America's Cold War converged in the fifteen years following World War II. By the late 1950s a rapid seesawing of political structures had combined with the trajectory of inter-American relations, the global upsurge of anticolonial nationalism, and the extension of Cold War competition into the Third World to create an unstable climate in both Latin American and international affairs. In this context the Cuban revolution served as a catalyst. It simultaneously expressed and sharpened the currents at work in the late 1950s, exacerbating internal radicalization, anti-Americanism, and *tercermundismo* ("Third-Worldism"), and drawing direct Cold War competition into Latin America to an unprecedented degree. More important, the revolution thrust these conflicts together, serving as their nexus in ways symbolic as well as concrete. In the short run, the volatile combination that resulted made Cuba the site of an intense confrontation. Over the longer term, this linking of domestic, regional, and global conflicts shaped Latin America's Cold War.

Latin America's history is one of exclusion and inequality. During the century following independence the legacy of the colonial order and the exigencies of agro-export development made economic exploitation and political marginalization the dominant themes of most people's relationship with the governing classes. Even in countries like Mexico and Chile, where electoral arrangements were nominally democratic by the first decades of the twentieth century, real economic gains and meaningful political participation eluded all but a privileged few. With few exceptions, the norm in Latin America was an economic system that delivered wealth and power to a small elite, a social system designed to maintain class boundaries and ensure a steady labor supply, and a political system meant to ensure that these arrangements were not seriously challenged. This characteristic engendered cycles of repression and revolt in many parts of Latin America, giving the region a built-in instability.[1]

Foreign influence also figured prominently in Latin American affairs. Following the collapse of Spanish and Portuguese imperial rule, Great Britain established its own "informal" dominance in the region's commerce and finances. European influence in Latin America was not to last, though, and during the late nineteenth and early twentieth centuries, Washington gradually displaced its rivals as the preeminent power in Latin America. During the three decades following 1890 the United States gained political and military supremacy in the Americas with an economic and financial sway to match.[2]

Washington's quest for preeminence in Latin America drew on various motives. Historically, the chief incentive had been strategic. Since their War for Independence, U.S. leaders had viewed American hegemony in the Western Hemisphere as an integral component of the nation's security. As far back as the 1780s the authors of *The Federalist Papers* argued that achieving continental dominance was crucial to avoiding the emergence of a balance of power in the hemisphere and thereby averting the constant quarrels that plagued Europe's anarchic relations. When John Quincy Adams laid down the explicit foundations of U.S. policy toward Latin America in the 1820s, his policies reflected the same basic precept, and over the next 130 years many of the major developments in U.S.–Latin American relations would issue from this belief.[3]

U.S. interests in Latin America were far from exclusively strategic, however. During the late nineteenth century American investors and exporters came to see the region as a lucrative potential market. Early efforts to expand the U.S. economic presence in Latin America were disappointing, but after World War I left Great Britain exhausted economically, Washington's influence grew rapidly. During the interwar period U.S.–Latin American trade shot up and U.S. corporations achieved favorable positions in extractive industries like Venezuelan oil and Chilean copper.[4]

American power was neither a purely benevolent nor an entirely exploitative influence in Latin America. Local populations benefited from some U.S. initiatives, such as public-health programs in Central America and the modernization of divorce laws in Puerto Rico. The infusion of U.S. technology and capital helped produce modest economic gains for some countries, and many Latin American observers viewed the United States as an agent of progress and modernization.[5]

In other respects the U.S. presence was more heavy-handed. Washington seized or otherwise obtained strategic territories like Guantanamo Bay, Puerto Rico, and the Panama Canal Zone, and occupied several Caribbean countries during the early twentieth century. U.S. officials used their financial leverage to reorient Latin American economies on lines more friendly to Washington's trade interests. By the 1920s writers like Argentina's Manuel Ugarte portrayed Washington as a "new Rome," an empire that dominated Latin America without acquiring the accompanying "dead-weight of areas to administrate and multitudes to govern."[6]

During the interwar period both U.S. influence and the oligarchic arrangements that had long structured regional affairs came under pressure. Internally, a series of economic and social changes altered Latin America's political landscape. Following World War I and the Great Depression, many Latin American countries turned inward, relying on import-substitution-industrialization (ISI) to reduce their vulnerability to the vicissitudes of world commerce. Beyond its economic import, this policy had major social ramifications. As late as 1930, three-quarters of the Latin American labor force worked in agriculture. Twenty years later, the balance had shifted notably toward industry and the cities, with only 53 percent of workers remaining in agriculture. As ISI shifted Latin America's human resources into the industrial sector, it promoted the emergence of a more coherent and concentrated working class.[7]

Along with a concurrent trend toward professionalization in the white-collar professions, the economic changes spurred by ISI also led to the expansion of the middle class. In many cases its members strained against existing political and economic arrangements. Disliking the fact that a small oligarchy dominated the best economic opportunities and wielded political power, they voiced their discontent by participating in the founding of new political parties that challenged the Conservative and Liberal establishments. By the outset of World War II the structures that had long dominated Latin American politics—limited and elitist democracy in some countries, military rule or other forms of despotism in others—were showing signs of wear.[8]

American influence also came in for a challenge. "Anti-Americanism" in Latin America dated back to Bolívar, and had often been expressed as an aversion to U.S. individualism and materialism. This sentiment built during the first three decades of the twentieth century, as military intervention and U.S. corporate culture became fixtures of the regional scene. Those wary of American influence found a hero in Augusto Sandino, who led resistance to the U.S. occupation of Nicaragua in the late 1920s and early 1930s. An Argentine newspaper called the U.S. occupation of Nicaragua "far worse and more unjust than was Belgium's invasion by Germany in 1914." Across Latin America, recounts one scholar, Sandino's struggle "concentrated scattered opposition to Washington into a focused movement."[9]

Anti-imperialism was prominent among the generation of political leaders that emerged during the 1920s and 1930s. Influenced by Marxist theories of imperialism and the reality of U.S. influence in Latin America, activists like Rómulo Betancourt (who would later lead Venezuela's Democratic Action party, or AD) and Víctor Raúl Haya de la Torre (head of Peru's American Popular Revolutionary Alliance, or APRA) criticized U.S. acquisitiveness and intervention. Washington, wrote Betancourt, "is currently committing, and is disposed to commit at every moment, the worst acts of banditry against our disorganized Latin American peoples."[10]

During the late 1920s and 1930s this opposition merged with pressing economic and strategic concerns to promote a reevaluation of U.S. policy.

Economically, the Great Depression made U.S. policymakers more conscious of the value of Latin American markets, and the corresponding worth of goodwill in the region. Strategically, the threat of European fascism and the proliferation of German military missions in Latin America revived the specter of foreign intrusion in the hemisphere. The result was a series of initiatives known as the Good Neighbor policy. U.S. officials abrogated the Platt Amendment (which since 1901 had made Cuba a protectorate of the United States), swore off the right of intervention that Franklin Roosevelt's cousin Theodore had claimed in his 1904 corollary to the Monroe Doctrine, and encouraged U.S. corporations to contribute to the economic well-being of their host nations. The most notable demonstration of this new approach came in 1938, when Roosevelt outraged U.S. investors by refusing to intervene in Mexico following the nationalization of the oil fields.[11]

The Good Neighbor was somewhat less a departure in U.S. policy than is often assumed. The United States still exerted considerable diplomatic and economic force in Latin America, the best example being intense U.S. pressure on Central and South American governments to intern German citizens and confiscate their properties. In some cases, too, the Good Neighbor reinforced authoritarian rule along the Caribbean rim. The same combination of economic interest and strategic concern that made Roosevelt conscious of the need to cultivate better relations with Latin America also made him willing to rely on friendly dictators to protect U.S. interests, a sentiment amply demonstrated by the president's cordial relations with Anastasio Somoza in Nicaragua and Rafael Trujillo in the Dominican Republic.[12]

During World War II, however, U.S. policy complemented the anti-oligarchic agitation occurring in Latin America. The emphasis on self-determination that was characteristic of U.S. diplomacy at this time, and the evident unpopularity of dictators like Jorge Úbico in Guatemala and Maximiliano Hernández Martínez in El Salvador, eventually caused Washington to withdraw its support from authoritarian governments it had hitherto supported. The rhetoric and policies of the Good Neighbor conduced to a striking improvement in the tone of U.S.–Latin American relations, a change reflected in the late 1940s in the formation of the Organization of American States (OAS) and the Rio Pact, two institutions that essentially institutionalized American hegemony in the hemisphere.[13]

Concrete U.S. policies mixed with the overall tenor of Washington's global diplomacy in encouraging democratization in Latin America. Beginning with the Atlantic Charter in 1941, themes of democracy and self-determination were central to Roosevelt's statecraft. Just as Woodrow Wilson's anticolonial rhetoric had sparked nationalist sentiment following World War I, this idea of a "New Deal for the world" had a pronounced ideological impact in Latin America.[14] In Guatemala and El Salvador demonstrators read from the United Nations (UN) charter. Honduran protestors invoked the Four Freedoms and the Atlantic Charter and wore headscarves bearing the UN emblem. Latin America's movement toward democracy in the mid-1940s was inextricably linked to the broader democratic optimism of that period.[15]

It was also tied to the brief Soviet–Western cooperation that prevailed during World War II. In hopes of improving relations with the Grand Alliance, Soviet dictator Josef Stalin disbanded the Comintern and instructed international communist parties to adhere to a popular front strategy. Faithful to Stalin's orders, Latin America's communists moderated their policies and forged alliances with other popular parties, adding breadth to the antidictatorial movements.[16]

Internal pressures and external encouragement came together between 1944 and 1946 in a remarkable wave of democratization. Popular parties joined with the Marxist Left to attack Latin America's dictatorial governments. Authoritarian regimes tumbled across the hemisphere, and democratic leaders initiated agrarian and labor reforms, expanded political rights, and unveiled social security programs. The degree of ambitiousness varied from country to country, but the general trend was unmistakable.[17]

This new order was fragile, though, and as it turned out, temporary. Reforms that empowered the lower and middle classes constituted a threat to Latin America's elites. Agrarian and labor reforms entailed a shift in economic influence, while mass political participation meant greater competition for control of state resources. During the late 1940s the conservative classes mobilized to check the progressive tendency. Trade unions were reined in, communist parties proscribed, and agrarian reforms reversed.[18]

The bloodiest example of the conservative reaction came in Colombia. Here the crisis of oligarchic rule during the 1930s and 1940s was symbolized by the rise of Jorge Eliécer Gaitán, a dark-skinned populist who rallied lower- and middle-class support. Gaitán's popularity spooked Colombia's Conservative Party, which following the 1946 elections systematically repressed its Liberal opponents. The Conservative government and its allies purged Liberals from public office and murdered Liberal supporters in the countryside—often as a pretext for opening up their land to commercial agriculture. Peasants formed self-defense groups to protect themselves, and Liberal and Conservative paramilitaries were soon doing battle in the Colombian countryside. The violence spiraled out of control after Gaitán was assassinated in April 1948. His supporters responded by razing much of Bogota; Conservatives, in turn, seized upon the rioting to launch a full-scale offensive against the opposition. For the next half-decade murder, rape, torture, and mutilation raged unchecked in many districts. *La Violencia* ultimately claimed perhaps 200,000 lives. It also led to the installation of a military dictatorship, placing Colombia firmly in step with the broader democratic retrenchment at work in Latin America.[19]

If world events and U.S. policy contributed to the opening of Latin American politics in the 1940s, did they choke off that *apertura* later in the decade? The emergence of the Cold War certainly heightened ideological polarization, debilitating the popular front and leading to a rash of anticommunist legislation in countries that had only recently been ruled by social democratic coalitions. U.S. support for popular alliances cooled as well, and few of the military governments that came to power found it difficult to establish good relations with Washington. Fletcher Warren, the U.S. ambassador to Venezuela, praised strongman Marcos Pérez Jiménez for his "constant concern toward the problem of Communist infiltration," and an American official in the Dominican Republic called Trujillo "an authentic genius." President Dwight Eisenhower downplayed violations of political freedoms and human rights in Latin America, and even presented Pérez Jiménez with the Legion of Merit.[20]

Yet U.S. policy hardly determined the conservative ascendancy. The military dictators that seized power beginning in the late 1940s, and the governments that imposed new restrictions on economic reform and political activity, needed little prompting from the United States. While rising Cold War tensions provided a climate conducive to the consolidation of conservative regimes, these leaders were reacting mainly to the expansion of working- and middle-class power that the democratic opening had encouraged. As the best survey of this period concludes, to the extent that U.S. policy figured in the conservative restoration, it was as a matter of neglect and indifference, rather than pro-authoritarian intervention.[21]

In fact, there remained a degree of flexibility in U.S. policy toward Latin America. U.S. policymakers viewed Latin America through a Cold War lens, but this did not always compel a rigid approach to the region. In 1948 the

Truman administration hardly responded to an incident in Bogota in which rioting crowds threatened to turn their anger against visiting Secretary of State George Marshall.[22] In 1952–1953 both Truman and Eisenhower supported Bolivia's National Revolutionary Movement (MNR), a revolutionary regime that nationalized the mines, expropriated U.S. properties, and enjoyed the support of the Communist Party. After Bolivian leaders made clear that they had no sympathy for Moscow and somewhat moderated their domestic course, U.S. officials made the MNR government the only regular South American recipient of U.S. economic assistance during the 1950s.[23]

Yet in other parts of Latin America, this Cold War framework gave a more reactionary tone to U.S. policy. In Guatemala the governments that succeeded Úbico promulgated a progressive labor code, expanded peasant rights, and initiated an agrarian reform that struck at the holdings of Guatemala's landed elite and the U.S.-owned United Fruit Company. Contrary to some earlier scholarship, these internal reforms did not determine U.S. hostility to the government of Jacobo Arbenz. When United Fruit officials schemed to overthrow the regime in 1952, the Truman administration helped kill the initiative. What ensured that Washington became antipathetic to Arbenz, even as it supported the MNR, was a series of indications (most notably the purchase of East-bloc arms) that he was moving toward Moscow. Following a well-worn path in U.S. policy toward Latin America, the Eisenhower administration concluded that it could not tolerate the establishment of an entry-point for external influence in the hemisphere. The CIA (Central Intelligence Agency) cooperated with dissident elements of the Guatemalan military to mount an anti-Arbenz sabotage campaign and launch an invasion through Honduras and El Salvador. In July 1954 Arbenz fled the country, allowing the installation of a conservative, pro-U.S. regime.[24]

It would oversimplify matters to say that the United States overthrew Arbenz. Although Washington's psychological campaign unnerved some Arbenz supporters and the United States provided strong support for the post-coup government, in reality the U.S. role in this episode was less decisive than is often assumed.[25] The president faced mounting opposition from Guatemalan conservatives and certain sectors of the military, and violence had erupted in the countryside even before the coup.[26] As the most detailed history of U.S. operations in Guatemala has concluded, it was these factors, rather than the dismal performance of the U.S.-backed forces, that caused the collapse of Arbenz's government.[27]

Regardless of what precisely forced Arbenz's ouster, U.S. complicity in this outcome was a serious misstep. Washington's blatant intervention in Guatemala reactivated the anti-Americanism that had lain dormant since the early 1930s. Protestors demonstrated outside American embassies, and Chilean socialist politician Salvador Allende rode his condemnations of U.S. policy to a greater national following. Assistant Secretary of State Henry Holland later conceded that Washington "paid a price in terms of prestige and good-will."[28]

U.S. intervention in Guatemala mixed with other Eisenhower-era policies toward Latin America—most notably Eisenhower's decision to direct U.S. economic assistance elsewhere and his support for unpopular dictators—to produce a broader alienation from American power. The bad feelings were best symbolized in Caracas in 1958, when a crowd of Venezuelans chanted, "We won't forget Guatemala," and nearly lynched Vice President Richard Nixon. In other capitals, similar incidents occurred.[29] While many Latin American politicians were less eager for a confrontation with the United States than these events might have indicated, they recognized the benefits of exploiting anti-Americanism and the dangers of opposing it. By mid-1958 the National Security Council identified "yankeephobia" as a primary threat to U.S. standing in Latin America.[30]

If opposing Arbenz exacted a price in U.S. standing with Latin Americans, it also marked a turning point with respect to the tactics of the Left. Until 1954, the World War II–era popular front remained the dominant strategy among Latin American leftists. While the repressive climate of the late 1940s led some to question this approach, it was the coup against Arbenz that truly energized radical dissent. To many younger activists, the bloody end to Guatemala's democratic path showed the futility of peaceful methods. Arbenz "could have given arms to the people, but he did not want to," wrote Argentine Marxist Ernesto "Che" Guevara, who had been in Guatemala in 1954, "and now we see the result." Only by waging war against the elite and its U.S. backers, he concluded, could Latin America liberate itself from the "hostile governments and social conditions that do not permit progress." "The struggle begins now," he asserted.[31] This sentiment was present in other countries as well; in the late 1950s Colombia's Communist Party approved the development of "popular armed resistance and the guerrilla movement."[32]

Broader global currents also called forth this shift in tactics. Following World War II, the exhaustion of the imperial powers produced an upsurge in nationalist movements and the collapse of European colonialism. Some two dozen new countries became independent in the late 1950s and early 1960s alone.

Decolonization and the spread of anticolonial struggle had a deep ideological impact in Latin America. For observers on the Marxist Left, where Leninist theories of imperialism had long promoted the view that Latin America was no less an exploited region than Africa or Asia, the anticolonial wars in Indochina, Algeria, and elsewhere illustrated the role of political violence in achieving liberation. These conflicts helped create a sense that the time had come for more dramatic action in Latin America's struggle against national oligarchies and U.S. imperialism. Uruguay's communists followed "every step" of the Algerian conflict, one militant later recalled, "from its birth to the final triumph."[33]

Decolonization also encouraged new thinking regarding Latin America's place in world politics. As decolonization proceeded, the notion of the Third World increasingly came to connote underdevelopment rather than nonalignment.[34] This evolving definition made it possible for Latin Americans to identify with the movement in a way that would have been unlikely only a decade earlier. If Latin America was hardly nonaligned, it was certainly underdeveloped, giving the region a similarity to the rest of the Third World that various observers were quick to point out. During the 1960s it became common to assert that Latin America belonged more to the group of underdeveloped nations than to the "inter-American community" led by the United States.[35]

Decolonization and the course of U.S.–Latin American relations constituted sources of growing conflict during the 1950s; the evolution of the region's internal political scene had a similar effect. Just as the conservative tide seemed to be waxing in the early 1950s, Latin American politics transitioned back toward greater openness. The late 1950s did see greater authoritarianism in countries like Guatemala, but in most of Latin America the *golpismo* of the preceding years faded. The military regimes that had come to power struggled with economic difficulties and the pressures that had fostered the democratic opening in the first place, and during the 1950s a series of dictators either were overthrown or relinquished power. Civilian rule was restored in Bolivia in 1952, and in Peru, Colombia, Venezuela, and Argentina between 1956 and 1958, leaving Alfredo Stroessner's Paraguay the lone dictatorship in South America.[36]

Yet this rapid shift in political arrangements created new fissures and divisions. The democratic institutions that emerged during the 1950s were fragile, as subsequent events would demonstrate. In many countries, the military possessed a veto on government policy and pressured civilian leaders to keep working-class movements and leftist parties excluded from national politics, and agrarian reforms were limited in comparison with the opening of the 1940s. For Latin America, Brazilian foreign minister San Tiago Dantas commented in 1962, democracy remained "much more an aspiration in the true sense of the word, than a political and social stage that we have achieved." U.S. diplomats reached the same conclusion. "There are few dictatorships left in the area," commented State Department analysts, "although it cannot be said that the seeds of representative democracy have yet taken deep root in most countries."[37]

The exclusionary tendency was most pronounced in Argentina. Since the mid-1940s, Juan Perón and the movement that bore his name had dominated Argentine politics. Perón rose to prominence in a military coup in 1943, and subsequently consolidated his position by forging an alliance with the trade unions and the downtrodden—the *descamisados,* or shirtless ones. Perón granted wage increases, the right to collective bargaining, and other favors to organized labor. The unions, in turn, provided armies of supporters that he could call into the streets. Perón's government was corrupt, authoritarian, and clientelistic, but it nonetheless brought about political and economic advances for the working class.

For Perón's opponents, it also brought about the specter of economic collapse and class warfare, and Perón fell victim to a military coup in 1955. The generals sought to purge Argentine politics of Peronism, banning the party and jailing many pro-Perón union leaders. Elections held three years later restored democracy, but only of a limited sort. Elected with Peronist support, President Arturo Frondizi eased the outright repression instituted by the military government. Frondizi remained beholden to a strongly anti-Perón military establishment, however, and the Peronists were forced to remain on the periphery of Argentine politics. Frondizi's austerity measures rolled back some of the working-class economic gains made under Perón, and the Peronists were banned from competing in elections. When Peronist candidates did run for and win office in the early 1960s, the military annulled the results. What one foreign diplomat called "that great force of two million Peronist voters" was in limbo, excluded from meaningful participation in a system that was only nominally democratic.[38]

As the plight of the Peronists showed, Latin American democracy was more conservative and less inclusive than it had been a decade earlier. To persuade the military to return to the barracks and avoid antagonizing the business community, populist parties throughout Latin America tacked right. In Venezuela Betancourt's AD forged a "pactocracy" with the other mainstream political organizations, pledged to respect private enterprise, and marginalized the influential Communist Party. Peru's Haya, long considered one of Latin America's more radical populists, shocked supporters by moderating APRA demands for agrarian and labor reform and pledging to support a conservative presidential administration in exchange for an end to the ban on the party.[39]

This rightward shift caused schisms within many popular parties. Hugo Blanco, an APRA dissident, charged that the party "has moved toward the dominant classes, away from the masses" and led an exodus of left-wing *apristas. APRA-rebelde*, a splinter group, would eventually renounce electoral politics and turn to guerrilla violence.[40] In Venezuela and Colombia the pacted democracies achieved in the late 1950s created widespread disillusion in trade unions, student organizations, and other groups where communist influence was strong. Similar dynamics were at work in Argentina, Costa Rica, Ecuador, and elsewhere. The return to electoral democracy in the late 1950s bred fragmentation rather than stability.[41]

The fluidity of Latin American politics increased due to a series of economic, demographic, and social changes occurring at mid-century. With respect to economics, the 1950s demonstrated that ISI had been at best a partial success. Despite accelerated industrialization, most of the region's economies remained highly dependent on commodity exports. When prices plummeted after the Korean War, a prolonged recession set in. Between 1955 and 1958 prices for Latin American exports dropped by nearly 10 percent, and the region's terms of trade fell by somewhere between 10 and 20 percent. For agricultural workers, this meant depressed wages and fewer employment opportunities, a situation exacerbated by the expansion of commercial agriculture. The concentration of arable land and increasing mechanization that accompanied commercial agriculture reduced full-time employment in the countryside and further skewed Latin America's unequal property-holding patterns.[42] In Peru one-tenth of a percent of the population now controlled three-fifths of the land under cultivation, leading to growing popular demands for corrective action.[43] "God does not will that some shall enjoy extravagant riches," a Santiago conference on rural life declared, "while others lack even the barest necessities."[44]

These economic patterns went hand-in-hand with striking demographic shifts. Latin America experienced a population boom in the mid-twentieth century, growing from 125 million inhabitants in 1940 to more than 200 million in 1960. As economic opportunities diminished in the countryside, urban populations swelled, increasing by roughly 5 percent annually between 1940 and 1960. Many urban migrants sought industrial employment, contributing to the nearly 75 percent jump in union membership (from 3.8 million to 6.6 million) between World War II and 1960 and the consequent growth of a politicized working class. Others wound up unemployed. Either way, these trends created tense conditions in Latin American cities.[45]

An equally important development of the 1950s was a region-wide boom in higher education. The growth of the middle class in the mid-twentieth century led to an explosion of university populations, symbolized by the construction of the National Autonomous University of Mexico's massive "university city." Between 1950 and 1960 college enrollments shot up across Latin America, with most countries registering a jump of somewhere around 100 percent, and signaled the beginning of a sustained boom that would become even more marked during the 1960s and 1970s. The outcome was a growing concentration of young people, many of them coming from a middle class that opposed the authoritarianism and oligarchic arrangements that had long persisted in Latin America, in universities that enjoyed autonomy from government supervision and had traditionally served as repositories of leftist thought. The potential political consequences of this situation became evident in Venezuela between 1956 and 1958, when students played a key role in the protests that brought down the military dictatorship.[46] Demographic, social, and economic trends were reinforcing Latin America's political ferment, accentuating fault lines in regional affairs.

The unsettled nature of Latin American politics was well matched to the context of international relations as a whole. The late 1950s and early 1960s witnessed fundamental changes in the Cold War. The traditional superpower struggle became sclerotic; nuclear stalemate and the emergence of a balance of power in Europe restricted opportunities for maneuver and promoted a cold peace of sorts in what had formerly been the Cold War's chief areas of struggle. Added to the concurrent collapse of European colonialism, these trends increasingly pushed U.S.–Soviet conflict into the underdeveloped world. Areas once locked safely into the Western camp were now up for grabs. In accord with the zero-sum logic of bipolar politics, Washington and Moscow competed fiercely for Third-World loyalties. They vied for access to the strategic real estate and resources of the underdeveloped countries, and looked to gain Third-World support in forums like the United Nations. Just as important, the White House and the Kremlin sought to use the Third World to demonstrate the attractiveness of their particular methods of organizing society. For the United States, this meant showing that democracy and liberal capitalism could serve as a path to wealth and political stability. For Moscow, it meant proving that state-directed socialism could bring about economic equity and social justice. The fight for the Third World revolved around ideology no less than economics or strategy.[47]

Moscow and Washington did not simply barge into the underdeveloped regions; in many cases they were invited. The nationalist leaders that came to power in the 1950s and 1960s often looked to the superpowers for support in fashioning postcolonial arrangements and institutions. Many of them viewed the United States and the Soviet Union as sources of economic aid, and were eager to play the Cold War game. Moreover, the Soviet model of development had considerable attraction for Third-World leaders. "You have been pioneers in many fields and you have transformed the vast tracts of your country before our eyes with a speed that has astonished humanity," India's Jawaharlal Nehru told Soviet officials in 1947. "Inevitably, when we want to produce great changes in India, we want to learn from your example." In this sense, the superpower presence in the Third World was constructed from below, rather than imposed from above.[48]

During the 1950s and 1960s the United States and the Soviet Union strove to mold the internal development and external orientation of the Third World. "We were guided," Soviet intelligence officer Nikolai Leonov later recalled, "by the idea that the destiny of world confrontation between the United States and the Soviet Union, between Capitalism and Socialism, would be resolved in the Third World."[49] Nikita Khrushchev made Soviet intentions clear in January 1961, pledging support for the "mighty upsurge of anti-imperialist, national-liberation revolutions" taking place in Asia, Africa, and Latin America. Soviet economic aid, technological support, and arms sales to the Third World grew exponentially under Khrushchev's government, and the KGB developed a "Third World strategy" to destabilize unfriendly regimes and bring pro-Soviet elements to power.[50] While Khrushchev and his advisers had initially concentrated mainly on expanding Soviet influence in Southeast Asia, by mid-decade they had moved to exploit opportunities in other regions.

Soviet diplomats supported the Bandung conference of nonaligned states in 1955, forged an alliance with Egypt's Gamal Abdel Nasser, and sought to capitalize on this momentum during the late 1950s by mounting a massive trade, aid, and technological effort in the Third World as a whole.[51] Decolonization, Khrushchev declared in 1961, would "bring imperialism to its knees."[52]

U.S. policy followed much the same trajectory. John Kennedy anointed "the whole southern half of the globe" as "the great battleground for the defense and expansion of freedom today."[53] The focus of U.S. foreign aid programs shifted from Europe and East Asia to Latin America, Africa, the Middle East, and Southeast Asia, and new institutions like the Peace Corps and the U.S. Agency for International Development (USAID) sponsored economic and social development programs. U.S. interventions in the underdeveloped world shot up during the 1950s and 1960s as well. As the Third World took shape, so did the contours of a new Cold War.[54]

By the late 1950s Latin American affairs had reached a sensitive juncture. Within the region, there was significant potential for conflict. During the 1940s and 1950s the structural changes of the early and mid-twentieth century combined with an evolving international environment to cause rapid shifts in Latin American political arrangements. The pendulum was swinging toward democracy in the latter half of the 1950s, but it was a form of democracy that entailed few advantages for those groups most affected by the social, economic, and demographic trends of the period. The exclusion of leftist organizations and working-class parties like the Peronists left substantial constituencies marginalized; the expansion of the middle-class and university populations created growing bodies of citizens that clamored for more meaningful political participation and a deepening of democracy; and the spread of commercial agriculture combined with the decreasing emphasis on agrarian reform to dilute democracy's benefits for many rural residents. In addition, trends in international politics—such as decolonization and U.S. intervention in Guatemala in 1954—had begun to weaken the appeal of the popular front and promote a greater attraction to revolutionary violence. In late 1950s Latin America, the prevalence of elections and electoral democracy concealed deep rifts and rising instability.

The region's external relations were also in flux. The course of U.S.–Latin American relations in the 1950s had undone the equilibrium established by the Good Neighbor and tapped into the reservoir of anti-Americanism in the region. Similarly, decolonization and the changing shape of the Third World encouraged ideological shifts regarding Latin America's place in international affairs. Finally, the evolution of the Cold War raised the prospect that Latin America's unsettled internal situation would increasingly interact with a more acute superpower competition over the Third World. By the close of the 1950s local, regional, and global conflicts had begun to coalesce in and around Latin American affairs, creating a volatile situation.

It was in this context that the Cuban revolution occurred. The revolution originated in 1953 as a middle-class revolt against dictator Fulgencio Batista. It subsequently gained more of a class element, as Guevara joined the leaders of Fidel Castro's July 26th movement and the rebels sought to cultivate support among the rural poor in the Sierra Maestra mountain range following a 1956 defeat at the hands of Batista's army. Castro's advocacy of agrarian reform and economic redistribution proved effective; the uneven development of Cuban agriculture over the previous decades meant that economic insecurity was a fact of life for many rural groups. By 1957 the anti-Batista struggle had become a cross-class phenomenon that drew on a variety of economic, political, and social grievances. Batista's authoritarianism and brutality merely added to his unpopularity, and the dictator soon faced opposition from Castro's movement, an urban underground, student organizations, and various political parties.

In 1957–1958 a series of victories by Castro's rural wing of the July 26th movement combined with the misfortunes of other rebel groups to leave Fidel at the front of the revolutionary coalition. In the second half of 1958 Batista's demoralized army, crippled by a U.S. arms embargo meant to disassociate Washington from the weakened dictator, disintegrated before a multifront offensive. The dictator fled Havana on New Year's Eve, leaving the country to the rebels. Over the next two years, Fidel and Raúl Castro, Guevara, and their supporters outmaneuvered other leaders to gain control of the new government and purged Cuba of Batista's followers and other political enemies. They displayed a strong antipathy toward the United States, moved Cuba rapidly to the left socially and economically, and eventually concluded an alliance with the Soviet Union.[55]

During the late 1950s and early 1960s the Cuban revolution interacted dynamically with the circumstances in which it occurred. At the broadest level, the anti-Batista movement was an expression of the issues that challenged governments across Latin America during this period. Middle-class discontent with authoritarianism, the political mobilization of student groups, the social effects of uneven economic development, and the way that the events of the 1950s radicalized revolutionary leaders like Guevara all figured prominently in Batista's ouster.

The Cuban revolution did not simply draw on the growing militancy at work in Latin American affairs; it amplified it as well. While Castro's revolution would undoubtedly have had a powerful impact on a region as plagued by poverty and inequality as Latin America regardless of when it occurred, the particular social and political context of the late 1950s gave it an especially powerful appeal. The revolution exerted its strongest influence on many of those groups affected by the rapid changes of recent decades. Amid falling wages, decreasing access to land, and the defeat or reversal of most agrarian reform movements, the triumph of a revolution with such a pronounced emphasis on rural redistribution had a catalytic effect in the countryside. In Brazil and Guatemala *campesinos* burned crops, held pro-Cuba demonstrations, and invoked Castro's exploits in calling for land reform.[56] In Chile Castro's victory energized efforts to organize rural workers.[57] In Peru APRA dissidents praised Castro's example as they turned toward land invasions, peasant organization, and even guerrilla violence.[58] Cuba became a mecca for agrarian reformers, hosting numerous conferences where they established contacts and studied the Cuban experience. "We Costa Rican campesinos also want a Revolution like Cuba's," declared one rural organizer.[59] In agrarian matters Cuba's revolution crystallized dissatisfaction with the status quo.

Among students and intellectuals, the revolution had a similar effect. Its antidictatorial nature and stress on economic redistribution proved popular with an expanding student class traditionally sympathetic to leftist ideas and skeptical of their prospects for advancement in an elite-dominated system. When Castro and Guevara visited Latin American universities during 1959 and 1960, huge throngs greeted them, and the Argentine University Federation announced that "a second front will open up in the streets" if the United States attacked Cuba.[60] In Mexico student groups mobilized the popular appeal of the revolution to press for political and social reform. Every year, student organizations held antigovernment demonstrations on the anniversary of the Cuban revolution.[61] Student leaders made pilgrimages to Havana, and Mexican youths even left school to join the various guerrilla bands active in

Central America.[62] Dissident leaders of Mexico's Institutional Revolutionary Party (PRI) took a similar tack, using a pro-Cuba message to rally support with the Mexican Left. Ex-president Lázaro Cárdenas helped found the National Liberation Movement, a group that mixed sympathy for Castro with calls for a struggle against the unholy trinity of "the dominant oligarchies . . . the political clergy and . . . North American imperialism."[63] By the early 1960s rising student and political activism greatly concerned the PRI security apparatus, and one newspaper commented that the Cuban revolution was responsible for "disrupting our political and civil morality."[64]

Working-class groups also seized on the revolution, seeing it as a more authentic, labor-friendly version of the democracy that prevailed in many Latin American countries. In 1960 a group of Latin American unions gathered in Havana to state their support for Castro's Cuba, "for the first time on this Continent, a truly democratic state that has the unlimited and unanimous support of the people."[65] Across the region, Cuba's rapid labor reforms led to a demand for similar measures, with some unions advocating violence as the way to obtain these aims. "We think Fidel is right," read one leaflet distributed at rallies in El Salvador in 1960. "He has stood up for his people, 'cleaning out' the capitalists who have no conscience."[66]

Cuba's impact in Latin America was all the more important because of the fractionated nature of regional politics in the late 1950s and early 1960s. Where parties like AD and APRA had become more conservative, the Cuban revolution created a strong temptation for groups marginalized by these changes to adopt more radical tactics. In Colombia, Peru, Bolivia, and several other countries, entire sectors of populist parties defected, either joining with the parties of the Left or forming altogether new organizations, many of which were dedicated to violent struggle.[67] In Venezuela these schisms rent the coalition that had toppled Pérez Jiménez. As Betancourt adhered to a relatively conservative program, student and union groups that had fought to overthrow the strongman concluded that their struggle had produced only "renewed domination by the old dominant classes and power groups." Effecting dramatic social change, they concluded, required the same militancy that had infused Castro's movement. The Cuban revolution "had a determining effect in the sense of orienting our political perspectives of the possible and the desirable," recalled one Venezuelan student leader, motivating the left wing of AD to break away and become the Leftist Revolutionary Movement (MIR).[68]

As these divisions indicated, the domestic impact of the revolution was nowhere more evident than in the burgeoning struggle for the soul of the

Left. Castro's triumph turned the gap between those who supported the popular front and those who advocated violent action into an unbridgeable gulf. The Cuban example and the subsequent dissemination of Guevara's *foco* theory of revolution (discussed in Chapter 2) shifted the balance of power decidedly toward the radicals. "The Stalinist cult was shaken to its very roots," recalled Peruvian Communist Héctor Béjar. "We all understood in those years that a new revolutionary period had begun."[69] In Paraguay the Communist Party split as several factions prepared for armed struggle. "The Cuban way," wrote the United National Liberation Front (FULNA), "has demonstrated to us how a united and determined people can destroy a despotic system."[70] Between 1959 and 1961 guerrilla uprisings modeled on the Cuban example occurred in more than a dozen Latin American countries.[71] Castro supported some of these movements directly, sponsoring exile attacks on Haiti, the Dominican Republic, Nicaragua, and Panama and promising to "convert the Cordillera of the Andes to the Sierra Maestra of the Hemisphere."[72] If Cuba stirred up the masses, it positively revolutionized the Marxists.

The spillover effects of the Cuban revolution created widespread apprehension throughout Latin America. Leaders in the region now viewed Cuba as the source of their internal problems and a frightening reminder of the need to restrict domestic dissent. Guatemala's Manuel Ydígoras charged that Castro "brought strikes upon us, riots, etc."[73] Colombian diplomats echoed this assessment, and Nicaraguan officials alleged that Havana wished to convert that country into a communist "beachhead" in Central America.[74] In October 1959 Nicaragua's National Guard fired on what the government called a "frankly subversive" student demonstration in Leon (press reports had it differently, terming the protestors peaceful), causing heavy casualties.[75]

As this incident showed, the Cuban revolution promoted a radicalization of the Right similar to that occurring on the Left. Following World War II, the professionalization of Latin American militaries and the emergence of the Cold War had led many officers to rethink the dictates of national defense. In institutions like Brazil's Superior War College (ESG), lecturers argued that the superpower conflict was not a heavily armed peace, but rather a "worldwide war that will decide the destiny of Western civilization." Nuclear weapons made war a Pyrrhic alternative, so communist advances would likely come from "ideological penetration" and subversion.[76] The radicalization of the Cuban revolution and the outbreak of insurgencies across Latin America reinforced these fears, causing near-panic in official circles. Paraguay's intelligence services warned Stroessner that "communist agents" were seeking to subject Paraguay "to the same process . . . that is observed in Cuba."[77] These perceptions led influential military strategists to advocate severe political restrictions as the price of preventing a Cuban-style revolution. To meet the danger posed by subversion, Brazil's General Golbery do Couto e Silva argued, citizens "must abandon the secular liberties, which had been won at such high costs, and place them in the hands of the state, the all-powerful lord of war."[78] By the early 1960s the Cuban revolution had stimulated the Left, terrified the Right, and intensified existing internal conflicts throughout the region.

The single dominant rhetorical trope of the Cuban revolution was the mixture of anti-imperialism and anti-Americanism that characterized Castro's public discourse. Having largely avoided open attacks on the United States prior to 1959, Castro turned the full force of his vitriol toward Washington once in power. He pledged to liberate Cuba from its "semi-colonial status," and in one of his more vivid declarations, promised "200,000 dead gringos" if the United States invaded the island.[79]

The anti-American flavor of the revolution came from several sources. In one sense it grew out of political expediency. Casting the revolution as a struggle between Cuban liberation and U.S. imperialism allowed Castro to paint his political opponents as Washington's lackeys and rally nationalist sentiment in support of his domestic program. As Felipe Pazos, the head of the Cuban National Bank, put it, "It was good politics to have someone as a whipping boy."[80]

Yet Castro's rhetoric, and that of other Cuban leaders, also drew on deeply held convictions about Washington's role in Latin America. For Guevara, a mixture of Marxism and a direct experience with U.S. power in Guatemala produced a decided antipathy to Washington. For his part, Castro viewed U.S. political and economic sway in Cuba as a manifestation of imperialism and a chief cause of the island's impoverishment. Cubans were "never before free in truth," he announced shortly after Batista's downfall; they had traditionally "been the victims of the powerful influence of the United States in the destiny of our country."[81] Moreover, Washington's long-standing support for Batista infuriated Castro. "When I saw the rockets being fired at Mario's house," he wrote in 1958 after Batista's U.S.-supplied planes had strafed rebel targets, "I swore to myself that the Americans would pay dearly for what they are doing."[82] The same perceptions of imperialism, exploitation, and support for dictators that informed regional anti-Americanism were thus present in the Cuban case as well.

If Cuba's new leaders stressed *anti-yanquismo*, they were also part of the growing *tercermundista* movement in Latin America. Guevara boasted that Cuba's new government was one with the "uncontainable forces of the Revolutionary Movement which has also shaken the colonial pillars in Asia and Africa where there are 1,600,000,000 people who support us with all their strength." Over the next decade and after, Castro and Guevara would give substance to this ideological connection, sponsoring revolutionary movements in various African countries and offering to send combat troops to Vietnam.[83]

Once in power, Castro's rhetoric and policies gave a significant boost to both anti-Americanism and Third-Worldism. As U.S.–Cuban relations deteriorated in 1960–1961, Castro sought to mobilize Latin American opposition to "these miserable imperialist gringos." "Latin America will soon march united and victorious," promised the Declaration of Havana in 1960, "free of the ties which convert its economies into riches alienated by North American imperialism."[84] Coming just a few years after U.S. intervention in Guatemala had decisively undone whatever remained of the warm feelings from the Good Neighbor era, these sentiments found a receptive audience. Trade unions, student groups, communist and socialist parties, and other groups trekked to Havana, declaring their backing for the revolution and their opposition to U.S. imperialism.[85] An estimated crowd of 200,000 demonstrated in favor of Castro in El Salvador, chanting *"¡Cuba sí, Yanquis no!"*[86] In Uruguay communist leader Rodney Arismendi declared, "We are a single force, the force of anti-imperialism in Latin America, whose heart beats in the Cuba of Fidel Castro."[87]

Held in Mexico City in March 1961, the Latin American Conference for National Sovereignty, Emancipation, and Peace provided vivid testimony to the anti-imperial sentiment evoked by the revolution. Thousands of students, laborers, and white-collar professionals attended the event, presided over by Cárdenas and other prominent regional figures. In his keynote address, Cárdenas declared that "the achievements of the Cuban revolution show the way to put an end to foreign domination," and pledged to defend Cuba "against all aggression."[88] When conference organizers displayed the flags of the Latin American countries at the outset of the gathering, the crowd complemented the now-standard chant of *"Cuba sí, Yanquis no"* with cheers of *"México sí, Yanquis no."* Other events at the conference emphasized nonalignment and resistance to U.S. power, creating a sense that the gathering represented a "Latin American Bandung."[89]

As this appellation showed, the Cuban revolution deepened the burgeoning ideological links between Latin America and the rest of the Third World. The rhetoric of speakers like Guevara and Castro popularized the idea that Latin America's history of economic exploitation and political subordination gave it much in common with the underdeveloped countries, a notion that was at the center of the dependency-theory movement that would sweep Latin American universities during the 1960s. More specifically, historian Alan McPherson has detailed how pro-Castro sentiment and an emerging anticolonial discourse infused Panamanian efforts to reclaim sovereignty over the Canal Zone. In riots that broke out in 1959 and 1960, shouts of *"Viva Fidel Castro"* complemented anticolonial slogans in encouraging popular opposition to the U.S. presence in Panama. During the 1960s Cuba would host conferences of students and revolutionaries from Africa, Asia, and Latin America in order to strengthen the bonds between activists in these regions.[90]

Castro's effective mobilization of anti-imperial and Third- World sentiment soon sharpened the crisis of U.S. hegemony in Latin America that had become evident with Nixon's close call in Caracas in 1958. Latin American statesmen, even those who detested Castro privately, found that it had become politically dangerous to support Washington as U.S.–Cuban relations grew more acrimonious during 1960–1961. To do so, wrote one Mexican diplomat, would cause "difficulties of internal order" in various countries.[91] In the first months of 1961 several Latin American leaders distanced themselves from U.S. policy. Brazilian President Jânio Quadros called the revolution "the just and powerful aspiration of a people for economic and social emancipation," and refused to follow Washington in breaking relations with Havana.[92] Mexican president Adolfo López Mateos publicly praised the revolution as "one more step toward America's greatness," and Mexico's public diplomacy came down firmly on Cuba's side.[93] As Castro's ideological influence rose, Washington's power in Latin America declined, and U.S. officials soon came to view the charismatic Cuban as a grave threat to American interests in the region. "Castro has been able to develop a great and striking personality throughout Latin America," Kennedy conceded.[94] The Cuban revolution had helped unsettle internal affairs in Latin America, and now exerted an equivalent effect on the region's external relations.

Nowhere was this fact more evident than with regard to Castro's most controversial postrevolutionary initiative, the decision to seek an alliance with the Soviet Union. While the predominant view of historians has long been that Havana's overtures to Moscow constituted a defensive response to U.S. pressure, it now appears that that Cuban policy owed primarily to reasons internal to the revolution. Guevara and Raúl, Fidel's most powerful advisers, were strongly attracted to the Soviet model. Raúl had secretly been a member of Cuba's Communist Party for years, and initiated contacts with Soviet intelligence officials during his Mexican exile.[95] Guevara belonged to the cohort of anti-imperial leaders who, like Nehru, looked to the Soviet Union as an exemplar of modernization and progress. In Mexico during the mid-1950s Guevara asked his Soviet contacts about "the concept of Soviet man." "How do they think? How do they live?" Additionally, amid the internal jockeying that followed Batista's ouster, Guevara and Raúl envisioned a partnership with the Soviet Union as a way of isolating non-Marxist members of the government and forcing them to the side.[96] As for Fidel, he viewed Soviet support as proof of the legitimacy of the revolution. "We are revolutionaries!" Castro exclaimed to a Soviet official in 1959. "Go . . . tell [Soviet diplomat Anastas] Mikoyan what kind of revolution this is—that it's worth him coming."[97]

Driven largely by ideological and political considerations, the move toward Moscow began well before the breakdown of U.S.–Cuban relations in late 1959 and early 1960. Moscow helped the July 26th movement acquire arms in late 1958, and in April 1959, Raúl obtained Soviet aid in organizing Cuba's security and intelligence services. After mid-year, the two governments exchanged secret envoys and arranged for the first official Soviet delegation to visit Cuba in February 1960.[98]

From a Soviet perspective, an alliance with Cuba was attractive for a number of reasons. On one level, it was just the sort of bold maneuver that Khrushchev so loved to employ. In an ideological sense, too, Cuba's steady move to the left during 1959 thrilled Soviet leaders who, under Stalin, had become accustomed to exporting socialism at the point of a gun. "We have been waiting all our lives for a country to go Communist without the Red Army," Soviet diplomat Anastas Mikoyan exclaimed. "It has happened in Cuba, and it makes us feel like boys again!"[99]

Cuba also looked to be an invaluable asset in the emerging superpower struggle for the Third World. Cuban socialism would present a striking contrast with the exploitation and underdevelopment present in much of Latin America and act, Khrushchev explained, as "a magnet that would attract other Latin American countries to Socialism."[100] More broadly, supporting Castro would allow Moscow to position itself as the patron of anti-imperialist social and economic change throughout the Third World. According to Soviet diplomat Yuri Pavlov, the Kremlin government envisioned Cuba as "a model socialist country," which would illustrate "the advantages of [the] socialist way of development" and thereby help "to force revolutions in other countries."[101] For Moscow, Cuba could be the key that unlocked the door to the Third World.

Mikoyan's visit to Havana in February 1960 marked the unveiling of Soviet–Cuban cooperation. Fortuitously for proponents of the alliance, Mikoyan's trip (which had been planned long previously) occurred just as U.S.–Cuba relations began a steady downhill slide. In January 1960, in response to Castro's anti-U.S. diatribes and the seizure of several U.S.-owned firms, Eisenhower asked Congress for the authority to suspend Cuba's sugar quota. These actions undermined opponents of a Soviet alliance within Cuba, and, from Castro's perspective, provided an additional rationale for cooperating with Moscow. Mikoyan took full advantage of the opening, promising to purchase Cuban sugar, give Havana $100 million in economic and technological assistance, and establish full diplomatic relations with Castro's government.[102]

This accord initiated a cycle of Cuban–Soviet cooperation and U.S.–Cuban discord. In March Eisenhower approved a CIA plan to aid anti-Castro exiles in overthrowing the Cuban government. At mid-year, U.S.-owned oil companies in Cuba refused to process Soviet crude delivered as part of Moscow's assistance package. In response, Castro nationalized the companies—and all other U.S. properties on the island—without compensation. Ike reacted by suspending Cuba's sugar quota, and the CIA stepped up its assistance to the marauding exile groups.[103] By late 1960 Castro quite justifiably feared a U.S. invasion, and was frantically arming 300,000 civilians in anticipation. "All the reactionary forces in the hemisphere are plotting against our revolution," he declared.[104] Castro deepened Cuba's economic ties with the Soviet Union, publicly praised Moscow's policies, and urgently requested arms deliveries from the Kremlin. The Kremlin responded by sending tanks and other heavy weapons to Cuba, and Khrushchev promised that the Soviets would "support the Cuban people with their rocket fire" if the United States invaded the island. Seizing on the revolution as the symbol of Moscow's aid to the underdeveloped world, Khrushchev publicly touted Cuba's triumph over the "tyrannical regime supported by U.S. imperialism" as the type of Third-World revolutionary struggle that Moscow would henceforth support. "Can such wars flare up in the future?" he asked. "They can. Can there be such uprisings? There can."[105]

The Cuban–Soviet alliance brought superpower conflict over the Third World to a new level. Khrushchev viewed Cuba as a particularly potent weapon in East–West ideological competition, while the KGB saw the revolution as a bludgeon with which to "beat the hell" out of Washington in Latin America.[106] For the United States, the alliance revived the old strategic dilemma of extra-hemispheric penetration, this time in the context of a global contest for influence in the Third World. The threat presented by the Soviet–Cuban alliance was evident in the hyperbolic language used by U.S. analysts. The Joint Chiefs of Staff forecast "disastrous consequences to the security of the Western Hemisphere," and the CIA labeled Cuba "an opportunity of incalculable value" for the Kremlin. Kennedy put the matter most directly, arguing that Latin America was now "the most dangerous area in the world."[107]

Even more so than the events of the 1950s, the Soviet–Cuban alliance brought the various conflicts involving Latin America to an intersection. Internally, the alliance added an East-West dimension to concerns about Cuban subversion and created fears that the Soviet presence in Latin America would encourage the violent Left. "Cuba has been invaded by the henchmen of all Moscow's satellites," wrote a contributor to Guatemala's *Prensa Libre*. "From there they are preparing their blows in order to overthrow the genuine and representative governments of our continent."[108] Similarly, Brazil's Interamerican Studies Society stated that Cuba and "its powerful sponsors" were preparing a subversive blitz by "Castroite, communist, Soviet, and Chinese agents."[109] In regional terms, the fact that Castro combined his angry denunciations of the United States with a move toward Moscow raised the prospect of a link between anti-Americanism and Soviet gains in the Western Hemisphere. "In this atmosphere of radical change, erratic leadership, and anti-US sentiment," wrote the CIA, "the most dangerous aspect is the opportunity given to international communism to strengthen its position in Cuba and the Caribbean."[110] Beyond intensifying anti-Americanism, *tercermundismo*, internal conflict, and superpower competition over the Third World, the Cuban revolution and its aftermath made these issues inseparable from one another.

That Cuba had emerged as the focus of the conflicts affecting Latin American affairs became evident with the Bay of Pigs invasion in April 1961. During 1960 and early 1961 a multilateral coalition led by the CIA prepared an operation meant to provoke a civil war in Cuba and destroy Castro's regime. Anti-Castro organizations in the United States and Central America provided the men, the CIA supplied money and arms, and the Guatemalan and Nicaraguan governments contributed bases for training and air support. On April 17, 1961, a force of roughly 1,200 Cuban exiles went ashore at the Bahía de Cochinos, or Bay of Pigs.

The rationale for the Bay of Pigs drew on the same themes that the Cuban revolution had helped bring together. For a number of Latin American leaders, the Bay of Pigs represented a chance to remove an incitement to domestic upheaval. As early as March 1960, Nicaragua's Luís Somoza had urged joint action with Guatemala against "the growing threats of international communism." Guatemalan officials called for "the extirpation of communism in Cuba" and continually pushed Washington to take more drastic action against Castro. For U.S. officials, the invasion offered the possibility of decapitating the anti-U.S. movement in Latin America and reversing Moscow's recent gains. The Bay of Pigs occurred at the intersection of Latin America's domestic upheaval and the regional and international crises of the early 1960s.[111]

The invasion was a disaster. Within hours of hitting the beach, the invaders were trapped, and it was clear that the operation would fail without direct U.S. support. Kennedy had never been inclined to go this far, a reluctance surely reinforced when Khrushchev threatened to give Castro "all necessary help to repel armed attack on Cuba." The president decided to cut U.S. losses, and abandoned the invaders to their fate. More than 100 were killed, all but a few of the rest captured.[112]

The Bay of Pigs had been conceived as an all-purpose solution to the crises converging in Latin America, but it ended up worsening each of the issues it was meant to resolve. Internally, the invasion complicated the delicate domestic balancing act being performed by many Latin American governments. The invasion trampled Latin American sensitivities regarding U.S. intervention, and incited pro-Cuba, anti-U.S. demonstrations from Mexico to Chile.

Student groups in Colombia proclaimed themselves to be "with Cuba to the death."[113] Mexican students organized volunteer brigades to aid Cuba, and governments with close ties to Washington came under a barrage of criticism.[114] The Bay of Pigs might have failed to undermine internal order in Cuba, but it succeeded in doing so almost everywhere else.

The fiasco also deepened the Soviet–Cuban alliance and Moscow's presence in Latin America. Castro publicly declared himself a communist, and Cuban officials told their East German counterparts that the island was passing from "the stage of the anti-imperialist agrarian revolution" to "the stage of the socialist revolution."[115] Internal opposition to Cuba's alliance with the Kremlin vanished. Whereas Cuban students had earlier protested Mikoyan's visits to Havana, waving banners that read "Cuba remember Hungary," there was now unprecedented enthusiasm for accepting Soviet protection. The Mexican embassy reported that Havana was covered in red stars and socialist slogans, and that the entire country remained on high alert for a follow-up invasion.[116] Guevara subsequently rubbed the noses of several U.S. officials in this outcome, telling them that he "wanted to thank us very much for the invasion—that it had been a great political victory for them."[117] Soviet arms shipments to Cuba increased dramatically, with the island now receiving sophisticated fighter planes and air defense systems. Moscow had become a major player in the hemisphere, a fact about which Khrushchev taunted Kennedy when the two leaders met at the Vienna Summit in June 1961.[118] By mid-year Cuba had joined Berlin as the most important issues in U.S.–Soviet relations, becoming, as Guevara put it, the "country in which the interests of both camps meet head on."[119]

The Bay of Pigs revealed the degree to which the Cuban revolution had brought the major trends at work in Latin America to a crossroads. In the period following 1959 the revolution sparked new levels of internal unrest and anti-Americanism, and linked these long-running issues to newer themes such as decolonization, *tercermundismo,* and the changing shape of the Cold War. The immediate result was to place Cuba squarely at the center of these struggles, giving rise to the multilateral effort to topple Castro at the Bay of Pigs. Rather than providing a quick solution to the overlapping problems dramatized by Castro's revolution, however, the invasion merely exacerbated these issues, contributing to the same volatile processes it had been meant to curb.

From a longer-term perspective, the Bay of Pigs and the events surrounding the Cuban revolution marked the transition from the period of accumulating conflict in the 1940s and 1950s to the more pronounced strife of the succeeding decades. During the 1960s and after the combination of issues described above would give rise to escalating superpower and Cuban intervention in Latin America, intense and increasingly violent polarization internally, and important shifts in the region's diplomatic climate. The conflicts that resulted would take on a ferocity that at times better resembled a hot war than a cold one. Thomas Mann, Washington's foremost Latin America hand, captured the climate of urgency and militancy that would prevail for much of the next thirty years in a comment made shortly after the Bay of Pigs: "We are at war."[120]

2

Intervention and the Limits of Power

The Third World was a Cold War battleground during the 1960s. U.S. policies toward the underdeveloped regions became increasingly militarized, culminating in the invasion of the Dominican Republic in 1965 and the deployment of more than 500,000 troops to Vietnam. Soviet policymakers, emboldened by the gains of the 1950s, expanded Kremlin influence and supported revolutionary movements in Africa, Southeast Asia, and Latin America. Cuba and China took on similar roles, backing Third- World revolutionaries and competing for power in the developing countries. Around the world, outside actors strove to mold the internal development and external orientation of the global south.

Latin America was at the center of this contest. Responding to the unrest that had built during the 1950s, Moscow, Havana, and Washington engaged in parallel quests to shape Latin American politics and society. Havana and Moscow supported insurgencies and looked to transform Cuba into what one Soviet official called a "beacon of Latin American revolution."[1] Washington encouraged economic growth and social reform via the Alliance for Progress, and combated the Left through counterinsurgency, covert operations, and military intervention. This intense competition informed the Cold War's most perilous moment—the Cuban missile crisis—as well as myriad other confrontations, and gave substance to Kennedy's characterization of Latin America as "the most dangerous area in the world."[2]

The initiatives launched by the superpowers and Cuba traced similar arcs. Geopolitically, all three powers had much to gain in Latin America. Moscow hoped to hammer on an American weak spot; Havana meant to win allies and a respite from U.S. pressure; Washington looked to shore up its traditional hemispheric buffer and contain or eliminate Castro's Cuba. In each of these cases, too, policy toward Latin America passed through a strong ideological filter. Modernization theory, the intellectual framework that structured U.S. policy toward the Third World during the 1960s, shaped the Alliance for Progress as well as certain aspects of counterinsurgency. Guevara's *foco* theory, an attempt to extract universal principles of revolution from the Cuban case, guided Havana's endeavors. For its part, Soviet policy was strongly influenced by Khrushchev's ideological predilections and Marxist-Leninist ideas about Third-World development. Importantly, each of these paradigms centered on a belief that the Soviet, Cuban, or American path to economic growth and social modernization could be replicated in other countries. Moscow, Havana, and Washington looked to gain influence in Latin America by remaking the region in their own images.

Ultimately, however, universalistic aspirations ran up against the entrenched realities of Latin American affairs. Guevara's *foco* theory proved terribly suited to the political, social, and cultural context of most countries, and in conjunction with the decline of the Soviet–Cuban alliance during the mid-1960s, led to disaster for the region's guerrilla movements. The development of Cuban socialism failed to exert much appeal, and generally made that island's example less rather than more attractive to mainstream observers. On Washington's side, the disappointing course of the Alliance for Progress exposed the contradictory nature of U.S. objectives and the flimsiness of American beliefs about the malleability of Latin American societies. Initiatives like counterinsurgency and military intervention seemed more effective, but often had unexpected—and deeply counterproductive—results. By decade's end neither Washington nor Moscow nor Havana had attained its desired ends in the region, and the ideological and intellectual paradigms that had guided their policies had been either weakened or overturned altogether. A decade defined by intervention wound up revealing the limits, rather than the extent, of foreign influence in Latin America.

Latin America's accumulating internal tensions provided the backdrop to U.S., Soviet, and Cuban policies during the 1960s. Violence and polarization were widespread. Guerrilla uprisings occurred in more than a dozen countries, and there were sustained insurgencies in Peru, Colombia, Venezuela, Guatemala, and Bolivia. In Paraguay dissidents from the Communist and Colorado parties sought to emulate "the example of the noble Cuban people" and launched an invasion of that country from Argentina. "The only form of struggle [is] that of the guerrillas," said one participant.[3] Radical Peronists adopted a similar strategy following leader John William Cooke's trip to Cuba in the early 1960s. "Nowadays," Cooke wrote in 1961, "nobody thinks that national liberation can be achieved without social revolution."[4] In Colombia the widespread rural bloodshed of the 1950s (as recently as 1958 there were 1,400 political murders in the department of Tolima alone) took on an increasingly ideological flavor as several pro-Cuba groups swung into action.[5] "Colombia began with bandits and now confronts an endless guerrilla war," lamented one official.[6]

The situation was most dire in Venezuela and Guatemala, reaching the point where Kennedy was prepared to send in the Marines should matters get out of hand.[7] Venezuela's guerrillas, who pursued a strategy of urban violence before switching to rural insurgency, consisted mainly of Democratic Action and Communist Party dissidents and had some support within the armed forces as well. With conservative officers concerned that Betancourt could not stem this "unrestrained criminal wave," it seemed likely that even if the guerrillas could not topple the government, their actions might cause a right-wing coup that would.[8] In Guatemala a group of nationalist military officers rose against Ydígoras in November 1960. "Come on General," they taunted, "and come personally to the massacre."[9] Loyalist forces put the revolt down, but several rebel leaders escaped to lead an insurgency. In 1962 demonstrations rocked Guatemala City, causing some observers to fear for the survival of the regime. Overall, CIA analysts predicted that "there is a good possibility that a few of the governments in Latin America will be overthrown and replaced by regimes which draw inspiration from the Cuban revolution and look to the Soviet bloc for outside support."[10]

Even among the majority of Latin Americans that wanted little part of guerrilla violence, dissatisfaction was widespread. In several countries average food consumption was less than 2,000 calories daily, and infant mortality was above 25 percent. Roughly 5 to 10 percent of Latin Americans dominated 70 to 90 percent of the land, and in some places the distribution was considerably more skewed. In Brazil more than 4 million farmers lacked access to arable soil.[11]

While misery and inequality were nothing new (although many markers of poverty had worsened in recent years), what made the early 1960s such a tenuous juncture was that these conditions were now coupled with a demand for immediate relief. As described previously, the Cuban revolution encouraged a belief that rapid change was both possible and necessary in areas like rural landholding and labor rights. Cheap radios disseminated Castro's exploits widely and stoked desires for similar reforms. ("The transistor," warned Chilean president Eduardo Frei, "is a much more revolutionary factor than Karl Marx.")[12] According to one poll, up to 75 percent of respondents in several South American countries voiced significant grievances about their socioeconomic situation, and similar proportions demanded immediate land and tax reform. U.S. analysts summarized the general feeling as "a high level of dissatisfaction with current standards of living . . . coupled with extremely optimistic expectations for improvement."[13]

The widespread unrest of the early 1960s created a sense that Latin America was on the verge of profound internal transformations. The CIA warned that "revolution or attempts at revolution are definite possibilities in twelve of the twenty-three countries to our south." Guevara agreed: "We are deeply convinced of the possibility of seizing power in a number of Latin American countries." This perception created strong incentives for foreign intervention.[14]

Beginning in 1960–1961, Moscow and Havana eagerly looked to exploit Latin America's turmoil and foster additional revolutions. From a Cuban perspective, this desire mixed strategy and ideology. In an ideological sense Cuban leaders viewed themselves as liberators who were destined to help the exploited nations of Latin America break free from imperial domination. Guevara advocated "a life-and-death struggle against imperialism from the very first moment," and referred to Cuba as "the hope of the unredeemed Americas."[15] In 1958 the July 26th leadership declared that it would fill "the need proclaimed long ago by Bolivar and Martí for the nations of America to become united," and Castro predicted that a "war" with the United States was his "real destiny."[16] During the 1960s and after this missionary impulse drove Cuban intervention not only in Latin America but in various African countries as well.

Intervention also served strategic purposes. From 1960 onward Castro viewed promoting revolution as a counter to U.S. hostility and a means of diverting Washington's attention. "If the United States believes it has the right to promote counterrevolution and reaction in Latin America," he declared in 1961, "Cuba too feels it has the right to encourage the Revolution in Latin America!"[17] Another revolution in Latin America, explained Cuban official Blas Roca in 1963, would mean that "we will cease to be the solitary Caribbean island facing the Yankee imperialists and we will have a nation on the continent to back us up." Even if these efforts were not fully successful, the chaos wrought by internal violence would force the United States to focus on containing Latin America's turmoil, rather than snuffing it out at the source. Washington "will not be able to hurt us," Castro forecast, "if all of Latin America is in flames."[18]

Soviet officials were ambivalent about Castro's interventionism, worrying that it might provoke a U.S. invasion of Cuba. Nevertheless, Khrushchev decided to support Cuba's revolutionary ambitions. In part he did so because Soviet officials wished to keep their foremost Third-World ally happy at a time when Beijing had begun to compete with the Kremlin for the loyalties of the socialist world.[19] More important, Soviet leaders saw real benefit in Castro's activities. "At any time other Latin American countries may follow after Cuba," Soviet official Sergei Pavlov argued. "Venezuela may blow up at any moment. There are mass strikes in Chile. The same applies to Brazil and Guatemala." Successful revolutions would presumably bring pro-Soviet governments to power, and would force Washington to reallocate diplomatic and military resources from other areas. In 1961 the Politburo approved a KGB plan to spur "armed uprisings against pro-Western reactionary governments" in Latin America with the aim of "diverting the attention and forces of the United States."[20]

Soviet policy also fit squarely within a Marxist-Leninist framework. Cuba's revolution exhilarated Soviet leaders, reviving the thesis (largely neglected by Stalin) that the Third World would inevitably turn to socialism. The revolution, Mikoyan remarked, "is a great success of Marxist-Leninist theory." Khrushchev felt similarly, viewing Cuba not simply as an ally but as validation of Soviet ideology and "a revolutionary example to the rest of Latin America." During the 1960s the prospect that other countries might follow the Cuban model helped override whatever worries Kremlin officials had about antagonizing the United States. "Socialist revolution in Latin America should develop and strengthen," Mikoyan told Castro in 1962.[21]

Moscow and Havana pursued a two-pronged approach to Latin America. First, they cooperated to build up Cuba's defenses against external attack and make it a shining example for the rest of the region. Cuba was "a beacon of Latin American revolution," said Mikoyan. It must "develop more rapidly in every respect and give a decisive example for mobilizing other peoples for struggle."[22] Moscow sent heavy machinery, oil, and other industrial components to Cuba, purchased Cuban sugar at above-market rates, and gave Castro generous credits. The Kremlin also delivered massive quantities of arms, giving Castro advanced fighter planes, tanks, and air defense systems, and allowing him to pursue a more assertive foreign policy.[23] Castro and Guevara undertook a crash program designed to spur industrialization and economic diversification, raise Cuba's standard of living, and demonstrate the achievements of Cuban socialism. "By virtue of the example it sets," Guevara wrote in 1962, Cuba "casts light for all the peoples of America to see."[24]

The second prong consisted of wide-ranging programs meant to destabilize existing governments and aid insurgent movements. Castro allowed Venezuelan guerrillas to set up their headquarters in Cuba, and regularly welcomed insurgent leaders to Havana.[25] Moscow arranged for East-bloc countries to transfer tens of thousands of infantry weapons to Cuba "for the needs of the revolutionary movements in Latin America," and Cuban and Soviet money helped sustain movements in at least twelve countries.[26] The amount of support varied by case: Castro gave Paraguayan communist leader Agustín Goiburú $300,000 in 1961, Cooke's wing of *justicialismo* received $750,000, and Moscow provided lesser sums to the nascent Sandinista movement in Nicaragua and other organizations.[27] Pro-guerrilla student groups and trade unions also received funding, and Havana disseminated copies of Guevara's book *Guerrilla Warfare* throughout the hemisphere.[28]

Perhaps most important was Cuban and Soviet operational assistance. Thousands of Latin American guerrillas traveled to Cuba for training, including at least 1,000–1,500 in 1962 alone.[29] As one Cuban official later recalled, the central part of the country (where many training camps were located) resembled a "frenzy of liberation." Under the aegis of a program known as "Operation Manuel," Soviet and Czech intelligence operatives transported these trainees to safe-houses in Eastern Europe, providing them with fake passports for the return trip to their home countries. Between 1962 and 1967 nearly 1,000 Cuban-trained operatives passed through Czechoslovakia, and others were repatriated through Algeria or the Caribbean.[30] Cuban advisers sometimes accompanied these guerrillas into combat. Guevara's ill-fated Bolivian trek is the best-known example of direct Cuban involvement in Latin

America, but Che's colleagues undertook similar tasks in Argentina, Paraguay, Venezuela, and elsewhere.[31]

In most cases Moscow played a secondary role to Havana in designing and implementing these programs. Guevara and Manuel Piñeiro, head of the Americas Department of the *Dirección General de Inteligencia,* selected targets and vetted applicants for Cuban support. Cuban leaders viewed Peru, Colombia, Bolivia, Guatemala, and to some extent Argentina as excellent prospects for revolution, but their highest hopes centered on Venezuela, referred to by the Cuban press as "the Vietnam of Latin America." This country had numerous guerrilla groups, a record of internal turmoil, and a president—Betancourt—whom Castro loathed. In conjunction with Cuban efforts in the Andes, a guerrilla offensive in Venezuela would allow Havana to mount what one intelligence officer called a "two-pronged attack on South America." Finally, Venezuela possessed immense oil wealth, which in the hands of a friendly government would be a godsend for the Cuban economy and the revolutionary movement as a whole. "When the people of Venezuela achieve their full independence from imperialism," said Roca in 1963, "then all Latin America will be ablaze, all America will move forward, all America will free itself once and for all from Yankee imperialism."[32]

Ideologically and strategically, Guevara's *foco* oriented Havana's revolutionary proselytism. Influenced by what one historian terms "the science of Marxism," Guevara set out in the 1950s to find the unalterable principles of revolution.[33] After the July 26th movement toppled Batista, he composed the lessons of that conflict into the *foco* (which means "focal point" or "center"). In *Guerilla Warfare,* the bible for a generation of Latin American revolutionaries, Guevara argued that the Cuban revolt represented "a change in the old dogmas concerning the conduct of the popular masses of Latin America." It demonstrated that revolutionary violence could precede, rather than follow, the creation of revolutionary consciousness among the masses. No longer was it necessary to wait until "all conditions for making revolution exist"; by inciting the masses and exposing the debility of the reactionary forces, "the insurrection can create them." In essence, Guevara proposed a shortcut to revolution.[34]

The *foco* dominated Cuban policy during the 1960s. Convinced that the *foco* "has a context approximating the universal," Guevara made ideological conformity the price of Cuban support. "Revolutionary conduct is a mirror of revolutionary faith," he wrote. "When someone who calls himself a revolutionary does not behave as such, he is simply a charlatan." Latin America's socialists must therefore forsake the "muddle-along strategy" of the popular front and launch the guerrilla struggle immediately, focusing on the rural areas.[35] "There is only one path," Castro declared; those movements that sought Cuban aid must adhere to the science of revolution.[36]

Fortunately for Havana, there were plenty of groups willing to do so. Coming at a time of ideological ferment and internal conflict, the *foco* had a transformative impact on the Left. Guevara explicitly directed his arguments against "the defeatist attitude of revolutionaries or pseudo-revolutionaries who remain inactive and take refuge in the pretext that against a professional army nothing can be done," and those Marxists who had argued against the popular front now seized on the *foco*. The Cuban example caused a "continental explosion," one Venezuelan guerrilla said. "In every young man, there took root a Fidel Castro, wanting to tie up his horse on the gate of Miraflores." By the early 1960s there were dozens of *foquista* guerrilla organizations active in the region, many of them drawing on Cuban support.[37]

As the 1960s progressed, Cuban interventionism became more strident. "It is not for the revolutionists to sit in the doorways of their houses waiting for the corpse of imperialism to pass by," stated the Second Declaration of Havana in 1962. "The role of Job doesn't suit a revolutionist." At mid-decade, Havana convoked meetings of the Latin American Solidarity Organization (OLAS) and other such groups in hopes of achieving closer cooperation between the region's revolutionary movements. "His approach is direct and simple," the CIA wrote of Castro in 1967. "Stop talking, get out there and fight, and this action will sooner or later create the conditions for success."[38] Seeking both strategic gains and affirmation of its own experience, Havana undertook a major offensive in Latin America.

U.S. policy toward the region was little less ambitious. The boldest move Kennedy made in Latin America during 1961 was not the Bay of Pigs, but rather a speech he gave at the White House in March. Kennedy announced "a vast cooperative effort, unparalleled in magnitude and nobility of purpose, to satisfy the basic needs of the American people for homes, work and land, health and schools." This "Alliance for Progress" was to be a ten-year program to aid committed Latin American leaders in stimulating economic growth and better distributing its benefits. The Alliance would "complete the revolution of

the Americas," redressing the region's pervasive underdevelopment and inequality and, in the space of only a decade, transforming it into a stable, prosperous area. By comparison, attempting to overthrow Castro seemed downright pedestrian.[39]

The Alliance, a greatly expanded version of an aid program begun under
Eisenhower, was primarily the result of the Kennedy administration's liberal
anticommunism. Alarmed by guerrilla violence, the administration concluded
that only thoroughgoing improvements in social and economic conditions would
alleviate the tensions underlying this turmoil. Rising expectations and intense
dissatisfaction meant that there was bound to be some sort of revolution in
Latin America, wrote adviser Adolf Berle; Washington's task was to "divorce
the inevitable and necessary Latin American social transformation" from "capture by overseas Communist Power politics." Alliance reforms would channel
social change into a "middle-class" revolution, thereby lessening the chances of
a "workers-and-peasants" revolution led by Castro. Kennedy himself put it
succinctly: "Those who make peaceful revolution impossible will make violent
revolution inevitable."[40]

The Kennedy administration was hardly alone in drawing this conclusion,
as certain Latin American leaders were moving in the same direction. "The
campesino has awoken from his centuries-long hibernation," wrote Betancourt,
"and urgently requests not only lands, but also credits, schools, roads, and rural
aqueducts." Frondizi offered a similar assessment: "What is required is a basic
attack on the conditions that produced Castro." The Alliance was to partner
U.S. anticommunism with the reformist inclinations of leaders like Betancourt,
Frondizi, and others.[41]

The Alliance was also the product of Kennedy's preoccupation with the anti-
Americanism that had grown during the Eisenhower years. "You remember
those people who threw rocks at Nixon," he remarked to an aide. "I'd like to
believe it was just Nixon's personality, but they were sending us a message."[42]
Politicians like Betancourt skillfully reinforced this perception, telling U.S.
officials that money would go far in redressing the hurt feelings of the 1950s.
Nixon's near-lynching in Caracas, he said, "was the result of Communist tactics
which found a ready atmosphere because when they said: 'Nixon, no!' there was
nobody in Venezuela who was prepared to say: 'Nixon, yes.'"[43]

Fears of communism and anti-Americanism provided the rationale for the
Alliance, but modernization theory gave the program its shape and ambition.
Developed by social scientists like Walt Rostow, Max Millikan, and Lucian

Pye, modernization theory was a body of ideas centered on the notion that there was a single, linear path to economic development. Due to their liberal institutions and early industrialization, the United States and its Western allies had gone farthest down this path, reaching the apex of social and economic development. In other countries, however, the persistence of feudal social arrangements and the lack of economic infrastructure had retarded progress and created the frustrations conducive to radicalism. With respect to U.S. foreign policy, modernization theory implied that spurring growth—and thus stability—was a relatively simple matter. "Social patterns and institutions in most underdeveloped nations are extremely malleable," an administration paper stated. By encouraging underdeveloped countries to abolish feudal institutions like tenant farming, and by helping them increase agricultural output, attract investment, and build infrastructure, Washington could propel these nations toward social and economic modernization. As one reviewer of Rostow's seminal work, *The Stages of Economic Growth,* put it, modernization theory was "a shaft of lightning through the murky mass of events which is the stuff of history." Guevara had come up with one way of accelerating history; Rostow proposed another.[44]

Modernization theory was central to U.S. foreign policy during the 1960s. It appealed to the need for a formula that would allow Washington to shape the internal development of the Third World while avoiding the taint of formal colonialism, and held out the prospect of replicating the American experience throughout the global south. Modernization theory underlay initiatives as diverse as the Peace Corps, the strategic hamlet program in Vietnam, and the Alliance for Progress. The point of the Alliance, wrote aide Arthur Schlesinger, Jr., was to help Latin American countries escape their "agrarian, semi-feudal economic structure" and thrust them toward Western-style industrialization. The extent to which American officials aimed to replicate the U.S. experience in Latin America was evident from the language they used. "What we are asking is that the philosophy of Jefferson and the social reforms of FDR be telescoped into a few years in Latin America," said Undersecretary of State Chester Bowles. Cuba was to be Moscow's exemplar of socialist development; the Alliance was Washington's counterargument.[45]

The Alliance for Progress took shape in 1961. U.S. officials promised to provide $20 billion in loans, grants, and investment over the next decade (to be matched four-to-one by Latin American countries) to pay for infrastructure, education and health programs, and an expansion of profitable activities like commercial agriculture and light industry. Latin American governments would undertake measures, such as land and tax reform, to ensure that the resulting growth benefited all strata of society. At the level of implementation, the Alliance was supposed to resemble the Marshall Plan, with Latin American governments taking the initiative in designing and enacting programs. In practice the Kennedy administration realized that strong U.S. pressure would be required to convince those threatened by economic reform that a moderate amount of pain now was preferable to infinitely greater trauma later. "This job is not just the administration of billions of dollars," said Alliance chief Teodoro Moscoso. "It is a job of evangelizing."[46]

If the Alliance for Progress represented Kennedy's hopes, other aspects of U.S. policy reflected his fears. From the start, U.S. officials worried that the Alliance alone would be insufficient to prevent revolution. Reform would take time, and would have to be carried out amid turmoil and violence. "Vitamin tablets," said Secretary of State Dean Rusk, "will not save a man set upon by hoodlums in an alley."[47] Even if these programs were successful, they would disrupt the balance of economic and political power in Latin America, generating additional instability. "Between the shattering of the old mold and its consolidation into a viable modern state," wrote U.S. officials in 1962, "a modernizing state is vulnerable to subversion and insurgency." The Alliance might represent the long-term salvation of Latin America, but in the short term it would be necessary to find additional ways of restraining upheaval.[48]

This concern underlay two essential elements of U.S. policy. The first was an effort to bolster Latin America's internal defenses. Following Khrushchev's "wars of national liberation" speech in January 1961, U.S. officials identified "subversive insurgency rather than overt aggression" as the tip of the communist spear in the Third World.[49] To meet this challenge, Washington developed a wide range of counterinsurgency programs. The U.S. Military Assistance Program kept Latin American militaries and security services well supplied in arms, helicopters, and infrared technology, while institutions like the School of the Americas and the Inter-American Defense College provided doctrinal and operational training. U.S. military missions traveled to twenty Latin American countries, supported the creation of regional defense and intelligence networks like the Central American Defense Council (CONDECA), and sometimes accompanied counterguerrilla units into the field.[50]

Counterinsurgency is sometimes thought of as a U.S. invention imposed upon Latin American governments.[51] This is incorrect; many Latin American militaries first learned counterinsurgency techniques from French and British trainers.[52] More generally, amid the insurgencies that erupted following the Cuban revolution, no Latin American officer needed to be told to be anticommunist. Brazil's Golbery wrote in 1959 that "Latin America now faces threats more real than at any other time," and that country's Interamerican Studies Society (SEI) warned of a "new subversive network" taking shape.[53] The Guatemalan Chiefs of Staff termed the "well-organized" coordination between revolutionary groups "truly terrifying," and Guatemalan officials estimated that up to 700 exiles had received training in Cuba and were preparing a guerrilla offensive for 1963.[54] Having seen how the Cuban revolution had impacted that country's armed forces (Castro disbanded Batista's army and had many officers executed), Latin American military men had an extra incentive for vigilance. The prominence of counterinsurgency was less a function of U.S. pressure than the natural response to a growing (if sometimes exaggerated) threat.[55]

Counterinsurgency was not simply about neutralizing the Left militarily. It also drew on the same ideas about social and economic development that underlay the Alliance for Progress. "The military officer operating in a less developed part of the world," Defense Department official Alexis Johnson told Latin American officers, "must be concerned with the economic and sociological demands for reform if he is going to be totally successful." An integrated counterinsurgency program would couple antiguerrilla operations with "civic action" projects like irrigation and road-building. These initiatives would simultaneously win the support of the rural population and break down the isolation that impeded modernization. "In every country," administration officials wrote of Latin America in 1961, "there are problem areas susceptible to attack by indigenous military forces in a civic action role." In this sense, counterinsurgency was less a replacement for than a complement to the Alliance.[56]

Yet what if invigorated counterinsurgency programs were not enough to hold back the Left? Both Kennedy and Lyndon Johnson after him viewed the prospect of a "second Cuba" with terror. A Soviet–Cuban ally in Central or South America, U.S. officials feared, would endanger the Panama Canal, provide an improved base for subversive activities, and allow Moscow to blackmail Latin American leaders.[57] It would also lead to ruin for the president who had "allowed" this to happen. Kennedy predicted that "the American people would not stand for a situation which looked as though the Soviet Union had leap-frogged over Cuba to land on the continent in the Western Hemisphere."

Johnson harbored the same fear. "If Castro and Communism had succeeded in a larger state in Latin America, why all of you would have been writing about it longer than you have about China," he told reporters in 1965.[58]

Both Kennedy and Johnson resolved to do whatever necessary to keep a "second Cuba" from coming to pass. "How many troops could we get into the Dominican Republic in a 12–24–36–48 hour period?" Kennedy asked Defense Secretary Robert McNamara. "How many into Honduras? How many into Venezuela?" In 1963 the president declared that the United States would use "every resource at our command to prevent the establishment of another Cuba in this hemisphere." Johnson made a nearly identical statement in 1965. If Alliance reforms and counterinsurgency could not keep the Left in check, American military power would.[59]

Kennedy was determined to prevent a second Cuba; he was no less adamant about destroying the first. During 1961–1962 the CIA launched Operation Mongoose. "My idea," said Bobby Kennedy in 1961, "is to stir things up on [the] island with espionage, sabotage, general disorder." The administration sponsored industrial sabotage and exile raids, sought to have Castro assassinated, and apparently considered "decisive U.S. military intervention" to topple the regime.[60] Mongoose assumed such proportions that it discomfited even Johnson, who termed it "a damned branch of Murder, Inc. in the Caribbean."[61]

Washington's stance toward Latin America was driven by the fear of revolution, but it also reflected the supreme confidence of superpowerdom. Kennedy's policies featured not just a willingness to use U.S. diplomatic and military power, but also the sincere belief that Washington's economic and ideological influence was sufficient to thrust Latin America into the modern age. In this sense U.S. officials had much in common with their Soviet and Cuban counterparts. Each of these powers sought not simply to influence Latin America, but also to make that region a showcase for its own model of social and economic development.

Yet Moscow, Havana, and Washington all failed to spur the changes they sought in Latin America. Soviet and Cuban programs encountered obstacles from the start. As Operation Mongoose unfolded in early 1962, Soviet officials worried that socialism in Cuba itself, let alone in Latin America as a whole, might not survive. "Wildly aggressive powers in the USA," wrote Soviet ambassador A. I. Alekseev, were pushing for "the most decisive actions against

Cuba."[62] For Khrushchev, this was a sobering prospect. "If Cuba fell," he later explained, "other Latin American countries would reject us, claiming that for all our might the Soviet Union hadn't been able to do anything for Cuba." If Cuba went, in other words, so would the chances of attracting other Latin American countries to socialism.[63] Accordingly, Khrushchev decided to undertake an "offensive policy" for protecting Castro. In mid-1962 Moscow began transporting ballistic missiles to Cuba.[64]

This gambit backfired when U.S. spy planes discovered the missiles in mid-October, triggering a diplomatic showdown. The Cuban missile crisis was the closest that Latin America's Cold War—and the Cold War in general—ever came to touching off a nuclear conflagration. In Washington Kennedy and his aides feared that a weak response to Moscow's endeavor would expose the administration politically, encourage Soviet probes in Berlin, and destroy U.S. prestige and credibility in Latin America. "If the missiles are not removed or eliminated," said Treasury Secretary Douglas Dillon, "the United States will lose all of its friends in Latin America, who will become convinced that our fear is such that we cannot act."[65]

On October 22 Kennedy announced a blockade of Cuba and initiated preparations for military action. After a week of tense diplomacy, caution and compromise ultimately prevailed. "We do not want to unleash a war," Khrushchev told the Politburo. "We only wanted to threaten them." On October 27 Khrushchev (negotiating without Castro's knowledge) agreed to remove the missiles in return for a promise not to invade Cuba and a secret pledge to withdraw U.S. missiles from Turkey.[66]

While the no-invasion pledge constituted a victory of sorts for Castro and Khrushchev ("the USA was forced to acknowledge that we have our own interests in the West hemisphere," the Soviet leader), the missile crisis was crippling to broader Soviet and Cuban aims in Latin America.[67] First, it gravely weakened hopes that Cuba might become an attractive model for the rest of the region. During the early 1960s Castro's ideological capital among Latin American moderates had steadily eroded. Castro's alignment with Moscow, widespread use of the death penalty for "crimes against the revolution," and limiting of political and civil liberties caused formerly sympathetic observers like Frei to label Cuba's regime "a totalitarian government."[68] Similarly, the decision to accept Soviet missiles horrified most observers. The OAS (Organization of American States) gave strong support to the United States during the crisis, and Adolfo López Mateos of Mexico called the missiles "a grave threat not only for the security of the peoples of the American continent but also for the peace of the world."[69] Moscow had hoped that its support would heighten the attractiveness of the Cuban model, but the end result was just the opposite.

The Latin American reaction to the crisis was emblematic of the thoroughly counterproductive nature of Cuban diplomacy. While Castro had come to power at a time of rising anti-Americanism, his alliance with Moscow and attempts to subvert Latin American governments soon convinced many observers that Cuban imperialism was more dangerous than the U.S. variant. In 1962 the OAS adopted a Colombian proposal to expel Cuba from the organization, and two years later the discovery of a Cuban arms cache in Venezuela led that body to impose sanctions on Havana.[70] When, in 1964, the Mexican government learned that Cuban agents were in contact with anti-PRI elements, Mexico secretly joined the anti-Castro coalition, imposing unpublicized travel restrictions on the island and sharing information on Cuban affairs with the United States.[71]

Economic underperformance undermined any remaining appeal that Castro's revolution might have had. During the early 1960s Castro's economic program failed badly. Agricultural output fell off, and poor management and a shortage of spare parts derailed the experiment in industrialization. The government, admitted President Osvaldo Dorticós, had made "undeniably costly" errors.[72] Cuba reverted to a heightened reliance on sugar, but this strategy produced dislocations in other sectors and culminated in the disastrous failure of the "ten-million ton harvest" of 1970. By the early 1970s Cuba was completely reliant on Soviet aid and isolated within the Western Hemisphere. Far from establishing an attractive, independent model of development, Castro swapped one form of dependency and dictatorship for another.[73]

A second effect of the missile crisis was to produce serious strains within the Soviet–Cuban alliance. Castro considered Khrushchev's retreat a betrayal. "The whole of Cuba was ready for defense," he told Mikoyan. "And suddenly— concessions." "Nikita, you fairy," chanted crowds in Havana, "What you give you can't take back."[74] Soviet officials recoiled at Castro's recklessness during the crisis (he had urged Khrushchev to launch a preemptive nuclear attack on the United States). "We do not want to die beautifully," Mikoyan told Cuban officials. "Socialism must live."[75]

The missile crisis pushed Khrushchev and Castro in different directions concerning the struggle for influence in Latin America. Khrushchev, hoping to dampen tensions with the United States, throttled back Soviet support for the guerrillas. "Revolution is not brought from outside on bayonets," he said. Castro took precisely the opposite lesson. Moscow could not be counted on to defend Cuba; "we must not go on expecting from anyone but ourselves." Following the crisis, Castro became more determined to win allies via support for revolutions abroad.[76]

These divergent strategies gradually drove Cuban–Soviet relations toward the breaking point. After Guevara issued his call for "two, three, or many Viet Nams" in 1966, Leonid Brezhnev (Khrushchev's successor) termed Cuban policies "dangerous." By this time Cuban and Soviet leaders regarded each other dimly. "Brezhnev thinks that Castro is some kind of idiot," CIA analysts wrote, "and Castro probably isn't very fond of Brezhnev either."[77] During the late 1960s Moscow decreased economic support to Cuba and Castro publicly criticized Soviet timidity. The alliance survived, but the cooperation of the early 1960s had broken down.[78]

The deterioration of the alliance weakened prospects for radical change in Latin America. An even greater obstacle was the *foco* itself. From early on, the *foco* emerged as a divisive force among Latin America's leftist organizations. The pro-Soviet Communist parties dismissed the *foco* as a perversion of Marxism and a dangerously premature call to arms. "It is impossible to create a vanguard arbitrarily or artificially," warned Luís Corvalán, the general secretary of Chile's Communist Party.[79] They also feared that the *foco*'s glorification of violence would leave them marginalized within the leftist hierarchy. Sure enough, the *foquistas* now portrayed themselves as Latin America's authentic socialists, dismissing the contributions of the old guard. "Those who deny the role that violence decisively plays in social transformations have no right to call themselves Marxists," declared one pro-guerrilla group. "The possibility of a 'peaceful way' in Venezuela is absurd," argued that country's MIR. These groups' ideological convergence with Castro gave them access to the reservoir of Cuban support, and the old guard found that its influence was on the wane.[80]

During the mid-1960s the influence of the *foco* combined with the ideological fallout from the Sino–Soviet split to provoke a series of clashes within the Left. In Venezuela Castro's denunciations of the communist leadership and his support for a breakaway faction under Douglas Bravo led to open polemics. "The rightist leadership of the Venezuelan party," Castro declared, "has succeeded in practically becoming the enemy of the revolutionaries and an instru-

ment of imperialism and oligarchy." The Venezuelan Central Committee re-
plied in kind, mocking Castro as a "revolutionary Pope."[81] In Bolivia Guevara's
insistence on directing the revolutionary struggle alienated the Communists
and caused them to disown the guerrilla movement. "The Bolivian Revolution
and the armed struggle must be planned and directed by Bolivians," they in-
sisted.[82] The Bolivian Left split into pro-Chinese (pro-guerrilla) and pro-Soviet
(anti-guerrilla) wings of the Communist Party, a Revolutionary Workers Party
(POR) that characterized Cuban policy as "a service to Yankee imperialism and
worldwide counterrevolution," and other organizations.[83] Across the region,
accusations of "revisionism" and "Trotskyism" flew.[84]

The resulting discord was present on a region-wide scale at the Tricontinental and OLAS conferences in 1966–1967. Castro denounced the popular front
and even urban (as opposed to rural) violence as "stupid" and "a crime." "Those
who say in any place in Latin America that they are going to achieve power
peacefully will be deceiving the masses," he announced.[85] The old guard retaliated by aligning with Moscow and temporarily blocking agreement on an
OLAS resolution calling for violent struggle in Latin America. At roughly the
same time, seven communist parties declared that "each party has the right to
pursue its own line in accordance with the conditions prevailing in the country," a clear swipe at Castro's domineering approach.[86]

Throughout the region, ideological divisions played havoc with attempts to
mount an effective revolutionary struggle. In Colombia the Communist Party
broke relations with Cuba and expelled "deviationist" leaders. The competing
wings of the party rarely cooperated with either each other or guerrilla groups
such as the Revolutionary Armed Forces of Colombia (FARC) or National
Liberation Army (ELN), leaving the violent movement markedly disjointed.[87]
The situation was similar in Guatemala; the Rebel Armed Forces (FAR) later
admitted that, after its split with the Guatemalan Labor Party (PGT) in 1968,
there was no "unity of action."[88] In Venezuela the divisions among the Left led
to constant leadership disputes and complicated logistical matters.[89] In Paraguay one faction of the Socialist Party took to assaulting and even murdering
its rivals.[90] The mobilization encouraged by the *foco* widened the internal gaps
that had emerged during the 1950s, throwing the Left into chaos.

Even more problematic than the divisions accentuated by *foquismo* was the
fact that the theory was not relevant to Latin American societies. There had
always been sleight-of-hand involved in the *foco*. One of Guevara's motives in
elaborating the theory was to outmaneuver his rivals for power in Cuba,

which led him to exaggerate the role of the rural guerrillas in the anti-Batista struggle and overstate the possibility of popular support for such movements. During the 1960s events demonstrated this essential superficiality of the theory. Time after time, *foquista* groups took up arms and waited for the *campesinos* to follow. Time after time, the *campesinos* kept them waiting.[91]

Why such disappointing results? For one thing, Latin America's "peasantry" was never as coherent a group as the *foco* implied. Land tenure was a problem in nearly every Latin American country, but the extent of the crisis varied considerably. In some regions of Guatemala landless tenant farmers constituted 15–25 percent of the population; in others the number was only 4–5 percent. Where most poor farmers had some access to land, the insurgents were viewed as troublemakers rather than liberators. In 1962 peasants in Huehuetenango helped round up the guerrillas and deliver them to the army, and between 1959 and 1967 there were similar happenings in Bolivia, Paraguay, Peru, Colombia, Venezuela, and El Salvador. In terms of its willingness to cooperate with the guerrillas, the peasant class that Guevara spoke of did not exist.[92]

Even where levels of tenancy were relatively high, revolutionary violence often had little appeal. In areas of Venezuela, Peru, Bolivia, and Colombia where land distribution was highly skewed, the initiation of agrarian and other reforms convinced many observers that local needs were more likely to be met by the government than by the guerrillas. After Betancourt oversaw the redistribution of 100,000 parcels of land and the expansion of sanitation and education services, peasants were reported to take up arms *against* the guerrillas. Civic action and rural development programs had a similar effect in Colombia, and even in Peru, where the agrarian reform stalled, the possibility of land redistribution diminished rural support for the insurgents.[93]

The guerrillas' failure to relate to the basic needs of the rural poor indicated a broader cultural divide. The *foco* identified the countryside as the only acceptable location for guerrilla struggle, but most insurgents had little in common with residents of these areas. Guerrilla organizers were mainly urban, *mestizo*, and middle class. They rarely spoke the languages of the countryside (Guevara actually learned the wrong language in preparation for his guerrilla campaign in Bolivia), and considered the rural masses to be politically ignorant.[94] This condescending attitude combined with the history of interethnic exploitation in Latin America to provoke mistrust and hostility from the rural poor. Security officials exploited these feelings, establishing networks of "rural military commissioners" that gathered and distributed information on insurgent activities.[95] The guerrillas soon found themselves isolated. As one Venezuelan leftist later admitted, "We saw the reality of the country through the eyes of *liceo* and university students, and we forgot that in the working class and the peasantry we had no support."[96] Guatemalan guerrillas also eventually acknowledged that "the great mass of the people did not participate actively in the revolutionary armed struggle."[97]

A final error of *foquismo* was its emphasis on exemplary violence. There has long been a cult of romanticism surrounding Guevarism, but the reality is that the *foquistas* were generally quite thuggish. Reflecting Guevara's call for "rivers of blood" and the belief that violence itself would revolutionize the masses, the guerrillas engaged in actions that were, quite simply, terroristic.[98] Venezuelan insurgents threatened to murder anyone who voted in the 1963 presidential elections, a stance that only alienated the 90 percent of registered voters that participated anyway. Guatemalan guerrillas murdered businessmen and other public figures and dissipated their support in the armed forces (the insurgency had, after all, begun as a military revolt) by executing eighteen soldiers in 1965. In Bolivia Guevara became so frustrated with the peasantry that, by the time of his death, he favored using violence *against* them to compel their cooperation. Such tactics rarely endeared the guerrillas to the broader public, and instead left them even more unpopular than before.[99]

In fact, the *foco* was better suited to radicalizing the Right than radicalizing the masses. In no case during the 1960s did a Latin American guerrilla movement achieve sufficient strength to seize power, but *foquista* violence and Cuban support provided militaries, security services, and conservative elites with both a reason and a pretext for internal repression. Whether as genuine fear or cynical rationalization (there was plenty of both at work), the notion that Guevara and his allies sought to spark, as Guatemalan military intelligence officers phrased it, "a revolution of the Cuban type," was elemental to the wave of anti-Left violence that swept Latin America during the 1960s and after.[100]

While it is often argued that U.S. intervention and counterinsurgency were decisive in defeating the radical Left, the reality is that the guerrillas did an excellent job of beating themselves. Lacking popular support and weakened by ideological divisions, these movements were easy prey for counterinsurgent forces. "The guerrilla was short-lived," boasted one Peruvian general, "we had infiltrated them thoroughly."[101] Venezuela's MIR admitted in

1964 that "the correlation of forces in Latin America . . . is favorable to imperialism at this time," and in 1967 Guevara himself was captured and executed
at the close of a disastrous (but hardly atypical) campaign in Bolivia.[102] By the
late 1960s the rural guerrilla movement had ground to a halt, done in by internal disagreements, tactical errors, and the very ideas that had helped spur
these initiatives in the first place.

The failure of the guerrilla challenge had a pronounced effect on the Left's
subsequent approach to the region. While in many ways the Left would never
get beyond Guevarism, later guerrillas would shift the fight to the cities in an
effort to avoid replicating the disaster of the 1960s. Diplomats in Moscow and
Havana also changed tactics. For Soviet officials, the frustrations of dealing
with Castro and the collapse of the guerrilla movement caused a turn toward
a less ambitious policy centered on building political and economic ties with
governments of all ideological inclinations. In Havana Castro certainly never
abandoned efforts to export revolution, but Cuban officials would dilute the
stridency of the Guevara era and emulate Moscow in building relations with
non- and even anticommunist governments. The strongly ideological content
of the policies of the 1960s would be tempered by a less romantic pragmatism
in the years that followed.

If the travails of the Left constituted a victory of sorts for the United States,
they also obscured the fact that Washington's initiatives in Latin America
had been no more successful than those of its rivals. The Alliance for Progress
symbolized this mediocre record. While the launching of the Alliance temporarily pushed anti-U.S. sentiment into the background, more substantively
the program left much to be desired. Per capita income grew at less than 2
percent annually during the 1960s, and as economic and social reforms stalled,
inequality increased in many countries.[103] In 1968 the CIA concluded that
while "revolution seems unlikely in most Latin American countries within the
next few years," over the next decade, "we see conditions developing throughout the area which will be much more conducive to revolution." Another U.S.
official called the region "a time bomb almost certain to explode a few years
hence."[104]

Why did the Alliance fare so poorly? Low commodity prices depressed
growth and produced balance-of-payments problems. USAID (United States
Agency for International Development) struggled to find employees with suf-

ficient language or technical skills to oversee development programs. U.S.-owned corporations opposed initiatives that might jeopardize their labor practices, privileged tax status, or land holdings. And as the Vietnam War escalated during the mid-1960s, U.S. aid to Latin America fell off. "We're just too damned anxious to give money away," said Johnson.[105]

Beyond these problems, the very ideas that drove the Alliance ended up weakening it. The one-size-fits-all approach to development promoted by modernization theory led to programs that were poorly fitted to their cultural or economic settings. USAID administrators in Bolivia concluded that it was "extremely difficult and expensive" to extend agricultural credits to scattered *campesinos,* and cooperated with Bolivian authorities to move the farmers into "hastily organized cooperatives." Predictably, the *campesinos* abandoned the cooperatives at first chance. In Costa Rica USAID-sponsored production increases glutted the agricultural market, drove down prices, and impoverished small farmers. "Our knowledge of what is economically productive and what is not is fundamentally deficient," reported one perceptive observer.[106]

In fact, the course of the Alliance gave the lie to the central premise of modernization theory. U.S. planners had assumed that development would breed stability, but in a number of instances the opposite was true. Projects meant to empower long-marginalized classes, while rarely carried through fully, upset internal power dynamics and provoked instability. The promise of reform and redistribution energized both opponents and defenders of the status quo, leading to polarization and exacerbating the very turmoil these programs were meant to control. "The pressures among organized groups and peoples for positive and radical changes in the inequitable and backward socio-economic structures and for gains in levels of living are mounting steadily," the CIA reported in 1964. "The hazards of governing may be increasing rather than lessening in Latin America."[107]

During the early 1960s these pressures combined with economic crises, long-standing political rivalries, and fears of insurgency to cause military coups in several Latin American countries. While not all the juntas that came to power during the 1960s were reactionary, in many cases they slowed or weakened domestic reforms. Nonetheless, Washington generally supported the *golpistas,* enthusiastically in some cases and with varying degrees of embarrassment in others. The military, wrote State Department higher-ups after one coup, constituted "a strong bulwark against possible disorders fomented by the extreme left."[108] Driven by the exigencies of anticommunism, U.S. officials weakened the progressive impulse at the heart of the Alliance.

The instability provoked by economic and political change—and the consequent marginalization of reform—had no better illustration than U.S. dealings with the Dominican Republic between 1961 and 1966. In 1961 Kennedy worked to oust Rafael Trujillo, an erstwhile ally who had fallen into disrepute. Fearing, as U.S. consul Henry Dearborn put it, that Trujillo's totalitarian rule was "softening up the D.R. for leftist extremists," Kennedy sought to have the generalissimo killed to open the way for a transition to democracy (or at least a less distasteful anticommunism).[109]

A group of Dominicans murdered Trujillo in May, and Kennedy dispatched a U.S. flotilla to guard against either a communist takeover or a restoration of the old regime. In 1962 the freest elections in Dominican history resulted in the ascension of Juan Bosch, an ambitious reformer who declared, "Agrarian reform *is* the Dominican Revolution."[110] Within months, though, Kennedy had cooled to Bosch and wavered in his support for Dominican democracy. Bosch proved friendlier to the Left than Washington had expected; U.S. officials called him "a lousy president" whose "tolerance of communist activities in the Dominican Republic is a dangerous risk."[111] Bosch's agrarian reform was highly polarizing, as it galvanized landless farmers and aroused the anxieties of Dominican conservatives. In September 1963 the Dominican military overthrew Bosch, earning a wink from Kennedy.

Yet Bosch would not go away. In April 1965 he sought to return to Santo Domingo at the head of a revolt within the military. Fearing that "the Castroites are taking over," Johnson sent in 26,000 Marines to pacify the island. After helping defeat the pro-Bosch forces, the Marines oversaw elections that brought Trujillo-era holdover Joaquín Balaguer to power. The outcome satisfied Johnson. "We did a pretty good job there," he remarked.[112]

The events of 1965–1966 capped a momentous shift in U.S.–Dominican relations, and in American policy toward Latin America. At the outset of this period, Kennedy had identified right-wing authoritarianism as a breeding ground for left-wing extremism, and thus pursued an equal-opportunity assassination policy that targeted dictators on both ends of the political spectrum.[113] Yet when reform and democratization, thought to be the antidote to internal upheaval, turned out to be themselves destabilizing, Kennedy and later Johnson shunted the progressives aside. A preference for the Right and a proclivity for intervention came to characterize American policy. Kennedy himself explained the basis of this shift amid the turmoil after Trujillo's death. The United States "wanted a democratic regime in the Dominican Republic; failing that we would prefer a friendly dictatorship, and the last thing we wanted was a Castro type regime." Reform was preferable, but stability was essential.[114]

This dilemma confronted U.S. officials in any number of cases during the early 1960s, and in the vast majority, reform lost just as badly as it had in the Dominican Republic. This trend underlay U.S. support for military coups, as well as Washington's stance on initiatives like land reform. While U.S. officials understood that land reform was the central element of the Alliance for Progress, ideological concerns led Washington to temper its initial enthusiasm. Congress declined to fund agrarian reforms, with conservatives terming these programs an attempt to "export socialist ideas to Latin America." In Brazil the suspicion that the radical Left had infiltrated the government's reform led U.S. diplomats to withdraw their support for the initiative. In this and other cases, anticommunism compromised the reformist zeal on which U.S. officials had always known the Alliance would rise or fall.[115]

Counterinsurgency fit the same pattern. To control the pressures released in the early 1960s, Kennedy and Johnson placed increasing importance on counterinsurgency as the decade progressed. American training and supply programs expanded rapidly, and in 1962 alone, 9,000 Latin American officers and soldiers graduated from institutions like the School of the Americas.[116] Under the aegis of CONDECA, U.S. advisers provided aerial surveillance and advanced telecommunications equipment in support of border sweeps and arms interdiction missions.[117] U.S. money funded organizations like El Salvador's National Democratic Organization (ORDEN), which oversaw the creation of a network of rural informers tied to the government. By the mid-1960s these programs were at the center of the battle against the insurgents. It was a U.S.-trained "Ranger Battalion" (with CIA officials attached to it) that eventually captured and killed Guevara. The episode "shows the soundness of our 'preventive medicine' assistance," wrote National Security Adviser Walt Rostow.[118] During Operation Cleanup, a counterinsurgent sweep in Guatemala in March 1966, a U.S. mission led by former FBI agent John Longan provided state-of-the-art communications technology and real-time intelligence to the government forces. The operation netted scores of detainees who were interrogated, tortured, and executed. As economic development failed to provide internal tranquility, more coercive tactics came to the fore.[119]

Even counterinsurgency was overshadowed by the rising prominence of covert and military intervention. Both Kennedy and Johnson made good on their pledge to use drastic measures to forestall any leftist takeover. Aside from backing the putsch against Bosch in 1963, U.S. officials supported a coup against their old ally Ydígoras in Guatemala. "We should be grateful" for the coup, concluded U.S. ambassador John Bell.[120] Kennedy also engaged in a prolonged campaign to bring down British Guiana's Cheddi Jagan, who had received aid from Castro and predicted that communism would "sweep throughout the world."[121]

Kennedy was no slouch when it came to intervention, but Johnson made the deceased president look like a piker. In 1964 Johnson backed a military coup in Brazil, spent millions to support Eduardo Frei in Chile's presidential elections, and had U.S. troops put down riots in the Panama Canal Zone. The next year, the Marines quashed the pro-Bosch revolt in the Dominican Republic, and in 1966 the United States sought to swing elections in Costa Rica. "We either got the power or we haven't," explained Johnson, "and if we got it, I'm gonna use it, period."[122]

Kennedy had initially conceived of intervention and counterinsurgency as complements to rather than replacements for internal reform. In practice, however, these methods sometimes debilitated hopes for evolutionary social change. Washington's reliance on military and covert intervention made Moscoso's "job of evangelizing" nearly impossible. For elites already inclined to resist far-reaching reforms, the knowledge that the Marines would come to the rescue helped weaken the fear of revolution and, by extension, the imperative to liberalize. Even high-level U.S. advisers realized that sending in the troops was but a palliative for Latin America's unrest. "We could easily have a few more revolutions even if we get San Domingo patched up," commented NSC (National Security Council) aide Robert Komer in 1966.[123]

Counterinsurgency proved even more corrosive to democratic reform. As Operation Cleanup showed, counterinsurgency could be a brutal business. Many U.S. and Latin American officials took a Manichean view of the Cold War and a no-holds-barred approach to counterinsurgency. An Argentine general declared that insurgency "today represents the clash between two civilizations."[124] CIA agents advocated torture as a means of extracting information from detainees, and one official recommended that the Colombian government utilize death squads to "execute paramilitary, sabotage and/ or terrorist activities against known communist proponents." Latin American military officials needed little encouragement, and such practices became common.[125]

These tactics exerted a chilling effect on Latin American democracy. The security services used violence and terror not simply against the guerrillas, but against anyone that challenged the privileges of the dominant elite. This was especially true in Central America, where close ties between the military and the oligarchies made counterinsurgency a tool of political control rather than national defense. In Nicaragua the response to what Luís Somoza termed the threat of "atheist Communism" was tinged with familiar racial and class overtones. One commander reacted to a series of land invasions by threatening to "leave Indians hanging by the same barbed wire that they cut."[126] The tactics used against union leaders, agrarian reformers, and other "communist sympathizers" by paramilitary groups such as ORDEN and Guatemala's National Liberation Movement (MLN) were indistinguishable from those long deployed by elites to protect their holdings. "Any individual with apparent leftist inclinations is a potential victim," reported the Canadian embassy.[127] By the late 1960s Longan acknowledged that the Guatemalan security forces were often used "not so much as protectors of the nation against communist enslavement, but as the oligarchy's oppressors of legitimate social change."[128] Here as elsewhere, measures originally intended to create space for reform actually helped make such changes less likely.

To assign the United States the primary responsibility for the course of events in Latin America during the 1960s, however, is to miss the point. While this decade saw a major diplomatic, economic, and military offensive on Washington's part, American officials found the region more resistant to U.S. influence than they had assumed. American policy toward military coups, for instance, owed not simply to anticommunism but also to a frank recognition of the limits of U.S. leverage. Kennedy had initially opposed the Peruvian coup of 1962, calling it a "ruinous setback" and suspending aid to the junta.[129] Before long, though, Kennedy realized that he had no good options for reversing events in Peru. The Peruvian officers knew that Washington could not long shun an anticommunist government. "When the U.S. knows exactly the reasons for our attitude," predicted one officer, "it will not only accept the *Golpe* but will support us."[130] Moreover, withholding recognition, terminating aid to Lima, or following Betancourt's advice in convoking an OAS meeting to halt "this contagious epidemic of *coups d'etat*" would undoubtedly be construed by many observers as unwarranted interference and probably do little to reduce the staying power of the government. Brazilian foreign minister Alfonso Arinos, for instance, made clear that his government had no interest in "interventionist" measures.[131] "We must not be deceived by [the] myth of U.S. omnipotence," warned U.S. ambassador Richard Loeb. Kennedy restored aid to the Peruvian government after it pledged to hold elections, and the administration concluded, as one official put it in 1963, that "a U.S. frown doesn't deter others from committing what we consider to be political sins."[132] Pressuring military regimes to give up power was not simply unwise, Kennedy believed; it was also unrealistic.

A tiff with Ecuador in the mid-1960s illustrated the dangers of too forward a stance on the Alliance for Progress. When Ecuadorian conservatives succeeded in weakening a tax reform measure by 30 percent, Washington reduced a $10 million loan to that country by a similar proportion. The Ecuadorian government cried foul, harshly criticized Johnson at a hemispheric summit, and snubbed certain subsequent Alliance measures. If not pressuring governments to honor their Alliance commitments was a losing strategy, taking the opposite tack seemed little more rewarding.[133]

The Ecuadorian and Peruvian cases hit on a fundamental reality of the Alliance: that it was generally Latin American actors that determined how development and aid projects played out. Where fairly progressive leaders could move strongly in support of reform, U.S.–Latin American cooperation produced decent results. In Venezuela Washington supported Betancourt's agrarian reform, civic action, and rural infrastructure initiatives, all of which weakened the insurgency. In Chile U.S. officials strongly supported a relatively successful agrarian reform, the enfranchisement of the rural poor, and an expansion of *campesino* labor rights. In Peru, while agrarian reform stalled amid political gridlock during the 1960s, this initiative nonetheless played an important role in undercutting the guerrillas. As one former insurgent put it, once the agrarian reform had begun, "the slogan 'Land or Death' no longer had such urgent meaning."[134]

These cases, however, were exceptions to the more common scenario. Governments with strong ties to the oligarchies supported the Alliance publicly, but in private they worked to ensure that reform would fail to alter the balance of economic and social power. Bowles had predicted in 1961 that many Latin American governments would make "no more than a gesture" in the direction of meaningful agrarian reform; events subsequently confirmed his analysis.[135]

The upshot was the perversion of Alliance programs. As U.S. planners had hoped, a number of governments used Alliance funds to expand commercial agriculture and light industry, a strategy that promised strong macroeconomic growth and benefited U.S. investors. El Salvador and Nicaragua saw surges in gross national product (GNP) during the 1960s, with the latter country averaging 6.2 percent annual growth. Industrial production rose by up to 100 percent in Central America, and South American countries like Brazil, Paraguay, and others registered impressive agricultural gains.[136] With redistributive projects having been gutted, however, this growth strengthened the oligarchies and weakened the poor. The increasing mechanization that came along with commercial agriculture depressed employment opportunities for agrarian workers, as did the shift of resources toward light industry. More dramatically, when not offset by land reform, the concentration of holdings characteristic of commercial agriculture worsened the plight of the rural poor.[137] By 1970 the top 10 percent of landowners controlled 81.4 percent of Guatemala's arable land. In El Salvador the numbers were roughly the same.[138] The *campesino,* complained one Paraguayan, no longer had "a single piece of land for his labors."[139] As implemented by many Latin American governments, Alliance programs actually *decreased* the availability of land to the rural poor. "We still haven't found a formula by which we can be sure that whatever we're doing is really getting through to the people," admitted one Alliance supervisor.[140]

Throughout the region, U.S. officials found that the progressive spirit evident at the founding of the Alliance did not translate into practical measures. The problem was hardly a lack of reformist leaders; politicians like Betancourt, Alberto Lleras of Colombia, and Fernando Belaúnde in Peru understood the need for redistributive programs, if only as a means of keeping themselves in power. The problem was that Latin American inequalities were so entrenched as to render even relatively bold reforms ineffectual. In Colombia the government's plan to distribute 20,000 farm plots per year was barely enough to keep pace with rural population growth.[141] Given the limited quality of Latin American democracy during this period, moreover, even reformist leaders often lacked the latitude necessary to take these steps. Frondizi constantly clashed with the military over reintegrating the Peronists, a conflict that eventually led to his ouster. The pacted nature of Colombian democracy kept reforms in that country limited, and Belaúnde also struggled to overcome opposition from Haya and Peruvian conservatives. When Ydígoras tried to allow Juan José Arévalo, a veteran of the "ten years of spring" and a proponent of "democratic socialism," to participate in presidential elections in 1963, the military overthrew him.[142]

Scholars have often faulted Kennedy and Johnson for not putting greater force behind their desire for reform in Latin America.[143] This criticism is certainly valid in that U.S. policymakers consistently chose anticommunism over potentially destabilizing reforms, but, insofar as this tendency is cited as a chief cause of the Alliance's demise, it ignores two essential realities. First, it makes the unreasonable assumption that U.S. browbeating could force Latin American governments to do something that they were convinced would lead to their own ruin. Second, even had U.S. pressure been capable of producing such an outcome, the Ecuadorian case indicates that reaching this destination would have required Washington to use the same heavy-handed tactics for which it is so often criticized. All told, seeking to compel Alliance-style reform would have surely produced considerable opposition and diplomatic outrage, and might well still have failed to produce the desired results.

Economic elites were not the only actors that obstructed reform. In Chile the Movement of the Revolutionary Left (MIR), which opposed the measured pace of Frei's initiatives, conducted illegal land seizures and effectively allied itself to the Right in opposing government programs. In other cases indigenous communities resisted land reform because it resembled the measures that had been used during the nineteenth century to break up their communal holdings.[144]

The frustrations attached to the Alliance were in few cases more apparent than in Brazil. The extreme poverty of Brazil's urban slums and Northeast made that country a key focus of U.S. concern in the early 1960s, and on the surface, President João Goulart supported many Alliance ideals. During 1961–1962 U.S. and Brazilian representatives met to discuss Alliance projects and Goulart's development program.[145] By 1963, however, U.S.–Brazilian relations had come apart. In some measure this falling-out resulted from the anticommunism of U.S. officials in Brazil, who viewed Goulart's proposals to enfranchise illiterate voters and his threat to use violence against Brazil's landowners as "demagoguery" and worried that his policies might empower the radical Left.[146] Goulart also refused to back "interventionist" measures against Castro, frustrating U.S. diplomats.[147]

Equally important, though, was that Goulart often seemed determined to make cooperation with the United States impossible. Even as he and his advisers sought U.S. aid, they condemned the Alliance publicly, hoping, as one official put it, "to ride the nationalist wave."[148] Even more damaging, Goulart had little grasp of economic affairs. Remarks one scholar, "He knew little about the subject and tended to view economic matters almost solely in terms of their political ramifications."[149] This approach led to a disastrous macroeconomic policy that caused massive debt and skyrocketing inflation, and brought the country to what the U.S. embassy termed the "brink [of] financial catastrophe."[150] This profligacy, combined with an aversion to Goulart's politics, led Washington to adopt an "islands of sanity" program that bypassed the national government and worked directly with state and local offices. The decision infuriated Goulart, and U.S.–Brazilian relations declined steadily until the 1964 coup.[151]

As these cases indicate, the fundamental reality of the Alliance was that its success hinged on a degree of cooperation and mutual effort that was in too many cases not forthcoming. This is not to understate the degree to which modernization theory, anticommunism, and other aspects of U.S. policy undermined the Alliance. Across Latin America, though, the success or failure of reform programs flowed most directly from the political, social, and economic conditions in which they were implemented. Even Juan Bosch, who had plenty of reason to blame Washington for the failure of Dominican reform, chose instead to explain this phenomenon as a result "of the Latin American character, and . . . our historical shortcomings." As Bosch recognized, it was local resistance to reform, rather than the flaws and contradictions of U.S. policy, that ultimately obstructed meaningful change.[152]

The same could be said of counterinsurgency. It is beyond debate that U.S. counterinsurgency programs contributed to the erosion of Central American democracy. In general, though, it was the local context rather than U.S. aid that determined how counterinsurgency programs played out. While the highly oligarchic nature of Central American society gave counterinsurgency a conservative, repressive flavor, in other countries the doctrine fit within a more democratic framework. In Venezuela, which received more counterinsurgency attention from Kennedy than any other Latin American country (Washington provided $60 million in military assistance, U.S. trainers worked closely with the Venezuelan army and air force, and Kennedy suggested installing a "hotline" to Caracas so he could stay abreast of developments there),[153] these programs led not to a reactionary but a democratic outcome. Driven by Betancourt's anticommunist reformism, the Venezuelan government partnered counterinsurgency with civic action programs. And as recent scholarship has shown, counterinsurgency provided the Venezuelan armed forces with the high-profile mission they had lost following the overthrow of the dictatorship in 1958, and was therefore crucial to consolidating an imperfect democracy. Counterinsurgency greatly affected Latin American politics, but its impact varied considerably according to local conditions.[154]

Even with respect to covert and military intervention, the areas in which American influence was seemingly at its greatest, the dynamics of U.S.–Latin American relations were more subtle than one might have noticed at first glance. The frequency of U.S. intervention during the 1960s, and the fact that Cuba remained the sole communist state in the region, obscured the reality that American initiatives often produced dubious results. Washington's efforts were only minimally responsible for the outcomes in Chile, where Frei's victory owed almost entirely to the decision of Chile's conservatives to abandon their own candidate in order to block Allende, and in Brazil, where the military moved so efficiently that U.S. plans to support the uprising never went into effect. In other cases U.S. policy was simply ineffective. Castro remained in power, and Washington's candidate failed to win the Costa Rican elections of 1966.[155]

Even where U.S. policy was more decisive, as in Panama, the Dominican Republic, and British Guiana, American intervention often missed the mark. In British Guiana the government that replaced Jagan's eventually turned to Castro for support—the very outcome that Kennedy had feared. In Panama and the Dominican Republic Johnson's fear of a "Castro operation" was misplaced, as Cuban involvement was basically nonexistent.[156] In the charged atmosphere of the 1960s, though, even a glimpse (albeit a mistaken one) of Castro's shadow was enough to override Johnson's reluctance to intervene. "I'm in a hell of a shape either way," he commented during the Dominican crisis. "If I take over, I can't live in the world. If I let them take over, I can't live over here." Time and again, Johnson's fear of "another Cuba" and the same superficial understanding of Latin American affairs that had long characterized U.S. policy produced a hair-trigger approach to intervention that slighted the complexity of events on the ground and brought only marginal benefits.[157]

Overall, the course of U.S. policy demonstrated that Washington's power in Latin America was not so great as it appeared. The Alliance for Progress, counterinsurgency, and military or covert interference had deep resonance in Latin American politics, but their meaning often corresponded more to the political and social context of the region than the intentions of U.S. planners. Modernization theory implied that it would be fairly simple for Washington to shape a dramatic departure in Latin American affairs; events on the ground told a different story.

By the late 1960s U.S. policy in Latin America had become unsustainable. Even in the short term, intervention weakened rather than strengthened Washington's position. While many governments were not necessarily opposed to the idea of intervening in the Dominican Republic, and a few countries later contributed troops to a peacekeeping force, they heatedly objected to Johnson's blatant disregard for OAS norms (the organization "ain't worth a damn, except window dressing" he remarked) in deploying the Marines unilaterally.[158] Radomiro Tomic, Chile's ambassador to the United States, noted that Washington's policy was "pregnant with the worst threats for the Interamerican System," and a Colombian official called the incident "the Waterloo" of the OAS. Sure enough, the fallout from this episode kick-started the evolution of the OAS from a tool of U.S. policy to an increasingly anti-U.S. organization. Johnson's policies helped wreck the very system Washington had constructed two decades earlier.[159]

Indeed, the Panamanian and Dominican interventions prompted a resurgence of the anti-American sentiment that had so troubled U.S. policymakers a few years earlier. In 1964 Frei criticized Washington for its "prolongation of a form of colonialism" in Panama, and Panamanian activists seized on the imperial overtones of the incident to mobilize worldwide diplomatic support.[160] In 1965 Uruguayan diplomat Carlos María Velazquez called the Dominican invasion a "new corollary to the Monroe Doctrine," while the Venezuelan press condemned this "return to the 'big stick.'" Colombian demonstrators invaded the U.S. embassy, chanting, "Down with yankee imperialism!"[161] By the latter part of the 1960s Washington was diplomatically isolated in Latin America and again seeking to deal with a rising tide of anti-imperial sentiment.

The United States avoided further gains by the Left during the 1960s, but upon closer inspection this victory was a Pyrrhic one. The bankruptcy of U.S. policies toward the region, evident in the stymieing of the Alliance and the outrage prompted by the Dominican episode, was confirmed by the rapid disappearance of modernization theory from Washington's stance toward Latin America. By the time that Richard Nixon took office in 1969 modernization theory was largely discredited, its faith in the possibility of exporting the American model replaced by a feeling that such projects were neither feasible nor necessarily desirable. "We can't do too much in the region," commented Nixon.[162] As with the *foco,* the failures and naivety of modernization theory led to its replacement by a more pragmatic alternative.

The superpower and Cuban initiatives of the 1960s were impressive in their scope, but less so in their effectiveness. The bold policies of that decade exerted considerable force on Latin American politics and society, but usually not in the way that their creators had intended. Khrushchev, Castro, and Guevara utterly failed to drive radical change in the region, and the Alliance for Progress was hardly more successful in spurring the thoroughgoing transformations envisioned by its founders. Naïve and simple-minded policies, derived not from an accurate reading of conditions in Latin America but from the ideological imperatives of the U.S., Cuban, and Soviet systems, proved utterly incapable of transforming a region as large and complex as Latin America. Time and time again the complexities of regional affairs punctured the illusions of foreign officials. In this sense the real story of the 1960s was perhaps not the extent of outside interference in Latin America, but the way in which the stubborn realities of hemispheric affairs exposed the essential superficiality of these programs.

For Moscow, Havana, and Washington, this was a decade in which grand ambitions proved not simply unrealistic, but self-defeating as well. Each power sought to expand its own influence and check that of its competitors, but did so in ways that were thoroughly counterproductive. Castro's clumsy interventionism ensured his diplomatic isolation, and the *foco* did the Left more harm than good. Khrushchev sought to spread socialism in Latin America, but his methods frightened and repelled the very audience he meant to woo. Washington avoided a "second Cuba," but its military interventions provoked a powerful backlash that more than canceled the limited gains accrued by sending in the Marines. By the end of the decade the superpowers and Cuba were thus grappling with the blowback from their own ambitions even as they struggled to meet the challenge posed by their opponents. The diplomacy of the 1960s had an ironic result: the Soviet Union, Cuba, and the United States attempted to contain one another, but wound up containing themselves.

Even so, the superpower and Cuban policies of the 1960s left an immensely influential legacy. In the unsettled domestic and international climate of the mid- and late 1960s, the fallout from these initiatives would contribute significantly to the evolution of Latin American politics. Superpower and Cuban intervention might not have fulfilled the aspirations of officials in Washington, Moscow, and Havana, but it nonetheless figured in forging the new landscape of conflict that would shape regional affairs during the 1970s and after.

3

From Crisis to Crisis

The decade that began with the Cuban revolution seemed to end with a whimper. The ebbing of the guerrilla threat and the Soviet-Cuban challenge eased the fear of revolution that pervaded the early 1960s, and lent an air of relative calm to regional affairs. Whereas in 1965 the CIA had predicted that up to twelve Latin American countries might soon confront revolutionary turmoil, three years later the agency offered a more sanguine assessment. "The fact is," analysts wrote, "that the establishments which now control the larger Latin American countries are much stronger than any proponents of revolutionary violence."[1]

If Latin America looked to be evolving toward greater equilibrium, the impression was misleading. On the surface the prospects for internal strife seemed to be fading, but at a deeper level the social and political tides were running in the opposite direction. In dominating the regional stage during the 1960s, the travails of the Left masked the rise of subtler, but no less momentous, influences that greatly increased the potential for turmoil. These forces drew on a complex combination of sources—the effects of the Vietnam War and slow Third-World economic growth, the internal and diplomatic conflicts dramatized by Castro's revolution, the blowback from superpower and Cuban interventions—and would soon thrust Latin America toward convulsions far more intense than those of the 1960s.

While the experience of the 1960s was, in important ways, one of diversity rather than uniformity, there were three such phenomena that stood out in their impact on hemispheric affairs. The first was the emergence of National

Security Doctrine, a set of ideas that dominated Latin American military politics as the decade went on. Centered on the premise that Latin American countries were now menaced by the twin dangers of subversion and insurgency, National Security Doctrine inspired numerous coups and augured the arrival of the assertive, ideologically driven military regime. The second was a regionwide political and social mobilization, symbolized by the growth of student and union activism in the cities and the surging influence of liberation theology in the countryside. The third was the ascent of dependency theory, an intellectual current that both reflected and drove a rising tide of *tercermundismo* and North–South conflict. By the late 1960s these forces and the events they informed had come to dominate the regional agenda.

That these influences would have such a wrenching impact was due to two factors. The first was that National Security Doctrine, liberation theology, and dependency theory channeled the various grievances and fears at work during the 1960s into more ideological—and therefore more potent—form. National Security Doctrine molded the anxieties provoked by revolution and upheaval into an encompassing, culturally charged worldview at the heart of military affairs. Liberation theology fused the power of religion to long-standing disputes over poverty and social injustice. Frustrations with slow economic development and ambivalence toward U.S. power found a new vocabulary and a social scientific cast in dependency theory. The events of 1960s crystallized issues like anti-Americanism, fears of revolution, and economic deprivation into powerful ideological frameworks that lent fire to the region's social and political affairs.

The second reason that these forces were so significant was that they were so incompatible. The North–South antagonism highlighted by dependency theory rubbed against the reality of U.S. power in Latin America and the recent record of American interventionism. More dramatically, the hyper-stable vision of society emphasized by National Security Doctrine clashed sharply with the protest, dissidence, and affinity for leftist ideas that characterized popular mobilization. By the late 1960s these influences were grating against one another, producing spasms of conflict that foretold the profound violence and upheaval of subsequent decades.

The 1960s were a bad stretch for democracy. Juntas came to power in El Salvador, Honduras, Guatemala, Panama, Peru, Ecuador, Bolivia, Brazil, Argentina, and the Dominican Republic, and the military controlled a veto on government policy in several other countries. After coming to power in 1969, Richard Nixon referred to Latin America's leaders as "the dictators," a label both derisive and essentially accurate.[2]

Why were military coups so prevalent during the 1960s? Civilian control of the military had always been weak in Latin America. Historically, the generals had rarely hesitated to take the statehouse in order to remove inept politicians or advance their own ambitions. Argentina's Juan Onganía, who would seize power in 1966, captured this notion that the military was above electoral politics—and thus elected politicians—in a speech given two years earlier. "Military obedience is ultimately owed and directed to the Constitution and its laws," he said, "never to the men or political parties which circumstantially hold power." Added to long-standing rivalries between the armed forces and parties like Peru's APRA and Argentina's Peronists, this attitude created a climate conducive to military takeovers.[3]

The instability that followed the Cuban revolution turned this long-standing civil–military discord into the rampant *golpismo* of the 1960s. Rising expectations and demands for reform fostered growing internal tensions. Simultaneously, the emergence of Soviet- and Cuban-backed guerrilla movements portended a revolutionary threat from within. Brazilian general Antônio Carlos Murici feared that Havana and Moscow sought to turn his country into "a new China," and Paraguayan officials alleged that Castro aimed at "the unleashing of insurrection in Latin America."[4] Guatemalan authorities wrote of Guevara's "weakly disguised" effort to provoke revolt, and pointed to "the tremendous danger that Castro represented for all America."[5]

Guerrilla violence and internal turmoil elicited an assertive reaction by the military. Fearing that the politicians would be unable to control this turbulence, officers in a number of countries decided that they must preempt the communist threat. A Chilean officer referred to Frei as "a Kerensky," language echoed by Brazilian officials before the 1964 coup.[6] An Argentine officer captured the general attitude, arguing that in the face of subversion and unrest, "We cannot continue on the defensive."[7] The Cuban revolution and subsequent guerrilla offensive failed to incite revolution, but succeeded in provoking an antirevolutionary response.

This fear of revolution was evident in the rise of National Security Doctrine during the 1960s. A collection of ideas based on the need for a centralized, integrated approach to fighting subversion, National Security Doctrine suffused Latin American politics following the Cuban revolution. It influenced coups in Peru in 1962 and 1968, Brazil in 1964, Argentina in 1962 and 1966, and various other countries as well. Even in Stroessner's Paraguay, often derided as an anachronistic backwater (one U.S. official called it "the kind of nineteenth-century military regime that looks good on the cartoon page"), National Security Doctrine and the fear that communist agents sought to foment revolution "at any price" informed a marked expansion of the national intelligence apparatus, to the point that government operatives reported the content of Sunday mass.[8]

Intellectually, National Security Doctrine was rooted in the characteristics of the postwar international system. The Cold War, many Latin American strategists argued, was a worldwide ideological struggle, a "permanent war" between communism and the West. "There is no longer a clear distinction between where peace ends and war begins," wrote Brazil's Golbery. In this contest traditional conquest had been replaced by subversion as the chief string in the communists' bow. It was therefore necessary to prevent the outbreak of actual violence by taking a proactive, comprehensive approach to the problem. "One must not wait for the illness to advance," one Argentine officer wrote. "It is necessary to proceed preventively, 'operating' with all possible means within our reach and making sure to remove the contaminated organs completely."[9]

National Security Doctrine coupled this fevered emphasis on combating subversion with an expanded definition of what subversion was. Having witnessed Castro's unexpected turn toward communism, and convinced that Moscow sought to weaken its enemies through "ideological penetration," many officers looked askance at any activity that challenged internal stasis or was even remotely connected to the Left. "A terrorist is not just someone with a gun or a bomb," said one Argentine general, "but also someone who spreads ideas that are contrary to Western and Christian civilization."[10] In this worldview, trade unions, student groups, and other organizations became suspect, a potential "wolf in sheep's clothing."[11] To meet this threat, national security theorists called for stringent restrictions on individual freedoms in order to limit the spread of pernicious ideas. In certain cases this broadened view of subversion created a belief that domestic politics had become a kind of internal war, to be conducted with the same urgency (and the same methods) as traditional military conflict. "The principal enemy of our civilization and way of life is to be found in the very heart of our national communities," concluded one report, and must be rooted out.[12]

If the threat was broad, so was the appropriate response. From a professional perspective, National Security Doctrine had its origins in the late 1940s and 1950s with the creation of institutions like Peru's Center for Higher Military Studies (CAEM) and Brazil's Superior War College (ESG). In these academies, officers took courses in a wide array of subjects, including geopolitics, economics and development, and political and social issues. Following the Cuban revolution, the expanded worldview that resulted from this education informed a belief that combating subversion required using all facets of national power. There could be no division between military, economic, and political initiatives; all must be geared toward the goal of internal security.[13]

The economic policies of the *golpistas* fit firmly within this paradigm. Argentina's Onganía government, which associated domestic instability with the working-class activism of *justicialismo*, attacked Peronist financial power by holding down wages, prohibiting strikes, and opening the economy to foreign competition.[14] In Peru the juntas that took power in 1962 and 1968 took a more redistributive approach to weakening the Left. The Peruvian soldier must be a "fighter against underdevelopment," said one officer.[15] In Brazil economic policy fell somewhere between these two poles, featuring *dirigiste* programs aimed at rapid industrial development as well as restrictions on unions and the working class.[16] Across the region, economic policy was part of a multipronged approach to national security.

Geopolitics and diplomacy fit the same pattern. The global nature of communist subversion, military strategists argued, demanded an equally internationalist response. "When it is a matter of continental defense," said Brazil's Artur da Costa e Silva in 1965, "borders pose no limit."[17] During the mid-1960s and after, various South American governments took the antirevolutionary fight beyond their national borders. In 1964 the Argentine generals, led by Onganía, quietly threatened war with Chile should Allende win the presidency. In 1965 Brazil proposed the creation of a "Defensive Hemispheric Alliance" to intervene in regional hot-spots, and a few months later Brazilian troops led an OAS peacekeeping force in the Dominican Republic. Shortly thereafter, the Argentine and Brazilian militaries tag-teamed a political crisis in Uruguay, threatening to invade if the government did not put down labor unrest.[18] Brazil "would almost certainly send in military forces it if considered a Communist takeover to be imminent," U.S. officials reported.[19] In 1967 Brazilian, Argentine, and Paraguayan officers promised their Bolivian counterparts aid in fighting Guevara's guerrillas, and conducted frequent border sweeps to this end. By the early 1970s the Paraguayan and Argentine armies had concluded secret protocols on intelligence and operational cooperation.[20] For proponents of National Security Doctrine, internal and external defense were one and the same.

The ideas that came to dominate Latin American military thinking had cultural and ideological significance as well. Like many Latin Americans, most officers viewed communism as more than a political threat. To them it was an atheistic, nihilistic creed fundamentally at odds with Christian values. Military regimes, especially those in Brazil and Argentina, portrayed themselves as defenders of Christian morality, and the Catholic Church hierarchy supported several coups during the 1960s.[21] In certain cases this convergence of religion and anticommunism led to the conclusion that, at the deepest level, eradicating subversion meant addressing the moral and cultural decay thought to encourage extremist politics. "The war that we confront is preeminently a cultural war," said one Argentine general.[22] The goal of communism was "to capture the minds of the people," commented another officer; the goal of the state must be to prevent this from happening.[23]

National Security Doctrine was thus as much an ideological and cultural project as a political one, and had implications for all realms of public affairs. Brazil's transition to authoritarianism after 1964 served as a model for how these ideas worked out in practice. Following the Cuban revolution, Brazilian military politics became highly charged ideologically. In 1961 the military withdrew its support from President Jânio Quadros after he publicly honored Guevara, an act that one general called a "violent shock for the armed forces."[24] Many conservatives were even more suspicious of Goulart, Quadros's successor. One newspaper editor warned that Goulart was simply a pawn in a plan to make Brazil a Soviet "beach-head." Once Goulart took office, his economic and labor policies and populist rhetoric created fears that the country might be "bolshevized" or devolve into "anarchy," while his meddling in military affairs provoked concerns about "communist infiltration and subversion" in the armed forces.[25] Tensions rose dramatically in early 1964, as rumors of a coup led Goulart's supporters to talk of popular resistance and a "counter-coup." In March 1964 General Humberto Castelo Branco urged his colleagues to end this "subversive agitation" and prevent Goulart from subjecting Brazil "to Moscow's communism." Several days later, the military overthrew Goulart and purged thousands of officers loyal to the ex-president.[26]

Following the coup, the Brazilian officers set about constructing a new, "protected" system based largely on National Security Doctrine. Although there was initially considerable hesitation and disagreement within the high command over what course to follow, by the late 1960s the "hard-liners" and "soft-liners" reached an uneasy equilibrium that allowed them to move ahead. After adverse results in early elections, the junta closed down the existing political system, creating new arrangements that preserved military dominance behind a façade of competition. The government reversed what Murici called "the complete handover of the unions to the communists," arresting union leaders and clamping down on labor rights.[27] The junta created new security and intelligence agencies, including the virtually all-powerful National Intelligence Service (SNI), launched broad "anti-subversive" sweeps, and instituted the widespread use of torture against political opponents. Finally, Castelo Branco sought far-reaching economic changes. He launched an austerity program designed to hold down inflation; opened the country to greater foreign investment; and used the centralized control afforded by military rule to promote certain capital-goods industries deemed central to the long-term maturation of the economy. While divisions within the armed forces often gave government policy a somewhat improvisational character, the Brazilian generals nonetheless established a paradigm of military politics that would ultimately take hold on the broader continental stage.[28]

One early adherent was Onganía. Convinced that Argentina's vulnerability to internal turmoil stemmed from the persistence of the Peronist problem, Onganía looked to "break the stalemate" with *justicialismo* and thereby destroy the threat. His government heavily censored Argentine arts and literature, passed measures to confront "a subtle and aggressive communist penetration in all fields of national life," created a National Security Council charged with co-ordinating the antisubversive effort, and met protests with violence.[29] Aiming to bring about "discipline in labor" and weaken the Peronists, the high command outlawed strikes, took a hard line in union negotiations, and unveiled a radical austerity program.[30] Onganía looked to overhaul Argentine politics as thoroughly as his counterparts had done in Brazil, proposing a quasi-corporatist system known as *participacionismo*. The language used to describe these measures captured their intended scope; Onganía (rather unrealistically, it turned out) termed his four-year dictatorship the "Argentine revolution."[31]

In Peru the junta of Juan Velasco Alvarado also pursued dramatic domestic changes, but of a different sort. Because much of the officer corps came from lower- and middle-class origins, Lima's variant of National Security Doctrine revolved around economic development and redistribution rather than the more conservative anticommunism seen in Argentina and Brazil.[32] Following the Cuban revolution, many officers concluded that Peru's vulnerability lay in its deep ethnic divisions and inequalities. As one said, "The country had 10 million inhabitants but very few Peruvians."[33] What was needed, wrote Colonel Cristián Sánchez, was "to furnish assistance to the citizenry in order to improve the standard of living and reduce suffering; with the end, among others, of earning for the armed forces the respect, support, and loyalty of the people."[34]

This belief guided the agrarian reform launched after the 1962 coup and gained strength after the guerrilla uprising of 1965. The guerrillas "rang the bell that awakened the military to the reality of the country," recalled one officer.[35] After conservative opposition stymied Belaúnde's reforms, the military exploited a dispute with the U.S.-owned International Petroleum Company (IPC) to remove him from power. The U.S. embassy deplored the incident as an "old-fashioned palace coup," but Velasco's dictatorship wound up being most remarkable for its reformist nature. Velasco nationalized foreign-owned companies, placed military officials at the head of major agencies and enterprises, initiated land and labor reforms, and took other measures that, one Ford Foundation fellow in Lima commented, "represent many of the major promises which progressive politicians in Peru have been unable to put into practice over the years."[36] At the same time, Velasco mimicked the more restrictive measures tested in Brazil and Argentina, shutting down the electoral system, jailing opponents, and creating new social and political organizations designed to keep mass activism within acceptable bounds. The Peruvian revolution featured a reformist yet thoroughly antirevolutionary centralization.[37]

The variations within National Security Doctrine bear emphasizing, if only because the doctrine is so commonly treated as a monolith. In the main, though, it was the shared elements of National Security Doctrine that made it of such signal importance to Latin American affairs.[38] National Security Doctrine represented the coalescence of antirevolutionary sentiment into an expansive and ideologically charged worldview. It produced a new type of junta, one that pursued transformative policies in the name of national security and subordinated individual and group rights to the need for internal cohesion. By the late 1960s National Security Doctrine was on the rise, shaping military policies toward domestic society and the world at large. When thrown together with the growing internal dissatisfaction of the period, it would feed the massive traumas that followed.

The pervasive influence and dramatic effects of National Security Doctrine require no exaggeration. Unfortunately, precisely this tendency toward caricature has long been present in scholarly interpretations of military politics. Of all the myths and misconceptions surrounding National Security Doctrine, none has proven more durable than the idea that the doctrine was a creation of the United States.

Almost since the birth of National Security Doctrine, the idea that this phenomenon was a U.S. invention foisted upon Latin America has been a staple of public and academic discourse. In 1970 one Uruguayan official charged that Washington had created military "Frankensteins."[39] Historians and other writers have variously termed National Security Doctrine "a U.S. export," labeled it a "U.S.-imposed" doctrine that Washington "assigned to its Latin American allies," and termed Latin America a "laboratory" for U.S. anticommunism.[40] While specialists in Latin American military politics dispute this notion, the consensus remains that "the ascendancy of national security doctrine within Latin America's armed forces was, above all, the result of U.S. resolve to prevent communist revolution in the hemisphere."[41]

There is little question that U.S. policy and National Security Doctrine shared the same basic thrust. The essential themes of National Security Doctrine—a preoccupation with subversion and the corresponding need for an energetic and even brutal response—were precisely those that often guided U.S. efforts to hold back the Left. Moreover, even a superficial survey of U.S. policies reveals apparently damning links to the ascendancy of National Security Doctrine. Institutions like Peru's CAEM and Brazil's ESG received U.S. funding from the late 1940s onward as Washington became the chief foreign sponsor of Latin America's militaries. The coup-plotters of the 1960s had in many cases spent time in the United States prior to seizing power, either as military attachés or as participants in training and professional development activities. The counterinsurgency programs of the 1960s emphasized certain ideas that would later inform the policies of the military regimes, and

Washington only rarely dithered in backing successful military takeovers. In this sense Washington's aggressive anticommunism found its equivalent in National Security Doctrine.

It is incontestable that U.S. policy fostered a climate friendly to the ideas that shaped Latin American military politics during the 1960s. Yet correlation is not causation, and upon closer inspection, the argument that the United States created or was otherwise "responsible" for National Security Doctrine falls apart. For one thing, the professionalization of Latin America's militaries, the institutional backdrop against which National Security Doctrine played out, was practically complete by the time the United States became the dominant foreign interlocutor of the region's armed forces. Just as European trainers first instructed Latin American soldiers in counterinsurgency, it was French and German officers that oversaw the rise of the region's professional militaries during the 1930s and the 1940s (and before, in some cases). To the degree that Washington was involved with this process, it was as a latecomer rather than as a catalyst.[42]

The connection between U.S. counterinsurgency programs and National Security Doctrine is also weaker than it initially appears. Latin American strategists identified insurgent violence as the primary threat to their countries in the late 1950s, well before Kennedy made counterinsurgency a focal point of U.S. relations with the region. Golbery issued his warning that "Latin America now faces threats more real than at any other time" in 1959, two years before Kennedy's inauguration.[43] The ideas that characterized National Security Doctrine did not derive from U.S. counterinsurgency initiatives; in many cases they predated these programs.

From a doctrinal perspective, in fact, Latin American officers were as likely to reject or adapt U.S. ideas on counterinsurgency as to embrace them. While Latin American officers were happy to accept U.S. equipment and training, they were often skeptical of the doctrinal advice that came along with this largesse. A number of Latin American theorists (who could see just how ineffective U.S. counterinsurgency programs were in Vietnam during this period) considered American conceptions of counterinsurgency to be flawed and incomplete. General Ramón Camps of Argentina preferred the French variant, honed in Algeria. "The French approach was better than the North American," he recalled. "It pointed to an all-around conception of the problem of subversion whereas the latter focused exclusively, or almost exclusively, on its military aspects."[44] Insofar as Latin American officials drew on foreign ideas in constructing National Security Doctrine, they did so selectively and independently.

The thesis that U.S. military assistance was decisive in the evolution of Latin American military politics fails to withstand scrutiny in other ways as well. The fact that Washington ramped up its military aid to Latin America just as a wave of coups swept the region has often obscured the reality that the relationship between these two variables was less direct than many scholars believe. Venezuela, for instance, received more military assistance during the early 1960s than any other country in Latin America, but its armed forces became steadily *less* interventionist as the decade progressed. In Peru, on the other hand, where the armed forces chafed against U.S. influence, cultivated new foreign suppliers, and even disbanded the units that American advisers had helped train during the mid-1960s, there were two coups in the space of six years. The argument that military aid programs were the primary factor in spurring coups becomes even harder to sustain when evaluated at the regional level. A detailed statistical analysis of the relationship between U.S. military assistance and the incidence of coups reveals that those countries receiving less assistance were more likely to experience a military takeover.[45] In other words, to argue that there was a straight line between the arrival of U.S. advisers and the rise of *golpismo* is to assert a correlation that, statistically speaking, simply did not exist.

The limits of U.S. influence in shaping Latin American military politics are even more clearly demonstrated by the fact that the governments inspired by National Security Doctrine often pursued policies that were sharply at odds with Washington's interests. The Peruvian variant of National Security Doctrine revolved around an assumption of antagonism toward rather than comity with the United States. The CAEM courses of the 1950s and 1960s taught not that Lima and Washington shared an affinity based on anticommunism, but that Peru was the victim of a dangerous economic dependency on the United States. "The sad and depressing reality," one report stated, "is that in Peru real power is not held by the executive, legislative, judicial or electoral branch of government, but by the large landowners, exporters, bankers and North American companies."[46]

This statement provided the intellectual foundation for the fiercely nationalistic policies of the Velasco regime. When the junta took power, Velasco promised the "definitive emancipation of our homeland," and declared that Peru "must stop being a colony of the United States." The government nationalized U.S.-owned firms and industries; opened commercial, diplomatic, and military relations with Moscow; and evicted the U.S. military mission.[47] These policies provoked serious tensions with Washington, and U.S. officials considered Velasco more of a nuisance than an ally. While the Peruvian junta was decidedly anticommunist, it was hardly passive or subservient vis-à-vis the United States.

In Argentina and Brazil conservative anticommunism conduced to more congenial relations with the United States, but here too assertions of diplomatic autonomy were common. These governments challenged Washington on economic and political issues and bought European military supplies in order to lessen their dependence on American manufacturers. Brazilian policy, the U.S. embassy judged in 1970, was one of "increasing independence of and divergence from that of the United States."[48] The tension that often existed between Washington and the South American military regimes led Nixon to worry about the emergence of a "different kind of military leader," one who pursued nationalistic policies rather than cooperation with the United States.[49]

The fundamental weakness of the argument that military politics in Latin America responded to the whims of U.S. policymakers is that this thesis slights the agency of the region's soldiers, treating them as mere ciphers that needed to be prompted to be anticommunist. This depiction badly misses the mark. Latin American officers needed no coaching on the dangers of internal violence and upheaval. The reality of Cuban-sponsored insurgency and the example of what had happened to Batista's army provided all the motivation they required. The alliance between Cuba and "its powerful sponsors," wrote Brazilian officials in 1960, represented the birth of a "new subversive network" that threatened the stability of countries throughout the continent.[50] Drastic measures, a close adviser to Stroessner argued around the same time, constituted "the only salvation from the danger that we currently confront in the most critical days of our Fatherland."[51] The Brazilian junta was so worried about the threat of ideological infiltration, one general later commented, that it prohibited a visit by the Bolshoi Ballet "as if it were a battalion of Russian paratroopers." When Latin American officers complained about Washington's policies, in fact, they often did so on the basis that these policies were not anticommunist enough.[52]

"Why are there no coups d'etat in the United States?" goes an old Latin American joke. "Because there is no U.S. embassy there." This joke, with its themes of powerlessness and dependency, well captures the thrust of much of the scholarship on U.S.–Latin American relations.[53] Too often this work reduces Latin Americans to mere pawns of the empire and depicts U.S. officials and economic magnates as the real movers of history. This tendency to deny the agency of Latin American actors is puzzling coming from scholars who so often deplore just this lack of regional autonomy vis-à-vis the United States. With respect to National Security Doctrine, moreover, it is simply inaccurate. The rise of National Security Doctrine was not a product of U.S. pressure or omnipotence; it reflected an organic reaction to trends that, for many Latin American military officials, seemed frightening indeed. It was this home-grown nature that gave National Security Doctrine its ideological power and endowed it with such devastating force.

As National Security Doctrine moved to the center of Latin American affairs, other trends posed a distinct challenge to this vision of an orderly, stable society. During the 1960s Latin America experienced an upsurge of popular protest in both urban and rural areas. Student groups, labor unions, religious activists, and *campesinos* embraced the very activities that many military thinkers deemed so threatening. They demanded reform and asserted the need for individual and group mobilization. They drew on the ideas of Marx, Gramsci, and radical Christian thinkers; they appropriated the symbols of Guevara and Mao. Their actions posed major challenges for military and civilian governments alike.

Latin America's urban movements drew their strength in large part from social and economic trends. While student populations multiplied up to fifteen-fold during the 1960s and 1970s, economic stagnation created a large pool of educated young people with few professional outlets.[54] With little to look forward to after graduation, and with tuition at public universities heavily subsidized, students lingered on campus for six, seven, or eight years and stridently criticized the system that seemed to limit their opportunities. For bored, frustrated students, political protest offered one of few apparent avenues for a meaningful release of their energies. Myriad political organizations popped up on campuses across the region; dissent became almost a social necessity. "If you were not associated with some group—some acronym—you were thought to be useless—a stray bullet," one former student later recalled.[55]

Economic crisis also drove working-class and professional activism. In Uruguay inflation averaged 60 percent between 1961 and 1967, decimating the earnings of the working and middle classes and causing considerable unrest. The number of man-days lost to strikes roughly doubled in the half decade ending in 1963, and in 1965 intense labor agitation cast the survival of the government into doubt.[56] In Argentina Onganía's regressive economic policies undercut real wages for professionals and the working class, exacerbating the perennial Peronist problem and producing a surge in labor turmoil. Peronist unions called a general strike in March 1967, and over the next two years repeated work stoppages and protests afflicted the automotive industry in Cordoba. When senior union officials hesitated to endorse this militancy, they gradually lost power to a new cohort of radicals.[57]

Modernization also destabilized existing social arrangements. In countries like Argentina and Mexico (the latter of which actually enjoyed strong growth during the 1960s) the expansion of the middle class and related socioeconomic changes created domestic dislocations. Youth cynicism and disillusion with paternalistic political arrangements became prevalent, and the pull of traditional social institutions like the family declined. Students who chafed at the restrictions imposed by conservative Latin American societies embraced symbols of disobedience like Che and the critique of bourgeois values offered by thinkers such as Gramsci. "We concocted a sort of cocktail in which Gramsci coexisted with Guevara and the Chinese Revolution," recalled one former activist.[58] Mexican youths rebelled against a patriarchal political culture, taking refuge in a rock-and-roll counterculture and burgeoning student activism. Here as elsewhere, these movements gloried in disrupting the established order. "It was a party," one participant later said, "an explosion after fifty years of good behavior."

> We slept in the dean's leather chairs; we breakfasted without paying in cafeterias that we'd taken over. We went to the rally feeling like a bullfighter before the pens were to be opened to let in the bull-as-riot policeman; we boarded the buses to give speeches to people, to sing, to present skits; we fled from the bull, delighted, when a patrol car would stop the bus; at night we'd light campfires and sing songs of the Spanish civil war; we'd form couples, and we'd look for the vacant cubicle to be alone with our lover; we'd swim at the pool without a credential. We did anything without any ticket or any permission.[59]

Popular dissatisfaction was no less the product of a restrictive political climate. While relatively open systems survived the 1960s in a few countries, for the most part these years saw a narrowing of Latin American democracy. In the context of economic underperformance and general disillusion this turn toward authoritarianism fostered a feeling that Latin American governments were illegitimate and unresponsive. In Argentina alienation was such that only 20 percent of students voted in elections (when there were even elections to vote in), and in Uruguay, massive majorities thought the government corrupt and incompetent.[60] As the Brazilian government imposed greater restrictions on political freedom during the late 1960s, it earned the enmity of student groups that fashioned themselves as the vanguard of public opposition to the dictatorship. In Mexico student leaders complained that graduates had only two options: to join in the exploitation of "the most oppressed classes of the population," or to become "one more employee who will also be repressed when he makes demands that put the sacred earnings of the owners of capital in danger."[61] Instead of creating stability, the authoritarianism of the 1960s bred dissent.

U.S. policies further accentuated this upheaval. As discussed previously, many student organizations, trade unions, and other social groups had rallied around the Cuban revolution as a symbol of resistance to Yankee imperialism and a foil to inequitable arrangements in their own countries. In these circumstances Washington's attempts to contain and roll back the revolution sparked large public demonstrations. Following the Bay of Pigs, protestors attacked U.S. government facilities in Mexico and Chile and took to the streets throughout Latin America. One Colombian group resolved that the invasion should be "the beginning of our own struggle to liberate the fatherland from foreign oppressors," sentiments echoed in other countries.[62] Similar events occurred following the invasion of the Dominican Republic in 1965, and incidents of vandalism and arson against U.S.-owned companies became more frequent as the decade wound down.[63]

As these episodes indicate, Latin America's popular movements were closely tied to the broader international trends of the period. During the 1960s intense disorders rocked Beijing, Berlin, Berkeley, and points between. "Dissidence," the CIA reported, "is a world-wide phenomenon." Protestors— students especially—demonstrated against the Vietnam War, social and economic injustice, and ossified political systems. A State Department "Student Unrest Study Group" estimated that student-led turmoil was "a significant factor in upwards of thirty countries and a potentially active element in at least as many more."[64]

The same currents that inspired this global upsurge were present in Latin America. The Vietnam War evoked strong responses throughout Mexico and Central and South America. Many students identified with the communist insurgents, seeing their struggle as a fight against the familiar evils of government corruption and U.S. hegemony. Mexican groups formed pro-Viet Cong committees, blending their support for the communist forces with calls for reform within Mexico. *"Viva el Vietcong,"* declared one organization.[65] More striking still, several Costa Rican students reportedly quit their studies and traveled to Southeast Asia to join the fighting.[66]

Latin American activists also drew strength from the general tumult of the 1960s. Facing an unsatisfying situation at home, young people looked abroad for inspiration. "We all thought that Argentina was going through the same process as that of May 1968 in France and the revolution of 1959 in Cuba," said one Argentine. Radical students lauded the revolutionary disorder of China's Cultural Revolution, brandishing copies of the *Little Red Book* and chanting *"Mao y Perón, un solo corazón."*[67] In Mexico government propagandists depicted the wave of international protest that crested in 1968 as central to that country's own disorders. For those disillusioned with domestic social and political arrangements, the global disruptions of the 1960s presented a thrilling alternate path.[68]

Popular dissent reached its peak in 1968–1969. University and labor unrest rocked Montevideo, Buenos Aires, Rosario, and Cordoba. Governments in Brazil, Guatemala, El Salvador, and Nicaragua faced mass demonstrations. In Mexico student strikes grew into a nationwide movement that demanded political liberalization, social justice, and "the defense of the rights won long ago by our people."[69] Most participants in this movement sought to reform the regime rather than topple it, but their actions nonetheless constituted a worrying threat to a PRI government that prized internal order and portrayed itself as the legatee of the Mexican revolution. On August 27, 1968, a crowd of 400,000 protestors filled the *zócalo* in Mexico City, taunting Díaz Ordaz with shouts of "come on out, monkey big-snout."[70]

Rising tensions in the countryside matched this urban upheaval. During the 1960s the agrarian discontent that had drawn such attention following the Cuban revolution grew sharper. The move toward commercial agriculture and light industry during the Alliance years produced decent macroeconomic gains for several countries, but worsened inequality and employment opportunities for the poor. Counterinsurgency and Alliance programs, meant to provide stability in the rural areas, sometimes aggravated this situation instead. In Guatemala the army used its prominent role in counterinsurgency to scoop up large tracts of arable land, establishing itself as a new economic elite and killing hopes for agrarian reform.[71] Similarly, Washington's sponsorship of road-building projects (U.S. funds paid for 75 percent of such programs in Central America) furthered the same opening up of the countryside that had such a devastating effect on the rural poor.[72]

Growing inequality and marginalization elicited resistance from *campesinos* who believed, as one Paraguayan put it, that they had been "abandoned by the Government."[73] There was no better measure of this discontent than the rapid spread of liberation theology. Liberation theology was a collection of dissident Christian ideas that emerged during the late 1950s and 1960s in response to Latin America's crushing poverty and exclusion. "The Latin American bishops cannot remain indifferent in the face of the tremendous social injustices existent in Latin America, which keep the majority of our peoples in dismal poverty, which in many cases becomes inhuman wretchedness," stated one Catholic Church document. Aside from offending the conscience, these conditions led religious officials to fear that, in the absence of amelioration, the Church itself might be swept away by revolution.[74] These concerns produced a theology predicated on the notion that the Church must combine its mission of saving souls with an emphasis on economic and social justice. "In Latin America," wrote Gustavo Gutiérrez, the most influential advocate of liberation theology, "the Church must place itself squarely within the process of revolution." Manifestations of liberation theology ranged from Paulo Freire's literacy campaigns in Brazil and Chile to organizing peasant cooperatives and advocating social reform to, at the most extreme, enthusiasm for revolutionary violence. "Revolution is not only permissible but obligatory for those Christians who see it as the only effective and far-reaching way to make the love of all people a reality," declared Camilo Torres, who in 1965 left the priesthood to join Colombia's National Liberation Army (ELN).[75]

Many advocates of liberation theology rejected this emphasis on violence, and support for the doctrine as a whole has frequently been exaggerated.[76] Nonetheless, liberation theology had momentously disruptive implications. It framed everyday disputes in religious terms, adding a strong ideological element to these conflicts. At the level of interaction between local priests and their parishioners, liberation theology put Latin America's most important social institution on the side of protest and, in some cases, revolt. "Third-World" priests (so named for equating the cause of the underdeveloped nations with that of Latin America's oppressed) used revolutionary rhetoric in mobilizing the poor. The rich "are sucking the sweat of the *campesinos*," declared one Paraguayan priest.[77] Radical priests linked up with the violent wing of the Peronist movement, and the writings of Freiere, Torres, and Gutiérrez were influential among the Uruguayan Left.[78] Mexican priests pledged to "create a consciousness in the people that they are being exploited," and called for the violent overthrow of the PRI.[79]

The ramifications of liberation theology were strongest in Central America. During the early 1960s several isthmian governments had tried to defuse the volatile combination of rural poverty, swelling cities, and unpopular authoritarianism (one Mexican diplomat called the area a "powder keg") by instituting a number of reforms.[80] Nicaragua banned presidential reelection and allowed a non-Somoza to take power, the Salvadoran military instituted proportional representation and a freer press, and several governments undertook modest agrarian and labor reforms. For the most part, though, these measures were swallowed up by economic changes that further impoverished the poor and counterinsurgency programs that strangled political discourse.[81]

Central America was thus fertile ground for liberation theology. As one religious worker in El Salvador later recalled: "When I first arrived in Tamanique, every time a child died the family would say, 'It's the will of God.' But after the people became involved in the Christian communities, that attitude began to change . . . They began to say, 'The system caused this.'" This tendency to attribute misery to oligarchic malevolence rather than divine intent translated into increased rural activism. Priests organized peasant leagues and Christian "base communities" and led invasions of large estates. In El Salvador the Christian Democrats (the main opposition party) used liberation theology and support for rural unions to garner greater popularity in the countryside. By the early 1970s liberation theology had begun to undermine the rural order in Central America.[82]

More often than not, Latin American officials responded to this surge in rural protest with the same repressive tactics long used to shore up inequitable arrangements. Semiofficial death squads targeted religious base communities and priests in El Salvador and Guatemala. "Several hundred bodies . . . have already been found during the past four months in various stages of mutilation and most of these have been directly attributable to the furtive right-wing execution squads," Canadian diplomats in Guatemala reported in 1967. "Any individual with apparent leftist inclinations is a potential victim."[83] In Paraguay Stroessner's agents termed the agrarian communes "an extremely dangerous focus of subversion and hostility against the authorities." Paraguayan officials roughed up the members, warning that they would "have problems" if they did not desist.[84] Farther north, Mexican soldiers murdered agrarian activist Rubén Jaramillo as part of a broader campaign of violence and intimidation. In one instance federal troops confronted Alfonso Garzón, a Tijuana peasant leader. The U.S. consulate reported: "Garzón was given a choice of: 1) either quieting down and fading into the background or 2) becoming a national figure in Mexico, along with Rubén Jaramillo. Garzón chose the first alternative, after some hesitation, being persuaded by the assurance that in his case, he would be martyrized by hanging rather than simply being shot."[85]

The response to urban activism was usually the same. While Peru's Velasco sought to co-opt student protest by instituting reforms and embracing a *tercermundista* foreign policy, most governments opted for coercion. In Argentina and Uruguay troops and police clashed with student groups, even taking the dramatic step of occupying the universities. Brazilian authorities tortured student leaders and further restricted the political system in an effort to stamp out protest.[86]

The most dramatic confrontation occurred in Mexico. As the student movement grew during the 1960s, the López Mateos and Díaz Ordaz administrations employed a two-pronged response, simultaneously wooing and repressing their opponents. López Mateos looked to undercut student dissent by declaring himself "on the extreme left within the constitution" and acting as Cuba's chief defender in Latin America.[87] In reality the administration took these measures largely to avoid making the more difficult changes demanded by the students and, as demonstrated by the experiences of Jaramillo and Garzón, had few qualms about old-fashioned political thuggery. As popular unrest spread later in the decade, Díaz Ordaz relied on the stick rather than the carrot. After first ignoring protests that expanded dramatically during mid-1968, he turned to more extreme measures. "Public peace and tranquility must be restored," he declared.[88] In late September, as Mexico prepared to host the Olympics, the government sent troops into UNAM (the National Autonomous University of Mexico), causing the rector to resign and sparking even larger protests. With the Olympics only days away, the government moved decisively. "The situation will be under complete control very shortly," Mexican officials reported. On October 2, troops surrounded several thousand protestors in Tlatelolco's *Plaza de las Tres Culturas* and opened fire, killing between 200 and 400 people.[89]

The students went back to classes after Tlatelolco, and the Olympics came off smoothly. Yet student protest would surge again in the early 1970s, this time accompanied by a guerrilla movement that robbed banks, kidnapped wealthy citizens, and killed Mexican soldiers.[90] In a deeper sense Tlatelolco was a self-inflicted wound from which the PRI would never recover. Political violence was nothing new in Mexico, but the killing of hundreds of peaceful protestors ensured that perpetual PRI claims to be the embodiment of a democratic revolution henceforth would ring hollow. The PRI had proven itself "irreversibly reactionary," proclaimed one student. The party "calls itself democratic," declared another organization, but "represses in violent form the right of liberty of expression that the people of Mexico obtained with so much blood and sacrifice during the Revolution." The link between the PRI and the Mexican revolution, so crucial to that party's domestic hegemony, was irreparably ruptured following Tlatelolco.[91]

The fallout from Tlalelolco symbolized the limits of coercion in dealing with popular movements. Repression failed to address the causes of public discontent, and merely reinforced the perception that Latin American governments were illegitimate. Tensions between students, workers, and the authorities grew sharper during the early 1970s. Uruguayan students and union members hurled Molotov cocktails at the police.[92] Disaffected Argentines rallied around the banner of radical organizations that would soon unleash a wave of violence. The People's Revolutionary Army (ERP) charged that the dictatorship had issued a "formal declaration of war against the Argentine people" and pledged itself to the concept of "the people in arms." Mario Firmenich, a product of the prestigious Colegio Nacional de Buenos Aires, formed a "politico-military" group, Montoneros, that glorified guerrilla warfare as "the highest level of political struggle."[93]

Trends in the countryside pointed in the same direction. Deteriorating economic conditions had convinced many *campesinos* that their situation was becoming intolerable. The repression of their efforts at redress convinced them that they would not escape this predicament through peaceful politics. One effect of liberation theology had been to build an intellectual bridge between two unlikely partners—the guerrillas and the Church. In its most extreme form, liberation theology related the Marxism espoused by the former to the teachings of the latter. Radical priests told young students that "Marxism is not incompatible with Christianity," and declared themselves "not merely tactical allies but strategic allies" of revolution.[94] In Central and South America small but growing numbers of rural farmers and laborers moved toward violence. Guerrilla warfare, argued one organizer, was "the only thing that could save the *campesinos* and the poor in general."[95]

Both ideologically and in their practical implications, liberation theology and the popular mobilization of the 1960s were fundamentally contradictory to the vision of society contained in National Security Doctrine. The latter discouraged protest as seditious; the former two influences revolved around just this sort of activism. National Security Doctrine identified Marxism as foreign and threatening; liberation theology stressed the relevance of Marxist ideas to the everyday struggle for dignity and survival. The worldviews that emerged during the 1960s were incompatible, and their rise prefigured the polarization and violence of the 1970s.

At the opening of the 1970s, these confrontations were already unfolding. One indication was the violence perpetrated against the religious base communities in Central and South America. Another was the "Bilateral Intelligence Agreement" signed in 1972 by the Argentine and Paraguayan militaries. The accord singled out Third-World priests and student organizations as threats to "the military, political, economic and/or psychological power" of the South American countries, and provided for greater cooperation to contain these groups.[96] "The nations that make up the non-communist world see themselves threatened by a totalitarian ideology that seeks their disintegration through subversion," stated Argentine intelligence analysts; stronger controls would be needed in response.[97]

New strains were also becoming evident in Latin America's foreign relations. During the early 1960s the Soviet-Cuban threat and the launching of the Alliance for Progress had forced conflict between the United States and its southern neighbors into the background. By the second half of the decade, though, anti-Americanism again competed with anticommunism for prominence in hemispheric diplomacy. Even as the rise of National Security Doctrine ensured that traditional Cold War issues remained relevant, inter-American economic disputes and a growing antagonism toward the United

States came to the fore. Largely fixed on East-West lines during the early 1960s, the axis of conflict in Latin America tilted toward a North-South orientation by decade's end.

The rise of dependency theory captured this shift especially well. Argentine economist Raúl Prebisch had sketched the basic outlines of dependency theory in the 1950s, and an adapted version, popularized by writers like Fernando Henrique Cardoso, Enzo Faletto, and Andre Gunder Frank, gained a wide following a decade and a half later. The basic thrust of the theory was that international economic relations were inherently unequal. The underdeveloped countries were excluded from meaningful development by dint of their status as junior members of a system that privileged the "industrial core" at the expense of the "periphery." Because the West controlled access to technology, capital, and markets, it reaped the benefits of international commerce and locked the underdeveloped countries into serving as producers of cheap raw materials and consumers of costly manufactures. Third-World countries therefore derived few gains from their abundant natural resources, which served mainly to line the pockets of rapacious foreign investors.[98]

Dependency theory represented an attempt to explain why the Third World was struggling economically during the 1960s. As Asia and Africa decolonized, many leaders had looked forward to what Ghana's Kwame Nkrumah called "jet-propelled" development.[99] In most postcolonial nations a combination of poor management and structural constraints quickly dashed these expectations. In assigning blame for this outcome, academics and Third-World thinkers focused more on the latter cause than the former. A sense of injustice and exploitation soon characterized international economic relations, and during the mid-1960s, organizations like the Group of 77 (G-77) (which Prebisch served as secretary-general) coordinated demands for "a new and just world economic order."[100]

Most of Latin America had been independent for more than a century, but this did not prevent similar ideas from taking hold in the Western Hemisphere. The fact that outside interests had long weighed heavily in Latin American economies, while the region itself languished, lent credence to *dependentista* arguments. Several Latin American countries joined the G-77, and leaders like Frei, Felipe Herrera, and Rafael Caldera called for united opposition to U.S. economic hegemony. Caldera, who would later become president of Venezuela, predicted the emergence of a "Latin American bloc," and Frei fought against "foreign strangulation" by pursuing the "Chileanization" of the copper companies.[101]

If the rise of dependency theory flowed from Latin America's lengthy experience with foreign economic influence, it was also an unintended legacy of the Alliance for Progress. The excessive optimism that accompanied the founding of the Alliance had created high and unrealistic hopes for rapid development. When Alliance programs fell short of these goals, the inevitable sense of disappointment led to a widespread rejection of modernization theory and created an ideological vacuum in which dependency theory would flourish. "The theory of 'dependency' grows out of the crisis of developmentalist theory," wrote one *dependentista*.[102]

Specific Alliance projects—particularly efforts to increase foreign direct investment (FDI)—helped drive this transition. From the start, U.S. and Latin American planners argued that foreign investment would spur growth and technological advancement in countries lacking adequate capital. During the 1960s the creation of the Central American Common Market (CACM) and the implementation of investor-friendly policies led to a marked rise in FDI. U.S. investment grew by 128 percent in Central America and by roughly 50 percent across the region as a whole.[103]

This inflow of foreign capital helped bring about gains in light industry, commercial agriculture, and banking. But FDI also displaced local producers, reinforced an already heavy foreign economic presence, and meant that profits reaped from these expanding sectors were partially repatriated to the United States or Europe.[104] Predictably, a backlash set in. Terms like "economic imperialism" and "cultural imperialism" became common, and economists like Celso Furtado warned that FDI was simply a tool used to "open up new fields for the future expansion of the multinational corporation."[105] FDI was not a means of development and modernization, *dependentistas* argued, but rather a cause of impoverishment. "Underdevelopment is not a preparatory stage preceding capitalist development," argued Brazilian professor Hugo Assmann; "it is a direct consequence of such development."[106] This growing antipathy to FDI was pungently demonstrated in 1969, when Nelson Rockefeller, the owner of various enterprises in the region, toured Latin America on Nixon's behalf. Demonstrators burned Rockefeller in effigy, and arsonists firebombed his grocery stores in Argentina. "Rocky, Go Home," crowds chanted.[107] To the extent that Latin American observers viewed FDI as an exploitative influence, they constituted a receptive audience for the *dependentistas*.

Dependency theory received a final boost from pure political opportunism. Dependency theory allowed Latin American politicians to blame underdevelopment and poverty on external factors, rather than acknowledging their own failures or confronting regressive economic structures. Luís Echeverría, Mexico's president from 1970 to 1976, relied on this rhetorical strategy. "Underdevelopment is not the absence of economic resources," he said, "but the burden of unbalanced structures imposed by external domination."[108]

In essence, dependency theory drew its power not from analytical rigor but from its relevance to both long-standing and more recent sources of Latin American frustration. Dependency theory offered a psychologically attractive explanation for the region's historical underdevelopment and the disappointments of the Alliance for Progress, and did so through a social scientific discourse that lent authority to its conclusions. Like National Security Doctrine and liberation theology, dependency theory was influential because it captured the resentments and fears at work in regional affairs and focused them into an ideologically powerful form.

Dependency theory swept Latin America in the mid- and late 1960s. *Dependencia* concepts became prominent in universities, in reports issued by the UN Economic Commission for Latin America, and in broader popular discourse. At the policy level, dependency reinforced certain precepts of ISI, contributed to a growing hostility to foreign investment, and helped inspire integration projects meant to pool industrial resources and thereby make participating countries less reliant on the developed world.[109]

The founding of the Andean Pact, an attempt at economic integration launched by Chile, Peru, Colombia, Ecuador, and Bolivia in 1969, demonstrated these dynamics. Economic integration had a long history in Latin America, and during the Alliance years enjoyed U.S. support.[110] In the late 1960s, though, dependency theory gave an anti-U.S. flavor to the Andean Pact. The agreement, Velasco explained, was a tool for overcoming "Peru's virtual subordination to the hegemonic centers of foreign power." Chilean Foreign Ministry official Aníbal Palma agreed, calling the Pact "a new form of diplomacy" to help the region achieve greater influence in "the world order."[111]

As such statements indicated, dependency theory was also a force in regional diplomacy. In 1969 twenty-one foreign ministers presented the State Department with a petition demanding lower tariffs on Latin American goods and a revamping of U.S. aid policies.[112] Perhaps more important than the content of the document was that it showed a unity of action that Washington had largely managed to avoid in its previous dealings with the region. By achieving this consensus, wrote one Chilean diplomat, Latin American countries would not "allow themselves to be seduced so easily by individual offers."[113]

By the early 1970s dependency-style language and ideas informed the policies of numerous Latin American governments. Mexican diplomat Alfonso García Robles declared, at the UN General Assembly, that the developing countries "have been for decades victims of a systematic and growing impoverishment," and the Peruvian junta based much of its foreign policy on dependency-related concepts.[114] Peru's future, Foreign Minister Edgardo Mercado declared in 1969, "must not continue to be tied in an economic knot with powerful industrialized countries whose interests are not in accord with those of the Third World."[115] Even as East–West conflict drove the rise of National Security Doctrine, the North–South tensions emphasized by dependency theory moved to the center of inter-American affairs.

The 1960s were a decade of major tectonic shifts. As guerrilla violence and superpower competition captivated the attention of observers within and outside the region, Latin America's political and social terrain moved beneath their feet. National Security Doctrine, liberation theology, and dependency theory injected ongoing disputes with a strong dose of ideological fervor. They rendered these conflicts more powerful and intractable, and soon began to rub against one another in increasingly dramatic fashion. Accordingly, as the guerrilla and diplomatic dramas of the 1960s wound down, they were quickly replaced by a new set of disruptions.[116]

The ferment of the 1960s cast a long shadow over Latin American affairs. The influences forged amid the foreign intervention, global turmoil, and domestic upheaval of that decade would shape patterns of regional conflict in the 1970s and beyond. The rise of dependency theory heralded a spike in North–South tension that soon became manifest in a major challenge to U.S. influence in Latin America. The friction between the imperatives of National Security Doctrine on the one hand, and the characteristics of popular protest and liberation theology on the other, drove polarization and bloodshed that ultimately made the fireworks of the 1960s seem small scale. The lasting legacy of the decade that saw the defeat of the rural guerrillas and the frustration of the Soviet-Cuban challenge was thus not stability, but rather the sharper conflicts that would take form in the early 1970s. Latin America had merely moved from one crisis to another.

4

The Third World War

Throughout Latin America, the 1970s were years of intense upheaval. The tensions that had taken hold in the decade following the Cuban revolution drove a series of prolonged crises that made the disruptions of the 1960s seem tame by comparison. Internal warfare and political turmoil wracked the Southern Cone, culminating in the establishment of radical military regimes defined by extreme anticommunism and institutionalized atrocity. The first half of the 1970s also saw a spike in diplomatic hostility between many Latin American countries and the United States, producing a sustained challenge to U.S. hegemony and provoking speculation that inter-American relations were on the verge of momentous change. At decade's end, Central America experienced the onset of a maelstrom that would last for more than ten years and cause a profusion of bloodshed. If the outcomes of the 1960s were instability and rising tension, the legacies of the 1970s would be dramatic conflict and massive body counts.

The following chapters cover the aforementioned episodes, beginning with the cycle of revolution and counterrevolution in the Southern Cone. Between the late 1960s and the mid-1970s the lower half of South America was the locus of a jarring collision between a revitalized leftist radicalism that found expression in urban guerrilla warfare and an intense, often brutal anticommunism embodied by National Security Doctrine. These antipathetic extremisms interacted potently with one another, causing profound polarization and violence.

This relationship played out across the space of roughly a decade. During the late 1960s leftist radicals like Raúl Sendic, Abraham Guillén, and Mario

Firmenich exploited sociopolitical strains to construct a new revolutionary movement in South America's major cities. Drawing on significant popular backing and a web of international support, the urban guerrillas soon established themselves as a major threat to internal order across the Southern Cone. In combination with the advent of a socialist government in Chile, their successes raised the possibility that the 1970s would be a decade of revolutionary change.

There were radical departures from the status quo—just not the type that the urban guerrillas envisioned. The effects of guerrilla violence and internal turmoil mixed with another legacy of the 1960s—the ascendancy of National Security Doctrine—to accelerate the radicalization of the Southern Cone militaries. During the mid-1970s the armed forces exploited the widespread fear and public disillusion that eventually resulted from left-wing violence to mount a devastating counterrevolutionary response. Juntas seized power in Uruguay, Argentina, and Chile, and initiated "dirty wars" against the Left. They conducted relentless campaigns against not simply the guerrillas, but leftist dissent as a whole. By decade's end most of South America was under the control of anticommunist military rulers, and the Left had suffered wounds from which it would not soon recover. The 1970s had started with the prospect of revolution; they concluded on a very different note.

Beyond eviscerating the South American Left, the events of the 1970s threw into relief one of the most important themes of Latin America's Cold War. More so than any previous episode, the convulsions of this period illustrated the fundamental interdependence of left- and right-wing extremism. The repression of the late 1960s helped sharpen the grievances that fed into urban guerrilla warfare; the violence employed by that ill-fated movement, in turn, called forth the military radicalism that dominated from the mid-1970s onward. Extremism begat extremism, producing vicious internal disputes.

Even before Guevara met his fate in Bolivia, the guerrillas' second act had begun. The urban guerrilla movement began in earnest in the mid-1960s, when a group known as the Tupamaros[1] declared war against the Uruguayan government and its U.S. backers. Led by Raúl Sendic, a Marxist union organizer and failed *foquista,* the Tupamaros carried out attacks that steadily escalated in audacity. They began by robbing banks and gun stores, and later graduated to kidnappings, bombings, takeovers of police and military installations, and the assassination of Uruguayan and foreign officials. By 1970 the movement had grown to the point that the Uruguayan government identified urban guerrilla warfare as a "new form of aggression to destroy Nations from inside."[2]

Tupamaro exploits inspired emulation. Chile's Movement of the Revolutionary Left (MIR) and a Brazilian group led by Carlos Marighella sprang up in the late 1960s, followed by Argentina's Montoneros and the ERP, Paraguay's Politico-Military Organization (OPM, which pursued a mixed rural-urban strategy), and smaller fronts in Mexico, Bolivia, and Colombia. When one Uruguayan official complained that his country had become a "laboratory" for urban warfare, he was not far off.[3]

Ideologically, the urban guerrillas differed little from the Guevarists of the 1960s. Leaders like Marighella, Firmenich, Sendic, and others believed that Latin American governments, whether democratically elected like Uruguay's or self-elected like Brazil's, were irredeemably reactionary and impervious to peaceful political mobilization. "One does not crush imperialism with speeches," declared ERP leaders, "but rather with struggle."[4] The OPM, Marighella's National Liberation Action (ALN), and Chile's MIR also demanded the establishment of revolutionary governments, with the latter group arguing that even a peaceful transition to socialism was insufficient.[5] Inspired by radical Catholicism, many Montoneros came to support the same basic end, demanding "the destruction of the capitalist State and its army, as preconditions for the taking of power by the people."[6] And while Tupamaro ideology was what one observer called a "political cocktail" of Trotskyism, Castroism, anarchism, and other schools, Sendic's violent Marxism ultimately oriented the group's strategy.[7]

The guerrillas railed against the iniquities of capitalism, but few of them actually hailed from backgrounds of crushing poverty. The rural poor were conspicuously absent from this movement, and while the working class was well represented, so were more affluent groups like intellectuals, professionals, and students. Moreover, though groups like ALN and the OPM sprang up in opposition to repressive military regimes, the Chilean and Uruguayan movements took form in two of Latin America's most democratic countries.[8]

How did these individuals come to head the revolutionary violence that roiled South America? In many ways, the mix of social and ideological currents that had taken shape during the 1960s was responsible. As discussed in Chapter 3, widespread social dislocations fostered a sense of rebelliousness among young people, while influences like U.S. intervention in Latin America, opposition to the Vietnam War, and solidarity with the global upheaval of the late 1960s pushed important segments of the population toward protest and political activism.

The economic downturn that affected the Southern Cone (especially Argentina and Uruguay) during the 1960s exacerbated these trends. The working and middle classes saw their purchasing power fall dramatically. This relative decline in economic status caused undeniable popular discomfort and mixed with the high degree of unionization in Southern Cone cities to produce a spike in labor turmoil. Economic crisis also hurt the employment prospects of South America's students, leading many to remain in college indefinitely and affording them prolonged exposure to an environment in which leftist ideas had traditionally flourished. The economic setbacks of the 1960s might not have pushed the working and middle classes to the brink of starvation, but they did certainly foster rising political alienation. "The crisis gets worse from day to day," declared one Tupamaro communiqué. "It is our best ally."[9]

Prominent ideological currents channeled this discontent in more radical directions. Among the heavily Catholic populations of the Southern Cone, the notion of "just violence" favored by radical exponents of liberation theology struck a chord with students, intellectuals, and labor activists. In Argentina and Uruguay, where labor priests had long propounded similar (if less extreme) messages, the students and unionists that served as guerrilla foot soldiers later reported being strongly influenced by the writings of Torres, Gutiérrez, and like-minded theologians.[10] Some Montonero leaders had worked with Paulo Freiere in Chile; Firmenich was a disciple of Carlos Mugica, a left-leaning Argentine cleric. Firmenich's writings trumpeted the "just violence of the oppressed," and when he took the Montoneros public in 1970, he declared that the organization was possessed of a "Justicialist doctrine, of Christian and national inspiration." From the outset, this extreme interpretation of liberation theology was central to urban guerrilla ideology.[11]

Dependency theory exerted much the same force. Although primarily an argument about the external sources of Latin American underdevelopment, dependency theory had important domestic implications as well. Foremost among these was the notion that Latin American governments were complicit in the systematic impoverishment of their own people. By forging alliances with foreign corporations and investors, *dependentistas* argued, Latin America's ruling classes had enriched themselves and their international patrons at the expense of their countrymen. In the context of a continuing economic recession, such beliefs lent themselves to rebellious responses. Abraham Guillén, a Spanish exile who became an intellectual godfather to the urban guerrillas, urged Latin Americans to overthrow the collaborationist governments that abetted Washington's domination. "A revolutionary war between the two Americas," he wrote, "between the plutocratic North and the proletarian South, is virtually inevitable."[12] Montonero ideologues drew explicitly upon dependency theory, terming the group's actions "a form of active solidarity with the Latin American, Asiatic, and African peoples, those of the so-called Third World exploited by colonialism and imperialism."[13] These appeals found a receptive audience. One student later recalled, "We thought that society was divided into two big blocs and that the domination was so powerful that there was no alternative to an armed struggle in order to overthrow the oppressors." In Uruguay books like Frantz Fanon's *The Wretched of the Earth* were popular among the Tupamaros.[14] Like liberation theology, dependency theory catalyzed Latin American dissent.

The final ingredient in urban radicalization was the coercion that many governments employed to limit domestic upheaval. In several countries the political and social restrictions promulgated during the 1960s simply exacerbated internal tensions. In Argentina coups in 1962 and 1966 and the military's persistent discrimination against the Peronists pushed disenfranchised trade unionists toward violence. The decision to nullify the 1962 elections undermined leaders willing to work toward accommodation with the military, and lent credibility to the extremists. "There will be a revolution," declared one Peronist candidate. "If blood flows, too bad."[15]

The radical ascendancy became more pronounced after the 1966 coup. Meant to lance the Peronist boil, Onganía's "revolution" robbed the political system of all remaining stability. The junta's regressive economic policies and no-strike stance isolated moderate Peronists and produced a sharp leftward swing among the rank-and-file.[16] A national plenary dismissed "illusory solutions" like compromise, radicals murdered accomodationist union leader Augusto Vandor, and groups like the ERP, Montoneros, and others rushed to fill the void. "With a regime like this," asked leaders of the Revolutionary Armed Forces (FAR), "what alternative is there but armed struggle?" Perón himself (less out of any sincere conviction than a desire to keep pace with his left wing) declared that "the dictatorship that devastates the Fatherland will not yield in its violence but before greater violence."[17]

Elsewhere the story was the same. In Uruguay the administration of Jorge Pacheco responded to labor and student unrest by suspending constitutional guarantees, ruling by decree, shutting down left-wing newspapers, and sending troops into the universities. Amid persistent economic difficulties, these actions simply reinforced public alienation and Tupamaro claims that Pacheco's was a "sell-out and anti-popular government."[18] Pacheco, declared one Uruguayan senator, "has systematically violated the Constitution," a charge seemingly confirmed when the president sought to alter that document to permit himself a second term. Pacheco's measures led to violent clashes between student and union groups and the authorities, and completed the radicalization of many Uruguayan activists.[19]

This radicalism took the form it did because of a simultaneous shift in the tactics of the violent Left. During the mid-1960s strategists like Sendic, Marighella, and Guillén concluded that rural *foquismo* had failed. It had isolated the guerrillas from their supporters (students, urban workers, and professionals), thrown them into an unfamiliar element, and resulted in utter defeat. The cities, on the other hand—now these were revolutionary environs. Santiago, Buenos Aires, Montevideo, and other Latin American cities were metropolises populated, Guillén wrote, by "a great human mass ruled by the tyranny of private capital."[20] Tactically, the city offered protection and anonymity. "The terrain of the urban guerrilla," wrote Marighella, "presents the police with a labyrinth that becomes an insoluble problem for pursuit."[21] Montevideo, explained one Tupamaro, was "a city which we know like the palm of our hand, in which we look like everybody else, and where we go from one place to another with the same ease as do the other million people who live in it."[22] The city would afford the urban guerrilla the sanctuary and support that had eluded his rural predecessor.

The city offered favorable terrain; the international situation seemed similarly propitious. Guerrilla leaders saw themselves locked in a struggle against not only their own governments, but also the American empire that propped up these regimes. From this perspective, the global trends of the late 1960s and early 1970s appeared to show a superpower in decline and offered leftists around the world an inspiring example of how guerrilla violence could thwart imperial domination. The Vietnamese people, wrote ERP leaders, "have carried popular war to its maximum expression nowadays, building a powerful army that holds the most powerful capitalist military forces of the earth . . . in check."[23] Along similar lines, guerrilla leaders interpreted signs of Latin

American diplomatic assertiveness vis-à-vis the United States, most notably the creation of the Andean Pact in 1969, as additional evidence of Washington's debility. The Pact, the Tupamaros reasoned, would throw "a diplomatic, economic, political and military wedge into the gears of the empire."[24] For Marxist rebels, the early 1970s presented an opportune moment for revolutionary action.

The urban guerrillas coincided with their Guevarist predecessors in drawing inspiration from Vietnam, but in other respects they differed from this earlier movement. Moving the struggle to the cities was one example of this divergence; guerrilla recruiting and propaganda provided another. In most cases the urban guerrillas sought to move beyond the strident rhetoric and doctrinal myopia that had weakened the *foquistas*. While the urban guerrillas never hid their Marxism or revolutionary ambitions, they initially tempered these characteristics in hopes of appealing to a broader public. "Words divide us," went the Tupamaro slogan, "action unites us."[25] Sendic declined to turn the Tupamaros into a formal vanguard party, a process that would inevitably bring ideological disputes to the fore. "The principle that guided them," wrote one Tupamaro captive, "was that of first making the revolution and only afterward the party." Early manifestos focused on issues like "high prices" and the "criminal intervention in Vietnam," themes sure to find resonance with students and the working population.[26] Tupamaro pronouncements were cast in broad terms, referring to the group simply as "the armed political organization of the students, the laborers, the white-collar workers, the rural wage-earners, the intellectuals, the unemployed."[27]

Argentine groups took a similar tack. The ERP and Montoneros combined their denunciations of capitalism with appeals to Argentine nationalism, invoking the legacy of José de San Martín no less than that of Guevara. The guerrilla struggle represented a "war of the second independence," the ERP declared.[28] Just as the Argentine people "did not hesitate in expelling the Spaniard," read one flyer, "neither will they hesitate today in struggling against North American imperialism."[29] Just as important, groups in Argentina and elsewhere assiduously exploited the sense of ennui at work among young people. The Montoneros and ERP recruited heavily in Peronist youth organizations, and Guillén framed guerrilla violence as an escape from bourgeois boredom. "The peoples of Latin America must have an heroic sense of life," he wrote; "they must abandon a decadent and flimsy nationalism."[30] In the climate of the early 1970s these tactics provided a steady supply of recruits. "We felt that we were part of the revolutionary history of Argentina," said one youth. "There was no possibility of being young and not being an activist; it was like a destiny."[31]

Guerrilla attacks were initially small, hit-and-run operations. To compensate for their numerical weakness (according to most accounts, the Montoneros had only twelve to twenty members when they went public), the guerrillas rejected what Guillén called "Homeric battles." They undertook operations that stressed speed and mobility, designed to bleed the enemy and augment guerrilla capabilities while not exposing themselves to a devastating counterstroke. "We are weak and it is going to be a long struggle," acknowledged one leader.[32] Robberies (euphemistically termed "expropriations") and abductions filled guerrilla coffers and kept their arsenals well stocked. "Armed propaganda," which entailed disarming factory guards and lecturing the assembled workers on the virtues of the revolution, provided a pulpit for guerrilla proselytism. The Tupamaros infiltrated and seized isolated government facilities, demonstrating the relative impotence of the Uruguayan authorities.[33]

At the outset, these tactics were successful in frustrating the authorities and rallying popular support. Daring guerrilla attacks captured the public imagination and made the Argentine and Uruguayan governments seem at once heavy-handed and incompetent. Robberies of foreign-owned banks and kidnappings of wealthy industrialists caused only slight discomfort to most Argentines or Uruguayans, while the massive—yet generally unsuccessful—dragnets launched in response occasioned considerably more annoyance. The ERP conducted Robin Hood missions such as forcing factory owners to raise wages and redistributing the contents of hijacked milk and food trucks.[34] When the guerrillas did shed blood (early on, at least) they did so selectively, targeting objects of widespread opprobrium. The Montoneros announced their presence in 1970 by murdering General Pedro Aramburu, an action that invited a harsh retaliatory blow but garnered significant approval from Peronists *cialistas* who recalled Aramburu's role in deposing Perón fifteen years earlier. Taking revenge on the general, Firmenich wrote, fulfilled "an old dream of ours."[35]

The political cachet of these tactics was evident from the growth of the guerrilla movement. By the early 1970s the Tupamaros numbered roughly 2,000 combatants and support troops (a large number given Uruguay's small population—2.8 million—and the fact that the armed forces had only 12,000 members) and had thousands more sympathizers.[36] Estimates of guerrilla strength in Argentina vary widely, but the ERP and Montoneros probably boasted between 15,000 and 30,000 combatants at their peak, with at least twice that number lending active support. By way of comparison, the Argentine army had 25,000 officers and noncommissioned officers and 65,000 conscripts, and this latter group was rife with guerrilla infiltrators.[37]

No less impressive, the guerrillas enjoyed substantial public support. The guerrillas' broadened public message, their image as plucky underdogs, and the discretion that they initially showed in using lethal force allowed the insurgents to win the sympathy (or at least the tolerance) of that dominant segment of the population that was dissatisfied with the status quo but not necessarily desirous of violent revolution. One poll revealed that 49 percent of residents in Buenos Aires, Cordoba, and Rosario (three of Argentina's major urban centers) had some sympathy for these radicals.[38] Clever tactics, shrewd propaganda, and the useful foil of repressive but seemingly hapless governments made the urban guerrillas a force to be reckoned with.

During the early 1970s South American governments claimed to be confronted with a continental conspiracy to foment revolution. Subversion "recognizes neither borders nor countries," resolved one meeting of South American security chiefs, "and the infiltration penetrates all levels of national life."[39] At the time, these allegations were widely disregarded as the paranoid delusions of security-obsessed regimes, and they are still received with more skepticism than credence.[40] In truth, however, there was a crucial international dimension to Southern Cone upheaval.

Much like the *foquistas,* many urban guerrillas saw themselves as part of a broader regional movement. An early Tupamaro manifesto declared it "impossible to think about liberation in national terms, independently from the rest of Latin America," and called for "the building and preparation of the continental strategy." Because Latin America was a single economic unit dominated by the United States, insurgent strategists argued, revolution was possible only on a continental scale. "The struggle must spread," Guillén wrote, "or become choked by the imperialism of the dollar, whether militarily or through an economic and diplomatic blockade."[41]

International cooperation had, in fact, been central to guerrilla warfare in South America for years. The Paraguayan guerrilla attacks of 1959–1960 were staged from Argentine territory, and the violent wing of *justicialismo* had long taken advantage of the same porous frontier.[42] This collaboration grew more systematic during the second half of the 1960s. Guillén dispensed wisdom to several groups, and the Tupamaros (which he called "a model of urban guerrilla warfare") explored the possibility of creating "a common front."[43] To this end, several organizations explored forms of operational coordination at the OLAS and Tricontinental conferences in 1966–1967.[44] In 1969 Paraguayan intelligence uncovered evidence that guerrillas from Brazil, Cuba, Argentina, and Paraguay were discussing joint operations, including the assassination of military leaders.[45]

As the urban guerrillas gradually integrated their efforts, they received support from several Marxist governments. Moscow was not among these; Guillén condemned the Soviets for conducting a "rapprochement with imperialism" following the Cuban missile crisis, and the Kremlin returned the insult by dismissing the Tupamaros as a "terroristic petty bourgeois group."[46] Castro took up the slack. While Cuban diplomacy in the 1970s was in many ways more nuanced than during the Guevara years (see Chapter 5), in no way had Castro relinquished the dream of spreading revolution. "Cuba will never renounce her right and her duty to collaborate with those who wish to change society when that is found to be impossible by the democratic method," Cuban official Carlos Rafael Rodríguez stated.[47] Moreover, Castro reasoned, the quagmire in Southeast Asia made it unlikely that Washington could do much to counter Havana's meddling. "We had a slight breathing space as a result of the Vietnam war," he later recalled. "Our activities in Latin America developed—our cooperation with these revolutionary movements was very active."[48]

Castro supported the Southern Cone guerrillas by various methods. He hosted a Tupamaro delegation in the late 1960s, and *Granma* (Cuba's official press organ) regularly carried guerrilla manifestos. Material aid soon followed. Sometime around 1974, Castro reportedly promised an anti-Stroessner activist named Agustín Goiburú "all the aid necessary to organize subversive groups" in Paraguay.[49] Cuban operatives trained members of the MIR, ERP, and Montoneros, and helped infiltrate the trainees through Mexico and the Caribbean en route to their home countries.[50] According to one estimate, Castro provided training to roughly 1,500 Tupamaros and at least $180,000 to fund their operations. In Chile Cuban intelligence agents used Havana's embassy to stockpile 3,000 weapons for use by the MIR.[51] Overall, Cuban backing for Latin American guerrillas was hardly less than it had been a decade earlier.

From 1970 to 1973, the Chilean government led by Salvador Allende joined Castro as a sponsor of revolutionary violence. The victory of Allende's Popular Unity (UP) coalition in 1970 was one of the signal events in Latin American politics in this era. It took many observers by surprise, and marked the unexpected outcome of a decade that had begun with hopes of constructing a sustainable Center in Chile. In 1964 Frei's Christian Democrats (PDC) won the presidency with 56 percent of the vote (an astounding number in a multiparty system where 30 percent was often enough to win). The size of this victory, and the fact that Chile's conservatives had backed the left-of-center Frei in order to defeat Allende, caused U.S. officials to hope that the PDC might serve as a model for nonradical reform in Latin America. American diplomats called the PDC "the best hope for popular democracy in Latin America," and during the 1960s Chile received more U.S. aid per capita than any other country in the region.[52]

Unfortunately, Frei's policies militated against the construction of a viable centrist coalition. Made arrogant by its electoral romp, the PDC dispensed with the trappings of coalition government and decided to rule as the *partido único.* Frei launched an ambitious "Revolution in Liberty," designed to spur economic growth while redistributing its benefits, and attacked opponents on both Left and Right.[53]

The upshot was polarization. The government did make strides toward strengthening the labor movement, extending an agrarian reform begun in 1962, and redressing what one government inspector called the "awful conditions of unhealthiness" in which many tenant farmers lived.[54] Nonetheless, the Revolution in Liberty—and the Chilean Center—soon began to crumble. The conservative parties rallied to the defense of economic elites, while the Left accused Frei of "hesitation and backtracking."[55] Frei now faced what he called an "unholy alliance of the extreme Right and Left," and many of his proposals were stymied. In 1970 the parties of the Right backed former president Jorge Alessandri, and younger members of the Unitary Popular Action Movement (MAPU) bolted Frei's bloc to support Popular Unity.[56]

The beneficiary of this turmoil was Allende. The venerable socialist politician had hardly seemed a winner at the outset of 1970. He barely secured the UP nomination, and even then it remained unclear how fully he actually represented the Left. During the 1960s various groups that now composed the

UP coalition had become more radical. In 1965 students at the University of Concepción founded the MIR, an organization dedicated to armed struggle, and in 1967 Chile's Socialists declared that "revolutionary violence is inevitable and legitimate."[57] While Allende did not discourage such methods, his own tactics were more in line with those of the Communists. (In 1961 Guevara inscribed a copy of his book *Guerrilla Warfare* "to Salvador Allende, who is trying to obtain the same result by other means.")[58] Even as Allende reclaimed the leadership of the Left, his ability to guide that group was open to question.

Despite these splits, the UP coalition held together, and Allende squeaked out a victory over Alessandri and PDC candidate Radomiro Tomic. This victory, it should be noted, represented less of a seismic shift than is often assumed. Though the 1960s saw a jump in unionization and rural electoral participation, both trends that might have been expected to help UP, the coalition actually *lost* strength between 1964 and 1970. Of the more than 400,000 new voters registered between the two elections, Allende claimed the support of only 13 percent, and his overall share of the vote declined from 38 percent to 36 percent. Yet if Frei's reforms had, to this extent, succeeded in weakening the Left, they had weakened the Center even more, and Allende's reduced share of the vote was good enough to win.[59]

The advent of a second socialist government in Latin America exerted a turbulent effect on regional affairs. It heartened proponents of revolution; Castro called Allende's election "the most important event after the Cuban revolution in Latin America," and closely allied himself with the Chilean leader.[60] It terrified those on the other side of this issue, provoking hostility from Washington (as well as several of Allende's neighbors) and giving rise to a variety of nefarious schemes to topple the Chilean president.

Allende's election also created a new source of solidarity for the urban guerrillas. While Allende was ambivalent about the guerrillas (and the MIR and MAPU were often downright hostile to him), he did nothing to stop them from exploiting his victory. The Tupamaros openly declared Chile a "bridge for logistical supply and base of operations."[61] Chilean officials held meetings with guerrilla leaders from across South America, and the MIR set up training camps for its regional counterparts. Various groups used Chile's long land borders to slip into Argentina and Bolivia, and beginning in 1972 these organizations held meetings in Santiago aimed at achieving greater collaboration.[62]

In 1973 these conferences produced the highest evolution of radical co-operation in South America: the formation of the Revolutionary Coordinating Council (JCR). The idea of creating a centralized continental command had long appealed to guerrilla leaders. Guevara had advocated forming guerrilla "Coordinating Councils," and as the insurgent movements grew during the early 1970s, their leaders looked to link efforts and thereby maximize the impact of their violence.[63] At a 1972 meeting in Santiago, guerrillas from Chile, Argentina, and Uruguay resolved to "unite the revolutionary vanguard" in order to "open the way to victory for the Latin American peoples." A year later, the Tupamaros, ERP, MIR, and Bolivia's National Liberation Army formed the JCR as the strategic command for all South America. Shortly thereafter the JCR issued a chilling manifesto that promised "a bloody and prolonged revolutionary war that will make the Latin American continent the second or third Vietnam of the world."[64]

The creation of the JCR frightened security services across South America. Guevara's vision of a continental struggle "is today a reality," wrote Paraguayan officials.[65] While South America's guerrillas never functioned as one, they did cooperate on matters of substance. Using Goiburú as an intermediary, the JCR established ties to Cuba and apportioned supplies and money to South America's various guerrilla groups. The JCR also created its own press and propaganda organs, doctored passports and other travel documents, and founded joint training camps run by ERP instructors.[66] Illicit arms flowed freely across the Río de la Plata and the long border between Argentina and Paraguay, and the Montoneros and ERP provided subsidies to smaller groups.[67] After abducting an ESSO executive and ransoming him for 18 billion Argentine pesos, the ERP distributed roughly 40 percent of this sum to comrades in Uruguay, Chile, and Bolivia. By 1975 Argentine police officials privately fretted about "the reach that subversion enjoys at the international level in Hispanoamerica."[68]

In spite of this revolutionary integration, not everywhere did the urban guerrillas find success. In Brazil, where there was no economic crisis to drive popular discontent, the movement fizzled. Brazilian president Emílio Garrastazu Médici declared that "we are in an undeclared war, but it *is* a war," and the sophisticated internal security apparatus quickly decapitated the ALN.[69] By the early 1970s Brazil's intelligence organs reported that there was "relatively little receptivity to the movement" among students and the population as a whole.[70]

In other countries internal order was harder to restore. Limited but persistent violence afflicted Bolivia and Colombia, and the Mexican government declared itself "at war" with the guerrillas that emerged following Tlatelolco. "A 19-year old girl armed with a submachine gun can be a deadly enemy," remarked one official.[71] In Paraguay the guerrillas pledged themselves to "the fundamental order of *Compañero* Guevara: the creation of two, three, many Vietnams." Drawing on financial and logistical support from their Argentine compatriots, they organized into small cells and prepared to launch the same type of attacks—robberies, sabotage, kidnappings—favored by other South American guerrillas.[72]

Uruguay and Argentina were the countries most affected by urban violence. In Uruguay early successes inspired Tupamaro leaders to embrace bolder and bloodier tactics. The guerrillas killed U.S. public safety adviser Dan Mitrione for his role in teaching the police "the art of mass repression and torture," held captives in crude "people's prisons," and assassinated police and security officials.[73] By 1970 Uruguayan democracy was teetering. Pacheco's failure to crush the guerrillas undermined public confidence in government, a decline that became even steeper when more than 100 Tupamaros staged a spectacular jailbreak in September 1971. Strikes and violence depressed economic activity and led to a flight of foreign capital.[74] Police morale plummeted. "We are on the front line of a . . . war against an invisible and murderous enemy," said one officer.[75] Government officials lamented that guerrilla tactics might "prove as effective as those conventional weapons used against fortifications or military installations," and by 1971 Uruguay's political and economic system seemed near collapse.[76]

The situation in Argentina was even more precarious. As in Uruguay, guerrilla attacks became more brazen and lethal during the early 1970s. Bank robberies, kidnappings, bombings, and assassinations were commonplace. "Acts of political terrorism are committed on a daily basis and the incidence of such acts is increasing," reported the U.S. embassy.[77] The military allowed Perón to return in 1973 in a bid to stem the violence, but even this failed. Perón had always been more of a caudillo than a revolutionary, and when he pronounced himself a "pacifier of spirits" upon his return, the guerrillas repudiated him.[78] Firmenich declared that "political power comes out of the mouth of the rifle,"[79] and the ERP leadership scorned Perón and "the sell-out bureaucrats" of *justicialismo*.[80]

Far from halting their violence after Perón's return, the guerrillas in-creased the pace and scope of their attacks. By mid-decade, one writer notes, Argentina was suffering "a political killing every five hours and a bomb ex-plosion every three hours."[81] The Montoneros and ERP mounted joint opera-tions against the "Peronist dictatorship" and made parts of the country virtu-ally ungovernable. The guerrillas operated with "impunity" in many areas, police authorities admitted; the Zárate-Campana area had become a "liber-ated zone."[82] Attacks became more audacious, as the ERP ambushed military convoys and the Montoneros sank a navy destroyer. The *élan* of the Argentine military eroded badly; Brazil's intelligence service reported growing "dis-belief and pessimism" within the ranks.[83] The perpetually unstable economy veered toward the precipice, with the guerrillas inflaming labor–management relations by killing factory supervisors and industrialists. Even more so than in Uruguay, the established order in Argentina looked close to unraveling altogether.[84]

Not even those states that supported the guerrilla movement were immune from its effects. In Chile Allende's grudging support for the urban guerrillas earned him little gratitude from groups like the MIR, MAPU, and the So-cialists. Though technically members of the UP coalition, these organizations wanted little to do with Allende's vision for Chile. Recognizing that more than 60 percent of voters had opposed his election ("I am not President of all Chileans," he commented upon taking office), Allende initially sought to soothe public fears by promising a gradual, peaceful transition to socialism. He respected democratic practices and throughout his presidency allowed the Chilean press to function freely. Predictably, these measures raised the hackles of the Chilean "ultra-Left." "We arrived in power, not in order to use the bour-geois State," declared the leader of MAPU in 1970, "but in order to destroy the state forms of bourgeois domination."[85]

Over the next three years, the ultra-Left ignored Allende's call for pru-dence. These groups illegally expropriated thousands of privately owned busi-nesses, alienating the owners and producing sharp social tensions. They mur-dered one of Frei's aides and bypassed the Foreign Ministry in establishing intimate ties with Havana.[86] The MIR, which had been arming for combat even as Allende took power, accumulated large illegal caches of weapons, and pledged to arm the workers in preparation for the final showdown with the Right. The general aim, one *mirista* would later recall, was to "bring matters to a head." While these measures never produced the same level of violence as in Uruguay or Argentina, they did provoke conflicts that fueled the unceasing polarization of the period. Right-wing groups like *Patria y Libertad* clashed with the ultra-Left, and the threat of internal violence was a constant in 1972 and 1973.[87]

Historians continue to debate the extent of internal upheaval and the seriousness of the guerrilla threat in Latin America during the early 1970s. Some see these movements as profoundly disruptive influences and even harbingers of revolution; others as overblown phenomena exploited by the generals to justify their own eventual seizures of power.[88]

As the foregoing analysis makes clear, the urban guerrilla was hardly a specter conjured by paranoid or cynical *golpistas*. Groups like the Tupamaros, Montoneros, and others boasted thousands of soldiers and supporters, enjoyed significant international support and cooperation, and had war chests filled with earnings from kidnappings and robberies. Their actions drove resurgent violence in several countries, left Argentina and Uruguay in situations that were dire indeed, and combined with the advent of a socialist government in Chile to set much of South America on edge. The revolutionary wave that had crashed following Guevara's death now crested again, this time with greater strength than before.

The radical change that occurred in the Southern Cone, however, would be of the counterrevolutionary type. Military coups—supported, in many cases, by large swaths of the population—toppled governments in Chile, Argentina, and Uruguay between 1973 and 1976, and augured an all-out offensive against the guerrillas and the Left as a whole. By mid-decade the Southern Cone was under the control of authoritarian governments linked by a common determination to eradicate leftist dissent.

This rapid reversal of fortunes reflected several factors, but there was a common pattern to events across the Southern Cone. In Argentina, Uruguay, and Chile alike, the violence and upheaval of the early 1970s eventually had two profoundly important effects: the alienation of much of the public, and the acceleration of the radicalization at work within the armed forces. This combination boded ill for the continuation of civilian government and set the scene for a rapid rightward shift.

This scenario first unfolded in Uruguay. As the Tupamaros grew more violent, the considerable public support that they had initially commanded dropped off rapidly. Mitrione's execution evoked widespread disapproval, and guerrilla actions garnered growing opprobrium. Large crowds in Montevideo chanted *"¡Policías, Sí! ¡Tupamaros, No!"* in late 1971, and a popular front coalition with ties to the MLN garnered less than 20 percent of the vote in national elections.[89]

Why did the guerrillas lose the sympathy they had only recently enjoyed? This would have seemed a paradoxical outcome, at least by the guerrillas' own standards. For all the ways in which the urban guerrillas differed from their rural predecessors, they agreed with the Guevarists on the exemplary value of bloodshed. The Tupamaros, one combatant explained, followed "the principle that revolutionary action in itself . . . generates revolutionary consciousness, organization and conditions."[90] Escalating violence, the Tupamaros calculated, would demonstrate the possibility of revolution and rally additional supporters to the cause.

Yet this logic was no more valid in the 1970s than it had been a decade earlier. Rather than inciting the masses to action, the Tupamaros' increasingly bloody attacks revealed the basic asymmetry between the objectives of the guerrillas and their hard-line supporters, on the one hand, and the broader communities that had initially tolerated insurgent activities, on the other. By and large, this latter group had not supported the guerrillas out of a desire for violent revolution. Polls taken in Uruguay revealed that even amid the difficult conditions of the late 1960s and early 1970s, only 3 percent of Uruguayans favored such an outcome.[91] They had tolerated the Tupamaros, rather, because the guerrillas had successfully portrayed themselves as a palatable form of opposition to unpopular governments. The Tupamaros had exposed the inadequacies of the Pacheco administration and dramatized the economic plight of the middle and working class, and early on they had done so in a way that was not excessively corrosive to the social fabric.

As the guerrillas grew more violent, they lost this crossover appeal. The guerrillas were no longer seen as "idealistic rascals"; they now exposed themselves as dedicated revolutionaries capable of throwing the domestic scene into chaos.[92] This ability did not endear the guerrillas to masses longing to burst free from oppression—it put them at odds with the vast majority of the population. In Uruguay polls showed that only 15 percent of the public would be bothered if the Tupamaros disappeared, and influential Uruguayans called on the armed forces to step in and restore order.[93] The guerrillas claimed to be the army of the people, but their actions drove the people away.

The Tupamaros ensured their own demise in more ways than one. The havoc of the early 1970s not only alienated the majority of the population; it also chopped the pillars out from under Uruguayan democracy. Labor strife and economic crisis had badly eroded public support for Uruguay's traditional parties and institutions during the 1960s, and Tupamaro violence created widespread doubts that the existing system could cope with the problems the country faced. In late 1971 U.S. State Department officials reported a "widespread sense of malaise and lack of national direction." Opinion polls showed deepening dissatisfaction with the Congress, the president, and the Blanco and Colorado parties, and only the military commanded broad-based public respect.[94]

This debasement of Uruguayan democracy occurred concurrent with a radicalization of the military. The Tupamaros had long ridiculed the Uruguayan armed forces as "one of the weakest organizations of repression in America," and the military eventually accepted the invitation to disprove this assessment. High-ranking commanders bristled at the idea that the Tupamaros represented a "police problem," and as guerrilla violence appeared to spiral beyond the control of the civilian authorities, the military pushed for decisive action to defeat the threat.[95] An opportunity arose in early 1972 when the Tupamaros began an assassination campaign against military officials. This decision ignited the fury of an already alarmed high command, and as one government minister commented, "unleashed the undeclared civil war."[96] From 1972 onward, the military—operating in conjunction with semiofficial death squads—inflicted severe casualties on the Tupamaros. Uruguayan forces killed and captured more than 1,000 operatives, including Sendic and other high-ranking leaders, and severely depleted the guerrillas' weapons stores.[97] "The Tupamaros are under control," Uruguayan officials could soon brag.[98]

This devastating counterinsurgency presaged even greater changes. The armed forces followed up their offensive against the Tupamaros in 1972 by gradually seizing power the next year. There was little opposition to this coup-by-stages; the military enjoyed unprecedented prestige after beating back the Tupamaros, and public esteem for the civilian government was at abysmal levels. A few protests marked the effective military takeover in early 1973, but for the most part public outrage was lacking. Even those officials displaced by the *golpistas* accepted their misfortune with equanimity. "Senior civilian officials appear to have little desire or ability to contest the military's encroachments," U.S. officials reported. A civilian president retained nominal control until 1976, but from early 1973 on the generals and admirals ran the show.[99]

The trajectory of events in Argentina bore striking similarities to the Uruguayan experience, though in the former country this saga played out with greater intensity. In Argentina as in Uruguay, the guerrillas suffered a severe diminution of their public standing as the turmoil they created came to dominate the national scene. By 1973, one historian recounts, the population had become aware that "the armed opposition that arose as a reaction to the military regime . . . appeared considerably more violent than the military." Firmenich basked in the bloodshed; he announced that he would gladly "sacrifice the organization in combat in exchange for political prestige."[100] Such statements alienated rather than attracted many Argentines. Public disillusion increased after Perón's return in 1973, when the guerrillas lost what had been their most formidable weapon: the ability to capitalize upon Peronist disenfranchisement. Within a year of Perón's return, much of the population had turned against the insurgents. The fact that the guerrillas were now attacking a democratically elected government, rather than a repressive military junta, produced widespread revulsion. Perón himself soon tired of the insurgents, who had now outlived their usefulness to him. In May 1974 he condemned the Montoneros as "stupid, screaming people" and ejected them from *justicialismo,* depriving them of what mainstream public support they still enjoyed. Over the next two years, the guerrillas would find themselves out of favor even with the Peronist unions, which had long been a principal source of solidarity.[101]

By the mid-1970s Peronism was at war with itself. Left and right-wing Peronists clashed on the occasion of Perón's return in 1973, and the civilian government subsequently organized a paramilitary group known as the Argentine Anti-Communist Alliance (AAA) to neutralize the Left. The AAA targeted ERP and Montonero leaders as well as leftist politicians, aiming at (as one member later put it) "the physical elimination" of these individuals.[102] The AAA issued public death sentences and murdered at least several hundred Argentines. "We declare WAR on those elements that disrupt the established order," read one proclamation.[103] "Leave [the country], or we will kill you," the AAA told suspected guerrilla sympathizers.[104] Union leaders that had grown wary of the insurgents began to cooperate with the AAA and counterguerrilla police units. The guerrillas responded by targeting members of the AAA as well as conservative unionists, and called for all-out war on the regime. By 1975–1976 U.S. officials reported that the bloodshed "approaches civil-war dimensions."[105]

Besides provoking public repudiation, the guerrillas' actions drove a radicalization of the military even more far-reaching than that in Uruguay. Argentina had long been home to the most extreme version of National Security Doctrine, and these ideas received a massive boost from the violence and general disorder of the period. The rapid growth of foreign-supported guerrilla movements and internal turmoil, and the apparent impotence of the democratic system, reinforced the notion that breaking the threat from the Left required drastic measures. High-ranking officers frequently stated that the Southern Cone had become the central front in a "Third World War" between communism and the West. "This is a struggle that entails the destruction of democracy or the annihilation of communism," declared one general.[106] Just as the repression of 1960s lent credibility to advocates of left-wing violence, the upheaval of the 1970s gave voice to those who argued for a draconian right-wing response.

Such sentiments probably would have found a receptive hearing in Argentina regardless of the prevailing intellectual climate. Guerrilla violence was significant by any standard, and constituted a challenge that no military establishment could have ignored. By mid-decade Argentine officials warned of a "wild orgy" of bloodshed, and one admiral feared "total chaos leading to [the] destruction of the Argentine state."[107] These worries were hardly unique to military officials. Interim President Italo Luder (Perón had died in 1974 and was replaced by his widow Isabel, who subsequently took leave to recover from exhaustion) conceded that "the institutional stability of the country" was at risk.[108] In these circumstances it is hardly surprising that the armed forces felt an impetus toward a strong response.

Yet the particular fire this upheaval sparked within the military also reflected the intellectual context of the period. Many Argentine officers interpreted the events of the 1970s as confirmation of the ideas that had come to influence military thinking over the past decade. This much was evident from a secret military intelligence protocol signed in 1972. "The street riots, the urban guerrillas, the kidnappings, the deaths and the fires that in the last months have devastated the principal cities of Latin America have not been caused by spontaneous generation," the authors wrote. "On the contrary, they have had—and have—a careful preparation whose origin is not unknown to our authorities." The fact of the matter was that "the nations that make up the non-communist world see themselves threatened by a totalitarian ideology that seeks their disintegration by means of subversion."[109] As this document indicated, the worldview promoted by National Security Doctrine found ample reinforcement in the course of Southern Cone politics.

Argentine military thought became increasingly extreme as the decade went on. High-ranking officers identified a comprehensive assault on the nation's political, social, and cultural institutions. Army Chief of Staff Jorge Rafael Videla warned that "international communism" had achieved "penetration of the schools and even the church."[110] His colleagues agitated for an "all out war on the terrorists," and looked forward to the "complete extermination" of the guerrillas.[111]

They soon got their chance. In February 1975 Luder issued an "annihilation decree" allowing the armed forces to direct the antiguerrilla struggle in the province of Tucumán. Eight months later that authority was extended to cover the entire nation. Videla promised "the annihilation of subversion in all its manifestations."[112] In early 1976, with inflation spiraling out of control and internal violence convulsing the country, the military took power in a broadly popular and long-expected coup. "Most Argentines were glad to be rid of Mrs. Perón's pathetically incompetent government," the U.S. embassy reported. Local comment confirmed this assessment. "The crisis has ended," declared *La Nación.*[113]

The rightist ascendancy in Uruguay and Argentine had its equivalent in Chile, where another Chief of Staff—General Augusto Pinochet—mounted another brutal but popular military takeover. Contrary to what is often thought, this outcome was not necessarily foreordained. For all the controversy Allende's election sparked, the UP government had actually enjoyed a fairly auspicious start. The president's pledge to adhere to democratic practices and allow freedom of the press earned him the criticism of the ultra-Left, but helped prevent an early blowup with the Center and the Right. Across-the-board wage increases stimulated the economy. UP scored follow-up victories in by-elections in 1971, indicating that much of the electorate was willing to consider Allende's "Chilean road to socialism."[114]

Allende's honeymoon ended quickly, though, and the situation began to unravel. The economy stumbled badly, as Allende's decision to staff crucial ministries with political loyalists rather than competent technocrats led to severe mismanagement. Economics Minister Pedro Vuskovic's wage hikes and loose monetary policy eventually resulted in galloping inflation, causing real wages to decline by nearly half between 1970 and 1973.[115] Ill-designed price controls made it impossible for farmers to market their goods profitably and led to shortages of consumer products. By 1972 Chile was experiencing severe economic disruptions and a worsening debt burden, leading Allende's ambassador to the United States, Orlando Letelier, to warn of "a powerful negative effect . . . on our internal political situation."[116]

These problems were not entirely of Allende's own making. Throughout his presidency, Allende faced unrelenting U.S. hostility. Worried that Allende's election would encourage revolutionary activity in Latin America and be perceived as a blow to U.S. influence, Nixon and National Security Adviser Henry Kissinger schemed to undermine the UP government. The CIA financed anti-Allende unions and press organs and cultivated disaffected military officials. Nixon squeezed the economy by withholding most development assistance, opposing World Bank and IMF loans to Santiago, and discouraging American investors from doing business with Allende. "Make the economy scream," he directed.[117]

This skullduggery contributed to the Allende's mounting economic difficulties. CIA financial support helped sustain anti-Allende strikers in 1972–1973, and U.S. pressure impeded his search for economic relief. The Paris Club did at one point approve debt rescheduling for Chile over U.S. objections, but Nixon's obstructionism was usually successful in reducing the chances of external assistance.[118] While U.S. officials were not directly involved in the coup that ultimately toppled Allende, Nixon's machinations certainly facilitated the economic destabilization that preceded this event. "We didn't do it," Kissinger remarked in September 1973, but the United States "created the conditions as great as possible" for Allende's overthrow.[119]

As much as Allende suffered from an adverse international environment, his most critical economic wounds were self-inflicted. International financial institutions like the World Bank needed no prodding to refuse Allende loans, because the Chilean leader's economic policies provided argument enough. "Nobody in their right mind would make a loan to Chile under Allende," World Bank president Robert McNamara later said. "The whole damned economy was being destroyed."[120] Allende further foreclosed the chances of outside relief by refusing to take corrective measures. He would not risk the wrath of his supporters by reducing public spending, a stance that ensured that the international financial institutions remained aloof.[121] All told, Allende did such a good job of wrecking the Chilean economy that Nixon could only pile on. "The present downward course of the Chilean economy," wrote one State Department adviser in late 1971, "is so well defined that the economic pressures available to us will add only marginally to its deterioration."[122]

Social conflicts exacerbated the tensions that resulted from this economic instability. Beginning in 1972, extreme right-wing groups exploited Allende's declining popularity to mount a violent antigovernment campaign. Organizations like *Patria y Libertad* attacked Allende supporters and conducted industrial sabotage. The chaos produced by these measures was greatly magnified by the practices of Allende's putative allies. As mentioned above, the ultra-Left often seemed determined to undermine Allende and ensure that his promise of a peaceful transition to socialism was completely bereft of credibility. Illegal expropriations, the accumulation of illicit arms, and other such measures provoked such a backlash that Communist leader Luís Corvalán accused the MIR of playing "reaction's game."[123] This was no exaggeration; *miristas* intoxicated with the prospect of revolution thrilled in provoking the opposition and the military. "I wanted a coup," recalled one MIR member. "I imagined myself as a leader in a liberated zone, fighting a revolutionary war in which the forces of good would sweep away the forces of evil forever."[124]

By 1973 the situation had become unmanageable. Mounting economic difficulties led to crippling strikes by truck drivers, farmers, and much of the middle class, and raging political and social tensions produced fears that the domestic order might collapse completely. Even those who benefited from Allende's rule admitted that the wheels had come off. A Montonero who visited Chile in 1973 reported: "I found myself in a desolate and—for me, at that moment—nearly incomprehensible situation. The road from the airport to the city was practically blocked by trash, trucks, and abandoned buses stretched across the road. The downtown bars without coffee or milk. The sabotage, the strikes, the shortages, had the city and the country paralyzed."[125]

As had happened elsewhere, this disorder produced two essential developments. The first was the isolation of Allende's government. Moderate and right-wing tolerance for Allende's socialist experiment, in rapid decline since 1972, evaporated completely the following year. In August 1973 Chile's Chamber of Deputies called for a coup, a stance echoed by newspapers, political parties, and swaths of the population at large. Even supporters referred to Allende's administration as a "shitty government," and the UP coalition was close to shattering. The Chilean road to socialism was hitting a dead end.[126]

The second development was an evolution of Chilean military thought similar to what had occurred in Uruguay and Argentina. The chaos of the late Allende period produced intense concern that Chile was on the brink of a generalized social breakdown. More alarming still, the emergence of well-armed and foreign-funded paramilitary groups, heated talk of arming the workers and abolishing the armed forces, and the presence of Allende support-ers within the ranks made high military officials fear that Chile was becom-ing "a new Cuba." These worries interacted with the preexisting influence of National Security Doctrine to create an extreme version of the anticommu-nism that had long prevailed within the Chilean armed forces. "The experi-ence of the UP years," writes one historian, "translated intellectual opposition to Marxism into a visceral hatred."[127]

Matters came to a head in the winter of 1973. A hastily planned coup at-tempt in June failed, but nonetheless completed Allende's isolation. "Its re-percussions have further strained the fabric of Chilean society and threaten to overwhelm what is left of the military and civilian commitment to constitu-tionality," the CIA reported.[128] In response to the *tanquetazo,* as it was known, Castro urged Allende to use violence against the Chilean Right. "Don't ever forget the extraordinary strength of the Chilean working class," he wrote. "In answer to your call that the revolution is in danger, it can paralyze those who are organizing a coup, maintain the support of the fence-sitters, impose its conditions, and decide the fate of Chile once and for all."[129] Allende himself seemed to be leaning in this direction. "If the coup comes, the people will be given arms," he declared.[130] This statement, combined with the fact that the MIR and other ultra-Left groups had reacted to the attempted coup by seiz-ing thousands of privately owned businesses, pushed elite and popular toler-ance for Allende's government past the breaking point. "The principal weapon of the Government," Foreign Minister Clodomiro Almeyda had said in 1972, "is to maintain public order and unconditional respect for legality. If this con-trol is lost, there would be pretext for the counter-revolutionary forces."[131] Almeyda was made a prophet in September 1973, when the military moved against Allende. Pinochet, who had refused to do so "until the overwhelming majority of the people call for such action," now joined a long-brewing plot against the government.[132] The coup occurred on September 11, toppling Al-lende and resulting in the deaths of at least 1,200 of his supporters.

There was thus a basic pattern at work across the Southern Cone. Internal turmoil reacted strongly with the precepts of National Security Doctrine, accelerating and intensifying the radicalization of the armed forces. At the same time, this upheaval exhausted public tolerance for the radical Left (specifically the urban guerrillas in Argentina and Uruguay, and the ultra-Left and Allende's government in Chile). Many officers were now convinced that only bold—and in many cases, bloody—action could save their countries, and large segments of the population seemed to agree. The result was the series of coups that swept the Southern Cone.

The Southern Cone juntas had strong popular backing at the outset, and in Chile, for at least several years thereafter. This support came from a range of groups: wealthy citizens whose worldviews had been profoundly influenced by fear of kidnapping or assassination; conservative Catholics who viewed the Left as an ally of godless communism and a threat to public morality; ambitious politicians who hoped that the military might soon turn power over to them; businessmen who had suffered from robberies, expropriations, and economic instability. A hard-line response appealed especially to industrialists, who had long complained that guerrilla exploits made it impossible to maintain discipline among their workers. The insurgents brought about "anarchy and disorder," lamented the management of one Argentine enterprise, disrupting the "elemental principal of [employer] authority."[133]

Support for the coups was not only prevalent among elites. These regimes also had good standing with segments of the middle class that had seen their savings and wages disappear amid runaway inflation. Many citizens in Chile, Argentina, and Uruguay had tired of endemic instability and violence, become frustrated with the inability of democratic leaders to set things right, and were willing to give military government a chance. These regimes enjoyed "passive legitimacy," a widespread belief that, for all its drawbacks, military rule might be the redress for seemingly insoluble problems.[134]

Yet if the Southern Cone military leaders could claim a mandate for defeating the guerrillas and restoring order, they had no intention of stopping there. The *golpistas* of the 1970s aimed at something grander. Drawing inspiration from the tenets of National Security Doctrine, they intended to remake their countries' politics so as to destroy the internal threat once and for all. Pinochet promised "to change the mentality of Chileans" to make a recurrence of the Allende years impossible, and Argentine admiral Emilio

Eduardo Massera voiced a similar opinion. The traumas of the 1970s had taken root "in the midst of the incredulity of some, the complicity of others and the stupor of many," he declared, and Argentina would not be safe until these weaknesses were corrected.[135]

Over the next several years, the Southern Cone governments initiated a multifront offensive against the sources of public disorder. Determined, as Chilean admiral Gustavo Leigh put it, to "cut out the Marxist cancer," they began by decimating the radical Left. The Chilean government ripped the MIR, MAPU, and other ultra-Left groups apart following the coup. During the next decade and a half Pinochet oversaw the killing of around 3,200 Chileans and the imprisonment, exile, or torture of tens of thousands more.[136] Even so, Pinochet looked like a moderate compared to the Argentines. The junta in Buenos Aires was responsible for perhaps 25,000–30,000 deaths during its six-year reign.[137] By 1977 Argentine officials could proclaim the "virtual annihilation of the subversive organizations," and three years later military officers estimated that "the Montoneros have no more than 20 activists and 20 sympathizers within Argentina."[138]

The guerrillas were hardly the only group to fall victim to government-sponsored violence. For proponents of National Security Doctrine, the guerrillas were just the tip of the subversive iceberg. The Third World War was a conflict "between ideologies," commented Leopoldo Galtieri, the commander of Argentina's notorious Battalion 601; destroying the enemy meant destroying those ideas that contributed to radical dissent.[139]

This expansive definition of subversion had always been a key tenet of National Security Doctrine, but like other aspects of that doctrine, it took on greater viciousness in the 1970s. In Chile and Argentina especially, and in Uruguay and Paraguay as well, the turmoil of the early 1970s had occurred amid growing labor, student, and in some cases agrarian unrest.[140] These trends were deeply disturbing to the military officials who took power between 1973 and 1976. Proponents of National Security Doctrine had always associated unions and student activists with subversion; the fact that so many guerrillas came from these backgrounds seemed to confirm these suspicions. Despite the fact that by the mid-1970s Argentine unionists were more likely to oppose the guerrillas than to support them, and that Allende too confronted significant labor hostility as his presidency wore on, the new military regimes were more convinced than ever that these groups were chief sources of the instability they meant to eradicate.[141]

The practical implications of this belief were nowhere more explicitly spelled out than in a memo written by Asuncion police chief Francisco Alcibíades Brítez Borges in late 1975 or 1976. In Paraguay as in Uruguay, Chile, and Argentina, the mid-1970s saw an assault on the Left. The decision of the OPM to dedicate itself to "armed revolution," and the growth of radical dissent within the universities, the unions, and the agrarian communes, led Stroessner to devise an across-the-board crackdown.[142] In bullet form, Brítez outlined this attack. The authorities must:

1. Destroy the subversive organizations.
2. Intervene in: Religious schools (Catholic and Protestant), Friendship Mission (center of subversion, contact with the ERP, economic support to subversives) . . . agrarian leagues and Institute for Integral and Harmonic Development (IDIA).
3. Energetically attack the causes (directors and indoctrinators) in order to weaken the effects: indoctrinated *campesinos*, workers and students.
4. Attacking only the effects, the struggle would acquire a state of permanence and the prisons would be filled with *campesinos*, workers, and students. The vital subversive organizations would remain intact.
5. Deal devastating blows to the subversive organizations and break them up.
6. Act with speed and without hesitation; it will require less effort and cost fewer lives and money.
7. Time will favor the subversives; they will continue indoctrinating.
8. A belated action would be dangerous; it will be difficult to control a coordinated, joint action by *campesinos*, workers and students (targets of the subversives to initiate the armed struggle).
9. Avoid at any price that the subversives initiate the armed struggle (guerrillas, armed robbery, kidnapping, sabotage, etc.). It will create a climate of anxiety, worry, and fear across the country, with disastrous consequences.[143]

Stroessner's government urgently took up these tasks. The regime targeted the founts of liberation theology and OPM recruiting, taking over prestigious Jesuit schools like the Colegio Cristo Rey in Asuncion. The authorities broke up the agrarian communes, arresting hundreds of members, deporting foreign priests, and subjecting detainees to torture and even death. Those lucky enough to escape the roundup were forced to go underground. "I have to disappear without leaving tracks," wrote one.[144] Stroessner's government prosecuted this offensive for years, seeking to squelch the spread of dissident ideas and dry up sources of guerrilla support.[145]

The situation in Paraguay resembled that of the Southern Cone as a whole, where military regimes deployed what one Argentine officer termed "preventive" violence against leftist organizations and individuals of all types.[146] Trade unions, student groups, and opposition parties all felt the brunt of this strategy. Chilean labor and student organizers were among the first to be "disappeared," and during 1974–1975 Argentine police and military officials prepared lists of union leaders who were then snagged following the coup.[147] The high command did not dissemble in describing the extent of their war. "We are going to have to kill 50,000 people," predicted General Luciano Menéndez; "25,000 subversives, 20,000 sympathizers, and we will make 5,000 mistakes."[148]

Nor did the generals blanch at the use of brutal methods. The dirty wars were characterized by disappearances, summary executions, rape, torture, and incarceration in secret jails. Prisoners were held in spaces measuring little more than a meter to a side, and forced to urinate and defecate within their cells. Torture sometimes went on for months. "The prisoner is a being without rights," said one Uruguayan jailer.[149] Favored tactics included the "submarine," in which prisoners were submerged in water until they nearly drowned, the "dry submarine," which used a nylon bag to achieve the same effect, and the *picana,* a kind of electric-shock torture. "Torture by picana," recalled one detainee, "is to feel death."[150]

Apologists later claimed that these incidents were anomalies, "excesses" committed by rogue soldiers. There was some truth to this; officers occasionally exploited military impunity to indulge their worst urges. In most cases, though, brutality represented not deviance from orders but compliance with them. "We conducted the war with doctrine in hand, with the written orders of the High Command," said Argentine general Santiago Omar Riveros in 1980.[151] Rape, torture, and murder were political tools, meant to destroy the solidarity of the urban guerrillas and instill fear in those who might be tempted to aid them. Torture, commented one Uruguayan official, "is a political instrument." "Its ultimate end . . . is the destruction of political opposition to the system."[152] An Argentine official put it even more bluntly. The purpose of torture, he said, was "to introduce widespread terror into the population to prevent the guerrilla from 'moving like fish in the water.'" The "excesses" of the 1970s and 1980s were not excesses at all, but played an essential role in military policy.[153]

The military regimes also created new administrative apparatuses to oversee these measures. The Uruguayan junta established a system of clandestine

prisons to house suspected subversives.[154] In Argentina the military divided
the country into five regions in order to apportion responsibility for deten-
tions and disappearances. Pinochet created the National Intelligence Directorate, or DINA (whose logo was, appropriately enough, a mailed fist). This
organization reported directly to the president and orchestrated the offensive
against the Left. DINA, comments one historian, was "the backbone of the
regime."[155]

The evisceration of the Left was accompanied by severe political, social,
and economic alterations. Convinced that the weakness of the democratic
system had conduced to the turmoil that preceded their takeovers, the juntas
undertook thoroughgoing domestic reconstructions. The transformation was
most profound in Chile. Following the coup, the junta suspended the legisla-
ture, placed the parties on indefinite recess, and ruled through decrees that
carried the weight of constitutional amendments. "The world beholds today a
generalized crisis of the traditional forms of democracy," Pinochet declared,
"whose failure and exhaustion, at least as far as Chile is concerned, should be
considered definite."[156] Over the next decade, Pinochet's success in consoli-
dating his own power allowed for a remarkable consistency of purpose in
overhauling Chilean politics. Chile would have a democracy, Pinochet explained, "but not one liable to attack from underneath as had happened before."[157] Military officials assumed control of nearly all cabinet positions,
many governorships and mayoralties, and even some of the universities. The
regime imposed various states of siege or emergency that allowed it sweeping
powers of detention and surveillance. It instituted a legal framework that
prescribed severe penalties ranging from loss of employment to exile (or
worse) for citizens with leftist sympathies, and used these measures to target
not simply the ultra-Left but the PDC as well. Many of these measures were
institutionalized in the constitution of 1980, which postponed congressional
elections for nearly a decade, effectively banned Marxist parties, and laid out
a path for Pinochet to remain president until 1997. Pinochet called the new
system a "protected democracy," but as U.S. officials noted, the adjective certainly trumped the noun.[158]

Pinochet pursued equally striking departures in the economic realm. After
some initial hesitation, he launched a drastic austerity program and instituted
a marked liberalization of the economy. His government lifted tariffs and price
controls, encouraged foreign investment, privatized industry and the banks,
and slashed social expenditures and public employment. The economic aims

of this program were to restart growth, restore fiscal balance, and redress the grave inflationary and debt problems that had accumulated prior to the coup. The political aim was to roll back the influence of organized labor and other sectors that had traditionally aligned with the Left. These groups benefited from high government spending, price controls, and a closed economy; with these protections stripped away, their power would wane. To further this latter objective, the regime prohibited strikes and assassinated, imprisoned, exiled, or replaced union leaders. Pinochet's economic measures entailed severe hardship for many Chileans, but as will be discussed in Chapter 8, they set a precedent that would later gain regionwide emulation.[159]

The juntas in Argentina and Uruguay also pushed for structural changes, though somewhat less decisively than Pinochet. In contrast to the Chilean regime, these juntas operated on a collegial basis, and interservice rivalries combined with regular personnel changes at the top to create greater inconsistency in policymaking. While both regimes introduced economic reforms that mirrored the Chilean emphasis on austerity and liberalization, implementation was halting and incomplete.[160]

All the same, these differences were ones of degree rather than strict demarcation. The juntas in Buenos Aires and Montevideo suspended electoral competition, proscribed or placed controls on the parties, and devised various means of controlling the population. The Uruguayan junta banned 15,000 politicians for a period of fifteen years, and the military classified all public employees according to loyalty. This small country, outside observers estimated in the late 1970s, had the most political prisoners per capita in the world.[161] Argentine leaders used shocking violence to cow the opposition, created a vast administrative apparatus for counterinsurgency purposes, and used press and artistic censorship to keep "subversive" intellectual currents out of circulation. The Argentine and Uruguayan generals even dabbled in social engineering by separating suspected guerrilla sympathizers from their infants. "Subversive parents educate their children in subversion and this must be avoided," one Argentine leader maintained.[162]

Although dramatic changes to economic policy were implemented less consistently in Argentina and Uruguay than in Chile, even a relatively brief experience with radical austerity and liberalization programs could cause wrenching transformations for many citizens. The liberalization initiatives pursued by the Argentine junta caused sweeping reductions in industrial employment, and by 1981, manufacturing employment stood at 65 percent of its

1975 level.[163] With price controls lifted, the cost of basic commodities rose by up to several hundred percent, while government efforts to restrain inflation meant that public sector wages stagnated and social spending fell dramatically. The working and lower classes took a beating from these measures, as reflected in the biting nicknames given to junta officials. Argentine minister of economics José Martínez de Hoz was known as a reverse Robin Hood, one who "takes from the poor and gives to the rich."[164]

The second half of the 1970s was the time of the radical military regime. Anticommunist juntas dominated the Southern Cone and most of South America, and the revolutionary violence of the early 1970s had been displaced by governmental repression. The guerrillas were demolished and the Left as a whole was reeling. A decade that began amid widespread revolutionary activism ended with a profoundly counterrevolutionary feel.

The violence of the 1970s left deep scars on the Southern Cone. Argentina, Uruguay, and Chile are still struggling to come to grips with these events several decades after the fact, and public memories of this period remain contested terrain.[165]

Consensus is little easier to find in the historiography. Scholars have advanced numerous explanations for the cycle of violence and upheaval that occurred during the 1970s. Some point to the sociopolitical dislocations caused by long-term economic changes; others to the gradual politicization of the armed forces; others to the imperatives of radically regressive economic programs; still others to the hidden hand of the United States.[166] A final group explains these traumas as the work of "master architects of 'radical evil'" like Pinochet and DINA chief Manuel Contreras. Such figures, historian Steve Stern contends, are undeserving of serious historical analysis. In their cases, "the dash of sympathy required for profound historical understanding proves impossible, pointless, or perverse."[167]

Leaving aside Stern's rather bizarre assertion about historical understanding (by Stern's metric, historians should steer clear of Hitler, Mao, Stalin, and Pol Pot), there is some truth in many of these arguments. The fact that Pinochet remained in power for seventeen years lends credence to the notion that his personal ambition figured strongly in charting the course of Chilean affairs from 1973 onward, and the long-term crises of the Southern Cone economies and other structural factors exerted an important influence as well.[168]

Yet these explanations downplay what is perhaps the most straightforward way of accounting for the events of the 1970s: the idea that the actions of the military regimes were the logical—if exaggerated—response to the leftist radicalism of the period. This notion has not traditionally received as much credence as one might expect, with many scholars arguing that because the right-wing repression practiced by the juntas dwarfed the leftist violence of the guerrillas, there must be some hidden reason for the scope and intensity of military brutality. The view of anticommunism as "a disingenuous façade," writes one scholar, "is now overwhelmingly the majority view among scholars of Latin American politics."[169]

But this idea that the virulent anticommunism espoused by the Southern Cone militaries was merely a guise for other, more dominant motives misunderstands both the nature of the dilemma in which these institutions found themselves in the 1970s and the power of the ideas that informed their response. While military officials were prone to exaggerating the extent of guerrilla violence, there can be no doubt that this threat was real. The urban guerrilla organizations included thousands of combatants (and perhaps more, in some cases) and enjoyed considerable foreign and mutual support. Their actions were deeply disruptive to the social fabric of the Southern Cone, and in many cases constituted a direct physical danger to police and military officials. In the same vein, the turmoil of the Allende years in Chile was highly corrosive to that country's political and social stability, and the actions of the ultra-Left provided an alarming reminder of the potential for internal violence. This upheaval had an immense impact on military politics, and when added to the potent ideas contained in National Security Doctrine, produced a violent anticommunism that—while outrageously disproportionate—was far from disingenuous or manufactured.

The essential sincerity of this mind-set was recognized even by the most unlikely of witnesses. As one Montonero combatant later recalled of the officer who tortured her, "He was fighting subversion and communism, not trying to get rich. His vision of the world was terribly Neanderthal, but he was convinced of what he was doing. He was there to 'save' his country."[170]

This recollection hits on an essential theme regarding the violence that wracked the Southern Cone during the 1970s. While utterly deplorable, the right-wing extremism that occurred during this period can only be understood as part of a larger cycle of radicalism and reaction. The period after the Cuban revolution witnessed growing extremism across the political spectrum, a phenomenon affecting those who favored dramatic social change no less than those who opposed it. These conflicting extremisms did not exist independently of one another, but rather interacted in a dialectical relationship that increased the intensity of both. The repression of the 1960s fueled public dissatisfaction and urban guerrilla violence, which itself drove drive the right-wing extremism that exploded in the mid-1970s. These mutually reinforcing radicalisms were at the heart of the traumas that occurred in the Southern Cone, and would figure in the even greater convulsions to come.

Dominican dictator and U.S. ally-turned-enemy Rafael Trujillo (right), shown here with Eleanor Roosevelt (front left) in 1934. Courtesy Franklin Delano Roosevelt Library.

Fidel Castro with Camilo Cienfuegos during the Cuban revolution. Cuban Revolution Collection, Manuscripts and Archives, Yale University Library.

Latin America's iconic revolutionary, Che Guevara. Cuban Revolution Collection, Manuscripts and Archives, Yale University Library.

Anastas Mikoyan (in hat) visits Cuba in 1960. Cuban Revolution Collection, Manuscripts and Archives, Yale University Library.

Veterans of the Bay of Pigs invasion at a reception with John F. Kennedy in 1962.
Courtesy John F. Kennedy Library.

Kennedy and Nikita Khrushchev meet in Vienna in the wake of the Bay of Pigs invasion. Courtesy John F. Kennedy Library.

Venezuelan president Rómulo Betancourt (shown here with Kennedy in 1961) was a star of the Alliance for Progress, and his country was one of the few in Latin America to emerge from the 1960s with democracy intact. Courtesy John F. Kennedy Library.

Lyndon Johnson and Dean Rusk at the Inter-American Summit in Uruguay in 1967.
Courtesy Lyndon Baines Johnson Library.

Chile's embattled reformer, Eduardo Frei (right). Courtesy Lyndon Baines Johnson Library.

Richard Nixon and Emílio Garrastazu Médici in 1971. "I wish he were running the whole continent," Nixon remarked of his Brazilian counterpart. Courtesy Richard M. Nixon Presidential Materials, National Archives and Records Administration.

Chilean president Salvador Allende. Reproduced with permission of the General Secretariat of the Organization of American States.

The man who overthrew Allende in 1973, Augusto Pinochet. Reproduced with permission of the General Secretariat of the Organization of American States.

Nicaraguan troops conduct a counterinsurgent sweep in rural Nicaragua in 1977. Reproduced with permission of the General Secretariat of the Organization of American States.

Jimmy Carter meets with Daniel Ortega and other members of the post-Somoza government in 1979. Courtesy Jimmy Carter Library.

Salvadoran army troops prepare for a patrol on the eve of the civil war in the late 1970s. Reproduced with permission of the General Secretariat of the Organization of American States.

Ronald Reagan meets with President Efraín Ríos Montt at the height of the Guatemalan counterinsurgency in 1982. Courtesy Ronald Reagan Presidential Library.

Reagan, on his way to Camp David in 1986. Courtesy Ronald Reagan Presidential Library.

The Latin American Diplomatic Challenge

Latin American leaders have long had an ambivalent relationship with U.S. power. At times they have enjoyed the protection it offers; at others they have looked to temper its exercise. The former tendency was evident in widespread Latin American support for containing Cuba in the early 1960s; the latter pattern went back to Argentina's uncooperativeness at the Pan-American Congress in 1889.

The pendulum swung back toward resistance during the late 1960s and early 1970s. Leaders of widely varying ideological orientations embraced bold foreign policies and contested Washington's hegemony in the region. They rejected the Cold War and the "inter-American relationship" as organizing frameworks for regional affairs and proclaimed their solidarity with the Third World. They sought new allies as counterweights to American power and proposed to collaborate to offset foreign economic influence. The resulting diplomatic friction provoked alarm in Washington and led a number of observers to predict that hemispheric relations were on the verge of a monumental shift. Inter-American diplomacy between the late 1960s and the mid-1970s might not have been as bloody as the concurrent disruptions in the Southern Cone, but it was tumultuous nonetheless.

As with so much of Latin America's Cold War, this diplomatic challenge occurred at the intersection of global trends and local dynamics. During the late 1960s and the early 1970s the post–World War II structure of international relations was groaning under the weight of three decades' accumulated strain. Washington's failure in Vietnam, the emergence of détente and the breakdown of Bretton Woods, and the oil shocks of 1973–1974 posed major challenges for the United States and the West in general, and even raised the question of whether the era of U.S. and Western preeminence had come to an end.

As the system creaked, Latin American diplomats sensed opportunity. For these statesmen, the signal international events of this era showed a decline in U.S. and Western power and the ascendancy of the Third World. Washington's defeat in Vietnam and concurrent rapprochements with China and the Soviet Union seemingly revealed a superpower in retreat, while the demise of Bretton Woods and the oil shocks looked to shift economic power toward the developing countries. Leaders schooled in *dependencia* concepts saw an opportunity to redress Latin America's persistent political and economic weaknesses, and moved energetically to do so.

Yet the growing assertiveness of these Latin American leaders had as much to do with domestic politics as geopolitics. The domestic ferment of the 1960s not only helped stoke the urban guerrilla challenge; it also drove the diplomatic crises of this period. By the late 1960s numerous Latin American governments found themselves facing seemingly intractable social and political problems. Confronted with pronounced domestic divisions, rising nationalism, and declining government popularity, Latin American officials tried to channel these forces outward via brash, confrontational diplomacy. To achieve consensus and legitimacy at home, Latin American governments fostered tension and conflict abroad.

The diplomatic movement that grew out of these factors was neither entirely coherent nor universally supported by Latin American governments. The Central American countries played little part in these events, and levels of enthusiasm for a collision with Washington varied significantly across the region. At a broad level, however, the desire to exploit geopolitical and economic change was present throughout Latin America, and, in conjunction with strong domestic impulses, shaped the diplomatic agenda.

Ambitious as it was, though, this Latin American challenge eventually ground to a halt. While a number of countries did modestly enhance their diplomatic position, the movement as a whole splintered, its momentum waned, and the United States escaped the early 1970s with its hemispheric preeminence largely intact.

In part, this outcome owed to the residual rigidity of the international environment. While the global disruptions of the 1970s did make the international order somewhat more flexible, this fluidity was not sufficient to permit the thoroughgoing changes envisioned by some Latin American leaders. Washington reacted strongly to challenges to its influence, and the other major powers hesitated to embrace the role of counterweight to the United States. More damaging still, the apparently favorable economic conditions of the mid-1970s quickly proved to be anything but. Ballooning debt burdens weighed on most Latin American and developing countries and undermined the autonomy of independent-minded governments. The international trends of the 1970s initially seemed conducive to a diplomatic revolution, but in Latin America they ended up reinforcing the status quo instead.

Yet if geopolitical factors impinged upon the designs of leaders like Allende, Velasco, and Luís Echeverría, so did ideological issues that originated much closer to home. The same surging nationalism that had helped inspire this movement ultimately had a divisive impact on Latin American diplomacy, as did the profound internal cleavages that emerged throughout South America during the mid-1970s. While leaders like Allende and Velasco argued that regional and Third-World solidarity must take precedence over Cold War loyalties, the guerrilla violence and domestic polarization of this period eventually led more conservative South American leaders to conclude otherwise. The radical military regimes that seized power in the mid-1970s made anticommunism rather than anti-Americanism the central tenet of their foreign policies, and the impetus for a confrontation with Washington declined accordingly. As the regional solidarity so often trumpeted by Latin American leaders once again proved to be fleeting, the diplomatic challenge lost force.

The diplomacy of the 1970s was an outgrowth of the strains of the late 1960s. Lyndon Johnson's interventionism earned stern rebukes from audiences throughout Latin America, and the winding down of the Alliance for Progress led many observers to decry U.S. "abandonment" of the region. These influences fed the antagonism manifested in the rise of dependency theory and initiatives like the Andean Pact and the Consensus of Viña del Mar.[1]

The regional dynamics of the late 1960s gave Latin American governments reason to rethink their position vis-à-vis Washington; global trends gave them the opportunity to do so. The early 1970s were a time of profound upheaval in world affairs. The Vietnam War laid bare the limits of U.S. influence, while the emergence of détente augured the restructuring of international geopolitics.

The gold and sterling crises of the late 1960s demonstrated growing shakiness in the major Western economies, and the subsequent abandonment of the Bretton Woods system brought down the postwar financial regime. The oil shocks delivered unprecedented profits to Third-World oil exporters and deep recessions to the industrialized nations, causing a sharp swing in economic power. The consequences of these developments were potentially immense; Henry Kissinger predicted that "the fall of the western world" could not be ruled out.[2]

The major international events of this period caused Latin American leaders of all ideological inclinations to question the durability of U.S. and Western power. Leftist elites saw the war in Vietnam as symptomatic of a general crisis of U.S. hegemony. Castro crowed that "the empire is not invincible," and Allende echoed this sentiment.[3] Non-Marxist officials concurred; Christian Democrat Domingo Santa María, Chile's ambassador to Washington, wrote that Vietnam had shown "the irrefutable truth" that American military might "could not destroy the limited material power of the Vietcong guerrillas."[4] By the late 1960s it was common to assert that Vietnam and the overall decline of U.S. power made American intervention in the region unlikely. Allende told a confidant that the United States' domestic and international traumas made it "more difficult for them to operate in Latin America," an assessment seconded by Peruvian foreign minister Edgardo Mercado.[5] Castro argued that the United States "is today much weaker, and in consequence much more limited in its possibilities of intervention."[6] Even Brazil's military government, which publicly denied that Washington's eventual withdrawal from Vietnam detracted from its status as "chief world power," worried privately about the consequences of the American defeat.[7]

The emergence of détente led to similar questions about the extent of American might. For many officials, the fact that the United States had been forced to make accommodations with its enemies in Moscow and Beijing confirmed Washington's strategic exhaustion. Leaders in Peru, Chile, and Cuba saw détente as "a reordering of power relations in the world," in which Washington, "whipped in Viet Nam," was "fending around trying to see what it can salvage."[8] U.S. policy, Chilean diplomats wrote, was "nothing other than a realistic accommodation to the crisis of empire."[9] Conservative assessments were much the same. In the wake of Kissinger's October 1971 visit to Beijing, Argentina's Alejandro Lanusse declared that "no state is so powerful" as to single-handedly manage the global balance of power, and Brazil's Emílio Garrastazu Médici announced the advent of a "new world order."[10]

This notion of hegemonic decline gained additional adherents amid the economic and financial disruptions of the early 1970s. At first glance, the breakdown of Bretton Woods should have given Latin American leaders little reason to be upbeat. Most Latin American economies had stagnated during the 1960s, and the general mood was one of pessimism. Viewed through the prism of dependency theory, however, the West's financial distress represented an opportunity. From this perspective, the disruption of the international financial order meant the end of the inequitable world system—"economic totalitarianism," Venezuelan president Carlos Andrés Pérez liked to call it—against which Latin American observers had railed throughout the late 1960s.[11] Accordingly, the collapse of Bretton Woods looked to be a moment of weakness for the developed nations, a window in which the Latin American countries might form what the Venezuelan Foreign Ministry termed "a united and strengthened bloc" and thereby exert greater influence in a reconstituted global economic order.[12]

This possibility seemed all the more likely after the oil shocks brought record profits to the Latin American petroleum exporters (Venezuela, Colombia, Ecuador, and Bolivia).[13] Even many non-oil exporters benefited during these years from high prices for commodities like copper, sugar, zinc, and cocoa. In 1974 the value of Latin American exports grew by 70 percent from the previous year, with the oil producers enjoying an uptick of nearly 200 percent. The region as a whole enjoyed a trade surplus of around $3 billion in 1973 and $4.8 billion a year later.[14]

The oil shocks and concurrent spike in commodity prices promoted a distinct sense of empowerment. "Oil moves history today," Pérez declared; exporters could now dictate the terms of their relations with importers. It was not just Venezuelan officials that were flush with optimism. ECLA (Economic Commission for Latin America), the closest thing to a truly Latin American organization, was positively exultant. The oil crisis confirmed "the vulnerability of the powerful and the strengthened position of the weak," the commission declared.[15]

The global trends of the late 1960s and early 1970s convinced many Latin American officials that the international system had reached a watershed. Coming on the heels of the Sino-Soviet split, the emergence of détente and Western economic weakness seemingly demonstrated that ideological confrontation and superpower preeminence, those most salient characteristics of the postwar era, had ceased to exist. "The appearance of new centers of power, the destruction of alliances that seemed unshakeable, the decrease of tensions and the understanding . . . between old rivals," declared Mexican president Luís Echeverría, "indicates with clarity that we have arrived at the end of the Cold War." The superpower-dominated order had given way, replaced by what Pérez called "a multipolar situation."[16]

Echeverría and his colleagues saw little to lament in bipolarity's demise. In Echeverría's view, the "antagonism of closed blocs" that defined the Cold War had restricted the flexibility of Latin American countries, locking them into either cooperation or confrontation with the United States.[17] As bipolarity broke down, Latin American countries could exploit the greater fluidity of a multipolar order to bolster their own diplomatic position. They could seek closer ties with Europe, China, or the Soviet bloc, using these partnerships to (in Mercado's words) "break the old patterns of intercourse that were always prejudicial to us." They might play the great powers off one another, gaining (according to Pérez) "a greater liberty of action" vis-à-vis the United States. With sufficient cooperation, they might form what Mercado called a "common economic front," vastly expanding Latin America's diplomatic and economic influence.[18] The major international events of the late 1960s and early 1970s had shown that the gap in power between the West and the rest was closing quickly, and created opportunities for those willing to practice bold, confrontational diplomacy.

The assertive diplomacy of the 1970s was also a response to pressing domestic considerations. From the late 1960s onward, Latin American governments looked outward in an attempt to ameliorate growing internal strains.

This strategy ruled foreign policy in several countries, none more so than Mexico. The youth activism, guerrilla violence, and rural unrest that had grown during the 1960s and continued following Tlatelolco convinced PRI leaders that they must regain the ideological legitimacy they had squandered by their own brutality in 1968. Echeverría, known in student circles as "the assassin of Tlatelolco" for his role in these events, was keenly aware of this problem.[19] Part of his solution was to portray himself as a reformer, even a revolutionary, in order to curry favor with the students. Echeverría "urges a posture of conscientious rebellion," U.S. officials wrote, as part of a "concerted effort" to capture youth discontent.[20] The liability of this approach was that it was a sham— Echeverría was no less authoritarian than his predecessors. He used a group of thugs called *Los Halcones* ("The Falcons") to assault protestors, and deployed paramilitary squads to crush manifestations of dissent. More broadly, Echeverría had no intention of seriously challenging the dominance of the Mexican elite. Echeverría "cannot hope to satisfy [the students'] economic demands," U.S. officials wrote, so he must "convince the less radical that he is moving the country in their direction."[21]

Like López Mateos a decade earlier, Echeverría used foreign policy as a means to this end. He presented himself as a dynamic diplomat dedicated to challenging the United States, affirming Mexico's solidarity with the Third World, and increasing his country's latitude in international affairs. He revived the issue of Cuba, positioning himself as a staunch defender of the Castro government. "By being outwardly somewhat leftist," he boasted, his government had forged "a social peace unknown to his seemingly more authoritarian predecessors."[22] During the 1970s Echeverría looked abroad in an attempt to re-create the PRI's ideological authority at home.

Peruvian leaders tried the same trick. From 1968 onward, Velasco and his top aides realized that they needed some means of solidifying their popularity and control of the government. Notwithstanding their general frustration with Peruvian politics, the junta members were perpetually divided over the proper pace of reform, and Velasco faced opposition from Peruvian elites jealous of their economic and social privileges. Accordingly, he turned to an issue that seemed certain to bolster his own standing and win broader public support for the "Peruvian Revolution": a nationalistic foreign policy. The junta promised the "definitive emancipation of our homeland," and subsequently nationalized IPC, seized U.S. fishing boats alleged to be operating in Peruvian waters, and evicted Washington's military mission.[23] This approach was popular among key domestic groups like students and intellectuals, whose backing Velasco cultivated, and Mercado later acknowledged that the junta's diplomacy had allowed it to overcome a "very difficult" internal situation.[24]

Similar dynamics were at work throughout South America. The Brazilian generals pursued a selectively independent foreign policy to tap into elite and popular nationalism and thereby ease the resistance provoked by their undemocratic rule.[25] In Argentina the military governments that ruled between 1966 and 1973 sought (as Lanusse put it) to "generate the image of an independent policy" in order to co-opt the Peronist legacy. Perón had left "an indelible leftist imprint" on Argentine politics, admitted Foreign Minister Luis María de

Pablo Pardo; an assertive foreign policy could thus provide domestic capital as well as diplomatic and economic gains.[26]

In Allende's Chile, fully on the other side of the ideological spectrum, there was also a strong internal impetus toward aggressive diplomacy. In a broad sense, Allende's *vía chilena al socialismo* ("Chilean path to socialism") required a forceful foreign policy. His promise to expropriate foreign holdings in the major industries, central to his project for revolutionizing Chilean society, implied a collision with Washington. The makeup of the UP coalition also continually pushed Allende to become more confrontational. The need to please the MIR, MAPU, and other ultra-Left groups moved Allende effectively to deny compensation to expropriated U.S. copper companies (by counting previously earned "excess profits" against them). Finally, railing against the "imperialist forms of dependency and exploitation" perpetuated by the United States served as a powerful rhetorical expedient. Casting Washington as the implacable enemy of the Chilean masses created the useful (and not inaccurate) image of a foreign foe opposing his revolutionary program, and allowed him to tar his domestic antagonists for their "complicity" with "U.S. monopolies."[27] Like his counterparts across Latin America, Allende found that confrontational diplomacy could serve domestic political ends.

There were other examples of the links between domestic and foreign policy. In Venezuela the trend toward increasingly nationalistic diplomacy during the late 1960s and 1970s occurred as the Caldera and Pérez governments sought to minimize social and political conflicts that might threaten that country's young democracy.[28] The cases discussed above, however, should suffice to establish that, at the same time many leaders became convinced that there was an opportunity for more energetic diplomacy, the internal dynamics of their societies pushed them in a similar direction. The dictates of domestic politics merged with the impulses created by global strategic and economic shifts, setting the stage for a confrontation with the United States.

The diplomatic activism of the late 1960s and early 1970s had its sharpest manifestation in the foreign policies of three countries that were sometimes considered to constitute an anti-U.S. axis in Latin America: Allende's Chile, Castro's Cuba, and Velasco's Peru.[29] In many ways it was the anticommunist junta in Lima, rather than the Marxist governments in Santiago or Havana, that blazed the trail of antihegemonic agitation. Notwithstanding Velasco's occasional dalliances with Washington (which reflected his strategic acumen as well as the divisions within the junta), the new diplomatic climate in Latin America owed substantially to the Peruvian example. After the 1968 coup, Velasco and Mercado implemented a number of measures to weaken U.S. power in Peru. They expropriated IPC and other U.S.-owned industries, joined the Andean Pact, and in 1971 successfully pushed the organization to adopt stronger controls on FDI. Self-styled "Nasseristas," they wooed Moscow as a potential counterweight to the United States.[30] In 1969 Mercado established diplomatic relations and signed a trade pact with the Kremlin, trumpeting "the end of an era in which our trade was channeled in only one direction."[31] Four years later, Lima imported two dozen Soviet tanks, a deal which one Foreign Ministry official characterized as a blow to Peru's "technological-military dependency on the United States," and subsequently purchased advanced artillery and antiaircraft systems from Moscow. Military ties between Washington and Lima had long been a source of U.S. influence in Peru; as these ties frayed, the junta would have less need to court American favor.[32]

More broadly, Peruvian diplomats mounted a concerted attack on the "special relationship" between the United States and Latin America. Seeing the underdeveloped nations as a source of diplomatic support, Velasco identified Peruvian diplomacy with the Third World, that "vast insurgency of the poor nations of the earth," rather than the U.S.-led "inter-American community." The junta assumed a prominent role in the Non-Aligned Movement (NAM) and Group of 77, supporting initiatives like the UN Charter of Economic Rights and Duties of States and the New International Economic Order.[33]

Velasco shrewdly maneuvered to ensure that Washington would not retaliate. He consistently declared his aversion to communism, but at the same time threatened to pursue closer ties to Moscow if the United States slapped economic sanctions on Peru (as mandated by U.S. law) in response to the IPC seizure. "We all remember what happened in Cuba," Mercado taunted.[34] The junta established tighter links with the Andean countries and Mexico in order to increase regional support for Peru and raise the costs of U.S. diplomatic pressure.[35] Initially, the strategy seemed to work. In 1969 the administration declined to impose sanctions on Lima, fearing, as Kissinger wrote, that doing so would "surely precipitate widespread and vehement criticism of the U.S. throughout Latin America." Nixon likewise conceded that Washington must accept a diminution of U.S. power in Peru. "We cannot succumb to the Aswan syndrome where Peru is concerned," he told advisers;

better to tolerate independence than make Velasco another Nasser (or another Castro).[36] In 1972 Nixon approved a $12 million road-building loan to Peru, and the administration later settled the IPC dispute on terms broadly favorable to Lima.[37]

Peruvian diplomacy provided a model for other Latin American countries, notably Allende's Chile. Chilean diplomats noted Velasco's ability to keep Washington at bay ("Peru nationalized IPC and the Marines were not sent there," commented Santa María) and sought to follow Lima's lead.[38] On the one hand, Allende aimed to avoid outright U.S. hostility that might prevent him from refinancing Chile's debt or obtaining foreign credit. Santa María's successor, Orlando Letelier, warned against creating "an acute confrontation with the United States."[39] Allende assured U.S. officials that he sought productive relations, and Chilean diplomats encouraged prominent American liberals such as Senator Edward Kennedy to portray the UP government in positive terms.[40] On the other hand, Allende moved energetically to exploit U.S. weakness. "Today it is not possible that a President of the United States can intervene in Latin America as President Johnson did in the Dominican Republic in 1965," Letelier wrote.[41] Allende expropriated U.S. holdings in mining, telecommunications, and finance, and made clear his determination to lead Chile out of the U.S. economic orbit. "We cannot continue to be exploited as an underdeveloped nation," he told U.S. officials.[42] Allende also supported several South American revolutionary movements, both directly and by turning a blind eye to the activities of the MIR.

To bolster his government against any U.S. response, Allende forged alliances with a variety of foreign leaders. He cultivated good relations with Cuba, recognizing Castro's regime and seeking aid in everything from intelligence cooperation to lessons on how to build "a revolutionary press."[43] As part of a strategy aimed at breaking what Foreign Minister Clodomiro Almeyda termed "the doctrine . . . of ideological borders," Allende also built bridges to Peru and Ecuador despite the historical enmity between Lima and Santiago and the non-Marxist nature of these governments.[44] Allende tried to position Chile at the head of the anti-U.S. movement in Latin America, lending full-throated support to economic integration and denouncing Washington's historical exploitation of the region. The countries of South and Central America must "overcome the fiction of the identity of interests . . . between the Latin American countries and the United States," Chile's Office of National Planning announced.[45]

No less important, Allende sought Soviet backing in order to keep Washington at a distance. Chilean officials received funds through the KGB, requested Soviet heavy weapons and extensive economic aid, and received Moscow's help in reorganizing Chile's security and intelligence services. After a visit to Moscow in 1971, Chilean representatives reported "excellent perspectives for collaboration between the Armed Forces of our two countries."[46]

The evolution of Chilean and Peruvian diplomacy presented Castro with new possibilities in his long-standing war against U.S. hegemony. Castro saw Allende especially as a potential ally. Chile represented a link to the South American mainland and an escape from the isolation of the 1960s. Castro made the most of the opportunity, exchanging visits with Allende and according preferential treatment to Chilean diplomats in Cuba. He also resolved to do all possible to keep Allende in power. Cuba's DGI armed the MIR and Allende's bodyguards, and Cuban security personnel stationed in the Santiago embassy prepared to swing into action in event of a U.S. invasion or a coup. "If Chile is attacked from abroad," Castro told Chilean diplomats, "[they should] not wait to ask him for help."[47]

Like Allende, though, Castro also realized that the conditions of the early 1970s provided opportunities not based solely on ideological sympathy. The fact that it was not simply Marxist governments striving against U.S. hegemony, but non-Marxist and even anticommunist regimes as well, allowed Cuban officials to work toward a broadened diplomatic presence in Latin America. Following Guevara's death, Cuban foreign policy underwent an important change. Guevara's demise and a series of disastrous economic failures ushered in what Cuban official Carlos Rafael Rodríguez called a "new period" in Cuba diplomacy, one based on setting Havana's policy on a more sustainable footing.[48] While Castro continued to foster revolution abroad, he simultaneously embraced a less abrasive approach to government-to-government relations. Castro made amends with Brezhnev, and Cuban officials admitted that he was aware "exactly how far he could go in asserting his independence of Moscow."[49] In 1968 Castro endorsed the Soviet policy of peaceful coexistence, desisted from criticizing Moscow's initiatives in Latin America, and supported the Soviet invasion of Czechoslovakia. In private, Cuban officials deplored this intervention as a "grave error," but in public Castro backed the Soviet move as the cost of avoiding "counter-revolution." Soviet–Cuban relations improved, and East Bloc arms and aid shipments increased. Although ties with Moscow would never return to their pre-1962 high, the relationship had been made workable once again.[50]

Castro also took a less vitriolic stance toward his neighbors. Recognizing "the growing influence of the progressive movement in Latin America," Castro married his diplomacy to the broader anti-U.S. sentiment of the period.[51] He cultivated ties with any regime that could plausibly be called "nationalist" or "progressive," and repaired relations with a number of the governments he had recently tried to overthrow. He called the anticommunist Velasco "a man of the Left," and sent a team of doctors to Lima after the dictator suffered an embolism in 1973.[52] Cuba supported a reformist junta that took power in Bolivia in 1971, and made peace with governments in Venezuela, Panama, and elsewhere.[53]

This strategy paid dividends. Velasco reciprocated Castro's friendship by recognizing Havana and launching an initiative to lift OAS sanctions on Cuba in 1972. This gambit failed, but regional enthusiasm for the idea grew over the next two years. By late 1974 it was Washington rather than Havana that was outnumbered. "We have to loosen up or we isolate ourselves," Kissinger concluded. In December the U.S. delegation took a position of "absolute neutrality" on a vote that ended OAS sanctions against Cuba.[54]

The breakdown of the sanctions regime provided a fitting marker of the diplomatic trends of the early 1970s and the consequent decline of U.S. sway in Latin America. Isolating Cuba had testified to U.S. success in beating back the radical challenge of the 1960s and organizing hemispheric affairs according to an East–West framework that stressed the common interests of Washington and the its neighbors. That this system collapsed even as Havana continued to support revolutionary movements in Latin America indicated not only an erosion of U.S. influence, but also the manner in which the Cold War alignments of the 1960s had given way to greater North–South conflict in the decade that followed.

As the loose and occasionally fractious concert led by Allende, Castro, and Velasco worked to undermine U.S. influence, another group of governments also contested long-standing dynamics of regional diplomacy. The unveiling of the Nixon doctrine, in which the president announced that Washington's allies would henceforth be expected to bear more of the burden of their own defense, was interpreted by leaders in Mexico, Venezuela, and Brazil as an invitation to move into the vacuum created by U.S. retrenchment. These nations were willing to concede the basic principle of U.S. hegemony in the Americas, but nonetheless sought to alter the terms of their relationship with Washington and carve out greater spheres of influence.

The most energetic of this group was Venezuela. With immense oil reserves, Venezuela was poised during the early 1970s to emerge as an important player both locally and globally. While Caldera and Pérez always considered the United States more of an ally than an adversary, they still brought Venezuela's new economic strength to bear on the relationship. Whereas in 1970 low oil prices had forced Caldera to trek to Washington to seek higher import quotas, following the oil shocks the tone of U.S.–Venezuelan diplomacy changed markedly. Caracas announced that it would nationalize U.S.-owned oil companies a decade ahead of schedule and publicly trumpeted the waning of American power. The emergence of multipolarity, Pérez announced, "has altered the bonds of economic, political, [and] cultural dependency" that restricted the developing countries, permitting "a greater freedom of action" with respect to Venezuelan natural resources.[55]

This activism had its counterpart in efforts to expand Venezuela's regional and global influence. On an international level, Pérez increased Venezuelan contributions to the IMF and World Bank and promoted greater coordination within the Organization of Petroleum Exporting Countries (OPEC). "It is necessary to preserve and strengthen the solidarity of the Third World," he wrote in 1974.[56] Regionally, Pérez aimed to displace U.S. influence in the Caribbean, long viewed by Venezuelan strategists as the country's natural geopolitical domain. He used oil revenues to launch aid programs for Central America and the Caribbean, and expanded Venezuela's diplomatic reach by making overtures to Haiti, Cuba, and the newly independent English-speaking states in the region.[57] Venezuela's regional influence was clearly on the rise; in 1974 a Guatemalan official wrote that Caracas was "almost equal to Washington" in the Caribbean.[58]

Venezuelan leaders also envisioned a rapid industrial ascent. In the mid-1970s Venezuela was awash with petrodollars. Brand-new skyscrapers sprang up in downtown Caracas and unprecedented wealth flowed into the economy. Pérez, who portrayed himself as "the man with energy," saw this money as the motor that would propel Venezuela toward modernization and a place among the developed countries. His government poured money into automobile construction, the production of heavy equipment, and other projects meant to give Venezuela a mature industrial base. The government also used significant wage increases to spur greater consumption and the expansion of the domestic market. Pérez sought to "sow the oil," to use this resource windfall to escape underdevelopment quickly and permanently.[59]

Mexico could not match Venezuela in resource wealth, but Echeverría took a backseat to no one in terms of ambition. After becoming president in 1970, Echeverría became a vigorous advocate of international economic redistribution and greater autonomy of the United States. The Mexican government tightened restrictions on FDI in the telecommunications industry, and Echeverría traveled to Moscow, Beijing, Canada, and Europe in an attempt to lessen Mexico's dependence on the U.S. market. "It is neither convenient nor healthy that three-fourths of our trade be exclusively with one country," he explained.[60] Rhetorically, Echeverría tried to outshout Velasco as the leader of the *tercermundista* movement in Latin America. "The Third World is not only a reality," he said in 1973, "it is also an ideology" derived from the Latin American peoples' awareness "of the external factors that prolong their misery." Echeverría lent strong support to initiatives like the New International Economic Order and railed against the "classist division of international society."[61]

Echeverría also looked to carve out an expanded sphere of influence in Central America and the Caribbean. His government encouraged investors to take advantage of the opportunities afforded by the Central American Common Market in order to expand Mexico's economic sway in the isthmus, and Echeverría strove to make Mexico the pivot in relations between Castro and the United States. He reversed Díaz Ordaz's cool stance toward Havana, exchanging visits with Castro and labeling him "one of history's leading heroes."[62] Echeverría then looked to parlay this relationship into diplomatic capital by offering his services as arbiter of the U.S.–Cuban conflict.[63] He also cultivated a warm relationship with Pérez, and the two leaders made OAS reform and the need for regional solidarity prominent themes of summits in 1974 and 1975.[64] This diplomacy was enough to exasperate Kissinger. "I find Mexico annoying," he complained in 1975.[65]

At the conservative end of the Latin American challenge was Brazil. The deeply anticommunist Costa e Silva and Médici governments were fundamentally friendly to the United States, yet they still viewed the late 1960s and early 1970s as a time of opportunity. With respect to the United States, these governments pursued what Médici called a policy of "firmness and tenacity."

Brasilia challenged Washington on issues such as territorial sea limits, bought Mirage fighters from France, and cast a cold eye on schemes through which the United States sought to limit the diffusion of global power. Brazilian leaders refused to sign the nuclear Non-Proliferation Treaty, arguing that this "discriminatory" regime did not impose a "just balance" between the nuclear and non-nuclear powers.[66] To the consternation of U.S. officials, Brazil subsequently imported reactor and uranium enrichment technology from West Germany. Brazil, announced Foreign Minister Antônio Azeredo da Silveira, must achieve "an outstanding position in the world," free from "the paths of hegemonic construction of the past."[67]

Riding a commodity-driven economic boom, Brazil also sought to exert greater sway over Latin American and South Atlantic affairs. Foreign Minister Mario Gibson Barboza (Silveira's predecessor), whom U.S. officials characterized as "the image of the suave statesman," gave a widely noted speech in 1970 in which he welcomed the end of the age of "two great poles of power" and heralded "a new phase" in Brazilian policy.[68] Brazil negotiated a series of economic arrangements with neighbors like Peru, and staked a claim to dominance in Paraguay by sponsoring construction of a massive hydroelectric plant along the Paraná River. Similarly, Médici and Gibson asserted a leading role for Brazil among the Lusophone countries. In 1972 Gibson made a monthlong tour of Africa during which he attempted to gain new markets for Brazilian goods and new stature for Brazilian diplomacy.[69] The aim of Brazilian policy, Silveira declared, was to "forge and shape opportunities for the future, to open niches for a broader and more effective action for a Brazil that grows and for this very reason needs a larger international presence."[70]

As Latin America's heavyweights maneuvered for leverage, so did its pygmies. During the Nixon and Ford years Panamanian strongman Omar Torrijos launched a crusade to obtain renegotiation of the Panama Canal treaties. To mobilize Latin American and Third-World support, he expertly cultivated the image of a Panamanian David confronting the U.S. Goliath. "Future generations will not be exploited . . . as their fathers were exploited," he declared.[71] To further up the pressure, Torrijos threatened to unleash saboteurs against the Canal should Washington refuse his demands. These tactics had the desired result, isolating the United States from regional and world opinion. "If there is no solution to the Panama Canal," warned one Central American president, "we, the traditional friends of the U.S., will have to hide because we will be on the receiving end of the stones."[72] In the end, Ford and

Kissinger chose not to confront Torrijos in an unwinnable diplomatic row. "The other Latins are getting into the act," Kissinger told Ford. "You have a personal letter from the President of Costa Rica, who said he and the Presidents of Colombia and Venezuela together with Torrijos would march arm-in-arm into the Canal Zone." In 1975 Ford agreed to a set of principles that cleared the way for the eventual revision of the treaties.[73] In the diplomatic climate of the early 1970s, even this most formal of Washington's imperial arrangements in Latin America was under fire.

This tendency toward greater autonomy was not only present in the foreign policies of specific countries, but had a broader multilateral relevance as well. The OAS, which had earlier been essentially a tool for confronting Castro, evolved into an increasingly anti-U.S. organization. Peru and Bolivia used the regional body to coordinate multilateral backing in a fisheries dispute with the United States, and some governments aimed to limit U.S. influence in the OAS by reforming the organization or abolishing it altogether. Latin American officials grew more attracted to the idea of coordinating policy through ECLA, which Inter-American Development Bank president Felipe Herrera called "a Latin American institution," rather than the OAS.[74] By the mid-1970s U.S. officials dreaded regional meetings. "Never has anything been scheduled that is such a guaranteed failure," griped Kissinger of one upcoming ministerial.[75]

Another area of contention was U.S. investment in Latin America. Economic nationalism had surged throughout Latin America during the 1960s, and by the 1970s the doctrine enjoyed what one scholar calls an "ideological moment."[76] Seeking to weaken the influence that Washington wielded as a result of extensive U.S. investments in Latin America, a number of governments attacked American capital. Bolivia seized U.S.-owned Gulf Oil, the Jamaican government moved against North American firms, and Guyana nationalized the bauxite industry.[77] The intensifying antipathy to "economic colonialism" was also obvious at OAS meetings. In 1971 Secretary-General Galo Plaza captured the general mood by demanding "the total exclusion of foreign capital from those sectors of vital national interest."[78]

This emphasis on redressing Latin America's traditional economic weakness vis-à-vis the United States was also prominent in the popularity of regional integration initiatives like the Andean Pact. Lanusse called for measures to build "an autonomous center of economic gravitation," sentiments echoed by Colombian president Misael Pastrana.[79] In the eyes of its proponents, regional integration would be doubly advantageous to the drive for economic independence. In one sense, it would allow the region to achieve a stronger, more unified position in international trade negotiations. The Venezuelan Foreign Ministry referred to the "urgent need" to construct "a united and strengthened bloc" of Latin American states, and Caldera cited Venezuelan participation in OPEC as an example of how underdeveloped nations might combine "so as not to find ourselves at the mercy . . . of the developed countries."[80] Additionally, regional integration would serve as a vehicle for industrial development. Many Latin American countries lacked the internal markets necessary to support large-scale industrialization, and in line with prevailing intellectual currents, prominent economists believed that the international environment was distinctly inhospitable to such an endeavor. "The developing countries have neither the resources nor the technical ability to compete with others even in the developing areas, and much less in the industrialized regions," ECLA concluded in 1967. To the extent that the Andean Pact and other such projects effectively expanded the domestic market for Latin American countries, they would, in theory, allow these countries to develop the sizable industrial enterprises that would serve as engines for future growth. Fittingly, Caldera, who had called for the creation of a "Latin American bloc" fifteen years earlier, led Venezuela into the Andean Pact in 1973, substantially increasing the group's political and economic clout.[81]

The growth of inter-American economic conflict went hand-in-hand with an ever-greater tendency for Latin American governments to align rhetorically and ideologically with the Third World. During the 1970s many leaders followed the Peruvian and Mexican examples in rejecting the primacy of the Cold War and placing foremost importance on the divide between developed and underdeveloped. Even Brazil's Médici, as strong an anticommunist as there was, acknowledged the "dichotomy" between the northern and southern hemispheres.[82] Between 1970 and 1975 several Latin American countries assumed leading roles in the NAM and Group of 77, and some leaders proposed setting up commodity cartels (modeled along the lines of OPEC) with other Third-World countries. By 1974 Kissinger was seriously troubled by the prospect of Latin America "sliding into the non-aligned bloc and compounding our problems all over the world."[83]

The desire to gain flexibility by establishing firmer ties with the Soviet bloc, China, and Western Europe was also present on a regional scale. Although Soviet–Latin American relations had warmed during the late 1960s, it was in the early 1970s that the idea of using outside powers to balance against U.S. influence took fullest form. Venezuela concluded a petrochemical contract with the Soviet Union; Argentina and other countries negotiated agricultural agreements with the European Economic Community; even the Central American regimes searched for new fruit and coffee buyers.[84] Brazilian officials outlined "a pragmatic and flexible policy, adjusted to the evolution of the world situation," in calling for the establishment of relations with Beijing, and a number of governments forged political and economic ties with Moscow.[85]

That so many governments were willing to draw closer to the Soviet Union showed the extent to which Moscow had succeeded in revamping its image in Latin America. Following the Cuban missile crisis, Moscow launched a charm offensive in the region. The Kremlin made overtures to numerous governments, even those that were strongly anticommunist, and offered advantageous trade and technological agreements. Moscow would no longer base its Latin American policy on ideological disagreements, the Soviet press announced, but would henceforth proceed on the basis of "businesslike cooperation and mutual understanding."[86]

This new approach had two purposes. The first was to avoid provoking the United States at a time when Moscow sought to improve relations with the West. In view of deteriorating Sino–Soviet relations, the Politburo resolved in 1967, Moscow should not become entangled in any "acute situation" with Washington. "We should avoid a situation where we have to fight on two fronts," Foreign Minister Andrei Gromyko wrote.[87] The enthusiasm for revolution characteristic of the Khrushchev period faded, replaced by a less threatening engagement with the region.

There was also a more opportunistic element to Soviet policy: the hope that establishing economic and diplomatic ties with Latin America would allow Moscow gradually to pry these nations away from the United States. Greater trade with Latin America, wrote Soviet analysts in 1967, would "further a weakening of their dependence on the imperialist powers, first of all the USA." By promoting normalized relations with Latin America, Moscow might expand its influence without the dangers inherent to the more adventurous strategy of the early 1960s.[88]

This strategy proved well suited to the general climate of Latin American affairs. Beginning with a Soviet–Brazilian trade pact signed in 1963, several countries moved to diversify their foreign commerce by establishing trade relations with Moscow. "Chile must take advantage of the vast Soviet market and its advances in the technical field," explained Foreign Minister Gabriel Valdés.[89] The Kremlin purchased raw materials and sold heavy machinery like tractors and industrial equipment. Soviet trade representatives impressed Latin American diplomats with their ability to speak "such a clear and perfect Spanish," and Moscow's trade with the region reached record levels.[90] By the early 1970s Moscow's image had evolved from that of an aggressive revolutionary power to that of a responsible commercial partner and perhaps even a useful balance against U.S. dominance.

Moscow's success in expanding its Latin American presence indicated both the extent of the diplomatic changes at work during the early 1970s and the potential threat these shifts posed to U.S. interests. Indeed, by 1973–1974, the diplomatic challenge had reached its high-water mark. Drawing on their interpretation of global events and the imperatives of domestic politics, Latin American officials as diverse as Echeverría, Médici, Velasco, and Allende attacked long-standing trends in hemispheric affairs and persistent imbalances of world power. Early on, their efforts reached across ideological boundaries, and displayed little of the subordination or passivity often thought to characterize the Latin American "side" of inter-American relations. Taken together, these diplomatic, political, and economic initiatives constituted an effort at a sharp departure in Latin American foreign relations—and a serious challenge to U.S. hegemony in the region.

Yet the Latin American challenge was only partially successful in delivering the results envisioned by its more aggressive proponents. During the mid-1970s the movement lost momentum, and what force it retained was channeled in new directions. While several Latin American countries did achieve an improvement of their international position, the broader antihegemonic tendencies that Kissinger had feared were largely diverted. "Latin America has shown signs of political will," Mexican foreign minister Santiago Roel lamented in 1978, but "we are not given the importance we deserve." At roughly the same time that the urban guerrilla offensive collapsed, the diplomatic challenge faded as well.[91]

There were three major impediments to the dramatic changes pursued by the likes of Mercado, Echeverría, and Allende. First, the major powers failed to conform to Latin American expectations, and Washington remained the only outside actor willing to take decisive action in the region. Second, for many countries the economic gains of the early 1970s proved temporary or even illusory, leaving them in a position of weakness rather than strength. Third, *tercermundista* unity and regional diplomatic solidarity soon eroded amid widespread ideological polarization, and the prospects for a broad-based mobilization against U.S. influence diminished as a result.

Regarding the first of these issues, Latin American observers seriously misjudged the ways in which global events would impact the behavior of the major powers. Whereas Allende and Castro had calculated that the decline of U.S. power would inhibit Washington from acting forcefully in Latin America, the actual outcome was precisely the opposite. Realizing that the unveiling of the "Nixon Doctrine" and U.S. withdrawal from Vietnam were tacit admissions that the United States was in relative decline, Nixon and Kissinger felt pressed to show that Washington would still act forcefully on behalf of its interests.

This policy of pairing "strategic withdrawals" with "tactical escalations" underlay the invasion of Laos, the bombing of Cambodia, and an abortive covert intervention in Angola, and was present in U.S.–Latin American relations as well.[92] While U.S. officials did make concessions on issues like the Canal treaties, in those cases where they perceived Washington's credibility to be at stake the Nixon and Ford administrations took sharp (if not always publicly avowed) action against their opponents. One example of this tendency was Nixon's response to the spike of expropriations in Latin America. Since 1969, U.S. officials had characterized this trend as a challenge that demanded an answer. State Department official J. Wesley Jones called the IPC dispute a test of U.S. "credibility and integrity," and argued that the Latin Americans would "certainly respect us more" if the administration demonstrated its resolve by imposing sanctions on Peru.[93] This counsel was not immediately adopted, but gained support after additional expropriations in Chile, Peru, Bolivia, and Guyana in the early 1970s. The Treasury Department argued that U.S. global credibility dictated a stern response. "The expropriation issue extends beyond its impact on our relations with LDC's," the department wrote. "A continued permissive attitude toward expropriations could have carryover effects in developed countries. The stakes are enormous." Treasury Secretary John Connally said that the White House should "get tough" on Latin American ex-propriations because "we don't have any friends there anyway." In late 1971 Nixon decided to deny foreign aid to any country that expropriated a U.S. company without "prompt and adequate" compensation.[94] Desperate not to appear feeble at a time of U.S. retrenchment, the administration became more—not less—likely to react strongly when provoked. "The United States renounced omnipotence," Brazilian officials noted in 1974, "but it did not re-nounce power."[95]

The same consideration prevailed in U.S. policy toward Allende. In this case, the fear of looking weak fueled Nixon's near-obsession with toppling the Chilean president. "Our failure to react to this situation," Kissinger told Nixon in November 1970, would be perceived "as indifference or impotence in the face of clearly adverse developments in a region long considered our sphere of influence."[96] Nixon put the matter more directly. "No impression should be permitted in Latin America that they can get away with this," he told the NSC. The United States must "show we can't be kicked around." While nu-merous concerns informed U.S. hostility to Allende, it was this need to avoid the appearance of another defeat that crystallized Washington's antagonism and gave it its urgent quality.[97] Though U.S. intervention was probably not the decisive factor in the eventual overthrow of the UP government, Nixon's in-trigues certainly exacerbated the problems that Allende grappled with as his presidency wore on. Allende expected to face a hobbled United States, but in-stead confronted a truculent superpower.

The extent to which Allende misread the United States was particularly evident in his reaction (or rather, nonreaction) to Nixon's meddling. Believing that Vietnam had irreversibly weakened the United States, Allende and many of his advisers consistently failed to appreciate the depth and danger of U.S. antipathy. Through early 1972, Chilean diplomats apparently allowed them-selves to be gulled by Kissinger's promises that the United States and Chile could establish a *modus vivendi*. "If we are reaching an agreement with the So-viet Union and with China," Kissinger told Letelier at one point, "How are we not going to be able to reach an agreement with Chile?"[98] Even after the *Wash-ington Post* revealed that Nixon had been trying to overthrow Allende since even before he took office, the Chilean president refused to respond. As a "show of good will," Allende decided to forego any number of countermeasures available to him, such as outing CIA agents in Chile (Soviet intelligence had excellent in-formation on Nixon's scarcely disguised destabilization program) or taking his grievances to the court of world opinion. Almeyda protested that conciliation would not diminish Washington's "obvious and evident intervention," but Allende refused to be swayed.[99] Persuaded of U.S. debility, and not realizing that it was the existence rather than the actions of his government that determined Nixon's hostility, Allende persisted in a policy of inaction that did nothing to reduce the mounting external pressure.

Latin American officials also misinterpreted the extent of other great powers' interest in Latin America. The early 1970s did see greater Soviet, Chinese, and European involvement in the region, but none of these powers emerged as a meaningful counterbalance to the United States. China was especially unhelpful. Premier Zhou Enlai was cold to a "Trotskyist," pro-Soviet Allende, and with U.S.–Chinese détente in prospect, Beijing refused to anger Washington by supporting anti-U.S. governments or otherwise meddling in America's "backyard."[100]

Europe was not much more forthcoming. Though leaders like Echeverría had seen NATO's growing independence of the United States as a sign that Western Europe might act as a diplomatic or economic balance to Washington, here too the results were disappointing. French arms sales and West German nuclear commerce did provide a few countries with modest autonomy from U.S. suppliers, but at no point was recourse to European support a meaningful option for a country embroiled in a dispute with Washington. NATO did not fragment during the early 1970s to the extent that many observers had believed it would, and while French, West German, and British officials continued to explore ways of expanding their presence in Latin America, they remained respectful of Washington's regional primacy.[101] This deference was not lost on Latin American officials; as early as 1972 the Chilean Foreign Ministry acknowledged that it was not practicable to exploit "the existing contradictions between the United States and the rest of the capitalist world."[102]

Equally disappointing to some Latin American leaders was Moscow's continuing diffidence. Some commentators speculated that the decline of U.S. power in the late 1960s might encourage Moscow to give greater support to its enemy's enemies in the Western Hemisphere, but here too reality fell short of expectation. This tendency was most evident in Moscow's dealings with Allende, whose election posed the single greatest threat to U.S. policy in Latin America—and offered the single greatest opportunity for an expansion of Soviet influence. Although Allende hoped that the Soviet Union would support Chile in any confrontation with the United States, Moscow often acted as though it was trying to ignore the Chilean leader. The consummation of dé-tente and the rise of Sino–Soviet tensions made Soviet officials increasingly solicitous of Washington's sensitivities in Latin America. "The USSR is not in competition with the U.S. in the areas of the Third World," Soviet ambassador to Washingon Anatoly Dobrynin told Chilean officials after Allende was elected.[103] Additionally, Soviet officials doubted that Allende could long hold power, and had little desire to pour resources into a losing cause. Allende's re-quests for aid, commented one official, "implies that the Soviet Union would have to accept conditions that have never been contemplated in the relations of the USSR with the developing countries."[104]

Even though Allende had been a KGB asset for years, official Soviet–Chilean cooperation never amounted to much. Moscow and East Germany shared intelligence with Santiago, sold a moderate quantity of arms to the UP government, and provided some economic and technological assistance, but on the whole Soviet support was considerably less than most observers had expected.[105] (The omens were inauspicious from the outset—shortly after Al-lende's victory, the Kremlin raised the rent on the Chilean embassy in Mos-cow by nearly 100 percent.)[106] Moscow made clear that it had no desire for a Cuba-style relationship with Chile, and offered little protest as U.S. intrigues against Allende became more obvious during 1972–1973. "We are living in a moment of convergence and understanding between the United States and the socialist countries," Letelier reported in 1972, and the possibility of strong Soviet support declined accordingly.[107]

This essential caution prevailed in other aspects of Soviet–Latin American relations as well. When Kissinger hinted that construction of a Soviet subma-rine base in Cuba might prevent further progress in arms control negotiations, Brezhnev discontinued the project. Moscow signed trade agreements with Peru, Venezuela, and other countries, and sold arms to Lima, but was unwill-ing to be drawn into more serious disputes between the United States and its neighbors or become a patron to additional Latin American clients. Soviet dis-bursements to regional communist parties remained at 1960s levels through-out the early 1970s, and quite low compared to the moneys given European parties.[108]

In sum, the large powers failed to conform to the expectations of many Latin American diplomats. Expanded economic relations with players other than the United States provided a marginal diversification of Latin American commerce, and Peru made some diplomatic and technological gains through its ties to Moscow. Overall, however, the Soviets and other outside actors refused to go beyond a very modest involvement in the area. Dreams of playing the powers off one another faded as it became clear that the United States was the only major actor willing to commit its influence and prestige—and aggressively at that—in the region. Ambitious Latin American diplomats had hoped the emergence of détente and multipolarity would herald decisive changes in regional diplomacy, but the geopolitical currents of the period tended to obstruct such changes instead.

The same was true of international economic relations. The oil shocks and the breakdown of Bretton Woods initially energized the Third World, but in most cases the effect was fleeting. By the second half of the 1970s it was obvious that much of Latin America—and the Third World as a whole—had been weakened, rather than strengthened, by the economic events of the previous years, and North–South stratification remained firmly intact.

The economic picture was not entirely bleak for Latin America after 1973–1974. High oil prices lifted Venezuelan profits; Brazil's military-directed success continued; Mexico went through a bust-and-boom cycle in late 1970s; and despite some lean years early on, Pinochet's Chile experienced relatively strong growth after 1975. By and large, however, the material gains that resulted from rising oil prices proved evanescent or simply nonexistent, and Western economic debility was temporary, too. What was not immediately apparent in the wake of the oil shocks, but soon became so, was that rising oil prices were in fact a disaster for most Latin American countries. For the non-oil exporters, high prices meant that import costs dwarfed export earnings, leading to serious debt problems. The high commodity prices of the early 1970s momentarily shielded Latin American countries from this reality, but as coffee, copper, and fruit prices subsequently fell, the extent of the trouble came into focus.[109] Latin America's external debt rose faster than the average rate for less-developed countries (LDCs) during the first half of the 1970s, and by 1974 the region possessed one-third of all LDC debt. In 1975 interest payments consumed 13 percent of export earnings, while debt service constituted another 27 to 30 percent. For most countries, the oil shocks exposed a new vulnerability rather than a new power.[110]

This vulnerability severely impinged upon the developmentalist projects launched during the 1960s and early 1970s. Rising oil and commodity prices imposed heavy burdens on industrial firms. Small and medium companies were hard-pressed to purchase necessary inputs, and while governments in Brazil and elsewhere kept state-owned firms productive via heavy borrowing and increased state spending, this strategy simply added to their growing debt exposure. As subsequent events would show, this trade-off was a disastrous one.[111]

Regional integration also lagged vis-à-vis the heady expectations of a few years earlier. The advantages of integration schemes accrued largely to the members with the most advanced economies, which were best placed to exploit lower trade barriers. This inequity led the less fortunate to solicit additional concessions; these demands, in turn, soured larger countries on the entire enterprise. Perhaps more important, countries that had spent decades pursuing ISI were reluctant to expose favored industries to new competition, and agreements on the most important categories of goods proved elusive. By the latter part of the decade the Andean Pact and regional integration more broadly had been exposed as false panaceas.[112]

While Latin America failed to make the economic gains many observers had expected, Western financial hegemony proved more resilient than predicted. The period following the oil shocks saw a marked rise in economic conflict between the West and the rest. Rising oil prices, and OPEC's perceived exploitation of this situation, created a sort of inverse dependency feeling: the idea that the rich were being gouged by the poor. Rising oil prices, recalled one World Bank executive, made it look like "the Third World was trying to beat the developed world into submission."[113] Officials in the United States, Europe, and Japan were determined to stunt the growth of Third-World economic power and restore their own dominance of international commercial and monetary relations. "We cannot accept the proposition that these nations can wreck the world economic system," said Kissinger, "and effect such a massive transfer of resources as to render worthless the very paper with which they are paid."[114]

The emerging Third-World debt crisis provided just such an opportunity. By 1974–1975 it was clear that countries in Latin America, Asia, Africa, and the Middle East would soon need financial relief. "The oil importing countries are faced with a massive increase in their import bill," the IMF reported in February 1974, and many developing countries would see a "very large deterioration in the current accounts of their balance of payments." As their financial situation deteriorated, these countries would find loans from private banks hard to come by.[115] This financial weakness presented the major developed countries with a chance to ensure that the evolution of Third-World economies occurred along lines favorable to the West. The Third-World debt crisis meant that organizations like the IMF, which had lost its original mission with the breakdown of Bretton Woods, quickly took on the role of emergency lender to the LDCs. Thanks to the severity of the debt crisis, the IMF was now in a position to impose stricter-than-before conditions on loan recipients. The organization could demand that borrowers reduce state involvement in the economy and allow greater openness to foreign investment and trade. "The industrial countries are dealing from a position of strength," noted a U.S. strategy paper. Coming at a time when the post–Bretton Woods liberalization of exchange rates and capital flows had unleashed the phenomenon now known as "globalization," this new strength vis-à-vis the developed world was all the more rewarding.[116]

Over the next two decades, this push to combine emergency debt relief with stricter "conditionality" defined Western relations with the Third World. The United States increasingly focused on the need "to achieve closer coordination among industrial countries on North-South relations, to make their leverage effective," and for the most part, they succeeded.[117] The latter half of the decade witnessed a proliferation of IMF stabilization packages, which required borrowers to adopt austerity programs, reduce state control of industry, and liberalize trade and investment regulations. The World Bank adopted similar policies in the late 1970s as part of its "structural adjustment" lending. By decade's end the international financial institutions and their predominantly Western sponsors had established economic reform as the price of debt relief.[118]

These trends undermined several leaders who had just recently attempted to assert their diplomatic autonomy of the United States. As Echeverría's presidency came to an end in 1976, government profligacy and general economic mismanagement sent the country into a balance-of-payments and currency crisis. These events spelled the end of the postwar "Mexican miracle" and, despite the discovery of new oil reserves that provided a temporary recovery, they marked the beginning of the downward slide to the debt crisis of 1982. The crisis also heralded a departure from Echeverría's confrontational style. The U.S. Treasury partnered with the IMF and private banks to provide a bailout to the Mexican government, but only after incoming president José López Portillo agreed to contract the state's role in the economy and ease restrictions on FDI.[119] These steps were difficult politically for López Portillo, who feared that austerity measures would antagonize the unions. Given Mexico's desperate financial state, though, he had few options. "Mexico is entering a period of turbulence," he told Ford in September 1976.[120] In order to create a climate of calm in the relationship with Washington, he significantly moderated Echeverría's public criticism of the United States over the next two years. As one scholar has noted, for all Echeverría's attempts to forge a more independent diplomacy, Mexico remained "as dependent as ever" on Washington and the international financial institutions.[121]

The same was true of Peru, where promiscuous borrowing combined with rising oil costs caused a quintupling of the country's external debt between 1970 and 1976. Velasco's attempt to maneuver out of these difficulties by nationalizing more U.S.-owned properties backfired, splitting an already-divided junta and leading to his overthrow in August 1975.[122] With commercial banks no longer willing to lend to Peru ("The whole damn place has gone to hell," remarked one potential lender), the junta that replaced Velasco moderated his policies to regain international support.[123] It promised that there would be "no more expropriations," and, like López Portillo, decreased criticism of the United States.[124] To convince the IMF to broker new loans from private foreign banks, the junta scaled back a number of Velasco's economic measures. The IMF put particular emphasis on holding down public spending via wage freezes, and on "dismantling Peru's far ranging system of import restrictions." In 1977 Velasco's successors finally took the long-resisted step of accepting an IMF stabilization package.[125]

The Third-World economic challenge that many had predicted in the early 1970s never really took shape. Within Latin America it was clear as early as 1975 that the international economic balance was not far removed from its earlier state. In contrast to its jubilance of two years earlier, ECLA now conceded "the sensitivity of the Latin American economies to changes in the international power and decision-making centers."[126] Over the next two decades it would be IMF conditionality rather than Latin American economic assertiveness that dominated the regional scene. The 1970s, which had begun so promisingly for those who hoped to upend the global economic order, ended with Western hegemony intact, if slightly worse for the wear.

This was true of Western economic relations with the Third World as a whole, where the 1970s saw not the emergence of a "common economic front" but the growing prosperity of a few petro-economies and the growing impoverishment of the rest. While Venezuela, Nigeria, and the Persian Gulf states reaped huge profits and played an expanded role in IMF lending and Euromarket finance, the majority of the underdeveloped countries received massive debt burdens as the chief financial legacy of the 1970s. The petro-economies escaped (in many cases temporarily), rather than elevated, a heterogeneous Third World.[127]

Ultimately, however, Latin American diplomatic assertiveness was diverted by internal splits as much as it was blunted by external opposition. While domestic divisions had initially helped spur the trend toward antihegemonic diplomacy, the upheaval and violence that erupted in South America during this period eventually had the opposite effect. The revival of the guerrilla threat and the advent of the Allende government polarized regional diplomacy, and the military regimes that subsequently came to power put anticommunism rather than anti-Americanism at the center of their foreign policies.

Although this trend would not become fully evident until the mid-1970s, it had actually been taking shape even at the height of the diplomatic challenge. Allende's election gave impetus to the antihegemonic movement in Latin America, but it also produced consternation among Chile's neighbors. The course of events inside Chile, and especially Allende's ties to the urban guerrillas, aroused the opposition even of governments that occasionally cooperated with him diplomatically. In Brazil U.S. representatives found that "practically everyone expressed concern about developments in Chile and the possible extension of 'Allendization' to Brazil's neighbors."[128] As his own country struggled to deal with guerrilla violence, one Uruguayan diplomat commented that "the only real hope he had for Latin America . . . was that the Chilean experiment would fail."[129] Even Peru's Mercado told U.S. officials that the two countries should make common cause "against the spread of Marxism in Latin America."[130] Allende had hoped to foster Latin American solidarity, but his rise to power caused ideological divisions instead.

This effect became all the more pronounced following the rise of the radical military regimes in the mid-1970s. Having seized power at a time of deep Left–Right cleavages and guerrilla violence, these governments contended that the primary threat to their countries came not from U.S. hegemony but from communist penetration. Whereas statesmen like Echeverría and Velasco had argued that the North–South conflict must take precedence in Latin

American diplomacy, the Southern Cone juntas viewed geopolitics through a Cold War lens. "Argentina is merely one theatre of operations in a global confrontation between Moscow and the United States," said General Ramón Camps.[131] This belief altered the context of regional diplomacy, as governments like Pinochet's placed primary emphasis on Cold War cohesion rather than *tercermundista* solidarity. Following the coup against Allende, Chile withdrew from the Andean Pact, severed relations with Cuba, and dismissed calls for regional cooperation as a "Cuban 'Trojan Horse.'" Worriedly noting the "growing influence of the USSR" in Peru, the junta reversed Allende's policy of building ties with Lima, and relations between the two countries soon deteriorated into talk of war. Pinochet staunchly opposed reform of the OAS or the Rio Pact, and he left no doubt that his allegiances lay with the First World rather than the Third. "We are behind you," he told Kissinger in 1976. "You are the leader."[132]

Kissinger reciprocated this gesture, praising Pinochet for his "great service to the West" in overthrowing Allende. And indeed, Washington eagerly encouraged the ideological fragmentation at work within Latin America. Aiming to avoid the feared scenario that Latin America might "form a bloc, united by its opposition to the United States," Kissinger worked assiduously to fracture any anti-U.S. coalition.[133] He did so primarily by cultivating relations with friendly authoritarian governments. The idea of a greater reliance on military regimes had been evident as early as Nelson Rockefeller's much-publicized report on Latin America in 1969, and fit well within the Nixon Doctrine's emphasis on finding supportive regional "sheriffs."[134] In the early 1970s Nixon, Kissinger, and Ford identified leaders that they hoped would advance U.S. interests in the face of a growing Latin American challenge. The Somoza government in Nicaragua and Argentine Foreign Minister Alberto Vignes received consideration for this role. At one point Nixon even looked to Echeverría, telling the Mexican president, "Let the voice of Echeverría rather than the voice of Castro be the voice of Latin America."[135]

Given Echeverría's strident *tercermundismo,* Nixon and Kissinger often found their dealings with the Mexican president more frustrating than anything else. They had greater success with other countries, particularly Brazil. Kissinger had little patience for Latin Americans, but Brazil occupied a privileged place in his worldview.[136] Due to its size, surging economy, and evident geopolitical ambition, Kissinger thought it certain that "in 50 years Brazil should have achieved world power status." On important political and security issues, moreover, Kissinger saw the military government as essentially friendly to U.S. aims. Médici aspired to a greater world role and might occasionally demonstrate his independence of U.S. policy, Kissinger believed, but in the main Brasilia sympathized with Washington's anticommunism. Brazil was "trying to be supportive," even though it needed to "lean enough towards the non-aligned to maintain a credible Latin American posture." Accordingly, Kissinger viewed Brazil as Washington's closest ally in Latin America. "Stay in close step with the Brazilians," he told subordinates.[137]

Kissinger's analysis was astute. Médici, though determined to expand Brazil's international influence, always considered Washington more of a partner than an adversary. "Any disagreement between the U.S. and Brazil should be considered a 'lovers' quarrel,'" he remarked.[138] As the Left took power in Chile and guerrilla violence wracked the Southern Cone, the forceful anticommunism that defined Brazil's internal policies suffused the country's diplomacy as well. "The situation was becoming ever more menacing," commented one Brazilian observer, making it indispensable that Brasilia "assume a more 'aggressive' security and foreign policy posture in this part of the world."[139] Médici eagerly cooperated with U.S. attempts to undermine the South American Left and "finish off subversive communism." He supported U.S. covert action against Allende, supplying arms to *Patria y Libertad* and telling Connally that "something should probably be done . . . very discreetly and very carefully."[140] In 1971 the Brazilian military conspired with Bolivian conservatives to stage a coup against that country's left-wing government, and kept thousands of troops stationed on the Uruguayan border in case the Left should come to power.[141] Rather than aiding South American movements and governments opposed to the United States, Médici collaborated with Washington in subverting them. "I wish he were running the whole continent," Nixon remarked.[142] Even after Médici left office in 1974, Brazilian diplomats privately characterized the bilateral relationship as "excellent" and "perfectly pragmatic." Kissinger envisioned Brazil taking "a decisive role in the course and fate of Latin America," they noted approvingly.[143]

As Brazil attacked the Left, it also undercut efforts to achieve greater economic integration and diplomatic solidarity vis-à-vis the United States. The military government opposed the formation of a purely Latin American body to replace the OAS, and argued against reforms that would make that organization a vehicle for regional "isolationism." Médici was equally cool to integration schemes. Brazil had less need for regional integration than some of its smaller neighbors, and the Brazilian government viewed many of these countries as potential enemies in any event. Development was a regionwide concern, Médici allowed, but in the last analysis economic growth must be "the exclusive responsibility of each state."[144] Brazilian diplomats also denigrated the "mythical entity self-designated as the Third World," and argued against "demagogic confrontations with the developed countries." The current configuration of global power was inequitable, Foreign Ministry officials recognized, but "the belligerency of the 'third world' countries" was a self-defeating strategy.[145] Because Brazil was by far the most powerful country in Latin America, its stance on these issues constituted a significant blow to any meaningful regional cohesion. As similar governments came to power in Uruguay, Argentina, and Chile, the pull of *tercermundismo* only became weaker.

Médici's policies underscored a fundamental characteristic of regional diplomacy during the mid-1970s: the often-contradictory nature of Latin American nationalism. The ascendancy of anticommunist, rather than anti-U.S., diplomacy in countries like Brazil did not signal a diminution of the nationalist tendencies that had driven Latin American foreign policies during the early 1970s. What it indicated was that Latin American nationalism was neither a monolithic nor necessarily a unifying force in regional affairs. Médici was no less a "nationalist" than any of his Latin American contemporaries—he pursued national power and influence no less vigorously than his left-leaning counterparts. Yet Médici's anticommunist nationalism proved largely incompatible with the leftist nationalism pursued by Allende and others, and constituted a check on these statesmen's policies.

There was no better illustration of the new diplomatic alignments taking shape in South America than the launching of Operation Condor in late 1975. A continental alliance against the Left, Condor built on the antiguerrilla cooperation begun by the military governments of the late 1960s and early 1970s. After the Chilean coup in 1973, Pinochet's Foreign Ministry solicited counterinsurgency assistance from Guatemala and proposed to join interested parties in forming "a united front to counteract the action of international Marxism."[146] In 1974 several South American militaries exchanged information on the various leftist groups active in their countries.[147] A year later, DINA director Manuel Contreras moved to institutionalize this cooperation. He invited representatives from Uruguay, Brazil, Bolivia, Argentina, and Paraguay to a meeting in Santiago to discuss a "strictly secret" proposal for "excellent coordination and better action in benefit of the National Security of our respective countries." Warning that subversion "does not recognize borders or countries, and the infiltration penetrates all levels of national life," Contreras proposed the creation of a "Security Coordination System" for the Southern Cone. This system would feature a centralized clearinghouse for information on guerrilla groups ("something similar to what Interpol has, but dedicated to subversion") and would eventually grow to include joint efforts to jail, torture, and kill Latin American leftists.[148] The guerrillas had long practiced revolutionary internationalism; the militaries now embraced internationalism of the counter-revolutionary sort.

Between 1975 and 1980 Condor developed into a full-fledged transnational network aimed at destroying what remained of the South American Left. Intelligence-sharing activities, facilitated by modest technical assistance from the CIA, allowed its members to track and capture high-ranking guerrilla operatives.[149] By 1977 the military governments had effectively closed the vise around the remnants of the JCR. The Argentine military routinely detained or murdered activists wanted by other governments, or clandestinely repatriated these individuals for torture and interrogation.[150] Argentine officers helped Bolivian paramilitary forces conceal the bodies of their victims, and several Argentine officials were involved in a coup in Bolivia in 1980.[151] Condor eventually went global, with Chilean intelligence operatives assassinating opposition figures in the United States and Europe.

Operation Condor showed that the feared "Latin American bloc" had, in South America at least, become an anticommunist league tacitly allied to the United States. In the early 1970s Washington had worried that Latin American diplomacy might coalesce around an anti-U.S. position, but by 1975–1976 there were few such fears. "The tone of U.S.-Latin American relations is better than at any time in the recent past," National Security Adviser Brent Scowcroft reported.[152]

By the mid-1970s the Latin American challenge had largely run out of steam. A few countries, like Brazil, Venezuela, and Panama, now enjoyed increased diplomatic influence, and U.S. hegemony in Latin America was not what it had once been. The United States would soon agree to revised Panama Canal treaties; the OAS no longer ostracized Cuba; both the outgoing Ford and incoming Carter administrations admitted that the paternalistic rhetoric of the "special relationship" needed junking.[153]

Yet the fundamental power relationships structuring Latin America's intercourse with the world remained at least temporarily intact. The advent of tougher, rather than more flexible, U.S. policies served notice that Washington was still willing to act boldly in the region, while the tepidness of other major-power involvement in Latin America meant that there emerged no real counterforce to American influence. The evanescence of the economic optimism of the early 1970s and the reassertion of Western financial hegemony eroded the material basis for increased Latin American autonomy, and rendered countries like Peru and Mexico more compliant with U.S. and IMF prescriptions. To the extent that a Latin American diplomatic bloc had taken shape, it consisted of South American military dictatorships that, whatever their disagreements with Washington (especially once Jimmy Carter became president),[154] saw U.S. power as a salutary rather than a harmful influence. Unable to overcome their economic weakness or form a united antihegemonic front, those Latin American nations that sought to transform the existing order were doomed to disappointment.

One of the ironies of the Latin American diplomatic challenge was that the demise of the movement actually vindicated certain of its intellectual premises. For *dependentistas* who claimed that Latin America was unfairly hemmed in by a rigid international system, this episode offered plenty of confirming evidence. During the 1970s Latin American ambitions ran up against a series of formidable obstacles: the opposition of the United States, the indifference of the other major powers, and the fundamentally disadvantageous economic position occupied by most countries in the region. Predictions of greater global fluidity were overblown, and the desires of the region's more optimistic statesmen were disappointed.

This outcome hinted at the larger reality that the global order changed less in the decade after 1965 than it might have seemed at the time. While the international system did become more flexible during the late 1960s and early 1970s, it ultimately retained sufficient resilience to avert the thoroughgoing transformations envisioned by certain Latin American officials. The United States was weakened by Vietnam and persistent economic difficulties, but was still willing and able to defend its interests vigorously. Great-power relations did become more flexible, but understanding between Washington and its erstwhile enemies had the unexpected effect of locking in the diplomatic status quo in Latin America. And while the international economic system became more fluid during the 1970s, it remained slanted toward the interests of the developed countries. The economic fluctuations and redistribution of world power that characterized this period were powerful enough to tempt ambitious Third-World diplomats into action, but not to permit them more than marginal success.

In other ways, however, the *dependentistas* would have been hard-pressed to explain the course of Latin American diplomacy. Perhaps the greatest impediment to a successful antihegemonic movement turned out to be internal rather than external, and the diplomatic assertiveness practiced by Latin American governments during the 1970s was not so much blunted as redirected. Countries like Brazil, Chile, and Argentina were hardly meek during the mid-1970s; if anything they showed what, to many observers, seemed an alarming aggressiveness. What happened, rather, was that they simply turned this energy in a different direction, placing primary emphasis on anticommunism rather than anti-Americanism. It was this change as much as anything else that dissipated the momentum of the challenge to U.S. influence and gave South American diplomacy its shape in the mid- and late 1970s.

This outcome, in turn, indicates two enduring themes with respect to Latin American diplomacy and relations with the United States. First, it underscores the dilemma that has long confronted ambitious Latin American diplomats: the fundamental disunity of the countries of the region. "Latin America" is a convenient political label, and as I hope this study has shown, a useful unit for historical analysis. At the same time, it is also a region of immense complexity and variation, as the course of Latin American diplomacy over the past 200 years has repeatedly confirmed. Since the time of Bolívar, enterprising statesmen have called for Latin American countries to combine forces against the United States or other looming powers. In most cases they have ultimately found that the unity perpetually trumpeted by regional leaders is only superficial. The conflicts between Latin American countries have often proved more powerful than the forces impelling them to cooperation, a reality once again manifested in the decline of the diplomatic challenge.[155] The Left–Right divisions that resurfaced during the mid-1970s gave the lie to invocations of antihegemonic unity and *tercermundismo,* and ensured that the region's traditional fragmentation continued. In diplomacy as in most other regards, Latin America's apparent uniformity proved to be largely overblown.

Second, the history of regional diplomacy between the late 1960s and the mid-1970s demonstrates the dynamic and ambivalent nature of Latin America's relations with the United States. Some historians have identified protective cooperation as the dominant theme of U.S.–Latin American affairs; more have seen the relationship as an essentially antagonistic one.[156] This episode indicates that neither of these characteristics permanently governs U.S.–Latin American diplomacy, and that the shape of this relationship depends more on circumstance than on any immutable affinity or hostility. In the late 1960s internal politics and global trends led Latin America's most important countries to contest U.S. power; a few years later, the explosion of Left–Right conflict in South America led a number of nations to rethink this approach. As had long been the case, inter-American relations thus revolved more around opportunism and calculations of temporary advantage than they did around any permanent state of conflict or cooperation. This characteristic of hemispheric affairs proved essential to the rapid swings of Latin American diplomacy between the late 1960s and the mid-1970s, and would be no less important to the dramatic changes that were to occur shortly thereafter.

6

The Revolution in Context

The Cold War is often thought of as a time of revolution in Latin America. In reality, successful revolutions were few and far between. In the early 1960s observers as disparate as Che Guevara and the CIA had forecast that triumphant insurgencies would soon sweep the Western Hemisphere; nearly two decades later, these predictions remained unfulfilled. There had been no shortage of revolutionary sentiment or violent revolts during this period, but since Castro's march into Havana in 1959, every one of these challenges had been turned back. ("Revolutionaries" like Allende, Velasco, and others had come to power via the ballot box or the palace coup, but these were hardly the sorts of transformations that Guevara had anticipated.) The twenty years after the Cuban revolution were hardly a period of stability in Latin America, but they were nonetheless an era of revolutionary failure and disappointment.

There were several reasons for this. The victory and subsequent radicalization of the Cuban revolution actually worked against the consummation of future revolts, setting Latin American security forces on edge and leading them to repress any sign of "subversion." The United States also strove to keep the Left out of power, using economic and military aid, covert intervention, and the occasional invasion to do so. Finally, the guerrillas and their allies often did considerable harm to their own cause, either by adhering to rigid ideological doctrines with no relevance to conditions on the ground or by producing such violence and havoc as to alienate much of the population. For all the exploitation and poverty that characterized regional affairs during the 1960s and 1970s, Latin America's "masses" simply were not that revolutionary, and they repeatedly turned away from the guerrillas as a result. This combination of factors tilted the balance sharply against the revolutionaries, whose flagging fortunes were symbolized by the utter destruction of the urban guerrillas.

Only three years after the Argentine coup capped the counterrevolutionary ascendancy in South America, however, events in Nicaragua put a close to the guerrillas' losing streak. During the late 1970s a broad revolutionary coalition rose against the Somoza dictatorship, toppling the tyrant and bringing a Marxist-Leninist guerrilla group, the Sandinista National Liberation Front (FSLN), to power.

Why this rapid turnaround? One explanation is that the Nicaraguan revolution was the unavoidable outcome of the socioeconomic inequity and political exclusion that had long generated instability in the region. Central America had usually outpaced the rest of Latin America in terms of repression and exploitation, and for years observers had referred to the isthmus as a "powder keg" (or something similar). In light of these conditions one might argue that the Nicaraguan revolution—as well as subsequent civil wars in Guatemala and El Salvador—were the inevitable result of oppression and marginalization.[1]

Repression and poverty did play an important role in the upheaval in Nicaragua. Yet if misery and injustice were sufficient to cause revolutions, Latin America as a whole would long have been in flames. The turmoil that shook Nicaragua was the result not of historical inevitability, but of a unique collection of trends that coalesced in the late 1970s and removed many of the barriers that had previously impeded radical change.

There were four principal factors at work in this regard. First, the Nicaraguan system—*somocismo*—was breaking down in the 1960s and 1970s. Economic change, official corruption, governmental repression, and blatantly dynastic practices reduced the flexibility of the Nicaraguan regime, magnified long-simmering internal conflicts, and produced widespread, radical dissent. Second, having learned from the travails of their predecessors, the Nicaraguan guerrillas embraced new strategies that allowed them to exploit these mounting domestic tensions and achieve an unprecedented breadth of public support. Third, the insurgents enjoyed substantial foreign backing—not just from Cuba this time, but from a variety of Latin American nations—that played a crucial role in steeling them against governmental responses. Fourth, the administration of Jimmy Carter implemented striking changes to U.S. policy toward Latin America. These departures, which had mainly to do with human rights and nonintervention, hardly lessened Washington's desire to avert radical revolutions in the region, but did leave U.S. officials with fewer tools to prevent such outcomes.

During the Cold War, Marxist elites perpetually declared that the "correlation of forces" was now in their favor. More often than not, these claims had more to do with ideology than reality. In the late 1970s, though, the factors described above finally did give the advantage to the revolutionaries, facilitating a successful revolt in Nicaragua and pushing Central America toward the generalized explosion that Latin America–watchers had long predicted.

The Nicaraguan revolution had its deepest origins in developments that predated the 1970s, the Cuban revolution, and the Cold War as a whole. The exploitation and marginalization that resulted from agro-export economics had long lent a degree of instability to Nicaragua's internal affairs, giving rise to waves of resistance and repression. The regime that dominated the country through the late 1970s had arisen out of just these dynamics. Anastasio "Tacho" Somoza cemented his power four decades earlier by putting down a widespread peasant movement, and following World War II his government oversaw an expansion of commercial agriculture and light industry that placed even greater pressure on the rural poor.[2]

These cycles of upheaval and oppression intensified following the Cuban revolution. The Somoza regime (now headed by Tacho's elder son, Luís) fully exploited U.S. largesse in the 1960s to further the shift toward commercial agriculture and light industry. And as happened throughout Latin America during the Alliance for Progress years, the government emphasized productivity at the expense of equity. "Each and every enterprise of this government should be to place us at a highly competitive level" in the world market, said Anastasio "Tachito" Somoza (Luís's younger brother), who would come to power in 1967.[3] Consequently, while Nicaragua's relatively low population density meant that land scarcity never reached the levels attained in Guatemala and El Salvador, these trends nonetheless had a serious impact. Growing numbers of *campesinos* were pushed off their land and into low-paying wage labor, ensuring that the ideological ascent of liberation theology became even steeper and leading to greater activism by Nicaragua's rural unions.[4]

The escalation of rural and working-class agitation was doubly important, because the Nicaraguan political system was simultaneously losing its capacity to ameliorate such discontent. *Somocismo* had always been an authoritarian system, but it had originally featured populist elements. After successfully weakening the peasant movement during the 1930s, Tacho employed a populist discourse and occasional concessions to the working class to cultivate an alliance with the unions and thereby use them as a counterweight to the Conservative opposition. Following the patriarch's death, this partnership came to an end. The "shadows of atheist Communism" that hung over Latin America after Castro came to power led Luís Somoza to repress labor activism in violent fashion.[5] These measures caused many unions to conclude that *somocismo* had become irredeemably reactionary, and marked the demise of labor's alliance with the regime. By the early 1970s labor upheaval was a constant in Nicaraguan politics. Rising food and gasoline prices produced major street protests in Managua in 1972 (prompting the National Guard to launch an "urban counterinsurgency"), and as the decade went on labor activism would come to the fore of both peaceful and violent opposition in Nicaragua.[6]

It was not simply (or even primarily) the downtrodden that confronted the Somoza regime in the late 1970s. Nicaragua's was a cross-class revolution, one that united the workers and peasants with students, merchants, Conservative elites, and even erstwhile *somocistas*. Of all the forces that helped produce this remarkable coalition, none was more important than Somoza himself.

Nicaragua's upwardly mobile classes had traditionally had an ambivalent relationship with *somocismo*. Students protested the lack of democracy, and Conservatives and the merchant class, while happy that the Somozas provided stability and protected their economic privileges, chafed at their political marginalization and the corruption that characterized one-family rule. To defuse this anger, the Somozas had at times stepped aside to allow friendly figureheads to govern, as Luís did in permitting René Schick to become president in 1963.

This equilibrium was undermined in 1967 when Tachito, already the commander of the National Guard, sought to win the presidency and revive dynastic rule. The younger Anastasio was widely considered to be dull yet hotheaded, simultaneously rasher and less intelligent than his father and brother. "He may not be equal to his aspirations," U.S. officials commented. Somoza's determination to be elected, as the embassy put it, "by fair means or foul" drew the ire of the political opposition as well as some Liberals who realized that a rejuvenated dynasty would preclude their own rise to the highest eche-lons of government.[7] Fearing (correctly) that Somoza would rig the poll, these groups formed a united opposition front and staged demonstrations in Mana-gua. The National Guard put down the protests with what the U.S. embassy called "bloody, heavy-handed, somewhat confused methods," and Tachito took power.[8]

The events of 1967 were signs of things to come. Tachito proved less flexi-ble and savvy than his predecessors, and dissatisfaction with his government increased. A major precipitant of this discontent was Somoza's 1971 pact with Conservative leader Fernando Aguëro, which was meant to allow the dictator to stand for another term in 1974. This power-grab alienated much of the po-litical class, and the Conservatives split into four factions, with the majority of the party now working to undermine the regime. Somoza only encouraged such intrigues with his blatant corruption, demonstrated most outrageously in his pilfering of tens of millions of dollars in emergency aid following a massive earthquake in 1972. By the time that Tachito ran for reelection in 1974 the opposition had begun to cohere around an anti-Somoza platform. Nine political parties and trade unions launched a campaign to disqualify So-moza from the presidency, and the Catholic Church also opposed his run. Somoza sought to reinvigorate the dynasty, but he was galvanizing the op-position instead.[9]

Undeterred, Somoza declared the opposition parties illegal and cheated his way to another smashing electoral success. Nevertheless, the foundations of *somocismo* had grown shaky. They would become even more so a year later, when Somoza overreacted to a series of relatively minor guerrilla attacks by imposing a state of siege and unleashing the National Guard against the in-surgents' suspected sympathizers. The assault failed to stamp out the FSLN. It did stamp Somoza as a tyrant, though, and provoked widespread public disgust.[10]

By the late 1970s *somocismo* was in deep crisis. Somoza now confronted entrenched resistance from the rural poor and the working class, pressure that an increasingly inflexible regime was poorly equipped to withstand. Somoza himself compounded this predicament, as his ambition, venality, and brutal-ity exacerbated the structural ossification of *somocismo* and turned actors of all classes against the government. Somoza had unwittingly given a heretofore fragmented opposition an unprecedented degree of unity, an accomplishment reflected in the comment of FSLN leader Carlos Fonseca. "Somoza was like a precious jewel," Fonseca remarked, "through which all the contradictions of the people were focused."[11]

From 1977 onward, the crisis of *somocismo* was manifest in two principal developments. The first was the formation of the Broad Opposition Front (FAO), a coalition of anti-Somoza parties, unions, and social organizations that encompassed a wide spectrum of society. The FAO demanded the end of the Somoza regime and a transition to democracy, and coordinated strikes, civil disobedience, and international pressure to this end. Somoza calculated that he could outmaneuver what he considered a "weak, divided opposition," but he misjudged his own isolation.[12] The murder of popular Conservative newspaper editor Pedro Chamorro in early 1978 (widely assumed to be the work of the regime or its sympathizers) produced a nationwide response, foreign sources reported, of "shock and repudiation." Demonstrations, a general strike, and blanket foreign condemnation followed, leaving Somoza weaker and more detested than before.[13]

The second development was the resurgence of the FSLN. That the Sandinistas would serve as the crucial element in toppling Somoza could hardly have been predicted just a few years earlier. During the 1960s the organization had been thoroughly spanked by the National Guard and enjoyed such little popular esteem that even FSLN leaders deemed themselves nothing but a "group of conspirators." In the 1970s military defeats and doctrinal disputes caused the organization to splinter into three factions, or tendencies (the Prolonged Popular War, or GPP, tendency; the Proletarian tendency; and the *tercerista*, or "Third Way," tendency).[14]

Between 1977 and 1979, however, the FSLN went from marginalization to triumph. The general decline in the quality of rural and working-class life, evident in the explosive popularity of liberation theology, produced an upturn in FSLN fortunes. "The humblest sectors of the population have been the groups most susceptible to penetration by the Sandinista movement," National Guard officials reported in 1978.[15] Similarly, the ever-increasing unpopularity of the dictatorship lent credibility to a group that had been trying to overthrow various Somozas for more than fifteen years. "The Sandinista movement possesses the sympathy and support of a good part of the Nicaraguan people," reported foreign diplomats, "who in their majority are not of leftist affiliation, [but rather are] motivated solely by condemnation of the Somoza dynasty."[16]

The growing influence of the Sandinistas was not simply a result of the populace coming to them; the guerrillas also implemented strategic changes that allowed them to exploit the opportunities offered by *somicismo*'s decline. FSLN leaders had originally been inspired by *foquismo*, but the disastrous defeats of the 1960s gradually convinced many of the survivors that Guevara's was a suicidal approach to revolution. Fonseca (who never identified solely with a single tendency, straddling the divides between the three) declared that "we have to avoid the notion that revolutionary war could ever be an operation carried out by a small number of individuals with absolutely no ties to the masses."[17] For the FSLN to prosper, Fonseca recognized, it must abandon the ideological rigidity of *foquismo* and find a strategy with greater relevance to the realities of Nicaraguan society.

During the 1970s each of the three tendencies sought a solution to this problem. For GPP leaders, the success of the Vietnamese insurgents during the 1960s and 1970s was an object lesson in political organizing and showed how to avoid the marginalization that had doomed earlier guerrilla offensives. The triumph of Ho Chi Minh's "people's war," they concluded, demonstrated the necessity of patient, long-term efforts to build support among the rural population. The communist forces spent years cultivating the peasants, Sandinista theorists argued, a practice that had ultimately sustained them during their twenty-year struggle against the United States. What was therefore needed, Fonseca wrote, was to achieve greater involvement in "the real day-to-day lives of the workers and peasants."[18] Only by elevating this "political work" to the same plane as "the military work" would the Sandinistas "transform ourselves from a group of conspirators to an organization that with the organized support of the masses attempts to win power."[19]

During the 1970s the GPP fanned out in the mountains, working to overcome the mistrust and hostility that had confounded earlier efforts to mobilize the peasants. This time around, GPP organizers did not simply exhort the *campesinos* to violence but sought to make the FSLN program more accessible and beneficial to the rural population. They offered reading classes for illiterate *campesinos* (a measure that also served indoctrination purposes) and promised access to health care, education, and above all, agrarian reform. To appeal to female peasants, they decried sexual discrimination and emphasized that women and men would enjoy equal rights and responsibilities in the FSLN.[20]

The Proletarians, for their part, fashioned a strategy meant to exploit changes in the Nicaraguan economy. Believing that the rise of commercial agriculture and light industry had created a nascent proletariat, this group focused its efforts on the working class. This meant organizing urban factory workers, a group largely ignored by the GPP, but also rural wage-earners, which were in many cases the same audience that the Popular War faction courted.[21] Like the GPP, the Proletarians eschewed the hope of "converting, from the first moment, every worker to a guerrilla," and aimed to establish a long-term relationship with the masses. They intervened on behalf of unions like the Association of Rural Workers in labor–management disputes, and encouraged wage-earners to press greater demands on their employers. Fostering labor militancy now, the Proletarians calculated, would make revolution possible later.[22]

As the GPP and the Proletarians sought gradually to revolutionize the masses, the *terceristas* established links to the noncommunist and even the anticommunist opposition. The largest and most important of the FSLN tendencies, the *terceristas* realized that Somoza's growing toxicity presented the guerrillas with a golden opportunity to gain mainstream support and forge a "broad anti-*somocista* front."[23]

Doing so entailed two tasks. First, the *terceristas* attempted to maintain fierce military pressure against the regime. Military action, *tercerista* leaders like Humberto Ortega averred, would provoke Somoza into overreacting and ensure continuing domestic polarization. Furthermore, by showing the FSLN to be a serious challenger to the throne, such tactics would improve the *terceristas'* position vis-à-vis the broader opposition. "We are in an open card game with the bourgeoisie," Ortega commented, "and the strongest and ablest will win." The *terceristas* launched a general insurrection in late 1977, which, though defeated, served notice that the group had not been destroyed (as Somoza had claimed) and captured international attention. The FSLN, Conservative leader Aguero remarked, "has created the best conditions for change in Nicaragua." The *terceristas* later launched even more brazen attacks, including an assault on the National Congress in August 1978 that severely embarrassed the regime.[24]

The second element of *tercerista* strategy was ideological flexibility, or to put it more bluntly, subterfuge. Recent recruiting successes notwithstanding, there was nowhere near a critical mass of Nicaraguans that favored socialist revolution. The people were "penetrated by anti-communist propaganda," Ortega wrote in 1979; their revolutionary consciousness had yet to develop. In these circumstances, open advocacy of Marxist revolution would destroy the popularity of the FSLN, creating "the danger of . . . isolating ourselves from the masses."[25]

The *terceristas* thus moderated their public message and obscured their more radical tendencies. In private, leaders like Humberto and Daniel Ortega remained committed to what the former called "our revolutionary, Marxist-Leninist content" and pledged that they would steer Nicaragua "toward socialism."[26] In public, however, they strove to make the FSLN palatable to the noncommunist opposition. "We have a concrete problem," explained one member of the FSLN national directorate, "which is the Somocist dictatorship. It is a dictatorship that has prolonged itself for more than 40 years. . . . For that reason, at this stage we are focused on the achievement of a broad national unity against the dictatorship."[27] On Humberto Ortega's orders, Sandinista militants were discouraged from uttering "ultraleftist phrases like 'power only for the workers,' 'toward the proletarian dictatorship,'" or from using the color red in public demonstrations.[28] Instead, the *terceristas* cultivated the image of a democratic, antidictatorial force. They emphasized that Somoza had violated "the most elemental Human Rights" of the Nicaraguan people, thereby identifying the organization with the worldwide human rights movement of the 1970s.[29] They denied any intention to set up a revolutionary government, pledging to work with "all anti-*somicista* forces" to create a pluralistic, nonaligned regime that would respect "the full observance of democratic guarantees and free union and political organization and . . . all economic, political, and social rights."[30]

Tercerista moderation was purely a tactical maneuver. The alliance with the bourgeoisie was always intended to be "temporary," FSLN *comandante* Víctor Tirado recalled. "We were still convinced of socialist theory," he said, of the need for "the single party."[31] In a letter written in early 1979 Humberto Ortega gave more elegant expression to this conviction. "We have not confused the essence with the appearance," he wrote.

> In *essence* we are ideologically and politically the representatives of the interests of the exploited, of the class historically destined to bury capitalism and imperialism: the working class. In *appearance* we have acquired the embellishments with which more easily to implement the tactics and modalities of politico-military struggle, which will allow us to attract to us NOT ONLY the workers conscious of their own class interests (which are very few due to the brutal imperialist domination in our fatherland, to the socio-economic as well as cultural backwardness of our people) but also,

fundamentally, all humble Nicaraguans, workers (even though they are not proletarians), who, praying to Jesus Christ because they are believers, shed their blood for the liberty of our people.[32]

From a logical standpoint, the strategies deployed by the three tendencies were contradictory. The GPP claimed that the mountain peasants would be the decisive revolutionary constituency, while the Proletarians believed that factory workers and wage-laborers would be crucial. And while at times these strategies overlapped, the *terceristas* took yet another stance, arguing that the critical audience was composed of actors who had no interest whatsoever in Marxist revolution. Not surprisingly, these divergences occasioned heated exchanges. Proletarian leader Jaime Wheelock accused the *terceristas* of being on the "side of the bourgeoisie," and Ortega found himself denying that he sought "Somozism without Somoza."[33]

In the peculiar context of Nicaraguan affairs, though, these disparate strategies turned out to be complementary. During the late 1970s larger numbers of peasants, women, and wage-workers joined the GPP and Proletarian tendencies, complementing the FSLN's traditional strength among students. Exact figures are difficult to come by; some observers put the number of full-time combatants in mid-1979 at 5,000, aided by hundreds of thousands of sympathizers and supporters, while the FSLN itself gave a higher estimate.[34] The marginalized were not uniformly supportive of the FSLN, of course—rural residents that enjoyed some economic security or otherwise mistrusted the guerrillas collaborated with the National Guard, and according to one analysis, only 5 percent of the Sandinistas killed during the revolution were *campesinos*. Nonetheless, this number still equated to greater rural support than previous guerrilla movements had boasted, and was augmented by the presence of thousands of factory workers and rural wage-earners, who accounted for more than half of all FSLN fatalities.[35] The Sandinistas had reached a new level of popular support, causing National Guard commanders to take note. In 1977 Somoza had dismissed the FSLN as a spent force; a year later his officers thought differently. "Nowadays, communism is a reality that bangs on our door, ready to knock it down," they wrote.[36]

The actions of the *terceristas* ensured that the FSLN achieved a political position commensurate with its growing military capabilities. The *terceristas* never fully allayed suspicions as to their ultimate intentions, but their change in tactics did eventually allow them to tap into the broader strain of anti-Somoza sentiment and win both domestic and international recognition as an

acceptable alternative to the dictator. This much was clear in 1978, when Somoza bent to international pressure and allowed a dozen political activists
linked to the FSLN (known as *Los Doce*, or "The Twelve") to return from their
exile in Costa Rica. The group received a rapturous public reception, and soon
grew powerful enough to exert a veto on the actions of the FAO. The FSLN
now commanded the support, or perhaps more accurately, the tolerance, of
much of the opposition. "There was a problem," Somoza groused in 1978, with
the "growing respectability of the Communists."[37] In early 1979 the three tendencies consolidated their recent gains, reuniting at a summit in Havana. As
Somoza had gotten weaker during the late 1970s, the Left had become stronger and smarter, and the Sandinistas now moved rapidly toward the forefront
of the Nicaraguan revolution.

The sight of a Marxist guerrilla group (albeit one that had claimed to have
moderated itself) marching at the head of an anti-Somoza coalition was profoundly unnerving to Jimmy Carter. Polarization in Nicaragua and the emergence of the FSLN as a viable alternative to the dictator led the U.S. administration to fear that the current path of events might end in a radical outcome.
The guerrillas had "previously . . . been isolated," commented Ambassador
Mauricio Solaún in early 1978, "but with the new militancy of the political
opposition and the private sector the revolutionaries were gaining respectability."[38] While his predecessors had condoned or at least ignored Somoza's brutality, the President Carter now told the dictator that he must relax political
controls and allow a transition to democracy. Carter dispatched U.S. military
representatives to Managua to warn Somoza that Washington would not save
him from the FSLN, and Solaún told him that the United States advocated "a
peaceful democratic solution" in Nicaragua rather than repression or a continuation of the dictatorship.[39]

The necessity of staving off the ever-present scenario of a "second Cuba"
was not the only force impelling Carter to push for reform in Managua. This
stance also reflected the president's desire for a broader reorientation of U.S.
policy in Latin America. Within weeks of taking office in January 1977, Carter
unveiled a slew of original initiatives toward the region. He opened negotiations with Castro, concluded the Panama Canal Treaties, and submitted
them to the Senate for what turned out to be a bruising ratification debate.
Most important of all, Carter made Latin America a central front in his

global fight for human rights, what one adviser called the "cardinal tenet" of his foreign policy.[40] The administration pushed authoritarian regimes to respect three essential categories of human rights—"integrity of the person," "basic economic and social rights," and "civil and political liberties"—and threatened punitive steps, such as terminating military and economic assistance, against those that refused.[41] As the Sandinistas sought to revolutionize Nicaragua, Carter envisioned changes little less profound in U.S. policy.

In part, Carter's endeavors reflected the prevailing worldview of his top counselors, most notably National Security Adviser Zbigniew Brzezinski. Brzezinski is often considered an inveterate Cold Warrior in an administration of idealists, but his ideas were actually central to what two scholars have aptly called a "post–Cold War foreign policy."[42] Brzezinski believed that U.S. diplomacy had become anachronistic. Decolonization and détente had led to fundamental changes in world politics, reducing the importance of Cold War concerns and heightening that of North–South issues. "Two essential themes" dominated world affairs, he said in 1978. "First, the world's population is experiencing a political awakening on a scale without precedent in its history; and second, the global system is undergoing a significant redistribution of political and economic power."[43] As the world had changed, however, U.S. policy had not. America's "inordinate fear of communism," Carter commented in 1977, had locked the country into a bipolar worldview and prevented it from adapting to a more diverse and fluid global scene.[44]

Nowhere was this myopia greater than in U.S.–Latin American relations. Brzezinski called the Monroe Doctrine, the foundation of numerous Cold War interventions in the region, "an imperialistic legacy which has embittered our relationships," and Carter made similar references to U.S. support for authoritarian regimes.[45] The key to correcting this short-sightedness was to place U.S. diplomacy on the side of the "political awakening" that was sweeping Latin America and the Third World as a whole. "As more people have been freed from traditional constraints" like colonialism, Carter said in 1977, "more have been determined to achieve, for the first time in their lives, social justice. . . . For us to ignore this trend would be to lose influence and moral authority in the world."[46] To preserve its position in Latin America, the United States must forego traditional expedients like military intervention and counterinsurgency and focus on cultivating the genuine sympathies of the region's people. In this sense, advocating human rights and democracy were central to protecting American power.[47]

If Carter's human rights policy represented an effort to modernize U.S. dealings with Latin America, it also reflected domestic political pressures. The fact that the United States had reacted to the communist threat by throwing its weight behind the dictators had long rankled liberals like Senator Frank Church, who criticized foreign aid on these grounds in the late 1960s and early 1970s. These sentiments became stronger following the South American coups of the early and mid-1970s. The brutality of these episodes, and Kissinger's unembarrassed support of brutes like Pinochet and Videla, outraged prominent liberals in Congress and elsewhere. AFL-CIO president George Meany declaimed Chile's "savage repression of its own people," remarking that the population of that country had become "one of the globe's endangered species." Such opinions had begun to influence U.S. policy even before Carter's election, as Congress enacted stringent curbs on aid to Argentina and Chile during the mid-1970s.[48]

Carter was not one to swim against this tide. Outraged by Kissinger's policy toward the South American dictators, he also recognized that human rights were a useful stick with which to beat Ford during the 1976 campaign. At one point he called Kissinger's relations with Brazil "a good example of our present policy at its worst." Once in office, Carter worked to ensure that his human rights policies did not lag too far behind those demanded by congressional Democrats.[49]

In the event, Carter's policy proved difficult to implement. Used to strong relations with Washington, Latin American military rulers were miffed at Carter's intrusiveness. The Brazilian foreign ministry termed Carter's approach "impertinent," and army officers warned that the U.S. administration aimed to create a situation in which "all of the country is against the Armed Forces and unsatisfied with the Revolution."[50] After Carter made clear that the United States would withhold military assistance from those governments that blatantly abused their citizens, seven Latin American countries renounced U.S. aid before it could be terminated. This break, which eliminated much of Carter's leverage in dealing with these regimes, was a sign of things to come. While Carter's human rights policies did prove effective in some cases (the administration persuaded Dominican president Joaquín Balaguer not to steal another election in 1978, and used financial leverage to compel Peru's post-Velasco junta to hold elections), the administration's experience was frequently a frustrating one.[51]

One reason for this was that Carter's human rights policies were continually contested and imprecise. The State Department, NSC, and Defense Department bickered over both the ultimate aim of the policy and how strictly it should be enforced. Did Carter simply desire a moderate reduction in abuses that would allow him to claim a diplomatic victory? Or did he hope to see the Chilean and Argentine regimes replaced by democratic governments that would embrace human rights out of something more than pure cynicism? Both sentiments were present in the Carter administration. Robert Pastor, Carter's top counselor on Latin America, argued that the president's rhetoric should be aimed at convincing the people of South America to "overthrow their military dictatorships." Other officials conceded that "our ability to change human rights practices in other societies is limited."[52]

These disagreements gave a lurching quality to Carter's diplomacy and seriously confused Latin American officials seeking to divine his intentions. Chilean diplomats identified "two currents in battle," in Washington, and noted "the real lack of coordination" between various U.S. officials.[53] At certain points, Carter succeeded in convincing Santiago that human rights were the "predominant factor" in his foreign policy. At others, however, the discontinuities in U.S. actions led Chilean diplomats to conclude that "economic-political and strategic interests overtook the ethical character of the Executive's foreign policy."[54] Uruguayan officials often voiced similar confusion, and U.S. diplomats reported that a "repeated question" in the region was, "Whom do we deal with in Washington?"[55] This uncertainty undermined Carter's attempts to bring concerted pressure on the region's oppressors and lessened the efficacy of his policies.

A second issue was that American leverage on these regimes was considerably less than Carter assumed. Security and economic assistance, though important to subversion-obsessed leaders, was hardly crucial enough to convince them to rescind measures that seemed to have kept the communists at bay. This dynamic was evident from the decision of several governments to renounce U.S. security assistance in 1977–1978. "The USA surely overestimated its capacity to influence Brazil," Brazilian foreign ministry officials wrote.[56] Beyond Brazil, the region's grossest rights violators turned a cold eye to Carter's blandishments. "Guatemalans had to protect their vital interests," that country's foreign minister told U.S. diplomats, namely, "preventing the communists from coming to power."[57] Pinochet dismissed human rights advocacy as an "international conspiracy against Chile . . . orchestrated by Marxism," and bluntly informed Carter that he planned "to leave a protected democracy so that it will not be broken from below."[58] Although the South American regimes did somewhat lessen the intensity of the "dirty wars" during Carter's presidency, they did so mainly because there were not many leftists left to kill.[59]

The vexations of Carter's policy were ultimately most consequential in his dealings with Somoza. As the situation in Nicaragua worsened, U.S. officials pressed Somoza to respect human rights, relax political controls, and, eventually, to step aside in order to allow free elections and a transition to democracy. Implementing these reforms, the administration believed, was the only way to reduce the relentless polarization that was paving the way for an FSLN takeover. "What is needed in Nicaragua is true reform to allow for democratic participation and avoid escalating conflict," Solaún counseled.[60] The U.S. embassy was particularly insistent that Somoza lift the state of siege, negotiate with the FAO, and refrain from imprisoning *Los Doce,* even though this latter group was openly calling for his overthrow. "My cabinet and I knew that if we touched them, the U.S. Embassy would come down on us with full force," Somoza later complained.[61] Solaún regularly threatened to desert Somoza altogether if he did not shape up. At one point, Solaún told the dictator that "there would be some temptation within the U.S. to support elements antagonistic to him if he does not act responsibly." U.S. pressure on Somoza was sufficient for the dictator to comment that the revolution was a "rebellion encouraged by bureaucrats in Washington."[62]

Somoza did heed U.S. advice at certain points, allowing *Los Doce* to operate freely and lifting the state of siege. Yet if Somoza was willing to compromise enough to avoid a full break with Washington, he had no intention of giving up power. He made clear that he intended to serve out the rest of his term (which ended in 1981), and coldly remarked, "I am not disposed to turn over power to the communists."[63]

Given Somoza's obstinacy, it was soon clear that the only way to secure a democratic transition would be to force the president out, either through direct intervention or the credible threat thereof. Toppling a disgraced, right-wing Latin American dictator in hopes of heading off a leftist takeover was not an unprecedented idea; Eisenhower and Kennedy had done just this to Trujillo two decades earlier. As it happened, the first months of 1978 presented Carter with a similar opportunity. Chamorro's murder united Nicaraguan society against the dictator, and, as Carter's advisers later admitted, gave Washington a unique chance to take decisive action. The United States could threaten to intervene in Nicaragua—multilaterally if possible, unilaterally if necessary—unless Somoza stepped down, while promising to let him keep his ill-gotten wealth and give him exile in the United States if he went willingly.[64]

Neither precedent nor necessity could convince Carter to consider this option seriously. He was consumed by the congressional fight over the Panama Canal Treaties during 1978, and had little political capital to spare on another risky endeavor in Latin America. Besides, Carter had always believed that any military intervention in Latin America—especially unilateral U.S. intervention—would be disastrous. Military adventures in the region would wreck his modernized, sensitive approach to Latin America and revive the imperial legacies that Carter sought to bury. One aid called intervention in Nicaragua "unthinkable," and Pastor opined that it would "toll the death of the President's Latin American policy."[65] Brzezinski weighed in too, saying that U.S. intervention "would unquestionably destroy the credibility of the policies you have developed to Latin America and the Third World and provoke virtually universal condemnation."[66] Even as the threat of revolution loomed, Carter decided that the cure (intervention) would be worse than the disease (an FSLN victory).

With intervention out of the question, Carter was left with few useful tools for influencing Nicaraguan affairs. He tried a carrot-and-stick approach to induce Somoza to make concessions to the opposition, but the Nicaraguan president refused to play along. In 1978 Carter sent Somoza a letter praising him for a series of essentially meaningless reforms, and released a small amount of military aid to Nicaragua. Somoza misinterpreted this decision, reading it as evidence that the United States might yet prevent his ouster. Seizing the initiative, he imposed martial law, launched a new campaign against the FSLN and the opposition, and deliberately sabotaged negotiations designed to produce a transfer of power. The opposition's proposals, Somoza's representatives announced, amounted to "a coup d'etat." "Somoza is taking the gloves off," the CIA reported.[67]

As Carter had feared, these measures led to further radicalization. By wrecking the negotiations and embarrassing the peaceful opposition in the process, Somoza discredited the moderates. Anti-Somoza sentiment rapidly gravitated toward the FSLN, less out of ideological fervor than out of a realization that the men and women with the guns were the only alternative to a dictator who refused to go. While the opposition feared "civil war, anarchy and a communist takeover," U.S. officials commented, "they fear three more years of Somoza in power even more."[68] Whereas earlier guerrillas like the Montoneros and the Tupamaros had lost mainstream support once it become clear that their intentions were far worse than the established order, Somoza's intransigence ensured that this dynamic did not recur in Nicaragua. His repression and stubbornness convinced much of the population that *nothing* could be worse than a continuation of the dictatorship, and thereby drove them to the FSLN. Even after a general strike and another *tercerista* insurrection in late 1978 forced Somoza to promise that he would step down after his current term ended, the polarization continued. The FAO splintered, with a number of members now calling for violence. "Somoza does not resign because there still does not exist a force capable of creating the situation that will force him to," wrote two FAO activists. "The national political problem will be resolved only by the overthrow of the Somocist dictatorship." One U.S. official summarized the situation: "The center in Nicaragua is being chewed up."[69] Somoza had succeeded in destroying the moderate opposition, but in doing so he strengthened a more dangerous enemy.

Carter had hoped to restrain Somoza, encourage reform and democracy, and thereby lessen the radicalization at work in Nicaragua. These efforts, though, stumbled on the central contradiction of Carter's Latin American policy. The administration was demanding fundamental changes in the way that Somoza and other autocrats did business, changes no less profound than those envisioned by the founders of the Alliance for Progress. But in the final analysis, Carter was not willing to exert U.S. power fully to achieve this end. The president who pursued the most interventionist strategy since John Kennedy was, ironically, repelled by the prospect of intervention, and the prospects of facilitating a moderate transition in Nicaragua faded. As a consequence, the door was open to those who favored a more extreme solution.

One such person was Fidel Castro. While Carter watched events in Nicaragua with a feeling of helplessness, Castro, who had backed the FSLN since its formative years, looked on with satisfaction. Castro's solidarity with the Sandinistas stemmed from the same motives that had long driven Cuba's revolution-for-export business: ideological conviction, antipathy to right-wing dictatorships, and the hope of finding a continental ally. The Sandinistas were "mature revolutionaries, sharing Marxist-Leninist beliefs," Castro reported in early 1979. "The fall of the dictator Somoza in Nicaragua is inevitable."[70]

Cuban policy during the late 1970s did not simply replicate the romantic interventionism of a decade prior. Just as the FSLN changed tactics after its early defeats, so had Cuban diplomacy evolved since the Guevara years. Following the breaking of the OAS boycott in 1975, Castro continued the regularization of Cuban foreign policy. Castro criticized his own "lack of political maturity" during the 1960s, and sought to give Cuba the image of a responsible power. Havana became active in the Non-Aligned Movement (NAM), challenging Tito's Yugoslavia for leadership of this group.[71] Even more strikingly, Castro extended feelers to the United States, raising the possibility of a comprehensive rapprochement. "We do not want to wallow in a new cold war," said one Cuban official in 1978.[72]

These initiatives did not signal a renunciation of support for insurgency. Castro remained a revolutionary at heart, and Allende's fall redoubled the Cuban leader's conviction that experiments in democratic socialism were doomed. "The Chilean example teaches us the lesson that it is impossible to make the revolution with the people alone," he remarked shortly thereafter— "weapons are also necessary!"[73] The rise of radical anticommunist regimes in the Southern Cone reinforced this sentiment, and Cuban officials pledged to seek the overthrow of Pinochet and Stroessner "with all our resources."[74] Accordingly, Castro coupled his overtures to Washington with a renewed revolutionary campaign abroad. Talking to Washington, Vice President Carlos Rafael Rodríguez said in 1978, "does not mean that we give up our principles." Havana's ultimately abortive negotiations with Carter coincided with an intensification of Cuba's revolutionary activities, first in Angola in 1976 and subsequently in Central America.[75]

Yet if Castro's revolutionary ambitions had not faded, he had become more sophisticated in pursuing this dream. The same ideological agility that was evident in Castro's dealings with the United States, the OAS, and the NAM proved even more crucial in his relations with the FSLN. Having seen how the factionalism and the strident ideological content of *foquismo* had wrecked the rural guerrilla offensive during the 1960s, Castro urged the FSLN not to repeat these errors. He demanded that the three tendencies unite and counseled his Nicaraguan allies "against giving publicity to their beliefs and speaking publicly about Marxism-Leninism."[76]

Once FSLN leaders agreed to these conditions and proved that they were a match for the National Guard in battle, the aid from Havana flowed. During the mid-1970s Cuban aid to Latin America had gone mainly to anti-Pinochet elements in Chile. Now the FSLN received pride of place.[77] Castro's intelligence services provided training to hundreds of FSLN combatants, and in a few cases Cuban advisers accompanied the insurgents into the field. Castro also lent the services of propaganda organs like Radio Havana and provided subsidies that filled the guerrillas' coffers. Cuba transported thousands of weapons to Nicaragua, allowing the FSLN to arm the new recruits that poured into the organization in the late 1970s. This materiel included infantry weapons and small arms, as well as heavier ordnance. In June 1979 U.S. officials marveled at the "unbelievable amount of arms, including anti-aircraft guns, heavy mortars, and recoilless rifles" traveling between Havana and Nicaragua.[78]

The evolution of Cuban diplomacy also figured in the alliances that Castro forged in seeking to overthrow Somoza. Whereas the Cuban regime had earlier scorned its neighbors and gloried in its isolation, Castro now cooperated with a variety of noncommunist and anticommunist governments. Chief among these were Mexico, Venezuela, Panama, Honduras, and Costa Rica. "Many leaders who are not communist," Castro later recalled, "helped the revolutionary movement." Efforts to topple Somoza were not the peculiar province of the FSLN's Marxist sponsors, but represented a truly regional affair.[79]

The motives of this anti-Somoza coalition were as varied as its members. In important respects, foreign support for the guerrillas boiled down to the same factor that had catalyzed the revolution in the first place: hatred for Somoza. Over the past forty years the Somozas had managed to irritate or provoke nearly all of their neighbors, who now looked to take revenge. Costa Rican leaders still harbored a grudge from the elder Somoza's invasion of that country decades earlier, and Honduran politicians were equally gleeful at Tachito's demise. Venezuela's Pérez and Panama's Torrijos both exhibited a visceral hatred for Somoza; the former leader accused the "bloodthirsty" dictator of genocide, and, according to the CIA, was "waging a personal campaign" against the Nicaraguan regime.[80] More broadly, Somoza's dynastic pretensions and flagrant authoritarianism were an embarrassment even by Latin American standards, and several governments (Mexico's especially) used their opposition to the regime to score points with the domestic Left.[81]

Cold opportunism complemented these factors in driving regional hostility to Somoza. As the dictator's position deteriorated during 1978–1979, many Latin American leaders concluded that the fall of the regime was inevitable. The president's status was in "irreversible decline," Mexican diplomats reported; there were now "great possibilities of the Sandinista guerrillas overthrowing him and themselves assuming power."[82] Once this transition occurred, those governments that had sided with Somoza would likely be treated as enemies by the new regime, while those that had aided the rebels

might gain additional influence in postrevolutionary Nicaragua. In these circumstances, why not back the FSLN?

For Mexico and Venezuela especially, it was this desire to use the revolution
as a springboard to greater regional clout that informed policy toward Somoza.
Caracas and Mexico City had long competed with Washington for influence
along the Caribbean rim, and Mexico had actually ruled Central America for
a time following independence. Though various factors had partially frustrated
Mexican and Venezuelan maneuvers during the diplomatic challenge of the
early 1970s, Somoza's glaring debility presented these countries with a new
opportunity to practice assertive statecraft. For Mexico, this path was made all
the more attractive by the discovery of additional oil reserves in 1976–1977,
which lifted the country out of its financial crisis and made it less dependent
upon U.S. support. "There are two classes of countries, those that have oil and
those that don't," said López Portillo. "We have it."[83] Somoza was a U.S. puppet, Mexican diplomats argued. The National Guard was "a creation of the
United States," and a victory by the dictator would allow Washington "to preserve its highly hegemonic presence in Nicaragua."[84] If Somoza fell, on the
other hand, those powers that had contributed to his fall would reap the benefits. The aim of Mexican policy, one adviser later wrote, was "to carve out a
sphere of influence in the only areas where such an ambition was feasible: Central America and the Caribbean Basin."[85] Venezuela's newly created National
Security Council reached a similar conclusion. Again tempted by a favorable
diplomatic conjuncture, Venezuela and Mexico sought to undercut U.S. imperialism in Nicaragua and replace it with an informal dominion of their own.[86]

Somoza's neighbors did their utmost to see him dethroned. Torrijos cooperated with Castro to ship weapons to Nicaragua. Venezuela provided large
quantities of arms and money. Mexico financed rebel activities and gave them
diplomatic support. Costa Rica allowed the FSLN to use its territory as a logistical base, safe haven, and staging point for attacks into Nicaragua.[87]

Latin American intervention was immensely influential. The warm reception the FSLN and *Los Doce* received in foreign capitals provided them with
greater public legitimacy, while access to the Costa Rican sanctuary and "modern arms of all caliber" proved even more vital.[88] While Somoza's National
Guard remained tactically superior to the FSLN through the close of the civil
war, the guerrillas' use of Costa Rican territory helped negate this advantage.[89]
Guard commanders continually complained about coming under fire from
the Costa Rican side of the border, and Nicaraguan officials bemoaned these

"constant invasions and armed attacks." When the Guard did cross the border in order to retaliate, the regional diplomatic climate ensured that Nicaragua rather than Costa Rica got the worst of the subsequent blowups in the OAS.[90]

All told, Somoza's allegations of an international conspiracy to unseat him were not far off the mark. He faced not only a more cunning and mature Cuban interventionism, but also the hostility of Castro's numerous enemies-cum-partners. The revolution from within drew substantially on aid from without, and this dynamic contributed substantially to the erosion of Somoza's position.

By early 1979 Nicaragua sat at the crossroads of several trends that favored a revolutionary outcome. First, *somocismo* was collapsing. Always an authoritarian system that created a degree of internal resistance, *somocismo* had been rendered more rigid by the economic changes and repression that followed the Cuban revolution. Somoza's dynastic aspirations shattered this brittle structure, and his actions produced massive elite discontent to complement the radicalism of the rural poor and the working class. The result was the rise of a cross-class revolutionary alliance held together by a common determination to end Somoza's rule.

Second, Nicaragua's guerrillas showed an adaptability that had been badly lacking in previous Latin American insurgencies. Having observed (and, for that matter, committed) the various mistakes made by their predecessors, the FSLN tendencies experimented with new strategic concepts that eventually allowed them to capitalize on the sociopolitical crisis described above. They thereby gained the increased military capacity that came with the growth of their ranks, as well as the political strength that derived from their appearance as an acceptable alternative to Somoza.

Still, these accomplishments might not have assured victory had the Sandinistas not operated in such a hospitable international environment. A third element in the Nicaraguan revolution, and one that should not be understated, was that the insurgents enjoyed a level of foreign support even greater than that provided to the *foquistas* of the 1960s. Castro's revised stance on revolutionary tactics and ideology served the FSLN well, as did the backing of those nations that loathed Somoza and viewed the guerrillas as proxies for their own interests in Central America. The combination of arms, money, advice, diplomatic support, and above all else, sanctuary, that the anti-Somoza coalition provided was critical in canceling out the military superiority of the National Guard and bringing the pressure against the government to unbearable levels.

The depth and audacity of Latin American intervention contrasted notably with the fourth essential factor in the revolution—the failure of U.S. policy. During the Nicaraguan crisis Washington did not play its traditional role as the firewall against Marxist revolution. Although Carter sought to prevent an FSLN victory, he jettisoned many of the measures that might have forestalled this outcome. The U.S. president never resolved the basic contradiction between demanding reform and eschewing intervention, and the last barrier to a revolutionary solution in Nicaragua evaporated accordingly.

This confluence of trends produced its logical conclusion in 1979. At the outset of the year, *Los Doce* used their political clout to defeat a proposed deal between Somoza and the FAO that would have left the FSLN empty-handed. The guerrillas now commanded the political initiative, and following the reunification of the three tendencies in March, they showed a military strength to match. In April the FSLN launched a coordinated, five-front offensive that put the regime under siege and forced Somoza to take refuge in a concrete bunker. As the regime teetered, hundreds of thousands of Nicaraguans rose to give the hated dictator a final push. FSLN-organized Civil Defense Committees organized barricades to keep Somoza's tanks and troops out of urban neighborhoods, and not even indiscriminate air attacks by the Guard could check the insurrection.

Realizing the gravity of the situation, Carter belatedly embraced the idea of a multilateral OAS intervention to oversee elections and a negotiated transition. With the Nicaraguan center destroyed and Somoza's neighbors having fallen in behind the FSLN, the proposal went nowhere. "We tried a multilateral approach toward finding a moderate solution," Pastor later recalled, "but Panama, Venezuela (under Pérez), Costa Rica, and Mexico were determined to help play a different role toward Somoza. Nothing we did deterred them."[91] The South American dictatorships were willing to intervene in Nicaragua to head off an FSLN victory, but the ongoing freeze in their relations with the United States made this option infeasible.[92] Castro gloried in the "disobedience" of the Latin American countries, and Pastor admitted that Washington could do nothing but "cross our fingers."[93]

Finger-crossing was not enough. Somoza finally gave up in July 1979 and fled to Miami, then the Bahamas, and then Paraguay (where he was soon murdered by the remnants of the Argentine guerrillas). He was succeeded by a short-lived provisional regime, which soon gave way to a Government of National Reconstruction (JGRN) composed of various members of the anti-Somoza coalition.

The Sandinistas quickly established themselves as the real winners of the revolution, despite the desperate maneuverings of the Carter administration, which even after Somoza's fall worked to prevent the revolution from turning truly revolutionary. Carter sent $75 million in reconstruction aid to Managua in early 1980 and approved a CIA initiative to support non-Sandinista elements of the new government. The idea was to strengthen the moderates and assure the Sandinistas of U.S. goodwill, thereby depriving them of any pretext for implementing extreme domestic measures. "The Sandinistas are wearing a moderate mask," one State Department adviser commented. "Our job is to nail it on."[94]

The strategy failed. Congressional opposition slowed the U.S. assistance package, making Carter's pledges of friendship seem hollow. More important, however, was the fact that the FSLN had never planned to share power or hew to a line that Carter and the Nicaraguan moderates thought appropriate. Although the *tercerista* representatives to the JGRN portrayed themselves as social democrats in the negotiations leading to the formation of the body, once in power they gradually revealed the face they had hidden during the revolution. "We are guided by the scientific doctrine of the Revolution, by Marxism-Leninism," Humberto Ortega announced. Having earlier promised that the FSLN would "walk a stretch together with the bourgeoisie" before seeking "to destroy them and throw their reactionary aspirations into the garbage," Ortega now made good on his pledge.[95] In 1980 the CIA reported that the Sandinistas had initiated the "use of force and intimidation" to move "toward a system that will probably feature a single party dominated by the FSLN."[96] The organization killed former National Guard commanders, postponed promised elections, and threatened to limit other political rights. "We support freedom of the press," said one FLSN official. "But of course the freedom of the press we support will be a freedom of the press that supports revolution."[97]

During 1979–1980 the FSLN established its supremacy within the JGRN, taking control of the armed forces and other crucial ministries. The FSLN permitted a Somoza-era official to serve as titular head of the military but, as Raúl Castro reported after a meeting with high-ranking Sandinistas, "he is mostly 'for show'; the army is being built without his knowledge and all real power in this area belongs to the commander-in-chief of the people's Sandinista army, Humberto Ortega."[98] FSLN insiders gave similar reports; only a few months after Somoza's fall, one Sandinista official wrote privately that the organization "has been clearly hegemonic in all aspects of the revolutionary process."[99]

At the outset, there was relatively little opposition to these measures. Due to its role as the essential element in toppling Somoza, the FSLN enjoyed widespread public sympathy. Moreover, those less enthused with the Sandinistas' hegemonic turn were stymied by the fact that, with the National Guard disbanded, the FSLN had an effective monopoly on military force. "We took power by arms," Humberto Ortega explained candidly, "and it should be clear who has power in Nicaragua today."[100]

The twenty years following Castro's triumph were hard times for Latin America's revolutionaries. Though the region was prone to radical upheaval, the record of the guerrillas since 1959 belied the notion that revolution was to be the ineluctable result of Latin American social relations. With powerful elites, the United States, and above all, the bulk of the population opposing violent revolution, neither the rural guerrillas of the 1960s nor their urban successors found much success. For most of the period following Castro's victory in Cuba, it must have seemed as though the trend in Latin America was not toward inevitable revolutions but inevitable *counter*-revolutions.

During the late 1970s the Sandinistas broke this pattern. Their ability to do so was the result of a peculiar historical moment in which a number of diverse but related factors came into alignment. These influences ranged from the long-term evolution of economic and political structures in Nicaragua, to the effect of the Cuban revolution and its aftermath on Nicaraguan affairs, to Somoza's noxious personality and dynastic ambitions, to changes in guerrilla strategy and tactics, to Carter's alteration of U.S. policy. In isolation, none of these issues would have been sufficient to produce the events of the late 1970s and early 1980s. Together, however, they knocked aside long-standing barriers to revolution and gave impetus to the forces of radical upheaval.

The Nicaraguan revolution was thus hardly "inevitable." It was a highly contingent affair that drew on a wide span of forces. And in certain senses, these forces represented some of the most important trends of the post–Cuban revolution era in Latin America. The continuing evolution of insurgent techniques and Castro's revolutionary designs; the effects of internal repression, counterinsurgency, commercial agriculture, and liberation theology; and the tendency toward opportunistic diplomacy on the part of Latin American statesmen: these dynamics came together in dramatic fashion in Nicaragua. Even Carter's policies, so much a departure from Washington's standard Cold War practices, fit within this context. In no small part, it was the belief that a continuation of such practices would lead to disaster—moral as well as diplomatic—that informed the president's approach to hemispheric events. In numerous ways, the Nicaraguan revolution drew together the influences that had flowed out of the Cuban revolution and its aftermath and subsequently exerted such strong pull on regional affairs.

It was fitting, then, that the Nicaraguan revolution would serve as the jumping-off point for the most intense phase of Latin America's Cold War. The Sandinista triumph presaged even bloodier revolutionary struggles in Guatemala and El Salvador, as well as a decade-long attempt by disaffected Nicaraguans to overthrow the FSLN-led regime. During the 1980s these conflicts—and the foreign meddling they elicited—would produce a torrent of violence in Central America.

7

Maelstrom

The period following the Nicaraguan revolution marked the culmination of Latin America's Cold War. In the wake of the Sandinista triumph the center of gravity in that struggle shifted to Central America, where the profound polarization and conflict that had figured in Somoza's ouster now played out on an isthmian scale. Persistent internal violence erupted into full-blown civil wars in Guatemala and El Salvador, with leftist guerrillas attacking murderous regimes. In Nicaragua, by contrast, it was the Left that faced an insurgent challenge, as a diverse coalition of the recalcitrant refused to accept the Sandinista victory and launched a guerrilla struggle against that government.

These episodes resulted in the most severe, sustained bloodletting in Latin America since *la violencia* in Colombia. Long-running struggles over political and social arrangements merged with the escalating extremism characteristic of Latin America's Cold War, and life in Central America took on an apocalyptic quality during the 1980s. The Guatemalan civil war ultimately claimed around 200,000 lives, and El Salvador lost more than 70,000 citizens. By comparison, Nicaragua got off easy. Its civil war took only 30,000 lives—in proportional terms, more than the United States lost in Korea, Vietnam, the Civil War, and World Wars I and II *combined*.[1] And as before, internal crisis begat external intervention, and the meddling of Washington, Moscow, Havana, and their respective allies simply intensified the upheaval at work in Central America.

Although the forces of radical change looked ascendant in the early 1980s, this bloodshed did not lead to the revolutionary transformations envisioned by a resurgent Central American Left. In Nicaragua a disillusioned electorate turned the FSLN out of power via the ballot box in 1990. In Guatemala and El Salvador the civil wars ended in peace agreements that provided for greater democracy but left most socioeconomic arrangements untouched. These three countries emerged from their civil wars with partially functioning democracies— itself a major departure from the past—but the transformations were hardly as far-reaching as the revolutionaries had hoped.

The failure (or in Nicaragua's case, the reversal) of the Central American revolutions was the product of several factors, not least of which were the massive violence and U.S. intervention deployed against these movements. Coercion, exemplified by Ronald Reagan's undeclared war on the FSLN, and repression, expressed most pungently in a Guatemalan counterinsurgency that killed around 100,000 people between 1981 and 1983, weakened revolutionary movements and played a key role in their decline.

Yet the Central American revolutions were not simply broken by force. Their failure also reflected the fact that the radical Left was ultimately unable to maintain the popular appeal that initially made it so potent. The Salvadoran and Guatemalan guerrillas found themselves marginalized by their own authoritarianism and the restoration of electoral democracy, while Sandinista incompetence and repression proved similarly injurious to that movement. This combination of influences ensured that while the Central American civil wars did not end in the simple restoration of the status quo ante, dreams of radical change were once more deferred.

The clearing of the dust kicked up by the Nicaraguan revolution revealed that El Salvador and Guatemala were experiencing severe convulsions of their own. The civil wars in El Salvador and Guatemala (and especially the latter) did not start in the late 1970s; alarming levels of violence had afflicted these countries for years. Since the early 1960s, many of the same trends that had provoked mass unrest in Nicaragua—brutal counterinsurgency practices, the accelerating commercialization of rural agriculture, and the resulting growth of liberation theology and social protest—pointed toward an eruption of domestic conflict in Guatemala and El Salvador as well. The fact that Guatemala and El Salvador had higher population densities and landholding inequalities than other Central American countries only worsened the situation, magnifying agrarian discontent and making the traumas that resulted all the more jarring.[2]

During the 1970s this cycle of marginalization, resistance, and repression became still more vicious. High commodity prices reinforced the expansion of commercial agriculture, and *campesino* displacement accelerated rapidly. The aggregate income of the bottom quintile in El Salvador fell nearly 40 percent during the 1970s, the percentage of *campesinos* without land rose from 27 to 65 percent, and three-quarters of the population now suffered from malnutrition.[3] In Guatemala real wages in the rural sector fell by half. "Everything points to an explosive sharpening of the crisis," Guatemalan Labor Party (PGT) officials reported.[4]

This was standard Marxist boilerplate, but agrarian unrest did soon reach a crescendo. Peasant and Christian cooperatives grew quickly. In Guatemala these organizations contained 132,000 members by 1976 in spite of governmental repression. Indigenous Guatemalans formed the National Integration Front (FIN), a party dedicated to protecting the rights of the poor, and groups like the Campesino Unity Committee (CUC) organized in the rural areas.[5] "No one answers the protests of workers and organizations," the CUC announced. "The door to dialogue is closed."[6] In El Salvador Christian base communities began to align with guerrilla groups like the People's Revolutionary Bloc, and the Catholic Church, represented by Archbishop Óscar Romero, offered a sharp critique of the established order. "Political power is in the hands of the unscrupulous military who only know how to repress the people and promote the interests of the Salvadoran oligarchy," Romero wrote. Romero soon became a magnet for popular resistance, as one observer put it, "a voice of the poor and the oppressed."[7] In both countries, confrontations between tenants and landlords became more common. Major landholders sought to push the *campesinos* off of what land they retained; the *campesinos* fought back by poisoning cattle, burning pastureland, and killing landlords.[8]

In neither Guatemala nor El Salvador was the political system capable of ameliorating these tensions. The oligarchic nature of these societies and the racism that permeated them had long militated against such flexibility. During the 1960s and 1970s these systems became even more unbending. The rise of the military as an economic elite made this institution largely immune to reformist tendencies, and the spread of National Security Doctrine predisposed conservatives to see political activism as subversion. "We have learned from experience that all trade-union and cooperative organizations fall into the hands of communist leaders who have infiltrated them," Guatemalan paramilitaries declared. "We have the organization and the strength to prevent this from happening. As long as we accomplish our sacred mission of freeing Guatemala from communism, it does not matter who dies."[9]

In both countries, the armed forces reacted to internal unrest by simply shutting down the political system. They rigged elections, censored dissent, and cooperated with landowners and anticommunist elements of the middle class to form death squads that tormented *campesino* organizers, union leaders, and anyone else who dared agitate against the existing order. The death squads, reported Canadian diplomats, "show not the slightest hesitancy to torture, mutilate or kill their victims."[10] Rural priests were singled out for punishment; the slogan, "Be a patriot, kill a priest" was often heard in El Salvador, and one notorious death squad, the "White Warriors Union," told all priests to leave the country or face death.[11] The bloodshed far surpassed previous levels of internal violence, and large-scale massacres became commonplace. "The heavily armed men systematically went from house to house and, using name lists, tracked down the Catholic, CUC, and cooperative leaders of the hamlet," recalled one Guatemalan. "By the time they were finished, fifteen people had been assassinated. . . . My brother, leader of the CUC, was crucified between two trees. After being stabbed in his side, he was strangled."[12]

Guatemalan and Salvadoran officials hoped that this repression would smother dissent, but choking off avenues for political opposition simply pushed dissatisfaction in more radical directions. Trade unionists, student organizers, and other activists now had no lawful outlet for their grievances and therefore embraced antigovernment violence.[13] Opposition parties followed the same path. Factions of Guatemala's PGT carried out attacks against the armed forces, and members of the Salvadoran Communist Party enlisted in a burgeoning guerrilla movement. As the death squads waged a brutal war against the political opposition, even moderates considered defecting to the insurgents. Vinicio Cerezo, the leader of Guatemala's Christian Democrats (PDC), warned that this "policy of indiscriminate repression . . . would lead to further polarization and radicalization of Guatemala," driving the country toward a general insurrection. After assailants dragged several members of the El Salvador's Christian Democrats out of a meeting and murdered them in 1980, parts of that organization did join the guerrilla ranks.[14] Amid rising discontent, political repression and authoritarianism simply provoked greater crisis.

Nowhere was this effect more evident than in the upsurge of rural radicalism during the late 1970s. More so than the Cuban revolution, the Nicaraguan revolution, or any of the uprisings that came between, the Guatemalan and Salvadoran revolts were essentially agrarian struggles.[15] As their living standards declined during the 1970s, the rural poor increasingly concluded that resistance was now worth the risk. The *campesino* "has nothing to lose," observed a Guatemalan officer. And because the ruling regimes had eliminated what little space there had previously been for peaceful mobilization, the activism that resulted tended toward the extreme. One Salvadoran guerrilla put the matter simply: "First they killed my mother and sister and threw them in a hole. Then they killed my husband and his parents. Then they killed my father and my brothers. So I fought harder for the [insurgents]."[16]

The growth of agrarian violence could be seen in the changing fortunes of the guerrillas. As in Nicaragua, the rural guerrillas—a motley collection of groups including Guatemala's PGT, Guerrilla Army of the Poor (EGP), Rebel Armed Forces (FAR), and Revolutionary Organization of the People in Arms (ORPA); and five Salvadoran groups led by the Popular Liberation Forces (FPL), that would eventually merge into the Farabundo Martí National Liberation Front (FMLN)—had suffered devastating defeats during the 1960s. As in Nicaragua, they came to see people's war as the answer to their problems.[17] This emphasis on people's war entailed a concerted effort to build links between the revolutionary aims of the guerrillas and the concrete needs of the *campesinos*. The overwhelming need, one EGP official wrote, was to overcome the "very deep resentment" that divided *campesinos* and insurgents. "When we organize the *indigenas* we must take into account their customs," EGP leaders wrote.[18] To this end, insurgent organizers in Guatemala and El Salvador took up residence in the countryside during the mid-1970s. They immersed themselves in the culture and politics of the *campesinos,* listening to their grievances and lending support to their efforts to achieve dignity and economic security. They stressed the need for agrarian reform, higher wages, and—in Guatemala especially—indigenous rights. Like the FSLN, they appealed to female peasants by invoking the language of gender equality.[19] Finally, adhering to the same practices that had proved so productive since the late 1960s, the organizers used the appeal of liberation theology to urge *campesinos* to take the step from dissatisfaction to violence. "Every Christian, if he is truly Christian, must be a revolutionary," declared one priest.[20]

By the late 1970s the sociological makeup of the insurgents reflected these organizing techniques. While most Guatemalan guerrilla leaders were still urban *mestizos,* peasants made up the majority of the rank-and-file. Although indigenous guerrilla fighters were rarer in El Salvador (mainly because that country had a smaller indigenous population), *campesinos* were nonetheless well represented in the FMLN.[21] This agrarian, rural flavor would ultimately limit the political appeal of the guerrillas, but in the late 1970s it seemed to have been an organizational masterstroke. At its peak, the Salvadoran guerrilla movement had perhaps 14,000 full-time combatants, 100,000 part-time fighters, and hundreds of thousands of sympathizers. Numbers on the Guatemalan guerrillas are difficult to come by, but a reasonable estimate would be a total membership of 6,000 to 10,000 at the outset of the 1980s, with hundreds of thousands of supporters.[22]

The growth of the guerrilla movements, and of radical dissent more broadly, set the stage for sustained, intense violence. In Guatemala the sharpest phase of the civil war kicked off in 1978, when the military collaborated with landlords in the town of Panzos to massacre peasants demanding "a just repartition of land."[23] The killings set off demonstrations throughout the country, and a PGT splinter group retaliated by murdering at least eighteen members of the military police.[24] These events presaged a descent into full-scale war. By mid-1978 the government and the death squads were engaged in a bloody assault on labor and agrarian activists, student groups, and opposition politicians. The guerrillas responded in kind, declaring war on the "murderous government and . . . its repressive army," and attacks by the PGT, EGP, FAR, and ORPA rose by more than 1600 percent between 1979 and 1982.[25] The insurgents occupied remote villages, destroyed critical infrastructure, and, according to their own estimates, inflicted 3,200 casualties on government forces in 1981 alone.[26] The EGP operated with impunity in many areas, conducting "executions" of wealthy landowners and "informants and collaborators of the murderous government."[27] The four main guerrilla groups eventually came together to form the Guatemalan National Revolutionary Unity (URNG), a joint command that coordinated insurgent operations and strategy. The government, still cut off from U.S. assistance, struggled to deal with this upsurge of violence, and guerrilla leaders anticipated the outright collapse of the regime. "Let's start the final battle now," wrote one PGT official.[28]

Salvadoran affairs were just as tumultuous. The military met guerrilla actions with a wave of repression, and U.S. officials commented that the government had "no instrument of public policy except murder."[29] There was hope that the situation might be stabilized in 1979, when a moderate junta seized power, promised major reforms, and again began to receive U.S. assistance.[30] The extreme Right sabotaged the reforms, however, and the extreme Left, now energized by its prospects, did likewise. The violence escalated, dramatized by the March 1980 murder of Romero. In what a U.S. official described as a "real 'Day of the Jackal' style" killing, a sniper shot him dead as he concluded his mass.[31] The slaughter of such an eloquent exponent of liberation theology, combined with the horrific imagery of Romero's blood staining the altar as he died, elicited sorrow and fury from both domestic and international observers. The resulting backlash helped derail Carter's plan to reestablish a military relationship with the Salvadoran government and provided an unintentional boost to the revolutionaries.[32] By late 1980 El Salvador's guerrilla groups had merged into the FMLN, and several opposition parties and unions banded together to form the Democratic Revolutionary Front (FDR), a political organization with close ties to the insurgents. The FMLN prepared for a "final offensive" to topple the regime. "We don't think the establishment of a popular, revolutionary government is very far away," one guerrilla predicted.[33] U.S. officials agreed, with Brzezinski giving the insurgents "a better-than-even chance to seize and hold power." With El Salvador and Guatemala on the brink, it appeared that much of the isthmus might go the way of Nicaragua.[34]

Throughout Latin America's Cold War, internal crisis was the father of foreign meddling, and the early 1980s were no exception. Of those looking to capitalize on the region's upheaval, the most energetic was Castro. Somoza's ouster, which he termed "the latest in a series of crippling defeats suffered by American imperialism," gave Cuban interventionism a boost, and the unsettled conditions of the early 1980s looked propitious to Havana.[35] Guatemala and El Salvador were in flames, and a coup in Grenada had brought to power a leader who mimicked Castro's exhortation, "*¡Hasta la victoria siempre!*"[36] "All Latin America" was a "powder keg," Castro commented. His advisers predicted that "during the coming decades at least five Latin American governments will fall to communist and leftist opposition forces." Havana, as always, looked to accelerate this process.[37]

This time around, Castro had superpower assistance. Although Brezhnev was less prone to ideological romanticism than Khrushchev had been, from the Kremlin's vantage point the late 1970s nonetheless seemed a time of opportunity in the Third World. The Soviet Union looked to be on the ascent during this decade. Moscow reached nuclear parity with Washington, expanded its power-projection capabilities, and Marxist movements (several of them allied to the Kremlin) took power in eleven countries between 1975 and 1979. These trends lent a new swagger to Soviet policy, and Kremlin leaders looked for favorable situations to exploit in the global south. The Soviet military "supports the national-liberation struggle," wrote Defense Minister Andrei Grechko in 1974, "resolutely resisting imperialist aggression in whatever distant part of the globe it appears."[38]

In few areas did prospects seem more promising than in Latin America. After Somoza's fall, Soviet officials hoped that additional revolutions might soon sweep the area. "Over two decades ago, there was only Cuba in Latin America," said Nikolai Ogarkov, chief of general staff of the Soviet military. "Today there are Nicaragua, Grenada and a serious battle is going on in El Salvador." Gromyko put it more artfully: "This entire region is today boiling like a cauldron." The current climate provided an excellent opportunity to make trouble in the "strategic rear" of the United States, Soviet officials argued, and thereby hobble Washington's ability to deal with crises elsewhere in the world. Central America, said Soviet diplomat Yuri Pavlov, was "the underbelly of the United States."[39]

Fifteen years after Moscow had distanced itself from the guerrillas, the Kremlin revised that policy. Social transformation would occur "by the armed struggle," an article in the Soviet press announced. "There is no other way." During the 1980s the Soviet Union aided Cuba in seeking to promote revolution in the Western Hemisphere, and the Kremlin issued pronouncements that channeled the confidence of the Khrushchev era. Moscow "will not accept the Monroe Doctrine in Central America," Soviet officials declared.[40]

Such statements were all the more credible because Moscow and Havana now had an ally in Sandinista Nicaragua. Through 1980, the outlines of Sandinista diplomacy were not fully clear. The JGRN pledged itself to a nonaligned policy and sought to obtain arms not only from Havana and Moscow but from Washington and Paris as well. Before long, however, the FSLN-led government effected a sharp turn to the East. The origins of this decision, which presaged a decade of U.S.–Nicaraguan hostility, remain hotly contested, with many writers judging this choice a reaction to Washington's hostility.[41]

This argument is not fully persuasive. From an ideological standpoint, the sympathies of the FSLN had always been with the Marxist-Leninist countries. The model the FSLN must follow, wrote Fonseca before his death, was that present "in the Paris Commune, in Russia, in China, in Korea, in Vietnam, in Cuba." Other leaders extolled the benefits of socialism. "No political,

ideological, and sociological theory, in all the history of humanity, has demonstrated such vitality, such capacity to spread and branch out," commented
Víctor Tirado. Marxist-Leninist principles, said another FSLN leader, would
be the Sandinista's "guide to action." The way that these beliefs translated into
a diplomatic affinity for the socialist states had been evident even before the
takeover. Of all the countries that supported the FSLN during 1978–1979, it
was Cuba that the guerrillas chose as the setting for the reunification of the
three tendencies in 1979.[42]

Moreover, the FSLN's top leaders never considered it feasible to seek a
long-term, cordial relationship with the United States. Despite the fact that
Carter provided more reconstruction assistance to Managua between 1979
and 1981 than any other leader, FSLN officials identified his administration
as an ineluctable foe of the new government. Concentrating on the history of
U.S. intervention in Nicaragua, rather than Carter's efforts to reverse that
trend, the FSLN viewed American antipathy to the revolution (as JGRN
head Daniel Ortega put it) as "inevitable." Before taking power, FSLN leaders declared the United States "the principal enemy of all the world's people."
Once in office, they incorporated this sentiment into the national anthem.[43]

These beliefs, when added to Carter's growing skepticism about the Sandinistas, opened the door to an alliance with the Soviet bloc. Cuba provided
arms, economic aid, technological assistance, and the services of some 2,500–
3,500 military advisers. In the event of a U.S. invasion or an internal uprising,
Cuban officials pledged, Havana would come to the defense of the regime.[44]
Moscow supplemented this assistance, providing subsidized oil shipments and
economic credits and helping the FSLN distribute Sandinista propaganda.[45]
The Soviet Union and its allies sent nearly $1 billion in military equipment
to Nicaragua in the years following the Sandinista takeover, and pushed Cuba
to deepen its support for the FSLN. "The idea," said one Soviet diplomat, "was to
make the price of the U.S military intervention . . . in Nicaragua so high that
it would be politically unacceptable for the United States to intervene."[46]

The FSLN also joined Soviet-Cuban efforts to promote revolution in Central America. Acting on both the "principle of revolutionary internationalism"
and the hope of bringing new allies to power, the FSLN worked with Moscow
and Havana to push the regional struggle forward. "Nothing you can say or do
will ever stop us from giving our full support to our fellow guerrillas," Bayardo
Arce told U.S. officials.[47] This support was fairly limited in Guatemala, but
much more substantial in El Salvador. The precariousness of the situation in El

Salvador, along with its proximity to Nicaragua, made that country a tempting target. The Soviet press depicted El Salvador as the "apex of revolutionary struggle in Latin America," while Ortega commented that the Salvadoran government was "practically defeated."[48] Beginning in 1980, Moscow, Havana, and Nicaragua cooperated to make this prediction a reality. Cuban advisers encouraged the Salvadoran guerrillas to unite into a single organization, trained 250–500 insurgents in 1980, and helped the FMLN pick targets and design operations. More important, Castro and his partners provided a steady flow of weapons—ranging from light arms to machine guns, mortars, and antiaircraft systems—to the guerrillas. While Moscow initially hesitated to send arms directly to the FMLN, the Kremlin did arrange shipments from North Korea, Vietnam, and Eastern Europe. These arms were delivered to Havana, then to Managua, and then transferred overland or via air or sea into El Salvador.[49] Nicaragua, Ortega commented, was the "logistical center of the Salvadoran revolution."[50]

Standing on the opposite side of the Central American conflict was the United States. U.S. policy toward Central America had begun to harden under Carter in 1980–1981, but the change fully crystallized under Ronald Reagan. Reagan was certainly aware of the local dimensions of Central American unrest (the need, he wrote in 1981, was to "correct the social inequities which make them ripe for Cuban inspired revolution"), but he also detected the guiding hand of Moscow and Havana. "The guerrillas are not embattled peasants, armed with muskets," he said. "They're professionals, sometimes with better training and weaponry than the government's soldiers."[51] This belief that the Central American revolts were part of a "bold attempt by the Soviet Union, Cuba, and Nicaragua to install communism by force throughout the hemisphere" provoked great alarm in the White House.[52] The spread of East-bloc influence in the Caribbean—"our lifeline to the outside world," Reagan termed it—would endanger U.S. commerce, cripple Washington's ability to act assertively elsewhere in the world, and eventually pose a direct danger to national security. "This is the moment of truth," Reagan said in 1984. "There is no time to lose."[53]

If the war in Central America was about protecting American interests, it was also about restoring American vigor. Following America's misadventure in Vietnam, Reagan believed, the United States had fallen into flaccidity, retreating from the world and demonstrating an alarming weakness. "It is time we purged ourselves of the Vietnam syndrome," he declared before taking office.[54] From this perspective, the conflict in Central America took on added salience. To shy from danger so close to home would signal that the United States was in irreversible decline. "If the United States cannot respond to a threat near our own borders, why should Europeans and Asians believe that we're seriously concerned about threats to them?" Reagan asked. "If the Soviets can assume that nothing short of an actual attack on the United States will provoke an American response, which ally, which friend will trust us then?"[55] Meeting this peril head-on, on the other hand, would restore American credibility and exorcise the ghosts of Vietnam. The task before the country, Defense Department official Nestor Sanchez explained, was one of reasserting "national will."[56]

This mind-set was clearly evident in 1983, when Reagan ordered the invasion of the tiny Caribbean island of Grenada in order to overthrow an authoritarian Marxist regime that had taken power four years earlier, and subsequently declared that "our days of weakness are over." In Central America the battle to restore U.S. prestige centered on El Salvador where, Secretary of State Alexander Haig announced, Washington would be "drawing the line" against Cuban-Soviet encroachments.[57] (Reagan had hoped to make a stand in Guatemala, but Guatemala's abominable human rights record kept U.S. assistance comparatively limited. For most of the 1980s, the Guatemalan army relied on fellow pariah-states like Argentina and South Africa for supplies.)[58]

Haig argued that the best way to resolve the Central American crisis was to "go to the source" and blockade or attack Cuba. "Give me the word and I'll turn that island into a fucking parking lot," he said.[59] Reagan settled for a less drastic approach.[60] U.S. officials pushed the Salvadoran government to reform and democratize, both out of a desire to lessen the polarization fueling the insurgency and a realization that liberalization would be necessary to ensure U.S. congressional support for Reagan's policy. "Our effort in El Salvador will succeed or fail first in the United States and not in El Salvador," wrote National Security Adviser Richard Allen.[61] Reagan also resumed large-scale military aid, sending $534 million worth of weapons and other supplies to the El Salvador Armed Forces (FAES) between 1981 and 1983, and U.S. advisers oversaw the training of 29,000 new military personnel. The goal, U.S. officials stated, was to "achieve strategic victory by destroying the insurgents' will and capability to fight."[62]

Reagan also sought to stop the flow of arms from Nicaragua to El Salvador via a covert military alliance with Argentina. Representatives of the Argentine junta, which supported Somoza during the late 1970s, linked up with Nicaraguan exiles—many of them former members of the National Guard—in Honduras in 1979–1980, and began to equip them as an anti-FSLN guerrilla force.[63] For Reagan, the *contras* (derived from the Spanish for "counterrevolutionary") offered a cheap solution to the problem of Nicaraguan support for the FMLN. In 1981 the CIA threw its support behind the rebels, working to transform them into a force that could interdict arms along Nicaragua's northern frontier. "We're proceeding with covert activity in Nicaragua to shut off supplies to the Guerrillas in El Salvador," Reagan noted.[64]

The *contras* not only rounded out Reagan's strategy for El Salvador; they were also the keystone of his policy toward Nicaragua. Reagan initially considered reconciliation with Managua, and U.S. diplomat Thomas Enders traveled to Nicaragua for negotiations. American officials warned the *contras* that Washington was "seriously attempting to find a modus operandi" with the FSLN, and that the insurgents therefore "should not count on [U.S.] support." The talks soon fell apart, though, as U.S. officials concluded that Managua would not cease its support for the FMLN or cut its ties to the Soviet bloc.[65] Convinced that the FSLN was "helping Cuba and the Soviets to destabilize our hemisphere," Reagan sought to turn the tables by destabilizing the FSLN. Congressional legislation passed in 1982 prohibited the CIA from seeking to topple the FSLN, but this rule was honored more in the breach than the observance. CIA operatives in Honduras trained the *contras* in guerrilla warfare and sabotage techniques and pushed them to mount audacious attacks. "Make the bastards sweat," CIA director William Casey ordered.[66] As the United States sought to staunch internal violence in El Salvador, it aimed to foment it in Nicaragua. Washington thus joined the international conflict over Central America, a struggle that would only feed the violence at work in the area.

In El Salvador matters came to a head in January 1981. Bolstered by arms shipments from abroad, the FMLN launched a "final offensive" that was meant to topple the government "before that fanatic Ronald Reagan takes over the presidency." The offensive proceeded briskly at first, and Salvadoran officials soon warned that the military had only a few days' ammunition left.[67]

These advances were soon checked, though, thanks to the timely intervention of the United States. Faced with the prospect of another leftist takeover in the days before he left office (and assured by the Salvadoran junta that it would take immediate steps to improve human rights practices), Carter authorized an emergency re-supply of the government forces. Reagan increased this assistance and the infusion of U.S. supplies helped avert an outright FAES collapse.[68]

Reagan hoped that the failure of the final offensive and the resumption of large-scale U.S. aid would allow the Salvadoran government to take the initiative and defeat the insurgency. Washington's assistance did ensure that neither the FAES nor the Salvadoran economy fell apart completely during the early 1980s, but for the most part, these ambitions went wanting. Corruption and nepotism impeded military efficiency, and the FAES never achieved the "strategic victory" that Reagan envisioned. In many ways U.S. military assistance turned out to be counterproductive. In the hands of a repressive army, U.S. weapons enabled the very practices that had alienated the population. The military used U.S.-supplied helicopters and planes in attacks that caused large numbers of civilian casualties and gruesome cases of "peasants' skin being burned off by white phosphorous bombs." In the most notorious case of FAES brutality, a counterinsurgent unit massacred, raped, and tortured hundreds of victims in the town of El Mozote. U.S. military assistance had been meant to create "breathing space" for political and social change, but in the early 1980s, had precisely the opposite result.[69]

Reconciling counterinsurgency and reform became even more difficult in 1982, when national elections gave ARENA (the Nationalist Republican Alliance), an extreme-Right party led by death-squad commander Roberto D'Aubuisson, a majority in the Salvadoran constituent assembly. ARENA was reactionary by any standard. One of D'Aubuisson's associates termed Jóse Napoleón Duarte, the progressive leader of the Christian Democrats, "just a Communist who happens to believe in God."[70] L. Paul Bremer called D'Aubuisson's policies "inimical to our interests," and other advisers labeled ARENA a "terrorist network led by D'Aubuisson henchmen."[71] With the insurgency raging, however, the Defense Department contended that now was not the time to be finicky about human rights. "When your house is on fire you don't call an interior decorator," one official explained.[72] Reagan sided with the hard-liners and continued to bankroll the activities of a repressive and reactionary government. (The administration also sought to distract attention from these practices, denying independent reports of FAES atrocities.) During 1982–1983 ARENA suspended implementation of an agrarian reform, provoking widespread rural outrage, and allowed the death squads to run wild. Many moderates contemplated abandoning the government altogether. "The situation is impossible," Duarte said.[73]

ARENA policies and the lack of progress against the insurgency eroded U.S. public support (never strong to begin with) for Reagan's involvement in El Salvador. Advocacy groups reported horrifying human rights violations, while other observers warned of a slippery slope leading to disaster. One congressmen declared that "the American people know that we have been down this road before," and a popular bumper sticker read, "El Salvador is Spanish for Vietnam." Resistance to Reagan's aid requests mounted, and administration officials feared that the program might be undone by domestic opposition. "The rug could be pulled out from under us," Secretary of State George Shultz (Haig's replacement) warned.[74]

The fact that U.S. support seemed only to be propping up a murderous regime led some observers to suggest that Washington should seek a negotiated settlement to the civil war. These suggestions were anathema to administration hard-liners, who doubted that the guerrillas would ever share power and sought to achieve an inspiring success in Central America. "We do not seek a military defeat for our friends," explained Undersecretary of Defense Fred Iklé, "We do not seek a military stalemate. We seek victory for the forces of democracy."[75]

Yet the United States was not the only one seeking victory. Ortega declared that the Salvadoran army "could fall apart at any moment," and Havana, Moscow, and Managua ramped up their support for the insurgency.[76] FMLN soldiers received training in Cuban and Nicaraguan camps, and Moscow continued to broker weapons shipments to the insurgents. (Plenty of these arms made it into El Salvador; there were simply too many routes—air, land, and sea—for a few thousand *contras* to choke off the flow completely.) Cuban and Nicaraguan advisers were integrated into the FMLN hierarchy, and urged the guerrillas to attack the cities and wage war against the country's infrastructure. Like Iklé, the guerrillas' patrons were willing to fight to the last Salvadoran. "The guerrillas [have] the morale to hold out indefinitely," Castro said; "time [is] on their side."[77]

This international solidarity was central to allowing the guerrillas to undertake several more offensives during the early 1980s. As Nicaraguan defense minister Roger Miranda later said, "These guerrillas would not have the strength that they have if they were without the direct support that the Sandinista government and the Cuban government have given them." By 1983–

1984 the FMLN controlled roughly one-fourth of Salvadoran territory and was maintaining a rhythmic assault on roads, bridges, power lines, and other vital pieces of the economy.[78]

On both sides, foreign intervention exacerbated the conflict in El Salvador. The United States backed a government that knew how to kill but was unwilling to reform, while Cuba, Nicaragua, and the Soviet Union gave sustenance to a guerrilla force that launched deadly attacks and wreaked havoc on the economy. Its fierce internal strife drawing fuel from abroad, El Salvador was trapped in a cycle of violent extremism. The majority of the estimated 70,000 deaths caused by the civil war occurred during the early 1980s (more than 80 percent of them caused by the military and the death squads), and plummeting economic performance made life miserable for the survivors. One historian puts it nicely: "The Four Horsemen of the Apocalypse appear to have taken up permanent residence in El Salvador during the 1980s."[79]

Circumstances improved somewhat beginning in 1983, as the Salvadoran government gradually eased back from its drastic course. In no small part, this correction was a result of U.S. pressure. By the close of 1982 the Reagan administration realized that continuing repression would likely lead to disaster in El Salvador. It might cause the U.S. Congress to terminate military assistance. It would almost certainly alienate the Salvadoran moderates and drive the country off a cliff. "The 'Mafia' must be stopped," one U.S. official told a Salvadoran audience. "Your survival depends upon it. The gorillas of this Mafia, every bit as much as the guerrillas of Morazan and Chalatenango, are destroying El Salvador."[80]

In late 1983 Vice President George Bush traveled to San Salvador with a blunt warning. A failure to rein in the death squads and permit political liberalization, he told his hosts, could cause irreparable damage to U.S.–Salvadoran relations. ARENA officials had previously rolled their eyes at such talk, assuming that the United States had no choice but to back them. In an ironic turn, however, the growing congressional skepticism that so troubled Reagan now worked in his favor. The prospect that Congress might force the White House to turn off the aid spigot lent Bush's admonitions a credibility that had heretofore been lacking, and ARENA chose to heed his advice. Death-squad violence dropped considerably from the horrific levels of 1981–1982 (though civilian casualties still numbered around 300 per month), and the paramilitaries largely ceased targeting the PDC. The government also restarted a long-delayed phase of the agrarian reform, proceeding with a "land-to-the-tiller" program that benefited 43,000 peasants. Overall, the reform redistributed roughly 20 percent of the country's arable land, and aided perhaps 25 percent of the rural poor.[81]

The reformist tendency grew stronger in 1984, when Duarte—with $2 million in CIA funds backing his candidacy—came to power on a platform promising to curb the death squads, lift political restrictions, and negotiate with the FMLN. Although the military and ARENA frustrated many of Duarte's initiatives, his election still marked a turning point in the war. The fact that the U.S. Congress could live with Duarte (once he was elected, the aid dollars flowed more freely) was not lost on the FAES, and convinced the generals that they must identify themselves with democracy and reform. Military officials took action against some of the most notorious human rights violators, and the FAES initiated civic action programs such as building roads, schools, and vaccination facilities.[82] "Troops moving into guerrilla base areas and occupied towns are treating local inhabitants with greater consideration," the CIA reported. The military also swung behind a gradual—and incomplete—democratic opening. Unions and other social groups were allowed to operate, political restrictions were relaxed, and relatively fair elections were held (though the FDR was not allowed to participate). These steps hardly ended repression against suspected "subversives," but they did mark a real improvement over the unrestrained right-wing terror of recent years.[83]

The opening of the political system destroyed the insurgents' greatest hope: that continued polarization would provoke a Nicaragua-style insurrection. The insurgents' agrarian themes, while useful in garnering rural support, had never held great appeal for urban, middle-class individuals whose dissatisfaction stemmed more from political marginalization than socioeconomic grievance.[84] Though the repression of the late 1970s and early 1980s tempted certain of these actors to make common cause with the insurgents, the *apertura* that followed removed any such desire. Most moderates and mainstream elites thought even a limited democracy preferable to an FMLN victory, and the chances of cross-class support for the guerrillas declined accordingly. The guerrillas, U.S. officials reported in 1984, found themselves "increasingly bowed in and with decreased options." FMLN spokesmen agreed, conceding, "The masses are not insurrectionary."[85]

By the mid-1980s the guerrillas were also losing *campesino* support. The agrarian reform, though it did little for the majority of landless peasants, did decrease guerrilla support among the beneficiaries.[86] The actions of the

FMLN itself also caused growing alienation in the rural areas. While the FMLN did at times take measures (such as constructing schools and hospitals) that bolstered their popularity in the "liberated zones," in many cases their actions tended in the opposite direction. Guerrilla sabotage attacks were extremely effective in wrecking the Salvadoran economy—GDP (gross domestic product) dipped 25 percent during the early 1980s—but they hurt the very people the guerrillas claimed to represent.[87] These economic disruptions were especially injurious to those who already lived on the brink, and guerrilla sabotage provoked a civilian backlash. The FMLN "claims to represent the people but cannot clearly prove it," declared the Salvadoran bishops, and "makes use of violence and sabotage as an essential weapon in its struggle."[88]

As the insurgents' situation grew precarious during the 1980s, the FMLN became more exploitive and coercive in dealing with the rural population. The FMLN levied "war taxes" on peasants and ran informal conscription programs. The insurgents murdered PDC mayors and other pro-government citizens to discourage support for the regime, and threatened to kill anyone who voted. This "revolutionary terror" did help the insurgents maintain their dominance in certain parts of the country, but it also made them seem little less repressive than the unjust order against which they railed.[89]

By the late 1980s guerrilla fortunes were on the wane. The FMLN still controlled large swaths of territory, but its number of combatants had fallen to 5,000–7,000, a decrease of 30 to 50 percent from a few years earlier.[90] Politically, the guerrillas found themselves marginalized by the democratic opening as well as their own destructive behavior. The decreasing popularity of the insurgency became evident in 1989, when a group associated with the FDR agreed to participate in national elections, only to receive less than 4 percent of the vote. The FMLN remained a large and powerful organization, but it was no longer capable of inspiring the widespread popular support necessary to overturn the state.

The FMLN might have been isolated, but it was not defeated. The group's agrarian message still resonated with some landless peasants, and the FMLN continued to receive massive weapons shipments from abroad. (This support was sufficient to allow the FMLN to make a wholesale conversion to East-bloc weapons in 1987.) Combined with the army's refusal to negotiate, these guerrilla strengths ensured that the civil war dragged on. The situation flared in 1989, when the election of an ARENA government threatened to derail political and social reform and the FMLN launched a major offensive. The war, admitted Juan Orlando Zepeda, the head of Salvadoran military intelligence, "is far from being resolved."[91]

In Guatemala, as in El Salvador, the battle between the guerrillas and the government reached a climax in the early 1980s. Believing that governmental repression had created a "decisive contradiction between the regime and the popular masses," the insurgents sought to strike the final blow. Guerrilla actions increased dramatically as the EGP and its partners looked to catalyze public discontent and make the jump from insurgency to general insurrection.[92]

This offensive set the stage not for a victorious march on the capital, but for a staggering counterrevolutionary blow. This scenario, a familiar one in Latin America, played out between late 1981 and 1983. First under Romeo Lucas García, and then more dramatically under Efraín Ríos Montt, the government unleashed a counterinsurgency that devastated the guerrillas—and much of the country in the process.

Ríos Montt, who took power in a coup in March 1982, exemplified Latin American military radicalism. His dedication to National Security Doctrine and his aggressiveness in dealing with "subversion" made even Pinochet and Videla seem like dilettantes. "I must do what I must," he remarked. "We here are fighting the Third World War." In late 1982 he deflected accusations that the government was seeking to destroy the economic livelihood of the indigenous peasants. "We have no scorched-earth policy," he said. "We have a policy of scorched Communists."[93]

Ríos Montt's strategy was to use widespread terror to destroy the guerrillas and their popular base. "Whoever is against the institutional government, whoever doesn't surrender, I'm going to shoot," he said. The purpose of this approach, note two analysts, was to "induce submission," showing that allegiance to the guerrillas would bring unspeakable horror and death.[94] Accordingly, the military targeted not only (or even principally) guerrilla combatants, but also entire towns thought to be supporting the insurgents. Beheadings, garroting, immolation, and massacres were commonplace. According to one estimate, more than 400 villages simply disappeared under Ríos Montt's rule. Indians were forced to kill suspected guerrilla sympathizers, or to watch as their loved ones were raped and executed. The ethos of the program was captured in a comment by one of Ríos Montt's officers. "Look, there can be no rules in guerrilla and counter-guerrilla warfare," he said. "It is the dirtiest war there can be."[95]

Toxic racism abetted this brutality. The belief that Guatemala's indigenous population represented "a lesser developed stage of humanity" fed the notion that the peasants were particularly susceptible to guerrilla penetration and allowed military officials to rationalize otherwise unconscionable violence.[96] "The guerrillas won over many Indian collaborators," said one. "Therefore, the Indians were subversives. And how do you fight subversion? Clearly you had to kill the Indians because they were collaborating with subversion." The resulting bloodshed was virtually genocidal. The number of people who lost their lives between 1981 and 1983 was probably around 100,000, at least 85 percent of which were killed by the security forces and death squads. One survivor commented, "I guess the government does not want any more Indian race."[97] Cold War radicalism mixed with long-standing social and ethnic tensions in Guatemala during the 1980s, producing cataclysmic violence.

Earlier repression had actually stimulated the guerrillas, but this most recent phase did the movement irreparable harm. Although most of those killed were noncombatants, the government did cast its net wide enough to devastate the guerrillas themselves. The insurgents had not been braced for such intense violence; PGT leaders noted that many *compañeros* were "poorly prepared militarily," and EGP militants later acknowledged, "We overestimated our capacities."[98] The PGT lost around 40 percent of its members in 1983, and the rest of the URNG suffered major losses as well. After Ríos Montt's "extermination campaign," the EGP admitted, "the enemy now has the initiative."[99] In general, the scope and brutality of the violence was sufficient to achieve the psychological effect that Ríos Montt sought. The guerrillas had claimed that resistance might lead to a better and more dignified existence; the government offensive showed that it would only lead to a gruesome death. The guerrillas soon found that even the marginalized were no longer so eager to join the cause.[100]

The Guatemalan government sought to build on this success by creating new rural institutions that would further separate the guerrillas from the masses. "We had to move people to areas where we could control them . . . and isolate the guerrillas," said one army supporter. The tools used for this purpose were Civil Defense Patrols (PACs), an initiative that required peasants to form anti-guerrilla militias; model villages, where traffic in and out was closely scrutinized by the army; and the *fusiles y frijoles,* or rifles and beans program which, according to one U.S. official, functioned as follows: "Those who are perceived to support the government are rewarded with food for work, housing if they have been displaced, and other forms of government largesse. Those perceived not to be in support of the government are met with whatever force is considered necessary."[101]

These programs were extremely effective. They allowed the army to keep watch over *campesinos*, who, after the maelstrom of the early 1980s, were often willing to accept safety wherever they could find it. While the model villages and PACs imposed economic burdens on the peasants and entailed a life under military scrutiny, writes one scholar, they nonetheless offered "some degree of security and tranquility after a period of chaos and violence."[102]

The promise of security was especially tempting because it came at a time of growing rifts between the guerrillas and the rural population. While the Guatemalan insurgents clearly enjoyed an organic connection with many *campesinos* during the late 1970s and early 1980s, this relationship suffered as the war intensified. As in El Salvador, the guerrillas sabotaged Guatemala's infrastructure throughout the 1980s in order to undermine "the base of [the state's] political and economic power." They destroyed power lines, roads, bridges, buses, and other targets. In Huehuetenango, the EGP boasted, it had committed "sabotage actions against . . . nearly all the towns."[103] These attacks seriously depressed economic activity and invariably hurt the poor more than the rich. Rural pastors began to lead their congregations out of EGP-dominated zones—a stinging rebuke from those who had, in many cases, earlier supported the guerrillas.[104]

The guerrillas undermined their own cause in other ways as well. Just as the intensification of the insurgency brought out the worst in the government, it highlighted the darker aspects of guerrilla behavior. For all their efforts to make themselves more appealing to the rural population, many insurgents still subscribed to a vanguard ideology that easily shaded into authoritarianism. The EGP, for instance, voiced a strong pro-Soviet tone and proclaimed "the need to carry out socialist revolutions in the style of Cuba, Algeria, Libya, and Nicaragua." This tendency became more marked in the early 1980s, as the ramping up of the struggle gave a militaristic tone to guerrilla activities. "What we had was politics, now we will act militarily," EGP organizers said.[105]

These attributes informed high-handed, coercive, and even brutal behavior toward the population. The guerrillas demanded food from the peasants, threatening them with violence if they refused. "One day, the guerrillas passed through [the] area, and they entered those houses and forced the people to give them food," recalled one *campesino*. "They told them that . . . if the people did not give them food, they would kill them."[106] Executions of "collaborators" and "army spies" were frequent, even though in many instances the victims were guilty only of failing to show full allegiance to the guerrillas. And as the pressure on the URNG grew, the insurgents more and more resorted to threats and intimidation to prevent *campesinos* from defecting to the enemy.[107]

These lingering traces of Guevarism led to a sharp decline in guerrilla popularity. No less damaging was the insurgents' tendency to invite violent retribution against the peasants. During the early 1980s the EGP would advance into a given area, provoke the military by attacking a patrol or killing a landlord, and then flee before the authorities could react. The idea was to escape the brunt of the army's response while at the same time exposing the *campesinos* to repression that would, hopefully, radicalize them.[108] This tactic worked in some cases, but it ultimately backfired. By leaving the peasants vulnerable to military reprisals, the guerrillas demonstrated that they could not or would not protect those who supported them. "The guerrillas only provoke the army, and then they go," said one rural pastor. "We are the ones who suffer the consequences."[109]

From 1982 on, these factors produced an important rural realignment. With the guerrillas showing themselves to be authoritarian and unreliable, many peasants accepted the safety offered by the army. "The presence of [the civilian patrols], coupled with the government's civic action programs, has impinged seriously upon the Indians' willingness to extend logistical support, safe haven, and good will to the insurgents," U.S. officials noted. Guatemalan officials offered similar assessments, and as the decade went on, the guerrillas found it difficult to win access to or sympathy among the rural population.[110]

As institutions like the PACs drove a wedge between the guerrillas and the *campesinos*, a final aspect of the counterinsurgency separated the insurgents from dissatisfied members of the political class. By the early 1980s unvarnished military rule and the stifling of the opposition had threatened to drive the moderates into the arms of the guerrillas and produce a Nicaragua-style outcome. In order to lessen this danger, Guatemalan officers realized, it was necessary to permit a gradual liberalization, to "design a political, economic and social model that would help change the huge contradictions that had

4 o

turned Guatemala into a country in constant political, economic and social conflict."[111] Beginning under Ríos Montt, but continuing more expeditiously under his successors, Guatemala experienced a limited democratic opening. Between 1982 and 1986 the military reduced death-squad violence against the PDC and other moderates, allowed unions to operate, permitted free speech and association, and supervised the drafting of a new constitution and the holding of multiparty elections.

The new system was hardly liberal or egalitarian. "Subversive agitators" were murdered or disappeared, although such occurrences were now less frequent. The new constitution made no meaningful provision for agrarian reform, but it did contain nods to indigenous rights. The military allowed moderate parties like the PDC to come to power, but maintained a veto on government policy. And, of course, this democratic opening began just as the army was waging an all-out war against much of the indigenous population.[112]

With respect to defanging the insurgency, though, liberalization accomplished its intended effect. Guatemala's political class, the majority of which was urban and *mestizo,* had never been comfortable with the agrarian, indigenous philosophy of the guerrillas, and would have supported the insurgents only if there had been no other alternative to a continuation of the old regime. The political opening eliminated this temptation. Guatemala's unions and opposition parties preferred a thoroughly imperfect quasi-democracy to a quixotic alliance with the insurgents, and the PGT admitted that the guerrilla movement was now "isolated from the rest of the popular sectors."[113]

By the mid-1980s it was clear that the guerrillas could not take power. Battered by violence, isolated by the democratic opening, and marginalized by their own errors and excesses, the insurgents were unmistakably in decline. As in El Salvador, though, insurgents that could not win could not be defeated, either. The URNG retained a significant—if much-reduced—contingent of experienced combatants, and a government "final offensive" in 1987 failed to eliminate the remaining guerrillas. The threat of revolution had faded, but peace was not at hand.[114]

Although the Nicaraguan civil war is often described, as one early account had it, as "Reagan versus the Sandinistas," the origins of the conflict had little to do with U.S. policy.[115] After taking power, the Sandinistas embarked upon what Allende might have termed a "Nicaraguan road to socialism." The gov-

ernment preserved a mixed economy and respected certain democratic practices, but did so with an eye to the longer-term goal of establishing a socialist
system. "The ideological attitude of the FSLN leadership is . . . fully clear,"
Cuban officials reported in 1981. "It wants Socialism in Nicaragua."[116] Sandinista officials referred to their party as the "vanguard," and made clear that political freedoms came second to the needs of the revolution. The FSLN "could not
lose sight of what had happened to other revolutionary governments in Latin
America," Daniel Ortega explained. "Others had taken advantage of the freedoms allowed to destroy those movements." Accordingly, the government
would permit democratic practices only so long as they comported with the
Sandinista project. National polls held in 1984, said Ortega, "are elections to
improve the power of the revolution, but they are not a raffle to see who has
power, because the people have power through their vanguard, the Sandinista
National Liberation Front and its National Directorate."[117]

During the early 1980s the FSLN combined progressive and sometimes
radical social policies with a determined drive for political hegemony. The government launched major initiatives in health, education, women's rights, and
other public services while at the same time institutionalizing Sandinista
power. The FSLN created a new army, militia, and secret police and channeled
mass political participation into organs overseen by the state. Sandinista Defense Committees (CDS) were given authority to grant drivers' licenses and
economic permits, thereby ensuring that loyalty to the FSLN was a prerequi-
site for obtaining even basic services. There was "a new reality" in Nicaragua,
Interior Minister Tomás Borge announced, with the FSLN now the nation's
"irreplaceable vanguard."[118]

This program was quite popular initially, and the FSLN would win a land-
slide victory in 1984 elections. Yet it also provoked violent resistance in some
quarters. Attempts to assert state control over the major industries led prominent Conservatives and economic elites to take up arms, while the Sandinistas'
rural policies soon produced what two scholars call a "virtual peasant insurrection."[119] The FSLN called itself the champion of the *campesinos,* but its rural
initiatives were based more on the ideological needs of the party than the long-
ignored needs of the peasants. Rather than giving landless peasants individual
plots of land, the Sandinistas placed them (sometimes forcibly) in collective
farms. Instead of allowing the Miskito Indians in the northeast to preserve
their long-standing autonomy, the government tried—often violently—to in-
tegrate them into Borge's "new reality."[120] The result was a fierce backlash. In

1979 residents of the mountainous interior formed the Anti-Sandinista Popular Militias (MILPAS), and thousands of Miskitos soon joined them in armed resistance. The reasons for rebellion, stated Miskito leaders, were "land, autonomy, the liberty of Indian people, freedom for our culture and people."[121] The *contra* armies eventually reached a peak of perhaps 30,000 combatants, the vast majority of them *campesinos,* making the Nicaraguan conflict the largest peasant war in Latin America since the Mexican revolution. The *contra* war was essentially a revolt, as one MILPAS member put it, of "a whole bunch of *really* pissed off peasants."[122]

To the extent that foreign involvement in Nicaragua provoked the civil war, it had to do mainly with the growing Soviet and Cuban role in the country. In one sense it was the need to assert Sandinista control over the ports of El Bluff and Puerto Cabezas—which sat at the terminus of the shortest maritime routes to Havana, Moscow, and other East-bloc allies—that made the government so eager to bring the Miskitos to heel.[123] More broadly, the tilt toward the Soviet bloc inflamed both violent and nonviolent opposition. The Catholic Church, led by Archbishop Miguel Obando y Bravo, charged that the government was "completely Marxist-Leninist and under Cuban control," presaging a decade of hostility between church and regime.[124] Other defectors criticized the "exaggerated sovieto-filia" of the FSLN government, an issue that pushed the Sandinistas' famed *Comandante Cero,* Edén Pastora, to turn traitor and form a guerrilla front in Costa Rica.[125] Early anti-Sandinista fighters tapped into this same fear, showing other peasants the Soviet-made weapons captured from the FSLN as proof, one fighter said, "that the Sandinistas were Soviet proxies and that the Cubans were invading Nicaragua to impose their political system."[126] Moscow and Havana may have helped the FSLN consolidate power, but their aid came at a price.

Reagan eagerly capitalized on the *contra* revolt, setting the stage for renewed U.S. intervention in Nicaragua. Few causes were dearer to Reagan than the *contras.* He called them "freedom fighters" and depicted them as America's first line of defense against Havana and Moscow. The administration worked (with varying degrees of success) to unite the anti-FSLN forces, and gave Honduras hundreds of millions of dollars in military aid in exchange for hosting the guerrillas. CIA operatives armed the rebels, trained them, and pushed them forward with an urgency well suited to Reagan's anticommunist zeal. "The only way to defeat Communism is by using the same means, the same tactics," one U.S. operative told the *contras.* "Kidnap, kill, torture, rob. Democratic means are not effective."[127] In accord with Reagan's desire to make the FSLN "say uncle," the CIA encouraged the *contras* to mount large-scale operations designed to capture and hold Nicaraguan territory, and used its own agents to mine Nicaragua's ports and attack Nicaraguan ships.[128]

In terms of the implicit—and later explicit—goal of overthrowing the Sandinista regime, the *contra* program was never particularly effective. The U.S.–Argentine alliance fell apart over the Falklands crisis of 1982 (see Chapter 8), and Pastora's "southern front" fizzled. Congressional skepticism kept *contra* funding more limited than Reagan would have liked ($322 million for the entire period between 1981 and 1990, as opposed to billions in Soviet and Cuban aid for Managua). This opposition eventually led to a cutoff of U.S. military support for the insurgents (which, in turn, led to the Iran-Contra scandal), and left the *contras* in worsening financial straits as the decade went on.[129]

What aid the United States did give the *contras* was largely counteracted by Cuban and Soviet assistance to Nicaragua. The fact that the United States was, as Gromyko said, "hurling gangs of mercenaries and terrorists against Nicaragua" led Moscow and Havana to step up their involvement in the conflict. Moscow delivered sophisticated helicopter gunships, which were sometimes flown by Cuban pilots. Cuban advisers helped the Sandinista Popular Army (EPS) create specialized counterinsurgency units, and East-bloc artillery allowed the Sandinista army to shell *contra* sanctuaries in Honduras.[130] Together these measures kept the *contras* on the defensive. The insurgency, U.S. officials reported in 1983, "does not yet pose a serious threat to the Sandinistas." Combined with the 1984 election results and Reagan's refusal to pursue a diplomatic solution seriously, this blunting of the *contra* offensive led to a stalemate. Reagan adviser James Baker called Nicaragua "our country's Vietnam of the 1980s," while State Department official Cresencio Arcos warned that U.S. policies "will give you nothing but attrition in the end."[131]

This stalemate may have been frustrating to Washington, but it was catastrophic for Nicaragua. *Contra* sabotage caused hundreds of millions of dollars in damages, and when added to the effects of a U.S. commercial embargo, it had severe consequences for a vulnerable Nicaraguan economy that had never recovered from the destruction of the 1970s. "The Contras are doing about as well as can be expected," wrote Reagan adviser Robert Pastorino, "not great;

but it apparently doesn't take much to disrupt the feeble economy and infra-structure of Nicaragua."[132] The costs of the war helped fuel inflation (which reached 36,000 percent in 1988), and real wages fell by roughly half during the early 1980s. The conflict also displaced tens of thousands of refugees and forced the government to implement a highly unpopular conscription pro-gram that, as the war dragged on, became more coercive and thus more po-litically toxic. Attrition worked both ways, and even a relatively ineffective resistance dragged down the general quality of life for Nicaraguans. When the U.S. Congress approved a "humanitarian aid" package for the *contras* in 1986, Ortega complained that this step meant only "still more death, destruction, and suffering."[133]

The *contra* war certainly made things difficult for the Sandinistas, but the FSLN made matters worse through its own errors and excesses. Ill-considered economic policies were no less responsible for Nicaragua's worsening plight than were U.S. pressure and civil war. Price controls seriously distorted the production and marketing of basic goods, while Sandinista agricultural prac-tices disrupted long-standing patterns of cultivation. Corruption and the appointment of incompetent loyalists to head important ministries further impeded effective economic measures, and the relentless printing of currency to finance growing budget deficits simply worsened the fiscal situation.[134] The Sandinistas had not given "our best performance," Planning Minister Henry Ruiz conceded. "The economy was on zero," Víctor Tirado later said, with inflation and rationing eliciting rising public discontent.[135] The fact that the upper echelons of the FSLN used their influence to insulate themselves from these hardships only increased popular resentment, and by 1985, Ortega identified a growing "alienation between the government and the Sandinista Front on the one hand, and the masses, the large majority of the population, on the other."[136]

The Sandinistas' problems extended to the political and social scene, as the government suffered fallings-out with numerous influential groups. The sus-pension of many political rights from 1982 to 1988, justified on grounds that there was an "enormous terrorist army" on the border, grated on moderates and the middle class. "The FSLN used coercive tactics," *Comandante* Jaime Wheelock later conceded, "which at times severely limited individual free-doms and civil rights." The banning of strikes alienated labor, and attempts to impose greater government control over the mass organizations caused a steep drop in their popularity. Then there was the debilitating feud with the Catholic Church. Although various factors produced this dispute, the FSLN handled the issue terribly, with Sandinista militants harassing priests and heckling a papal mass in Managua. The FSLN was isolating itself, losing the support of groups of the Right, Left, and Center.[137]

As the 1980s went on the FSLN became increasingly repressive in dealing with this discontent. There is a continuing debate over human rights abuses in the civil war, and neither side was innocent. The *contras* perpetrated exemplary murders of FSLN sympathizers; burned pro-government villages; and raped, kidnapped, and killed volunteers in the Sandinista literacy program. They tortured EPS soldiers or "collaborators" that fell into their hands. There was "no time to carry on due process," one *contra* official recalled; "you wanted to have answers very soon because otherwise you would be risking your own troops."[138] These practices diminished in the late 1980s as Reagan pushed the *contras* to show that they were "the real democratic alternative to the Sandinistas," but the insurgents' reputation for brutality was well earned.[139]

The FSLN also made use of such practices, although in this case the abuses mounted during the mid- and late 1980s. "We cannot renounce in these times the use of revolutionary terror," the FSLN directorate resolved in 1987. The government sought to blunt support for the *contras* by belatedly introducing a limited agrarian reform, but also through more coercive measures. The FSLN forcibly relocated perhaps 100,000 peasants, and tortured and executed suspected insurgent sympathizers. In one episode intelligence agents masqueraded as *contra* recruiters and, after enticing 200 peasants to join the cause, had them summarily killed.[140]

As had happened so often in Latin America, though, state terror had unintended effects. Sandinista repression was not sufficient to crush the opposition outright, but it was enough to alienate an already disgruntled rural population and drive more *campesinos* to the insurgents. By the late 1980s *contra* sympathizers were ubiquitous in the rural areas. "All these sons of bitches are Contras," exclaimed one EPS brigade chief. (The depth of rural hostility to the FSLN was confirmed by the 1990 elections, in which the FSLN polled poorly—around 36 percent—among *campesinos*.)[141] By 1987–1988 declining public support indicated that the revolution was running out of steam. "The social basis of the revolution" was eroding, commented Bayardo Arce. "The destabilization of the country" now loomed.[142]

Yet if the FSLN was losing its political footing, it was hardly in danger of being swept out of office by a mass insurrection. The Sandinistas still enjoyed the loyalty of a broad swath of the population, and the EPS remained far stronger than the *contras*. In Nicaragua as elsewhere the war seemed set to drag on indefinitely.

The Central American imbroglio only began to move toward resolution in the late 1980s as the international context surrounding the crisis evolved. Washington, Moscow, and Havana, whose involvement had done so much to fuel this conflict, each eventually concluded that their Central American policies were unsustainable. In the United States the Iran-Contra scandal threatened to undo congressional support for the *contras* altogether. Diplomatic backing for the program was also in jeopardy, as Honduras began to wonder if its Nicaraguan guests would ever be going home, and the Honduran government even consulted with the United Nations regarding the possibility of evicting the *contras* by force. Similarly, ARENA's return to power and the flaring of the insurgency in 1989 revived congressional opposition to an open-ended commitment to El Salvador. In these circumstances, the new administration of George H. W. Bush was ill disposed to brawling with Congress over Central American aid. The former vice president had never really identified with Reagan's anticommunist crusade, and with the Cold War winding down, he was most interested in removing what Baker (now secretary of state) called "the bleeding sore of Central America" as a point of executive–congressional discord.[143]

Moscow was also reconsidering its policies toward the region. The costs of supporting the FMLN and FSLN (not to mention Cuba) had become extremely onerous. The Kremlin was providing hundreds of millions of dollars per year in aid to Nicaragua and $8–10 million *per day* to Cuba, all as the Soviet economy underwent a slow-motion collapse. "The colonial regions are exploiting the Soviet Union!" U.S. officials joked. During the mid- and late Reagan years, moreover, Soviet officials worried that their support for these movements, far from deterring U.S. intervention in Central America, might actually provoke an invasion that Moscow could do little to impede.[144]

These considerations came to the forefront of Soviet policy under Mikhail Gorbachev. Contrary to conventional wisdom, Gorbachev did not effect a Third-World retrenchment immediately upon taking office. Early on, Gorbachev combined liberalization at home with ideological fervor abroad. Even as he began overdue reforms within the Soviet Union, he restated Moscow's support for the "struggle of the peoples for liberation from the colonial yoke." Moscow brokered a full-scale rearmament of the FMLN in 1987, and Gorbachev pledged "solidarity with the struggle waged by Nicaragua against the aggressive intrigues of imperialism."[145]

Gradually, however, economic and geopolitical realities forced Gorbachev to scale back Soviet involvement. Seeking to "introduce a certain stabilizing element to the relations between the USSR and USA," Gorbachev looked to defuse regional conflicts that would further tax the economy and might escalate into a U.S.–Soviet confrontation.[146] Moscow wanted "neither a beachhead nor a stronghold" in Central America, Soviet representatives averred. The Kremlin cut its material support for the FMLN after 1989, pledged to cease arms shipments to the Sandinistas, and reduced economic aid to Managua.[147] The Kremlin also pushed its Nicaraguan and Salvadoran allies to negotiate with their adversaries. The Central American crisis would have to be settled "with the partners God gave us and not with some ideal partner," Soviet radio commentators announced. In Managua the implications were clear. "The concerns of our strategic allies in the Soviet Union are concentrated around the geopolitical problems the worldwide struggle against imperialism poses," the National Directorate reported, "and not in acting sympathetically with the Revolution."[148]

Castro initially rejected this retreat. He announced that the Salvadoran guerrillas "have all our support" and pledged to match any increase in *contra* aid with additional military assistance for the EPS.[149] "Imperialism is in a deep crisis," he told East German officials in 1986.[150] Castro's fighting spirit remained intact, but his capabilities were in decline. For all Castro's diplomatic independence of the Kremlin, Cuba was heavily reliant on Soviet and military aid, and the changes occurring in Moscow soon had a profound effect in Havana. *Perestroika* left Castro ideologically isolated, while decreasing Soviet assistance crippled Cuba's ability to sustain military endeavors abroad or even to provide for the Cuban population. "Cuba is undergoing what is probably one of its most traumatic periods since 1959," UN diplomats reported.[151] Forced to turn inward, Havana looked to limit its exposure in Central America. Castro publicly restated his support for the FMLN and FSLN, but urged them to negotiate before East-bloc support dried up entirely. Havana, Moscow, and Washington had plunged into Central America a decade earlier; after years of inconclusive struggle, they now looked for a way out.[152]

That avenue was the Central American peace process. This process, which began in the early 1980s, had previously had an unhappy existence. Reagan rejected the Contadora peace initiative in 1984, and the FSLN accepted the plan, as Ortega put it, only to "expose" U.S. antipathy to the negotiations. Contadora died at mid-decade, but the peace negotiations (now known as the Esquipulas process) received new life in 1986, when isthmian leaders headed by Costa Rica's Óscar Arias called for talks on arms limitation, terminating aid to guerrilla forces, democratization and free elections, and other subjects.[153]

In Guatemala and El Salvador enthusiasm for the negotiations was muted. The guerrillas realized that a peace settlement would mean giving up on revolution, while the militaries disliked the idea of sitting down with enemies they claimed to have defeated. Given the alternative of continuing the civil wars, though, these parties eventually found a reason to embrace negotiation. The Guatemalan government signed onto Esquipulas in the late 1980s, opening talks that ultimately led to a peace settlement in 1996. In El Salvador the Bush administration pushed the FAES to do the same. Bush dispatched Vice President Dan Quayle to San Salvador to warn that any resumption of death-squad activity risked ending U.S. aid altogether, and gave the FAES a shove by gradually drawing down military assistance. Negotiate now, Bush threatened, or face the guerrillas without U.S. support. Combined with the sobering effect of the 1989 FMLN offensive, this pressure led the armed forces to accept the principle of negotiation, and a peace accord took effect in 1992.[154]

Ambivalence about Esquipulas was even stronger in Nicaragua, where all of the major parties had serious reservations about the process. U.S. officials feared that the negotiations would leave the *contras* denuded of supplies, and hard-liners doubted that the Sandinistas would abide by any agreement. "Communists win these kinds of negotiations," State Department adviser Elliot Abrams fumed. The Soviets were worried, as one diplomat put it, that the United States could bring "many and diverse pressures" on the small countries of the region. For its part, the FSLN realized that lifting political curbs, as the accords required, would energize a boisterous opposition. "The mix of leaving the ideological enemies of our process free in front of the means of communication and popular discontent," FSLN leaders warned, "has an explosive, highly dangerous potential for the revolutionary power."[155]

As elsewhere, though, the participants ultimately found virtue in necessity. U.S. diplomats realized that only by committing to the negotiations could the administration wring any more *contra* money out of Congress, and Reagan and then Bush traded their acceptance of Esquipulas for two final appropria-tions.[156] The Soviets thought that the peace process might lead to rapproche-ment between Nicaragua and the United States, and thereby allow Moscow to retreat from Central America in good order. A Sandinista electoral victory "would contribute to the international prestige of the Sandinistas and would be a very strong card in the normalization of relations between Managua and Washington," opined Soviet diplomat Dmitri Titov.[157] The FSLN eventually accepted Esquipulas as a way of restoring internal "legitimacy" and opening the door to aid from non-East-bloc sources. The peace process would also force Washington to end its support for the *contras*, the National Directorate ex-pected, allowing Managua to "leave the counterrevolution without resources." "We will win this war in Washington," the FSLN predicted. The Sandinistas began direct talks and signed a cease-fire with the *contras*, and the two groups agreed to hold national elections in early 1990.[158]

The polls took place in February, with the FSLN facing off against a hast-ily assembled coalition (the National Opposition Union, or UNO) whose chief advantages were $9 million in U.S. aid and the benefit of being anyone other than the Sandinistas. Few observers expected UNO to win. But a de-cade's worth of anger at economic hardship, conscription, political restrictions, and Sandinista repression, as well as the expectation that a UNO victory would mean peace, ensured that the FSLN's electoral gambit backfired. In a surprise result, Violeta Chamorro (widow of the murdered newspaper editor) defeated Ortega by a comfortable margin of 55 to 41 percent. The FSLN re-spected the decision; Chamorro took office in April; *contra* demobilization was largely completed two months later. The civil war was over, leaving Nicaraguans—like their neighbors in Guatemala and El Salvador—to rebuild a country wrecked by decades of dictatorship and violence.[159]

This would be no easy task, for the destruction was catastrophic. The ag-gregate death count of the Central American civil wars was probably upwards of 300,000, a staggering figure given the population of the countries in ques-tion. The economic cost was also great. Nicaragua, El Salvador, and Guate-mala each lost sizable portions of GDP during the 1980s, and the scorched-earth campaigns, loss of economic providers, and debilitating injuries took a heavy toll on many families. The conclusion of the peace accords did not eas-ily bridge the social and political divisions exacerbated by years of bloodshed, nor did it erase the collective psychological trauma that resulted from this vi-olence. Neither, in some cases, did the agreements even end the fighting fully:

dozens of *contras* were murdered upon their return to Nicaragua in 1990–1991, while some of these insurgents refused to lay down their arms. The cataclysmic bloodletting of the civil wars had largely subsided, but the legacies of those struggles remained.

The Central American conflicts were a fitting, if tragic, culmination to Latin America's Cold War. During the 1980s the combined furies of that struggle came together in Central America, and the result was a period of violence that dwarfed even the South American dirty wars in intensity and duration.

The civil wars ended in negotiated settlements, but the practical result was the frustration of revolutionary ambitions. The Guatemalan and Salvadoran accords reintegrated the guerrillas into systems that, while much more democratic than before, were still highly inequitable. The FSLN was turned out of power and watched as the Chamorro government rolled back a number of its reforms. Central America had not returned to the status quo ante, but it had not much progressed toward the vision of the revolutionaries.

Were the Central American civil wars, then, a case of the aspirations of the masses being thwarted by murderous elites and their foreign accomplices? Did these events demonstrate that the slogan *el pueblo unido jamás será vencido*— the people, united, will never be defeated—was wrong? In part, yes. The Central American revolutionary movements did embody the hopes of large segments of the population for a better, more dignified life, and, at certain points, each of these organizations enjoyed strong, organic bonds with "the masses." And these movements were defeated, in no small measure, by unrelenting U.S. hostility and the willingness of their opponents to act in bloody—even genocidal—fashion.

Like all of Latin America's Cold War, however, these episodes cannot be reduced to a simple morality play. The Central American crisis was more complex and ambiguous than is often realized. Take, for instance, the U.S. role. Washington backed a thoroughly thuggish army in El Salvador, but also supported efforts to open the political system and restrain death-squad violence. "U.S. officials behind closed doors did not wink and nudge each other when they spoke of promoting democracy in Latin America," writes Thomas Carothers, but rather were quite sincere—if simplistic—in their commitment to democratization. With respect to Nicaragua, U.S. policy was aggressive, cynical, and destructive, but it also aligned with the aspirations of pro-democracy elements and *campesinos* who found the FSLN little better than Somoza. Cresencio Arcos, the diplomat charged with demobilizing the *contras* in 1990, summed it up nicely: "We supported some very unsavory people and some very good people at the same time."[160]

Moreover, to view the U.S. role in Central America in isolation is to distort the complicated reality of foreign intervention in the area. Washington was but one of several self-interested meddlers that supported a mix of admirable and despicable characters as their needs required. Each of these powers had a hand in the Central American bloodbath; one could easily say that Soviet, Cuban, and Nicaraguan support prolonged the war in El Salvador by giving sustenance to an increasingly unpopular guerrilla force that spared little effort in its attempts to destroy the nation's economy. To make this comparison is not to weigh the relative morality or immorality of foreign involvement in Central America, but simply to point out that external intervention during the 1980s was not a one-sided affair.

Internally, too, the Central American wars were hardly unambiguous. "The masses" were never that cohesive, it turns out, nor were they unwavering in their support for the revolutionary Left. While these revolutionary movements did initially enjoy strong popular solidarity, their actions— while nowhere near as brutal as those of the Guatemalan or Salvadoran governments—eventually alienated many of those who had previously backed them. By the late 1980s, in fact, it was clear that *el pueblo* simply did not support the idea of social revolution, at least not as it was advocated by the FMLN, FSLN, or URNG.

And while repression and violence played a key role in this disillusion, other factors also mattered. In Guatemala and El Salvador, the decision of mainstream and moderate actors to shun the guerrillas was intimately linked to the political openings that occurred during the mid-1980s. These changes were hardly comprehensive ("low-intensity democracy," one scholar writes[161]), and were in both cases undertaken for reasons that were at least partly cynical. But they did leave Guatemala and El Salvador with more open political systems, and they drained support from the violent Left. If there was a positive outcome of the civil wars, this move toward democratization was it.

While it is thus necessary to recognize the complexity of the Central American conflicts, one should not go too far. The 1980s were a period of hellish devastation for Central America. Nicaragua, Guatemala, and El Salvador suffered massive human and economic losses, profound cultural and social traumas, and were left with broken institutions and legacies of fear that persist today. One historian has recently argued that the closing years of the Cold War represented a "triumph of hope." The residents of these countries might be pardoned for disagreeing. If anyone won the Cold War in Latin America, it was certainly not they.[162]

8

The End of History?

The tragedy of the Central American civil wars was impossible to deny, but that didn't stop Ronald Reagan from trying. In December 1982, with Ríos Montt's counterinsurgency in full swing, Reagan gave an upbeat appraisal of events in Guatemala. Ríos Montt was "getting a bum rap," he told reporters, and had not received credit for taking steps to increase political participation. "He is totally dedicated to democracy."[1]

That Reagan could make such a comment reflected his abiding anticommunism and his simplistic definition of democracy. All the same, Reagan's analysis did capture an essential transformation occurring in the region.

During the 1980s Latin America went democratic. At the close of 1978 there were only four democratic regimes in the region. Over the next dozen years, dictatorships fell or elected governments came to power in thirteen countries. Guatemala and El Salvador held elections and broadened political participation, even as the armed forces waged bloody counterinsurgencies. Honduras had its first democratically elected president in decades take power in 1981, and U.S. intervention toppled Manuel Noriega in Panama. Events in South America followed a similar course. Juntas in Peru, Bolivia, and Ecuador returned to the barracks, while Stroessner of Paraguay was overthrown in 1989. Negotiated transitions occurred in Brazil, Uruguay, and Argentina, and the seemingly omnipotent Pinochet was undone by a national plebiscite in 1988. By 1990 even the Institutional Revolutionary Party (PRI) in Mexico looked far less invincible than before. Whereas Cold War authoritarianism had swept Latin America during the 1960s and 1970s, the 1980s were dominated by the retreat of the dictators.[2]

In no two instances was the process of democratization identical, and the circumstances under which authoritarian rulers left power varied widely. Looking across these cases, though, there were several factors that loomed large in the region's political transformation. Democratization had much to do with the relationship between the dictators and the violent Left. The strength of the guerrilla forces compelled governments in Guatemala and El Salvador to embrace a degree of liberalization, while in South America the devastation of the extreme Left eventually robbed the radical military regimes of their raison d'être. Latin America's authoritarians also faced growing diplomatic pressure as the 1980s went on, with a variety of foreign actors—most notably the United States—impelling the movement toward democracy. Most important of all, democratization was a product of debt. Dictatorial regimes had sometimes struggled to deal with the sociopolitical ramifications of economic growth, but when the Latin American debt crisis unfolded, few of these governments survived the fallout from economic disaster.

If debt helped bring Latin America to a political watershed, it was even more crucial to a concurrent shift in regional political economy. During the 1980s Latin America largely abandoned the venerable ISI model. The emergence of the debt crisis brought together long-standing Latin American critiques of ISI with U.S. and international efforts to deepen the region's integration into the global economic order. Over the course of a decade, these forces ensured the ascendance of a new economic paradigm. Governments slashed spending, privatized state-owned industries, lifted trade barriers and price controls, and allowed their currencies to float. They denounced state interventionism and swore fealty to the market. As Latin America returned to democracy, it turned to neoliberalism as well.

Coming at roughly the same time as the Central American civil wars, the economic and political changes of the 1980s provided a fitting coda to Latin America's Cold War. In one sense the events of that decade rolled back the political arrangements—radical military regimes inspired by National Security Doctrine—that had been so central to that conflict. More important, the events of the 1980s seemed to settle the long-running ideological battle for Latin America. For decades the superpowers and Cuba had sought to use Latin America as a showcase for their respective models of economic and political development. Similarly, actors within the region had competed to determine what social, economic, and political system would emerge supreme. By the late 1980s this struggle appeared to have ended in a blowout. Latin America was rushing headlong toward free-market capitalism and electoral democracy, while the Left had given up dreams of radical change. "The United States and capitalism have won," judged one observer, "and in few areas of the globe is that victory so clear-cut, sweet, and spectacular as in Latin America."[3]

In reality that victory was less decisive than it often seemed. Democracy was no panacea for the region's problems, and neoliberal reforms could be quite painful for the poor. Social and political conflict persisted, casting doubt on the idea that Latin America's internal struggles had been conclusively resolved. Even for the United States, the apparent winner of Latin America's Cold War, the results were often unsatisfactory. Neoliberal reform was not without pernicious consequences for Washington, and democratic elections brought unexpected blowback. Appearances aside, there was ambivalence and ambiguity aplenty in the close of Latin America's Cold War.

In important respects, the sources of both democratization and neoliberalism boiled down to one word: debt. The Central American civil wars captivated many observers during the 1980s, but for the rest of the region, economic troubles took center stage. "External debt," IMF analysts commented in 1989, "has become a household word."[4]

The Latin American debt crisis is generally thought to have begun in 1982, but in certain countries it dated back to the mid-1970s. In Peru the debt crisis hit in 1975–1976 as the post-Velasco military government wrestled with its predecessor's economic legacy. Velasco had borrowed heavily to finance domestic projects and keep up with the rising price of oil. By the close of his presidency the Peruvian debt had quintupled and commercial banks had grown skittish of lending to Lima. The result was an economic crisis that severely depressed growth and would last through the 1980s and beyond.[5]

The Peruvian affair presaged the broader debt crisis that erupted in the early 1980s. As in Peru, this crisis had its immediate origins in the oil shocks of the previous decade. This "harsh test," as Brazilian officials called it, led nearly all Latin American governments to borrow furiously.[6] The importers did so to pay rising petroleum bills, head off crippling recessions, and finance politically popular—but financially unsustainable—social programs. The exporters did so in the belief that loans contracted now in order to foster industrialization and expand social spending (which in Mexico, for instance, went from 17.6 percent of GDP in the late 1960s to 48 percent in 1982) could easily be repaid with petro-profits later.[7] With borrowing fueled by the easy availability of funds from U.S. and European banks, the region's debt grew dramatically. It rose from $59 billion to $331 billion between 1975 and 1982, with much of this debt contracted via short-term notes with variable interest rates.[8]

This strategy of debt-led growth seemed workable in the short term. Annual growth in Latin America was nearly a full percentage point higher in the 1970s than it had been in the prior decade, and Brazil, one of the heaviest borrowers, maintained 7 percent annual growth from 1973 to 1979.[9] By the early 1980s, however, the swelling debt burden was causing inflation and depressing growth, which *fell* 3.6 percent regionwide between 1980 and 1982. The bottom dropped out entirely in 1982, when interest rates jumped, causing debt service payments to skyrocket. A simultaneous crash in oil prices meant that not even the high rollers were immune from the crunch that resulted. In August 1982 Mexico set off the debt crisis proper by announcing that it could no longer meet its obligations to foreign banks.[10]

The debt crisis would consume much of the 1980s and ultimately set the stage for sweeping economic liberalization. This move toward "neoliberalism," which in its simplest terms represented a return to the laissez-faire concepts discarded decades earlier in favor of Keynesianism, ISI, and other interventionist policies, had both internal and external sources.[11] Within Latin America, it reflected growing disillusion with inward-looking development strategies, particularly ISI. By the late twentieth century it had become clear that ISI was a thoroughly problematic economic model. By protecting domestic firms from foreign competition, ISI perpetuated inefficient business practices and conduced to the production of shabby, overpriced goods. Similarly, high trade barriers and an emphasis on domestic production discouraged the development of export-oriented industries. This latter outcome was particularly damaging because it led to recurring balance-of-payments problems and left Latin America poorly positioned to take advantage of the postwar liberalization of world commerce.[12]

The liabilities of ISI gave rise to an alliance of economists, politicians, and entrepreneurs that agitated for a new economic model. This group had its intellectual origins in the 1950s, when the Economics Department at Catholic University in Santiago established a partnership with its sister department at the University of Chicago. Over the next two decades, dozens of young Latin American economists—supported by grants from USAID and the Fulbright, Rockefeller, and Ford foundations—pursued graduate studies at Chicago,

Harvard, Columbia, and other U.S. universities. There they synthesized a critique of ISI with the monetarist doctrines expounded by Milton Friedman and the neoliberal ideas coming to prominence among top U.S. economists. Upon returning home, these "Chicago School" economists argued that it was not foreign exploitation, but rather the distortions promoted by excessive government intervention that were responsible for Latin American underdevelopment. Trade liberalization, privatization of government-owned industries, deep cuts in public spending, and a general opening of the regional economy would be necessary to reverse what one Chilean called a "half century of errors" and make Latin America prosperous.[13]

This movement found support from members of the political and business classes. Across Latin America, entrepreneurs increasingly concluded that while ISI benefited some privileged firms and industries, it injured the rest. Government control of banking, the extractive industries, and other profitable sectors limited opportunities for private profit. High tariffs, the need for licenses, and other restrictive arrangements discouraged firms from exploiting Latin America's low labor costs and profitably joining the export sector. Multiple exchange rates and restrictions on foreign investment impeded capital and currency flows. During the 1960s and after, important sectors of the business community mobilized in opposition to these arrangements. Entrepreneurs formed business associations dedicated to economic liberalization, and threw their support to political parties—such as the National Action Party (PAN) in Mexico and ARENA in El Salvador—that supported this program. They used television and other mass media to take their arguments to the public, and funded think tanks staffed by Chicago School economists. Intellectual currents, entrepreneurial sentiment, and political activism converged, forming a "New Right" in Latin America.[14]

Neoliberal doctrines influenced several military regimes during the 1960s and 1970s, but it was in Pinochet's Chile that the New Right really got a chance to turn criticism into policy. After two years of hesitation, Pinochet embraced the counsel of the "Chicago Boys" in 1975. The junta slashed import duties, lifted price controls, privatized industries and social services, aggressively courted FDI, and cut government spending. These measures were not without victims—civil servants whose jobs were eliminated, industrial workers whose factories now faced foreign competition, poor people who benefited from price controls and social programs—but they did drive down inflation, produce economic growth, and win the admiration of free-market devotees around the world.[15] Reagan termed Pinochet's economic program "amazing," a sentiment shared by George Shultz. "They stand on Adam Smith," he noted approvingly.[16]

Through the 1970s, though, Chile remained an outlier. For all its drawbacks, ISI retained substantial political currency. It appealed to *dependentistas* who viewed ISI as a way of shielding their countries from the inequities of world trade, as well as to "developmentalists" who argued for a strong state role in nurturing industry. It boasted the support of those industrial elites who had grown rich from their privileged access to the domestic market, as well as the blue-collar workers they employed. As a consequence, various forms of ISI became entrenched across Latin America, and while Pinochet was willing to make a clean break with this model, the majority of its practitioners were not. Even under authoritarian regimes, neoliberal reforms proceeded in fits and starts. Where there was not a single dominant personality to drive policy, or where authoritarian governments had to worry about transitions between one military leader and the next, the will to see a neoliberal program through to completion was often lacking. The Uruguayan and Argentine juntas allowed prices to rise, lowered tariffs, and restrained government spending, but in the face of growing public discontent, they eventually pulled back.[17] The Brazilian government embraced fiscal discipline and stimulated foreign investment after 1964, but maintained selectively high tariffs and a strong government role in industry. Transitions between presidents often saw a relaxation of austerity measures, and as the "Brazilian miracle" came under strain in the 1970s, the military government relied on interventionist policies to prevent a fall-off in growth.[18]

It took the shock of the debt crisis to displace ISI entirely. In one sense the debt crisis confirmed what the New Right had long been arguing—that the old economic model was broken beyond repair. It also opened the door to an alliance between the New Right and powerful foreign supporters of neoliberalism. For officials from the international financial institutions (IFIs) and the developed countries, particularly the United States, the debt crisis was both threat and opportunity. On the negative side, the crisis promised to depress exports to Latin America (U.S. sales to Mexico fell by 60 percent between late 1981 and early 1982) and raised the prospect that the debtors might default, thereby throwing the world financial system into chaos. Financial turmoil could also inflame social and political tensions in Latin America. One U.S. official who visited the region in 1983 reported "a generalized sense of despair and a wave of nationalistic, anti-American sentiment and, in some cases, violence."[19]

Yet the debt crisis also represented a decisive rupture, a chance to push Latin America down a more liberal economic path. This prospect was appealing for several reasons. Officials in Washington, whether they worked for Reagan, the IMF, or the World Bank, genuinely believed that neoliberal reform would be good for the region. In private as in public, these individuals averred that liberalizing trade, restraining spending, and privatizing industry were essential to providing macroeconomic stability and laying the foundation for growth. These measures had produced prosperity in Europe and the United States; why would they not do the same in Mexico and Uruguay? "The need for adjustment," remarked one high-ranking IMF official in 1980, "is simply a fact of life."[20]

The notion that the liberal model was universally applicable was nothing new in relations between Washington and the developing world, but this theme received a jolt of energy when Reagan took power in 1981. Reagan's presidency, which witnessed revitalized U.S. interventionism in Latin America, also saw resurgent certitude in the exportability of the American political and economic model. Carter's emphasis on human rights had already partially overthrown the post-modernization theory disinterest in democracy promotion displayed by Kissinger, and Reagan's election now brought political and economic proselytism back to the center of U.S. policy. Reagan's near-visceral aversion to "statist" economic policies and his dedication to free-market principles shone through in his rhetoric. "History has demonstrated that time and again, in place after place, economic growth and human progress make their greatest strides in countries that encourage economic freedom," he said in 1981. The "critical test is whether government is genuinely working to liberate individuals by creating incentives to work, invest, and succeed. Individual farmers, laborers, owners, and managers—they are the heart and soul of development. Trust them."[21] The strength of these beliefs, combined with the ideological assertiveness evident in Reagan's Central America policy, made the spread of free-market economics an essential theme of U.S. policy. "We apply the principles of economic freedom at home," Reagan said; "we should not export central planning and statist economics abroad." In appearances before international audiences, Reagan touted "the magic of the market," and argued that the developing countries would find success only if they emulated the U.S. example. There was only "one true path" to prosperity, Reagan intoned, and the Third World would do well to follow it.[22]

Reagan sincerely believed that economic reform would benefit Latin Americans, but his emphasis on this subject was hardly disinterested. As before, U.S. officials calculated that they could use Third-World debt problems to ensure that the world economic balance continued to favor Washington and the West. Sobered by the transfer of wealth caused by the oil shocks of the 1970s, the developed world reacted (as one World Bank executive recalled) by seeking to "draw up its wagons in a circle and to . . . keep the market economy intact."[23] The need to do so was all the more pressing given the recent liberation of capital and currency flows, which opened new frontiers for major First-World firms. Given the proper investment climate, these enterprises could now more easily relocate their productive facilities to Third-World countries, exploiting low labor costs to achieve considerable economies. The Reagan administration thus resolved to adhere to the model established after the 1973–1974 oil crisis, making debt relief contingent on greater receptivity to foreign goods and investment. Washington would thereby defeat the upsurge of Third-World economic nationalism, facilitate the advances of transnational enterprises, and deepen the liberal economic order. "The debt," Reagan administration officials wrote candidly, "can and should be used as leverage."[24]

For the World Bank and the IMF, too, the prospects of overhauling Latin America's economies carried powerful incentives. The fact that these banks moved with such alacrity into Third-World debt relief reflected not just the preferences of their major capital subscribers, but also the imperatives of institutional aggrandizement.[25] The IMF saw its influence and budgets grow considerably after it became a player in Third-World debt relief during the 1970s, and the World Bank looked to keep pace with its own "structural adjustment" programs. While some officials argued that the World Bank, whose original mission had been to rebuild postwar Europe, should proceed cautiously in entering this few field, the prospect of being left behind by its sister institution led Bank higher-ups to push ahead rapidly. The World Bank plunged into the debt crisis, setting the goal of expanding Bank lending by 150 percent.[26]

During the 1980s the IMF, the World Bank, and commercial banks in the United States, Europe, and Japan established a basic model for debt relief. The IFIs would provide stabilization packages to countries in distress and broker new loans from commercial banks. (The commercial banks, already risking the loss of billions on bad loans, were unenthusiastic about this scheme, but the IMF and World Bank forced their hand by refusing to lend without commercial bank support. Because a failure to provide external financing to Latin America would likely lead to default—and the collapse of the commercial banks in question—they had little choice but to go along with the plan.) These countries, in return, would commit to implementing far-reaching economic reforms, upon which full delivery of foreign funds would be contingent. For its part, the United States would use its diplomatic and economic influence to encourage Latin American countries to hold to these pacts, and would help the tenets of the New Right take root by sponsoring organizations, such as the Salvadoran Foundation for Economic and Social Development (FUSADES), that would serve as incubators of neoliberal concepts. The United States, the IFIs, and the commercial banks would thereby ease Latin America's debt burden while pushing it toward greater economic liberalism.[27]

World Bank and especially IMF agreements proliferated across Latin America during the 1980s, symbolized by a $4 billion IMF loan to Mexico in late 1982 that was accompanied by a promise of $5 billion in commercial lending. For much of the decade, though, these programs produced disappointing results. New lending helped Latin American countries avoid default, but accomplished little else. Most of the money that flowed into the region simply flowed back out as debt service. Regional debt continued to increase, and by the close of the 1980s, debt service payments were more than three times export earnings in Latin America.[28] The fact that the region was still hemorrhaging cash provoked considerable anger at the IFI lending model. The governments of Brazil, Colombia, Argentina, and Mexico complained that they were facing "forced insolvency," and demanded greater relief. A plan promulgated by U.S. treasury secretary James Baker failed to alleviate these concerns, and in 1985, Peru again raised the specter of default by serving notice that it would pay no more than what it could afford.[29]

Such sentiments figured in an attempt by various Latin American countries to bolster their bargaining position vis-à-vis the multilateral banks by banding together into a regional bloc. "It is neither just nor rational that the countries of the region have been converted into net exporters of capital," read a multilateral declaration issued from Quito in 1984. Latin American statesmen insistently called for "regional unity" as the "essential requirement of our development," and sought to coordinate support in the Organization of American States and the Non-Aligned Movement.[30] Eager to steal a march on the United States, Castro got into the act, holding a debtors' conference in Havana. In Washington U.S. officials worried about the "de facto or de jure formation of a debtor cartel" that might seriously impinge on Western leverage in dealing with the debt crisis.[31]

In practice, however, regional and Third-World unity were elusive. By the 1980s the NAM had become so fractious as to dissipate any leverage it might otherwise have wielded. Castro's efforts to take charge of the movement in the late 1970s and early 1980s alienated conservative members, exacerbated ideological disputes, and led, Mexican diplomats reported, to "an evident weakening of the movement." Within Latin America, solidarity was mostly rhetorical. Countries led by anticommunist presidents were loath to cooperate with Castro or Ortega, the larger nations resented being lumped together with the smaller ones, and the possibilities for a broad debtors' front faded.[32]

Even so, most Latin American policymakers hesitated to give neoliberalism their full endorsement. While they largely conceded that liberalization and austerity were necessary ("we all want free-trade policies," wrote one official; "we all agree that our private sectors must be strengthened and encouraged"), they blanched at the implications.[33] Ratcheting back public spending and opening industries to foreign competition would depress growth and hurt employment, while liberating prices would drive up the cost of food and other essential goods. The short-term consequence would be economic hardship for large sectors of society—and political hardship for their leaders. World Bank officials conceded that neoliberal reforms entailed "very painful adjustment measures," an evaluation confirmed when massive protests rocked Peru after the junta tried to impose an IMF stabilization program in the late 1970s.[34]

This threat of upheaval caused Latin American leaders to think twice before enacting their own reforms. During the Mexican financial crisis of 1976 López Portillo commented that the IMF was giving "the correct advice," but that heeding that counsel would lead to "political difficulties." During the early 1980s few statesmen would have disagreed.[35] "The traditional IMF medicine simply will not wash in Mexico," Mexican officials argued. "We have to keep growing to solve our chronic unemployment." "The effort to adjust our economies is necessary," agreed Mexican foreign secretary Bernardo Sepúlveda Amor, "but its social cost cannot be ignored."[36]

These concerns produced a stop-and-go approach to liberalization. Nearly all Latin American governments implemented at least some of the measures recommended by the IMF, such as devaluing their currency, lowering trade barriers, and reducing spending. Yet in few cases did they follow this approach comprehensively. Some governments, like Venezuela's, delayed or canceled the most controversial aspects of stabilization, leaving the truly wrenching decisions to the next government. Others, namely Brazil, Peru, Argentina, and Mexico, sought to square the circle by launching "heterodox" plans that contained certain liberal reforms but also left price controls in place, avoided wholesale privatization, and maintained deficit spending.[37] The move toward economic liberalism entailed potentially severe social and political costs, and Latin American governments avoided paying this price as long as they could.

Alternatives to the liberal model were fast disappearing, though. After often-promising starts, the heterodox programs ended in disaster. They were recessionary enough to depress employment and growth, which across Latin America fell by 1.6 percent between 1980 and 1986. While price controls did keep inflation under wraps, the eventual lifting of these restraints combined with the inflationary effects of persistent government deficits to send prices to astronomical levels. In 1988 inflation for the region averaged nearly 300 percent, and at various points the number exceeded 1,000 percent in Argentina, Brazil, and elsewhere.[38] The heterodox programs produced the worst of both worlds—stagnation and hyperinflation—and made economic conditions even more precarious.

Latin American officials eventually accepted that drastic reforms were unavoidable. The pill was sweetened by the Brady Plan (named after Bush's treasury secretary, Nicholas Brady), which for the first time promised actual debt amortization (rather than simply providing new loans) in return for "major structural changes."[39] Across the region, politicians that had recently condemned IMF programs now endorsed them as the only solution to hyperinflation and economic ruin. In Brazil the government proclaimed a far-reaching *abertura comercial,* slashing tariffs and working toward the creation of the Common Market of the South (Mercosul) with Uruguay, Paraguay, and Argentina. The Peruvian government of Alberto Fujimori undertook a radical austerity program, as did its Bolivian counterpart. President Armando Calderón of El Salvador declared that he wanted to turn his country into "one big free zone."[40]

The tide crested in Mexico and Argentina, where newly elected presidents broke with their parties' traditional economic platforms and undertook far-reaching reforms. Carlos Menem of Argentina harshly criticized the IMF while running for president; once in office, he pledged to pursue "carnal" relations with the United States and sold off more than 300 state-owned companies. There would be no tolerance, his government announced, for "activities that limit the decisiveness of economic agents at any step of the productive process"[41] Carlos Salinas of Mexico did likewise, privatizing hundreds of state-owned enterprises, opening new paths for foreign investment, and declaring that government spending must fall dramatically. "A larger state is neither a more effective nor a more just state," he said.[42] In the early 1990s Salinas negotiated the North American Free Trade Agreement (NAFTA) with Canada and the United States. By 1991 Brady could declare that Latin America was undergoing a "revolution," as "a whole new generation of leaders spells out their hopes for economic reform."[43] ISI was dead; the New Right and neoliberalism were ascendant.

Yet to what extent were this revolution, and the series of events that produced it, good for Latin Americans? From a macroeconomic standpoint, the consequences of the neoliberal turn were, in most cases, beneficial. Trade increased, deficits and debt fell, and foreign investment spiked. Inflation tumbled to a manageable 14 percent. The region averaged 3.5 percent growth during the 1990s, the highest rate in decades. Chile's mark of 6.7 percent placed it among the world's leaders, and in 1993, more than 90 percent of Chilean voters cast their ballots for parties that favored continuing the neoliberal model.[44]

These improvements came at a price, though. The investment that poured into Latin America was predominantly of the highly mobile and speculative type known as portfolio investment, rather than more stable direct investment. The fact that portfolio investments could easily be withdrawn from a country tended to exacerbate the severity and impact of financial crises, as demonstrated in Mexico in 1994–1995 and in Argentina at the turn of the millennium.[45]

When one zoomed in from the macro to the micro, the balance sheet became still less favorable. The negative growth and inflation caused by the debt crisis took a severe human toll, especially on the poor. Unemployment rose dramatically. In Mexico the potential labor force grew by 2 million between 1981 and 1984, while not a single new job was created.[46] Even those who could find work saw their purchasing power fall sharply. The real minimum wage dropped by 31.3 percent in Mexico, forcing millions of workers into dire economic straits. Rising food costs posed a growing burden for the impoverished. In Peru poor households were now forced to spend 70 percent of their income on this category of goods.[47] Across the region, recession and inflation left many people struggling to survive. For the poor, the World Bank acknowledged, "the 1980s was a lost decade."[48]

Stabilization programs eventually brightened the macroeconomic picture, but the poor again bore the brunt of the accompanying difficulties. The policies promoted by the IFIs and the United States suffered from the same flaw as the plans dreamed up by the modernization theorists twenty years earlier. In the 1960s World Bank president Eugene Black had been skeptical of the grandiose aims of the Alliance for Progress. "It takes time to understand a country," he said. "You can't just run out and set up a plan, set up a program . . . You just can't whip up these plans overnight." Black was right, but twenty years later the IFIs made much the same mistake, implementing policies that drew on an abstract, supposedly universal model of growth rather than a sophisticated understanding of local circumstances. The Bank's management, one employee later recalled, acted as though "it knows all the answers" and "it's never wrong." In the highly oligarchic context of Latin America, neoliberal policies had immensely unbalanced effects. They often benefited entrepreneurs and the rich, allowing them to scoop up privatized industries at bargain prices. The rich got richer, and income inequality increased. Neoliberal reforms, one U.S. diplomat later acknowledged, were "fixed for the people on top."[49]

For the poor, there was much less to celebrate. Eliminating government social programs hurt mainly the impoverished, while opening Latin American economies forced down wages and employment. Unleashing market forces ultimately helped curb inflation, but in the short term it pushed up the cost of food and other essentials. The human costs of adjustment were exposed in the early 1990s, when a cholera outbreak in Peru—caused in no small part by the fact that many Peruvians could not afford cooking oil or heat to boil their water—claimed around 2,000 lives. The traumas caused by adjustment programs were acknowledged even by their sponsors. "When structural adjustment issues came to the fore," World Bank officials wrote, "little attention was paid to the effects on the poor." On his way to ink a deal with the IMF in 1990, Fujimori put it more starkly. "If the economic shock were to work," he said, "the Peruvian people would no doubt forgive me."[50]

These social dislocations led some Latin American officials to fear a resurgence of revolutionary upheaval. "The way things are going," wrote Brazilian official João Leitão de Abreu, "there will be a convulsion that threatens the entire social and political structure." For the most part, the revolutionary threat did not materialize. Latin Americans fell back on mutual aid strategies and the informal economy, sent children and women into the work force, and managed to survive.[51]

Yet the economic crisis was not without deeply disruptive ramifications. In the Andes, increasingly severe rural poverty led *campesinos* to become more involved in the commercial cultivation of coca. Added to rising demand for cocaine in the United States and Europe, this shift led to an explosion of drug exports from Latin America—and in countries like Colombia, an equivalent surge in drug-related violence. In Central America and Mexico, falling wages and limited economic opportunity caused a spike in undocumented migration to the United States.[52]

The effects could be even more jarring. Anger at economic reforms provoked massive rioting in Venezuela in February-March 1989, and clashes between the protestors and the security forces caused hundreds of deaths. The deteriorating plight of Peruvian peasants informed the growth, if not the origins, of the brutal Shining Path insurgency that ravaged the country into the early 1990s. The Zapatista rebels in southern Mexico termed NAFTA "a death sentence for the Indians," and on January 1, 1994—the day that the trade agreement took effect—they rose in revolt. Finally, resentment at neoliberal reform would soon be translated into support for politicians, such as Venezuela's Hugo Chávez, Bolivia's Evo Morales, and even a resurrected Daniel Ortega, who railed against the new order. Capitalism was not the answer to Latin America's ills, Morales charged, but rather "the worst enemy of humanity." With economic security still elusive for many Latin Americans, the social and political conflicts that had so long afflicted the region continued.[53]

The economic shocks of the 1980s were also central to the second great departure in regional affairs—the return to electoral democracy. Nearly all of the authoritarian regimes that seized power during the 1960s and 1970s did so amid economic crises, and they subsequently made restoring economic stability no less a priority than restoring political stability. Their success in doing so varied considerably, but in some cases the generals did achieve growth over a period of several years or more. Uruguay's economy grew for the first time in twenty years between the 1973 coup and the late 1970s. In Brazil GDP rose at more than 10 percent annually between 1967 and 1973 and roughly 7 percent per annum in the six years after that. Chile's performance, though marred by high unemployment during the 1970s and a sharp setback in 1982–1983, was strong enough for the economic model established by Pinochet to be embraced by the democratic governments that succeeded him.[54]

Even when implemented successfully, though, economic policy was a mine-field for the juntas. On the one hand, economic growth provided the regimes in Chile, Brazil, and elsewhere with a source of domestic legitimacy. On the other hand, the economic policies employed by authoritarian governments eventually produced political problems for the generals. Restricting credit helped curb inflation, but it hurt business owners who could not get loans to finance their operations. Reducing tariffs facilitated trade, but that annoyed inward-looking industrialists and other producers who were not keen on fac-ing stiffer foreign competition. The attempts of many military governments to maintain a degree of control over the economy—whether by colonizing its most profitable sectors, as in Central America; imposing a web of regulations on business activity, as in Brazil; or privileging state-run industries at the ex-pense of the private sector, as occurred in numerous countries—produced ris-ing entrepreneurial discontent. By the late 1970s the Argentine, Uruguayan, and Brazilian regimes confronted growing opposition from groups such as businessmen, industrialists, and agricultural producers—just those sectors that might have been expected to appreciate the political tranquility and economic stability provided by the juntas.[55]

More damaging still was the fact that economic growth gradually led to the expansion of the middle class. As usual, these individuals grew restive in a system in which their economic success brought them few political rights. Throughout South America, lawyers, businessmen, and white-collar workers eventually emerged at the head of coalitions demanding political change.[56]

The Brazilian case demonstrates how these tensions helped produce initial moves toward democratization. After Ernesto Geisel donned the president's sash in 1974, he initiated a gradual political opening. The guerrillas had been defeated and the Left thoroughly defanged, he argued, making the regime's intense preoccupation with subversion unnecessary. Confronted with rising dissent from middle-class groups, the business community, and human rights activists, Geisel looked toward "a greater normalization for the political life of the country."[57] Brazil must reconcile its system of government with the social and political changes wrought by recent growth. "We can think of ourselves as being a developed country and we can also think of ourselves as being, re-ally, a democracy that stands the test of time," he said.[58] Geisel allowed rela-tively free elections, permitted labor unions and other groups more room to organize, and repealed the most restrictive of the Institutional Acts passed by the hard-liners following the 1964 coup. He sought to decrease external tensions by moderating Brazilian foreign policy and getting away from Médici's inter-ventionism.[59] The government must maintain a "climate of order, peace, and stability," but should simultaneously build legitimate political institutions and reduce the strains that threatened to derail economic development. Geisel's philosophy, he told his ministers, was "the maximum possible development, with the minimum essential security."[60]

If economic success was problematic for the military, economic failure was far worse. The debt crisis had momentous consequences for the authoritarians. Of the juntas in Brazil and the Southern Cone, only Chile's survived the immediate fallout from that event. The fact that the generals had chosen such a disastrous economic path, and that in doing so they had inflicted such pain on the population, destroyed one of the major points of esteem long enjoyed by Latin American militaries—the perception that they were more competent than the politicians. "People thought that when you have big problem in society it was better to give it to the military because they were so clever and so intelligent," said one Argentine of public perceptions during the 1960s and 1970s.[61]

The debt crisis shattered this image of professionalism and stability. In Chile deteriorating living conditions provoked mass protests in the slums of Santiago and intense anger from a middle class that saw its recent gains evaporate. The Pinochet regime faced its greatest challenge since 1973, with crowds in the streets chanting, "He's going to fall!"[62] In response the government lashed out in ways that only compounded its problems. Pinochet, predisposed to see any sort of antigovernment activism as subversion, launched brutal military sweeps of the slums, outraging much of Chilean society. Amid the "worst economic slump since the depression of the early 1930s," U.S. officials reported, "Chilean opposition to the Pinochet regime has increased sharply."[63]

As usual, the Argentine junta outdid its Chilean counterpart. Economic hardship catalyzed resurgent labor activism in Argentina during the late 1970s and early 1980s, manifest chiefly in a general strike in 1979 and massive anti-regime demonstrations in March 1982. Desperate to regain political momentum, the generals launched an ill-advised invasion of the Falkland Islands, a British possession. Argentine leaders believed that the Monroe Doctrine and their aid to the United States in Central America would convince Reagan to stay London's hand, but Washington came down firmly on the side of its NATO ally. A British task force routed the Argentines in the war that resulted, showing the junta to be incompetent militarily as well as economically.[64]

This pattern held true across Latin America, as the measures that authoritarian governments took to deal with the debt crisis simply undermined their positions further. IMF stabilization programs, while often undertaken hesitantly by governments afraid of provoking public outrage, still led to increased unrest. Peruvian labor unions reacted strongly to wage and spending cuts in 1977–1978, staging protests so severe as to force a retreat from the stabilization program and cause the military eventually to return to the barracks.[65]

Mexico's various bouts of stabilization between 1976 and the late 1980s produced similar results. *Campesinos* and other groups protested cuts in social spending made by López Portillo from 1976 to 1978 while trade unionists argued that austerity programs and rising prices left them unable to afford food and other necessities.[66] The student movement, reenergized by this dissatisfaction, issued harsh critiques of the government. López Portillo's adjustment plan, announced one group, was another attempt "to increase the exploitation of the working classes."[67] During the 1980s more intensive stabilization efforts produced road blockages, land invasions, and in some cases, violence. One group announced that they would cease paying their taxes, "with the end of suffocating" the local PRI government.[68]

By the end of the 1980s PRI supremacy was under strain. The protests of 1976–1977 and their role in revitalizing the Mexican student movement convinced the PRI to institute a political reform in the late 1970s. Only by broadening political participation, announced Mexican officials, "will the social tensions be driven out."[69] In the 1980s the anger provoked by economic crisis and adjustment led political sentiment to gravitate toward organizations like the PAN and the Party of the Democratic Revolution (PRD). The PRI, in turn, was forced to become more coercive in limiting the electoral successes of these challengers. The government, fearing "even a partial vote of no-confidence," used blatant fraud and intimidation to prevent the PAN from racking up victories in local and regional elections in 1984 and 1986. "Several popular PAN figures suddenly found that unforeseen legal or personal circumstances prevented them from standing as candidates," U.S. officials reported.[70] These tactics helped keep the PAN in check, but also produced protests that U.S. intelligence analysts termed "the most energetic challenge to the ruling PRI in many years."[71] In 1988 a strong PRD showing in the presidential polls caused the PRI to panic and perpetrate even grosser electoral manipulation. The PRI remained in power, but its hold had become tenuous. "The PRI will not be able . . . to reconstitute itself as it existed in the past," U.S. officials correctly predicted. Neoliberal reforms would continue to destabilize the Mexican political system in the 1990s, and were central to the PRI's eventual eviction from power in 2000.[72]

In many instances the political consequences of economic reform promised to be so traumatic that military governments left the toughest decisions to the civilians that eventually followed them in power. This being the case, why did these new, untested democracies survive an experience that entrenched military regimes could not? For the most part, this was because the debt crisis and the pains that followed were not widely seen to be the civilians' fault. In most cases—Peru, Argentina, Uruguay, Brazil, Chile, Bolivia, and elsewhere—the onset of intense economic difficulties preceded the transition to democratic rule, ensuring that most of the blame fell at the generals' feet. Accordingly, while citizens of these countries showed little patience with particular political parties that failed to bring about better conditions, they demonstrated greater forbearance with respect to the democratic system as a whole.[73]

In certain respects, the debt crisis and the dire need for solutions actually strengthened democratic governance. The tendency of unpopular military regimes to punt on taking decisive economic action led some commentators to conclude that only a government with democratic legitimacy could make the bold moves required to rein in inflation and instability. "The dark clouds accumulating on the horizon . . . will only be dissipated with an authentic and democratic government," one Brazilian business publication opined.[74]

Once implemented, moreover, neoliberal reforms helped discourage conservative authoritarianism from making a comeback. Macroeconomic stability continued to go wanting in some countries during the 1990s, but in most cases inflation fell and the economy no longer seemed to teeter on the brink. The establishment of this equilibrium removed what had traditionally been a chief stimulant to *golpismo* in Latin America, depriving the generals of the dramatic circumstances that they had long exploited to seize power. Similarly, the fact that many entrepreneurs benefited handsomely from the reforms showed that democracy could be good for business, and reduced the possibility that economic elites might support resurgent authoritarianism. Conservative businessmen gave up "the right to rule for the right to make money," and another traditional stimulant to *golpismo* faded in consequence.[75]

If the debt crisis and the neoliberal turn had pernicious consequences for broad swaths of Latin America, there was a silver lining. These same events discredited the military regimes, promoted democratization, and helped bring down the curtain on the radical authoritarianism that had long been such a central aspect of Latin America's Cold War.

Economic trends were not alone in pushing Latin America toward democratization. Political, social, and diplomatic dynamics figured as well. One influence of particular importance was the relationship between the military regimes and the radical Left. This relationship took different forms across the region, but from Guatemala to Argentina, it played a key role in forcing authoritarian retrenchment.

In Central America it was the strength of the radical Left that propelled this change. In El Salvador and Guatemala the need to isolate strong guerrilla movements led the military to back a closely supervised return to constitutionality. Democracy, U.S. officials commented, was "a bulwark against the Cubans and Nicaraguans." Fearing that a continuation of naked military rule would polarize political opinion and force the moderates to side with the guerrillas, the Central American officers allowed democratic practices to take root even as they worked assiduously to limit the effects this transition would have on the socioeconomic balance.[76]

In South America, by contrast, it was more often the weakness of the Left that undermined dictatorial rule. From the 1960s onward, the radical military regimes inflicted severe blows on the guerrillas and the Left in general. The Tupamaros, MIR, ERP, and other insurgent groups were virtually decimated. The Montoneros had been all but "eliminated," bragged one Argentine officer; they could detonate "a bomb or two" but posed no real threat to the state.[77]

This repression not only crippled the guerrilla movements, but also led to a broader taming of the Left. Marginalized, brutalized, and in some cases nearly exterminated, activists on the Left simply lost the militancy—whether violent or nonviolent—that had inspired them in years prior. Chastened by their earlier errors—and the heavy price paid for them—leftist groups across the continent now called not for revolution but for a return to even a limited and conservative form of democracy. "Experience with dictatorship has made liberation theologians appreciate political rights," noted Gustavo Gutiérrez.[78] Those groups that did pursue a violent strategy, such as Chile's Communist Party and Manuel Rodríguez Patriotic Front (FPMR), found themselves comparatively isolated as the 1980s went on. After years of violence and defeat, the Left was scaling back its goals.[79]

Military leaders counted the emasculation of the Left as their greatest accomplishment. "This is a war and we are the winners," boasted Roberto Viola of Argentina.[80] In reality this development set the stage for the authoritarians' demise. The destruction of the Left robbed these governments of their reason for being. The juntas had come to power at times of intense internal turmoil, and in many cases their initial efforts to restore order enjoyed substantial popular support. But once the chaos subsided, these governments—which, as U.S. officials pointed out, were born "in battle against the extreme left"— faced the daunting question of what to do next.[81] Few military officials were eager to return to normality or hand power back to the civilians. They held that eliminating the radical Left was only the first step toward protecting their countries from "subversive communism," and feared what such a transition might mean for those with blood on their hands. "Some of those most deeply involved in the 'dirty war' are terribly frightened that . . . they are being moved closer to the time when they must account for their acts and suffer retribution," reported one Argentine official. "On the other hand, if the 'dirty war' can be kept going they are protected—and . . . in some cases doing what they like best."[82]

The Southern Cone dictatorships, and especially that of Argentina, followed this latter strategy, purporting to see an existential threat from the Left well after that threat had been eliminated. Although murders, disappearances, and other abuses decreased sharply after the initial phase of the "dirty war," these practices continued through the early 1980s. "The continued tactic of murdering Montoneros without due process is no longer necessary from a security point of view," U.S. officials reported, but persisted nonetheless.[83] Detainees that had been tortured were executed even if found innocent, one Argentine officer said, "lest their release constitute a risk for 'the system.'"[84] Such practices were not unique to Argentina. In Brazil hard-liners in the intelligence services warned that the radical Left would exploit Geisel's *abertura* to mobilize against the regime.[85] Long after any serious subversive challenge had been defeated, the Army Intelligence Center warned that dissident groups were planning "the institution of a socialist regime, in preparation for a communist dictatorship."[86] In hopes of derailing the *abertura*, the hard-liners staged car bombings and other incidents meant to revive fear of the violent Left.[87]

These tactics backfired. Though many South Americans had been willing to accept blood as the price of internal stability, they found the persistence of political murder following the virtual evisceration of the Left distasteful. There had always been resistance to the human rights violations perpetrated in these countries, mainly on the part of the Catholic Church in Chile and advocacy organizations in Uruguay and Argentina. As the abuses continued without any apparent justification, these protests gained a wider audience. In Argentina groups like the Mothers of the Plaza de Mayo, which demonstrated weekly on behalf of their disappeared children, became a symbol of resistance to military abuses. Political parties and lawyers' associations registered their disapproval by ceasing to cooperate with the government.[88] In Brazil extrajudicial killings drew strong rebukes from religious and student groups as early as the mid-1970s, and these protests subsequently mounted in intensity. "Only God owns life," declared one Brazilian priest in response to the government-sanctioned murder of a student activist. "He is its origin, and only He can decide its end."[89] In Uruguay the political parties—which, while harassed and marginalized, had largely escaped the fury of the military offensive after the coup—reemerged as centers of popular activism in the early 1980s. In Chile, too, groups that had initially supported Pinochet's takeover, including moderate parties and lawyers' guilds, now denounced the brutality of the regime. This resistance usually took the form of restrained, patient opposition rather than massive civil disobedience—the tumult of earlier periods remained a not-so-distant memory—but the rise in discontent was unmistakable.[90]

More broadly, decreasing leftist radicalism left the military with a narrowed political base. The threat of the Left—whether elected, as in Allende's case, or violent, as with the urban guerrillas—had initially led the Right and much of the Center to support the *golpistas*. Amid the tumult of the 1960s and 1970s, these groups sacrificed certain political rights in return for a guarantee that the Left would be kept in check. With the Left clearly in decline, this pact no longer seemed such a bargain. The fact that much of the Left had concluded, as Brazilian industrialists believed, "that radicalism was a self-destructive path," greatly decreased the risks that democratization posed for the Center and the Right.[91] These groups now agitated for the freedoms that they had surrendered to the juntas. Pinochet confronted dissent from a "broadly based, moderate coalition" by the early 1980s, U.S. officials reported, and the situation throughout the Southern Cone was much the same.[92]

The South American militaries won their Third World War, but in doing so they lost their political legitimacy. The rise of the radical Left had helped bring these regimes to power; its destruction now pushed them toward a fall.

The isolation of the military regimes also had a diplomatic component. Beginning in the late 1970s, and more so in the 1980s, the dictators encountered growing pressure from abroad. The worldwide human rights movement that emerged in the 1970s led organizations like the OAS to become increasingly active in cataloguing abuses, criticizing oppressors, and ultimately in monitoring elections and promoting democracy. The UN Commission on Human Rights played a similar role in ostracizing tyrants, and as the European Economic Community (EEC) developed a foreign policy voice, it too supported dissidents and funded human rights campaigns.[93]

In the main, though, foreign support for democratization revolved around the policies of specific states. The Soviet Union and Cuba, which had earlier backed guerrilla movements in Central America, resolved in the late 1980s to support the Esquipulas process and the democratic reforms it entailed as a way of extricating themselves from that morass. For very different reasons, Raúl Alfonsín of Argentina adopted a vigorously pro-democracy stance after taking power in 1983. Argentina was "surrounded by countries in which possibilities of democratization were either remote or very fragile," recalled one official. "We were besieged, and we did not like it as this situation could encourage sectors within our own population that had no respect for democracy." To remove this danger, Alfonsín pressured the Stroessner regime to liberalize, as did Brazil once that country returned to civilian rule in 1985.[94]

The United States was even more active in promoting democratization. This process had begun anew under Jimmy Carter, who revived the reformist thrust that had lain dormant since the early 1960s. Carter had less success than he had hoped in convincing the hemisphere's worst offenders to mend their ways, but his policy was not an utter failure. Carter helped secure a democratic transition in the Dominican Republic in 1978, and the administration used U.S. economic leverage to reinforce the return to civilian rule in Peru. Additionally, while U.S. policy had little direct impact on the situation in the Southern Cone, Carter's efforts did lend encouragement to antidictatorial activists in that area. The administration funded human rights advocacy groups in Argentina and Brazil, and years later, Uruguay's first post-junta president, Julio María Sanguinetti, would praise Carter's stance. "In those dark years of dictatorship, those of us in the opposition had to struggle practically in the dark," he recalled. "One of the few significant sources of support we had was the policy of the U.S. government, which was constantly looking for human-rights violations."[95]

Reagan's stark Cold War rhetoric made it seem unlikely that he would maintain Carter's emphasis on democracy. "We cannot play innocents abroad in a world that's not innocent," Reagan intoned, and Cold War practicality seemed poised to displace Carter's post–Cold War humanitarianism.[96] Reagan's anticommunism led him to back brutal counterinsurgencies in Central America and to attack an FSLN government that, while ideologically authoritarian, was in practice more inclusive than many U.S. allies. In 1981, moreover, Reagan dispatched confidants like Jeanne Kirkpatrick and Vernon Walters to South America to repair relations with the military regimes. Chilean diplomats were pleased with what these visits seemed to augur. "Ambassador Kirkpatrick's thinking with respect to world problems . . . broadly agrees with our government's approaches," they wrote.[97]

From 1982–1983 onward, however, the Reagan and Bush administrations took up the mantle of democracy promotion even more forcefully than Carter. In some cases this policy had less to do with democracy writ large than with knocking off a specific regime. The Bolivian junta's involvement in narcotics trafficking drove Reagan's support for democratization in that country, and in Nicaragua, U.S. calls for elections were really a means of undermining the Sandinistas.[98] "If the Sandinistas are serious" about democratizing, said Reagan, "the battle is won."[99] This tendency found a more dramatic illustration when the Bush administration invaded Panama in December 1989. If this intervention had the consequence of restoring democracy to Panama, its chief motive was to depose Manuel Noriega, a former CIA asset who had become involved in drug trafficking and whose flagrant flouting of U.S. power seemed to call Washington's overall credibility into question. The need to reaffirm, as Chairman of the Joint Chiefs of Staff Colin Powell said, that the "superpower lives here," was the deciding factor in the overthrow of Noriega.[100]

Yet there were also several broader concerns underlying Reagan's solicitude for democracy. The first had to do with the diplomacy surrounding his efforts to unseat the FSLN. Administration officials realized that if Reagan's calls for the Sandinistas to liberalize were to have any credibility with the Contadora and Esquipulas countries, Washington would have to hold itself to the same standard in dealing with U.S. allies. "To get more help from the Contadora countries regarding the need for democracy in Nicaragua," aide Jacquelline Tillman explained in 1986, "we had to be more visible about Chile."[101]

Second, like Carter, Reagan harkened back to the original spirit of the Alliance for Progress in believing that undemocratic systems fostered leftist radicalism. The United States would "stop the advance of communism," Reagan told several congressmen, "by doing what Americans instinctively do best—supporting democracy." This was the case not only in insurgency-plagued El Salvador, but also in seemingly more stable countries like Chile. Here and elsewhere, the extreme Left was weak, but if mainstream Latin Americans concluded that the authoritarians would never leave, that debility might not last long. "If Pinochet stays," wrote Elliot Abrams, "tensions will increase, strengthening the far left . . . and endangering long-term U.S. interests."[102]

Third, Reagan believed that democratization and economic liberalization were two sides of the same coin. There was a "vital nexus between economic and political freedom," he said. "These democratic and free-market revolutions are really the same revolution." Democracy and free markets represented the liberty of the individual against the encroachments of the state, Reagan believed, and neither economic nor political freedom could long survive in isolation from the other. Accordingly, by promoting political reform, the United States would reinforce Latin America's neoliberal turn as well.[103]

This belief in the inextricable links between economic and political freedom touched on a fourth factor, which was Reagan's deep ideological commitment to democracy. Reagan was hardly a liberal, but he was a dedicated Wilsonian. For Reagan, democracy represented the highest form of political and social organization and the universal aspiration of mankind. People everywhere, he believed, wanted what the United States had. "This is not cultural imperialism," he declared.

> It is providing the means for genuine self-determination and protection for diversity. It would be cultural condescension, or worse, to say that any people prefer dictatorship to democracy. Who would voluntarily choose not to have the right to vote, decide to purchase government propaganda handouts instead of independent newspapers, prefer government to worker-controlled unions, opt for land to be owned by the state instead of those who till it, want government repression of religious liberty, a single political party instead of free choice, a rigid cultural orthodoxy instead of democratic tolerance and diversity?[104]

Combined with the economic and political arguments in favor of democratization, Reagan's ideological attachment to the idea ensured its centrality to U.S. diplomacy. "The cornerstone of our policy in Latin America is support for democracy," administration officials wrote in 1985.[105]

Support for democracy did not prevent Reagan from supporting the Salvadoran army, nor did he make much effort to ensure that economic and social equality accompanied elections in Latin America. Anticommunism, an aversion to social engineering, and a rather simplistic view of what constituted democracy led Reagan to conclude, as Thomas Carothers writes, that "any country with an elected government was a democracy, no matter how undemocratic the government was in practice, or how much it was curtailed by other power sectors within the society."[106] Confronted with a "Communist dictatorship seeking to expand," Reagan explained, the United States would not shun "the imperfect democracy seeking to improve." The democracy that Reagan favored, in other words, was often shallow, sometimes repressive, and above all anticommunist.[107]

The U.S. role in democratization varied by country, and in many cases Washington played little or no part in the reversion to civilian rule. In Brazil and Uruguay the transition was already underway by the time Reagan came to power. In Guatemala the Reagan administration lent strong verbal support to the democratic opening but had scant influence in causing or steering this process.[108] U.S. support for democratization in Argentina was important only in a negative sense, as Reagan's decision to back Great Britain in the Falklands War (which led the Argentine generals to complain that they had been "stabbed in the back") ensured that the high command would embarrass itself so thoroughly as to make a retreat from power unavoidable.[109]

Washington was more proactive in other episodes. Reagan declined to take military action to force Noriega out of office in 1988, but Bush did so a year later. In Bolivia the United States forcefully pushed the junta to hold elections, and in Peru the U.S. ambassador sternly warned the armed forces not to mount a coup in early 1989. The administration also used institutions like the Inter-American Defense College to advocate a new political role for Latin American officers. "Your generation must be a generation of pioneers," Abrams told the graduating class at the Inter-American Defense College in 1986. "You are now the guardians of the new democracies. Your highest calling must be—not to replace failed regimes—but to protect successful democracies."[110]

Along the Central American isthmus, U.S. policy took on similar tones. As discussed previously, Reagan used U.S. military assistance as leverage to push the Salvadoran government to liberalize. Washington strongly supported democratic governance in Honduras, threatening to terminate military aid to that country if the generals staged a coup. Pro-democracy activists credited this stance with helping stave off a military resurgence. "The threat of a coup d'etat is a latent condition in our country," commented a group of Honduran politicians and professionals, "that is curbed only by international pressures."[111] Bush (then vice president) was exaggerating when he said that "I can summarize our position in one word—democracy," but the United States did substantially encourage democratization in Central America and the Andes during the 1980s.[112]

This policy would be put to the test in Chile. Reagan had long admired Pinochet, criticizing Democrats and "Americans on the political left" for acting "as if Fascism has been imposed on the Chileans."[113] He appreciated the Chilean president's solidarity with respect to Central America; Pinochet called for "drastic action" against the FSLN and assured U.S. officials that they "could count on Chile's support."[114] Reagan and his advisers also esteemed Pinochet's economic reforms. "They have managed to put into effect the best economic policies you can find anywhere," said Shultz. "None of this would have happened without the consistent support of Pinochet." Well into his second term, Reagan was reluctant to break with the Chilean dictator. "He saved his country," he reminded advisers in 1986.[115]

By the mid-1980s, though, the administration was moving toward a rupture with Santiago. It was clear that Pinochet had no intention of leaving office; he sidestepped a dialogue with the opposition in the early 1980s, and in 1986 he gave a speech hinting that he might remain president for another decade. "Pinochet's bottom line is to stay in power," commented Shultz. If he succeeded, U.S. officials feared, he would simply encourage polarization and disorder. If he succeeded with U.S. support, moreover, Reagan's efforts to rally diplomatic pressure against the FSLN would collapse. If, on the other hand, the United States could encourage a political transition in Santiago, Reagan would have a shining example of economic and political freedom marching hand-in-hand. "If Chile can join the [democratic] parade in Latin America keeping their economic program underway," Shultz said, "if we have an example to point to based on economic freedom coupled with political freedom, well, they'll knock your eye out!" Accordingly, from 1986 onward the administration resolved to work for a negotiated transition in Santiago, even at the risk of a break with Pinochet. "If we only do things that are agreeable to Pinochet, we won't get anywhere," Shultz said. "We need to be willing to rock him a little."[116]

U.S. diplomats henceforth sided firmly with pro-democracy forces in Chile. The administration obstructed loans from the multilateral development banks and voted to censure Chile in the United Nations. Ambassador Harry Barnes, who called Pinochet "an anticommunist Cassandra," infuriated the Chilean government by attending the funeral of a teen burned to death during an anti-regime rally.[117] After Pinochet agreed to hold a plebiscite on whether or not he would remain in power, U.S. officials pressed him to respect the integrity of the voting process. Organizations like the National Endowment for Democracy helped fund the National Campaign for the No, the unified opposition front that opposed the regime, and Barnes informed Chilean businessmen and bankers that the United States would look askance at even a fair victory by Pinochet. When the "No" did triumph in the plebiscite, Barnes impressed upon the defeated dictator that a refusal to heed the vote would lead to economic sanctions.[118]

In Chile as elsewhere, international pressure did not cause the democratic wave of the 1980s any more than foreign influence caused the rash of coups in prior decades. In nearly all cases—the exception being Panama— the impetus toward democratization came primarily from within. On the whole, though, international pressure was a boon to reform in Latin America. Diplomatic ostracism deprived the dictators of international legitimacy and added impetus to internal agitation for change. Isolated abroad as well as at home, Pinochet and others found that their position had become untenable.

The multiple factors that undermined Latin America's authoritarian regimes came together in Paraguay in 1989. Just months before the collapse of communism in Eastern Europe brought the Cold War to a close, Stroessner's venerable dictatorship—then the longest-running in Latin America—crumbled as well.

Stroessner had never been anything but an authoritarian, and his power derived from his firm grip on the military and the Colorado Party. Nonetheless, his ability to maintain order in Paraguay, as well as the strong economic growth of the 1960s and 1970s, had long made him one of Latin America's more popular tyrants. During the 1980s, though, *stronismo* came under fire. The debt crisis caused rising inflation and unemployment, and those actors that had previously backed Stroessner—notably business elites and the middle class that had taken shape in recent decades—grew hostile to his rampant corruption and cronyism. The Catholic Church demanded greater respect for human rights, and the Reagan and Alfonsín administrations called for a transition to democracy. Stroessner, who had once labeled Marxism "a true historical crisis," found that he could no longer invoke the specter of the Left to legitimize his regime, and his popularity plummeted.[119]

As Stroessner's health declined during the late 1980s, this situation set off a succession dispute within the regime. The *militantes,* led by Stroessner's son, wished to repress the growing discontent. The *éticos* argued that the system could be saved only if the government cleaned up corruption and instituted electoral processes to alleviate criticism at home and abroad. This conflict climaxed in February 1989. A botched attempt to marginalize the *éticos* set off a coup, which ended in Stroessner being dispatched to a Brazilian exile. Over the next few years the *golpistas* held elections, publicized certain crimes of the Stroessner dictatorship, and heralded the triumph of democracy.

The new Paraguay system, however, was only marginally more liberal than before. The Colorado Party and the military still dominated national politics, and the essential socioeconomic dynamics of the old order remained intact. Popular groups had played no role in deposing Stroessner, and their participation would remain limited in the years that followed.[120]

The Paraguayan episode thus indicated a final theme relevant to democratization in Latin America: that its effects were less than revolutionary. While Latin America had made great strides with respect to elections and other procedural norms, the region's democracies remained tightly circumscribed. The emphasis on controlled, consensual transitions succeeded in limiting the disorder caused by handovers of authority, but also in limiting the degree to which these changes altered existing political and socioeconomic relations. The need to ease the armed forces out of the statehouse meant that these institutions usually retained substantial power. In Chile, for instance, Pinochet commanded immense authority as commander-in-chief of the military and senator-for-life. The socioeconomic bases of democracy were also weak, as landholding and financial power remained more skewed than in any other region of the world. Checks on executive power were feeble, and whether

Latin American presidents could actually be made responsible to democratic laws and institutions was still an open question. Latin America was much more democratic in the 1990s than it had been for decades, but the transition was far from complete.

This is not to deny that democratization was a force for good in Latin America. Human rights violations fell dramatically as elected governments replaced repressive military regimes, and by the early 1990s Latin Americans were safer from the threat of state-sponsored terror than they had been for decades. The return of democracy also offered avenues for social activism and opposition protest, provided mechanisms for the peaceful resolution of disputes, and, in conjunction with the taming of both the violent Left and the violent Right, made Latin American politics a less deadly game.

Yet electoral democracy was no silver bullet. Authoritarianism lingered in many countries. Alberto Fujimori dissolved the Peruvian Congress and ruled by decree in 1992, joining several of his counterparts in pushing the envelope with respect to executive power. For all the gains in human rights, politically motivated violence continued (albeit at much reduced levels) in various countries. Even where this was not the case, the perpetrators of past abuses were generally above any real reckoning. In Argentina an attempted coup in 1987 forced Alfonsín to halt the trial of former military officers. In Chile Pinochet used his power to thwart investigations into the crimes of his regime. "The day they touch one of my men, the rule of law ends," he said.[121]

The benefits of democracy were especially scanty for the poor. The transition to democratic rule provided little relief for those devastated by the debt crisis and subsequent economic reforms, leading many of Latin America's poorest to doubt that they had it any better under the civilians than under the generals. Polls taken during the 1990s and early 2000s revealed declining confidence in democracy, as citizens questioned whether the new system could meet their basic needs. Over time, these sentiments facilitated the ascent of leaders like Chávez and Morales, populists who promised to combat the effects of "savage capitalism" by lavishing subsidies and other benefits on the impoverished.[122]

The democracy that took hold in Latin America during the 1980s was a decided improvement over what came before, but the changes were less substantial than they sometimes appeared. As had been the case for centuries, inequality, injustice, and popular marginalization—and the consequent potential for conflict—remained prominent features of the regional landscape.

There were plenty of striking judgments passed on the Cold War's end, none more so than that issued by State Department Policy Planning official Francis Fukuyama. The demise of communism, he argued, represented the "unabashed victory of economic and political liberalism." Alternative forms of government and socioeconomic organization had been utterly discredited by the events of the past decades, and the world could now look forward to "the universalization of Western liberal democracy as the final form of human government." If history represented the continuing clash between rival ideologies, the events of 1989 represented not simply the end of the Cold War, but "the end of history" as well.[123]

Fukuyama was interested more in the collapse of communism in Eastern Europe than in recent trends in Latin America, but in many ways his thesis seemed well tailored to the course of events in the Western Hemisphere. By all reasonable measures, the decades-long competition over political and economic arrangements in the region looked to have ended in a decisive victory for the United States and its allies. The radical Left was a shell of its former self, Moscow and Havana had retreated, and Washington remained economically, strategically, and ideologically preponderant. Free markets, electoral competition, and democratic procedures were now the norm. Latin America had become "a prime testing place for core U.S. values," one observer wrote, the showcase Washington had long desired. "The lessons of the last two years are clear," echoed Brady in 1991. "Freedom works. Free markets work. These simple principles have moved nations; they have altered the course of history."[124]

But whether the new system "worked" for many of its residents was open to debate. Brady was certainly right insofar as democracy represented a major advance from the radical authoritarianism of the 1960s and 1970s; not even the most hardened cynic could deny that. In the same vein, neoliberalism did provide, in most countries at least, a respite from chronic inflation and perpetual macroeconomic instability. In this sense the political and economic order that took hold in Latin America at the close of the Cold War was probably better than most realistic alternatives.

In other ways, though, the situation was more muddled. Latin American democracies were limited by residual authoritarianism and ubiquitous socioeconomic inequality. Neoliberalism widened the already yawning gap between rich and poor, exerted pressure on the vulnerable, and led to considerable resentment on the part of many impoverished Latin Americans. The fact that the system did not work was evident in any number of trends: the rise of coca cultivation and narcotics production, the influx of illegal immigrants to the United States, the Zapatista revolt, and the rise of Chávez and his ilk. In other words, while the advances made during the 1980s should not be ignored, "victory" was probably not what came to mind for many Latin Americans as the Cold War wound down.

Even for the United States, the outcome of that conflict was not entirely positive. Illegal immigration and the drug trade, which drew in large measure on the reforms of the 1980s, soon replaced the red menace as chief bogeys in U.S.–Latin American affairs. The freeing of regional financial flows benefited U.S. investors, but also threatened to make economic crises contagious, as became clear from the Mexican meltdown in 1994–1995. Nor could the United States necessarily take much satisfaction from the spread of democracy in Latin America as the 1990s rolled on. The military's return to the barracks seemed to affirm the political example set by the United States, but eventually opened the door to the ascension of radical populists who contested U.S. hegemony and the neoliberal order. The United States came out of Latin America's Cold War in better shape than the other competitors. Yet its victory was hardly an unambiguous one, and the events of the Cold War in general and the 1980s in particular merely set the stage for future conflict in the region. In Latin America and U.S.–Latin American relations alike, history rolled on.

Conclusion

The events of the late 1980s and early 1990s did not constitute the end of history for Latin America, but they do mark the end of *this* history of Latin America's Cold War. What, in looking back, can we say about this episode? What was it all about? Why were its effects so traumatic? Who won it, and what, if anything, did it settle?

The defining themes of Latin America's Cold War were the persistence, pervasiveness, and intensity of the upheaval that characterized the period. Conflict unfolded on multiple levels, from the highest realms of superpower diplomacy to the "low" politics of everyday life, and played out with an often-astounding ferocity. Stability was fleeting or even illusory, and crises followed hard upon one another. Regional affairs traced an arc of strife running from the gathering turmoil of the 1940s and 1950s to the Cuban revolution, the rural insurgencies, and the foreign interventions that followed; to the urban guerrilla movements, the shocking military violence, and the diplomatic disruptions of the 1970s; to the torrential bloodshed and economic trauma of the 1980s. Re-democratization and the ebbing of superpower competition finally allowed the region to catch its breath, but even here domestic and diplomatic tensions soon resumed anew. In Latin America, as in much of the Third World, the Cold War was a time of little respite.

Why was Latin America's Cold War such an intense experience? The answer lies in the complexity of that episode. In Latin America the Cold War was not a single conflict but a series of overlapping conflicts, and it was the interaction between them that made the period so tumultuous.

The post–World War II period in Latin America was defined by four interrelated themes. The first was the perpetual clash over domestic arrangements and internal power structures. This dispute had long produced cycles of repression, resistance, and instability, and it again played out during the Cold War. The second was the continuing tension regarding the boundaries of U.S. power in Latin America, an affair manifest in the dynamic nature of inter-American relations during the second half of the twentieth century. The third conflict revolved around the emergence of the Third World, an event that generated recurring ideological ferment and social tension. The fourth and final issue was the superpowers' zero-sum struggle for ideological and strategic hegemony in the global south.

These diverse layers of conflict spanned the local, the regional, and the global scenes. They converged in Latin America in the decade and a half following World War II, they were firmly fused together by the Cuban revolution and its aftermath, and they henceforth became inseparable. East–West tensions and the effects of *tercermundismo* heightened internal turmoil and provoked occasionally dramatic shifts in the hemispheric diplomatic climate. Instability on these fronts elicited foreign intervention, as Moscow, Washington, Havana, and their allies sought to protect or expand their influence amid this flux. These endeavors, in turn, had a range of effects on the regional scene, but one notable outcome was to exacerbate the convulsiveness—both diplomatic and internal—that had elicited foreign meddling in the first place. The struggles comprising Latin America's Cold War were not only linked; they were mutually reinforcing.

This relationship was evident in any number of instances, from the fallout caused by the Bay of Pigs in 1961, to the confluence of *tercermundismo,* anti-Americanism, and rising domestic tensions in the diplomatic challenge of the 1970s, to the reciprocal effects of internal tumult and external intervention in the Central American civil wars. One conflict fueled another, and this dynamic gave the clashes of the period their sharpness and intractability. It was thus the multilayered nature of Latin America's Cold War that ensured its volatility; complexity bred intensity.

This notion of complexity provides an appropriate jumping-off point for analyzing the more specific issues—ranging from inter-American diplomacy to foreign intervention to internal polarization and violence—whose interaction drove Cold War conflict in the region.

This is certainly the case with respect to Latin American foreign policy and U.S.–Latin American affairs. The Cold War added new dimensions to this relationship, as the prospect of foreign intervention, the ideological pull of *tercermundismo*, and the need to divert rising internal tensions complemented the ambivalence toward American power that had traditionally characterized hemispheric affairs. The way that these influences worked themselves out in Latin American diplomacy varied across time and space. The outbursts of anti-Americanism that followed Guatemala in 1954 and the Bay of Pigs in 1961; the way that most countries aligned with the United States and against Cuba in the early 1960s; the subsequent rise and fall of the regional diplomatic challenge; and the various interventions and diplomatic initiatives that accompanied the Central American crisis: these events demonstrated the manifold ways in which Latin American leaders sought to reconcile these competing demands.

Fifteen years ago, Peter Smith criticized the paucity of quality literature on Latin American foreign policy.[1] Notwithstanding the subsequent publication of several excellent studies,[2] Smith's judgment is still accurate today, as interpretations of this subject remain rather one-sided. Bemis's "protective imperialism" argument has been thoroughly discredited, only to be replaced by equally simplistic suggestions: that anticommunist leaders in Latin America were "puppets" of the United States, or that coercion and domination have been constant themes of hemispheric relations. The principal tendency of the literature, notes Max Paul Friedman, is one "that ascribes all agency to U.S. policy-makers, even as it criticizes their actions."[3]

There were, no doubt, fundamental imbalances of power in the U.S.–Latin American relationship. The invasions of Panama and the Dominican Republic, as well as the U.S. part in destabilizing Allende's Chile and Ortega's Nicaragua, testified to this asymmetry. Reagan's use of U.S. economic leverage during the debt crisis, his brushing aside of the Central American peace process in the early 1980s, and Washington's success in weathering the worst of the diplomatic challenge of the 1970s indicated the same disequilibrium. This latter case in particular revealed that Latin American statesmen seeking to throw off U.S. preeminence faced a constellation of formidable impediments: a disadvantageous economic position, the resolute opposition of American officials, and the indifference of those that might have stepped in to offset Washington's sway. Inter-American relations were never conducted on an even footing, and the Cold War furnished ample evidence of this fact.

Yet U.S.–Latin American ties during this period were hardly monodimensional. To begin with, certain of the episodes listed above demonstrated a more complicated reality of hemispheric affairs. During the debt crisis the bargaining position of many Latin American countries was so weak not just because these countries were less powerful than the United States, but also because the regional and Third-World solidarity that they sought to invoke simply did not exist. Similarly, in the mid-1970s it was internal obstacles—the ideological splits that led numerous South American countries to ally with the United States rather than their *tercermundista* brethren, and the intraregional schisms wrought by rising nationalism—that did much to undermine the Latin American diplomatic movement. These episodes therefore showed not simply the durability of U.S. power, but also the impact of political divisions that conspired against Latin American unity.

Viewed more broadly, Latin American diplomacy during the Cold War cannot be reconciled with analyses that disregard or downplay the agency of actors within the region. Latin America's anticommunist leaders, for instance, were rarely in thrall to or controlled by the United States. They needed no encouragement to be anticommunist or to embrace the tenets of National Security Doctrine, and their ideological sympathies for Washington did not always translate into strong U.S. influence with these regimes. U.S. officials frequently expressed irritation at their inability to bend military presidents to Washington's will—witness Carter's frustration in dealing with Somoza, Pinochet, and Videla, or Kennedy's abortive showdown with the Peruvian coup-plotters in 1962. At countless other points it was the United States that struggled to keep pace with Latin American anticommunism. Luís Somoza and Ydígoras were far more enthusiastic about the Bay of Pigs than were many officials in Washington, and the subsequent formation of the anti-Cuba coalition during the early 1960s was less a result of U.S. pressure than of the fact that any number of Latin American governments were genuinely frightened by Castro's interventionism. This same pattern was at the heart of the *contra* program. As Ariel Armony points out, Argentina beat the United States into Central America in the late 1970s, and it was Washington that adopted Buenos Aires' project for supporting the Nicaraguan resistance.[4] The relationship between the United States and Latin American anticommunists was often (though not always) close, but rarely was it one-sided.

Exploitation also worked both ways, and Latin America's shrewder statesmen were as likely to manipulate as to be manipulated by the United States.

For these leaders, it was relentless opportunism more than anything else that guided Latin American diplomacy during the Cold War. In the 1960s Betancourt skillfully used the specter of anti-Americanism to cajole Kennedy into stepping up U.S. financial assistance. For their part, leaders in Central and South America gratefully pocketed Alliance for Progress funds and then declined to undertake the reforms they had promised in return. A decade later, Torrijos expertly cultivated regional and international opinion to get the best of various U.S. administrations in the Canal Treaty negotiations, and leaders in Venezuela and Mexico exploited the contradictions of Carter's Nicaragua policy to seek their own sphere of influence in Central America. During the late 1980s, finally, the participants in the Esquipulas process utilized the approaching exhaustion of Washington as well as Havana and Moscow to lay the basis for a negotiated settlement to the Central American wars. U.S.–Latin American affairs did not represent a relationship among equals, but the lines of influence and causality in that relationship still ran in both directions.[5]

Recent scholarship on the Cold War has emphasized the ways in which lesser powers influenced superpowers and found room to maneuver within a bipolar system.[6] Latin America was no exception to this dynamic. The internal and international strife of the Cold War era presented dangers and dilemmas for Latin American statesmen—but opportunities, too. As a result, while the relationship between the United States and Latin American leaders was not usually one of tails wagging dogs, neither was it one of puppet masters pulling strings.[7]

Scholars would also do well to reexamine a closely related subject, that of foreign intervention and its consequences in Cold War Latin America.

Beginning with U.S. complicity in Arbenz's overthrow, and proceeding more rhythmically from the Cuban revolution onward, external interference in the region was perennial. Driven by both geopolitical and ideological imperatives, Washington, Havana, Moscow, and their respective allies maneuvered to advance their own agendas and thwart their rivals' aims. The particular policies they pursued to this end changed considerably over time. In Washington modernization theory gave way to the darker anticommunism of Nixon and Ford, which itself faded amid Carter's efforts to distance Washington from military adventures in the region. The diplomacy accompanying Castro's guerrilla aid programs evolved greatly from the 1960s to the 1980s, and the Kremlin got out of the guerrilla business altogether for roughly fifteen years between the mid-1960s and the late 1970s. On the whole, though, this was a period of near-constant foreign competition in Latin America.

With few exceptions, studies of this issue focus on the U.S. part in maintaining an inegalitarian, repressive order in the region. Starting in the late 1940s and 1950s, and especially after the Cuban revolution, many scholars argue, Latin American elites used anticommunism as the basis for a partnership with U.S. officials desperate to prevent any more red from seeping into the hemisphere. Washington subsequently worked to preserve conservative rule and stifle social change, sometimes directly, more often by providing the expertise and the repressive apparatus—the "technologies of terror"—that allowed Latin American governments to do the dirty work themselves.[8]

This thesis is eminently reasonable; the connections between Washington and Cold War repression practically draw themselves. The United States helped construct the counterinsurgency state in Guatemala; maneuvered against leftist leaders like Jagan, Ortega, and Allende; fueled violence in El Salvador by providing aid to the FAES; and frequently pushed its conservative allies forward with Manichean urgency. Even where Washington was only peripherally involved in such practices, U.S. diplomats did little to discourage them.

Yet the stronger version of this argument—that U.S. policy *caused* such terror—is harder to sustain.[9] If counterinsurgency programs and military missions ineluctably led to state terror, then how did Venezuela (which claimed a greater amount of such assistance than either Guatemala or El Salvador under Kennedy) emerge from the 1960s with one of Latin America's least repressive democracies? The answer is that the political and social context in which U.S. aid was received made all the difference. Venezuela had a strong president committed to democratic reform; El Salvador and Guatemala were run by predatory leaders and acquisitive elites. U.S. military aid certainly *enabled* state terror in various countries, but to hone in too narrowly on this variable as the *source* of such terror is to risk ignoring the importance of local circumstances.

The Venezuelan case also reminds us that anticommunism led U.S. officials to pursue a broad range of policies in Latin America, not all of them repressive. The United States helped shore up reactionaries in certain countries, but backed reform and democratization in others. Viewing Betancourt as the best bulwark against the Left, Kennedy planted himself firmly on the side of an imperfect constitutional democracy in Venezuela. A decade and a half later,

Carter staked his Latin American policy on his ability to persuade the dictators to stop murdering people. During the 1980s Reagan's fear that authoritarianism would encourage extremist elements and derail economic reform led him to support democratization in numerous countries. Anticommunism was a constant in U.S. policy, but support for dictators and repression was not.[10]

Even granting that U.S. policy often contributed to polarization and violence in Latin America, to view this contribution in isolation is to obscure the broader reality of foreign intervention in the region. The Cuban revolution presaged not simply a jump in U.S. interference in Latin America, but also persistent involvement by Moscow, Havana, and their partners. The fact that these East-bloc measures were sometimes overstated at the time (one Stroessner-era official, comparing Paraguay's role in Latin America to "the position that West Germany occupies in Europe," estimated that the regime must arrest a Soviet spy every five days just to keep pace with infiltration) has led historians to *understate* this phenomenon.[11] In retrospect, it is apparent that while both Soviet and Cuban policies evolved considerably from 1959 onward, East-bloc—and especially Cuban—intervention was the rule rather than the exception. The rural insurgents of the 1960s, the urban guerrillas of the 1970s, and the FSLN and FMLN thereafter all drew on significant international support. The United States lent its backing to the counterinsurgents; its rivals threw their weight behind the insurgents.

These competing interventions had widely varying outcomes, and from the perspective of Havana and the superpowers, the results were often less than satisfying. For every time that foreign meddling went off as planned, there was an instance in which such interference had unanticipated consequences, played only a marginal role in bringing about the eventual product, or simply failed. During the 1960s neither Washington nor Moscow nor Havana succeeded in molding Latin American societies as they had hoped, and their efforts to do so frequently generated an unwelcome backlash. The U.S. invasion of the Dominican Republic in 1965 elicited such ideological and diplomatic fallout as to wreck the inter-American system that American officials had long labored to perfect, while Cuban intrigues ended any chance of Castro building a regional diplomatic bloc against the United States. Two decades later, Central America became a quagmire for all involved, eventually leading Moscow, Washington, and Havana alike to look for a graceful exit from the isthmus. As viewed by its practitioners, then, the story of foreign intervention was often one of ill-designed initiatives running up against the stubborn realities of regional politics. All too frequently, these intrusions produced not the successes envisioned by their designers but the frustrations and blowback that accompanied exaggerated ambitions.

Yet what looked like a failure from Washington or Havana could still exert an immense impact on the local scene. Here too, there were substantial parallels between Cuban, U.S., and Soviet policies. U.S. diplomacy stoked tensions in numerous countries by strengthening the radical Right, and it also pushed the Left toward greater extremism. U.S. interventions were critical in radicalizing leftists like Guevara during the 1950s, inspiring the student movement and the urban guerrillas thereafter, and in feeding other disruptions. U.S. policies helped sustain the conservative order in a number of Latin American countries, but they inspired challenges to that order as well.

Cuban and Soviet policies could be even more incendiary. After all, it was precisely turmoil and violence that Castro and his counterparts in Moscow sought to sow. To be sure, Latin American guerrilla movements were not controlled by Moscow, Havana, or Managua, and foreign support for groups such as Shining Path and the URNG was minimal to nonexistent. In general, though, international solidarity greatly aided the campaigns waged by the violent Left. The example of the Cuban revolution was central to the emergence of the *foquista* movements of the 1960s, and from this point forward, any number of guerrilla organizations benefited from supplies, money, training, and occasional combat support acquired abroad. Though this backing was rarely successful in bringing about guerrilla victories, it surely abetted the violence the insurgents practiced.

Cuban and Soviet policies helped energize the violent Left; they also radicalized the Right. It is fashionable to attribute the emergence of counterinsurgency, virulent anticommunism, and National Security Doctrine to U.S. diplomacy, but if scholars seek to identify a foreign impetus for military extremism, they would do better to interrogate the ramifications of East-bloc initiatives. As discussed in Chapters 2 and 3, the accurate (if exaggerated) perception that Moscow and Havana sought to stoke insurgency and upheaval in Latin America was crucial in stimulating the anxieties that brought National Security Doctrine to the forefront of military politics. At other points, Soviet and Cuban policies influenced not simply the Right, but also a wider range of political actors. In 1980s Nicaragua, Soviet and Cuban aid to the FSLN alienated moderates, former members of the anti-Somoza coalition, and even erstwhile Sandinistas like Pastora, and thereby stoked the *contra* war. As with U.S. intervention,

Soviet and Cuban intrusions had a radicalizing effect across the political spectrum.

To a greater degree than is often recognized, then, there was substantial symmetry to the struggle for the soul of Latin America. Tempted by the twin prospects of geopolitical gains and ideological victories, Moscow, Havana, and Washington all found it difficult if not impossible to resist the temptation to dive into the region. In Latin America's Cold War, foreign intervention— and the polarization to which it contributed—was hardly a one-way street.

This polarization was the central theme of Latin American domestic politics during the Cold War. Internal radicalization, already underway at the time of the Cuban revolution, metastasized in the period that followed. The prospect of revolution, the influence of currents like *tercermundismo,* National Security Doctrine, and dependency theory, and the effects of East–West discord and foreign intervention inflamed preexisting social and political tensions and pushed domestic interactions toward the extreme.

This tendency had two principal outcomes for Latin America, both of them devastating. The first was the militarization of internal conflict, as seen most notably in Argentina in the late 1970s and Central America in the 1980s. The second was the asphyxiation of democracy, demonstrated vividly in the *golpismo* of the 1960s and 1970s. A few fortunate countries escaped the worst of these trends, and the re-democratization of the 1980s somewhat eased their effects, but for the most part, the Cold War was a period in which moderation gave way to extremism and violence.

There is much to support the common argument, advanced most forcefully by Greg Grandin, that these ills were primarily the outcomes of a "savage crusade" perpetrated by the Right in collusion with the United States.[12] Driven by anticommunism and simple self-interest, and in numerous cases acting with Washington's support or acquiescence, Latin American elites and their rightist allies were never shy about using violence or extralegal methods to maintain control of the political system. Most (but not all) of Latin America's coups were the work of conservative military officers, and in the region's bloodiest internal struggles—Guatemala, El Salvador, Argentina—the Right bore preponderant responsibility for the carnage.[13] Right-wing violence, conducted by the security services, death squads, or both, took a vast human toll and had a chilling effect on participatory politics. If body counts are an indication of effectiveness in the stifling of Latin American democracy, then in many cases the Right was without peer.

But Cold War polarization and trauma cannot be explained solely as a function of Right repression and U.S. complicity; here, as with respect to foreign intervention, some appreciation of symmetry is necessary. The postwar period, and especially the years following the Cuban revolution, witnessed not just a spike in right-wing radicalism, but also a flourishing of extremism across the political spectrum. The internal and international trends of the era dramatically intensified ongoing conflicts, inciting the passions of those who sought to spur radical change no less than those who sought to strangle it. Right-wing extremism centered on National Security Doctrine and government-sponsored terror; left-wing extremism took the form of *foquismo,* insurgency, and revolutionary terror.

The fact that successful revolutions were quite rare in Latin America after 1959 should not obscure the fact that violent revolutionary movements—often boasting considerable foreign support—were ubiquitous during these years. The *foquistas* had hardly been defeated before the urban guerrillas took up the standard of the revolutionary Left, and this latter movement was succeeded in short order by the even more powerful insurgencies that roiled Nicaragua, El Salvador, and Guatemala. In retrospect, the fears of revolution expressed by Latin American officials may appear exaggerated, but at the time, radical change seemed far from a remote prospect.

It was the perverse symbiosis of these dueling Left and Right radicalisms that made the Cold War so devastating. As noted throughout this book, these polar opposites were in fact quite interdependent, fueling one another in a dialectical process that augmented the intensity and destructiveness of both. Guerrilla violence terrified conservatives, leading to *golpismo,* authoritarianism, and repression. And while in a few cases these measures did restore a semblance of internal stability, just as often they ended up feeding the discontent that informed subsequent generations of insurgents. Cold War radicalisms were mutually reinforcing, and from the Southern Cone to Central America, this escalatory spiral drove the polarization and bloody conflict that dominated Latin American politics.

Together, these rising extremisms constituted a pincer movement that Latin America's fragile democracies were ill-prepared to withstand. Right radicalism had a devastating impact on hopes for meaningful political change; Left radicalism could be similarly toxic. Many insurgent groups had the express intent of derailing democracy, a goal that organizations in Venezuela, El Salvador, Peru, and elsewhere pursued by threatening to murder anyone who went to the polls. Groups like the FMLN and URNG, which distanced themselves from some of the more destructive practices of *foquismo,* nonetheless killed moderate officials and uncooperative civic leaders and behaved coercively toward the peasants they claimed to represent. Rural and urban guerrillas alike caused economic chaos via sabotage, a strategy that hurt the poor no less than the rich. The guerrillas were even known to obstruct efforts at agrarian and other reforms, as when Salvadoran insurgents deliberately impeded the program announced by the junta that took power in 1979. Finally, in countries like Argentina and Uruguay, the violence and turmoil wrought by the guerrillas imposed such strain on the sociopolitical system as to convince many previously devout democrats that only decisive military intervention could salvage the situation. Latin America's democracies were not just attacked from the Right; they faced an assault from both sides. Too often, the Center could not hold.

During the Cold War conservatives blamed the Left for making democracy impossible. Since then, scholars have largely faulted the Right for the violence and political illiberalism of the time. In reality, responsibility for internal polarization in Latin America was not the peculiar province of either end of the political spectrum. At each stage during the Cold War, Latin America's dueling radicalisms exacerbated one another, empowering the extremists and doing gross harm to the prospects for evolutionary change. In 1967 Eduardo Frei had warned that the far Left and the far Right were forging an "unholy alliance" against progressive democracy. Later events made him a prophet.[14]

If the Center came under immense strain as a result of Cold War extremism, the Left did not prosper either. The generally disappointing performance of the radical Left was one of the most striking aspects of Latin America's Cold War. In the early 1960s a variety of informed observers had predicted that leftwing takeovers were imminent in countries across the region. The fact that this did not happen, that there was only a single successful insurgency between 1959 and 1991, and that the two leftist governments that did come to power—Allende's administration in Chile and the FSLN in Nicaragua—ultimately failed to stay there, would have come as quite a surprise. In Latin America the period following Castro's triumph was one of great revolutionary agitation and even greater revolutionary disappointment.

What caused these travails? One venerable answer is that this outcome resulted from the violence, repression, and above all foreign intervention that battered the guerrillas and the Left in general. As Timothy Wickham-Crowley observers, "Perhaps no theory is more widely held by the left in Latin America and in the United States itself than that U.S. military aid . . . to Latin American regimes has been the main cause of revolutionary *failures* in Latin America since 1960." James Petras echoes this argument, writing that U.S. military assistance programs "are responsible for the repression of popular movements" in the region.[15]

There is plenty of truth in these assessments. The example of the Cuban revolution and the threat of future upheaval terrified Latin American security services and officials in Washington, and these groups worked diligently to kill radical change. The deaths of 200,000 Guatemalans, the lesser but still shocking slaughter in El Salvador and Argentina, the not-so-covert wars waged against Allende's Chile and Sandinista Nicaragua, and numerous other instances testified to the immense obstacles faced by the Left and the lengths to which their opponents would go to block them. In the frustration of the Central American insurgencies, the destabilization of the Chilean and Nicaraguan governments, and the generally poor performance of the Latin American Left, these factors must not be obscured or underestimated.[16]

Coercion was therefore integral to revolutionary failure. It was not, however, the only element at work in destroying the dreams of the Left. The fact remains that the guerrillas never proved particularly effective in attaining or holding the popularity necessary to bring them to power. The *foquistas* were marginalized from the start, and while the urban guerrillas and the Central American insurgents cultivated much greater public followings, they eventually grew isolated from the moderates and many erstwhile backers as well. In the 1970s one informed observer wrote that "neither the peasants nor the urban masses . . . are particularly revolutionary, in spite of the unspeakable conditions in which both groups live," and this problem continued to plague the guerrillas throughout the Cold War. The insurgents invoked the solidarity of a *pueblo unido,* but in reality, that revolutionary unity was often lacking or difficult to maintain.[17]

While this declining support reflected the widespread use of terror against suspected guerrilla sympathizers, it also bore the mark of two additional causes. The first of these was, quite paradoxically, reform. The Cold War was anything but an era of progressivism in Latin America. As discussed above, the competing Left and Right extremisms of the period dramatically narrowed the possibilities for meaningful democracy and peaceful social change. In various instances, though, regimes menaced by insurgency or the threat thereof embraced just enough reform to avert disaster. Incomplete agrarian reforms, civic action programs, and closely scrutinized democratic openings did not come close to ameliorating the appalling economic and social conditions that prevailed in the region, but they did release sufficient pressure to deprive the insurgents of widespread support. This effect was evident in Venezuela, Colombia, Bolivia, and Peru during the 1960s, and in Guatemala and El Salvador two decades later. Guerrilla violence, though generally quite deleterious in its political effects, thus unintentionally fostered a degree of reform that ultimately helped do the insurgents in.

That these incomplete and often cynical reforms were so politically effective points to the second factor—that the guerrillas consistently failed to present an attractive alternative. In the decade following the Cuban revolution the high-handedness, cultural and social insensitivity, and thuggishness of the *foquistas* ensured that even the exploited and oppressed took a dim view of the insurgents. The post-*foquista* guerrillas changed tactics accordingly, but they never cast off the self-defeating aspects of Guevarism. The use of revolutionary terror and exemplary violence; the reliance on sabotage attacks; the tendency to abuse or intentionally expose the local population: in South America during the 1970s and again in Central America ten years later, these practices revealed the darker side of guerrilla ideology and eventually deprived the insurgents of organic support. Latin America's revolutionaries suffered grievous injuries from state terror and repression, but their wounds were also self-inflicted.[18]

The exception to this pattern of revolutionary failure proved the rule. In Nicaragua the Sandinistas succeeded largely because they avoided—either by luck or design—the various issues discussed above. Somoza's dynastic predilections and allergy to reform convinced most Nicaraguans (and a broad coalition of foreign observers) that a continuation of his rule would be even worse than a guerrilla victory, a perception reinforced by the public moderation of Sandinista rhetoric and political tactics during the late 1970s. Combined with the effective withdrawal of U.S. support from Somoza, these factors canceled out the multiple disadvantages that generally impeded leftist takeovers in the region, and made Nicaragua the sole example of revolutionary triumph in Castro-era Latin America.

Yet the Sandinistas would be turned out of power in 1990, like Allende nearly two decades earlier. For scholars like William Robinson, U.S. intervention was far and away the dominant factor in this reversal. External pressures, he writes, made the maintenance of socialism in Nicaragua impossible, "independent of behavioral factors such as Sandinista state conduct."[19]

As with the disappointments of the guerrillas, though, the picture is more complicated than this. In both Chile and Nicaragua U.S. intervention was only one of several ingredients in undermining these regimes. Allende's gross economic mismanagement and multiple political errors, along with the unbridled radicalism of the ultra-Left, badly eroded the footing of the UP government, and may well have been more consequential than Nixon's interpositions in leading to its fall. With respect to Nicaragua, Reagan's unrelenting antagonism to the Sandinistas undoubtedly constituted a major—perhaps *the* major—impediment to the consolidation of FSLN rule. Here too, though, domestic issues such as economic bungling, state repression, and the perceived unresponsiveness of government officials were integral to driving the public away. "There were no *contras* in the ballot boxes," Víctor Tirado later acknowledged.[20] Leftist governments in Nicaragua and Chile were beaten down from the outside, but they helped beat themselves as well.

Coercion, intervention, and violence were elemental to revolutionary disappointment in postwar Latin America; to ignore this reality would be to sanitize the history of the period. But these failures had a more complex genesis than is sometimes assumed; to smooth over this fact would be equally inappropriate.

The Left thus did poorly during the Cold War. The far Right, though apparently ascendant in the 1960s and 1970s, also saw its luck run out in the 1980s. Amid a confluence of causes—ranging from economic trouble to foreign pressure to the reactivation of powerful social movements—the authoritarians lost their grip. The limits of democratization were as notable as its extent, but this change nonetheless represented a departure from the radical authoritarianism that had dotted the regional landscape only recently.

Democratization was not the only momentous domestic development of the 1980s. Major economic changes were also in the offing, as a long-standing critique of ISI merged with the shock of the debt crisis and U.S. pressure to promote a dramatic turn toward liberal reform. By the 1990s Latin America had thrust itself firmly into the neoliberal age.

Combined with the failures of the violent Left and Soviet and Cuban retrenchment from the region, these events appeared to signal a clear victory for Washington and its allies in Latin America's Cold War. Capitalism and electoral democracy reigned up and down the Western Hemisphere, and strategic threats to U.S. hegemony were nowhere to be found. U.S. officials basked in these triumphs, grandly asserting that Latin America had joined a worldwide movement toward political and economic freedom. Observers on the Left agreed—grudgingly, in some cases—that the Cold War had come out splendidly for Washington, democracy, and neoliberalism. Castro forecasted "a unipolar world under American hegemony," and in Venezuela former insurgent leader Teodoro Petkoff reconciled himself to the new order by becoming a proponent of privatization.[21]

The sense of finality and triumph that accompanied the close of Latin America's Cold War was not entirely misplaced. Neoliberalism, democratization, and the winding down of superpower conflict constituted dramatic departures for Latin America, changes that were largely to the good. The weakening of both violent Left and violent Right permitted a general decompression of regional affairs, and in some countries eventually conduced to the establishment of healthy political systems.

Yet pronouncements heralding the dawn of an entirely new era in the region were premature. By the close of the 1990s, and especially as the 2000s unfolded, Washington's "victory" no longer looked so decisive. Drugs and immigration, both in some sense related to the debt crisis and economic reforms of the 1980s, replaced communism as sources of tension in inter-American relations. The rise of radical populists like Chávez and Morales eventually led American observers to wonder whether Washington was again on the brink of "losing" the region. As Chávez increased his military cooperation with a resurgent Russia in 2006–2007, conservative commentators in the United States grumbled that it had become "open season on the Monroe Doctrine." Even for Washington, the aftermath of Latin America's Cold War was a thoroughly muddled affair.[22]

Nor was it really correct to argue that democracy had emerged from this conflict triumphant. After all, if Latin America was largely democratic by the late 1980s, the breadth of that democracy was only slightly greater than during the late 1950s, and its quality was probably less than it had been in the wake of World War II. Between the Cuban revolution and the late 1970s, in fact, Latin American democracy had suffered a massacre, and if the 1980s were a period of re-democratization, it was only because the previous two decades had been years of de-democratization.

The ambiguous nature of Latin American democracy and inter-American relations hinted at a broader reality, which was that the end of the Cold War marked less of a break from the past than most observers had initially assumed. The strands of continuity were strongest in the region's internal relations, where it was often questionable what, exactly, had changed. Not vast economic disparities: income distribution in Latin America was still more skewed than in any other region. Not mass deprivation and poverty: in many countries, the predicament of the poorest worsened considerably as a result of the debt crisis and subsequent reforms. Not the persistence of authoritarian tendencies: democratic and undemocratic practices coexisted uneasily in many political systems. Not social and ideological strife: Latin America's politics, though less violent than before, were soon roiled anew as populist politicians worked toward "21st century socialism." Nor, finally, had Latin America left the devastating legacies of the Cold War behind. Broken states in Central America, persistent human rights violations, and gaping psychological and social wounds served as reminders of the lasting impact of that period.

Latin America's Cold War featured several overlapping layers of conflict, and the course of regional affairs following the close of that period showed that many of these laminas were yet to be peeled away. One historian has written that the Cold War "settled fundamental issues once and for all."[23] Such finality was nowhere to be found in Latin America.

Just as polarization was often the essential feature of the Cold War in Latin America, so, too, with the dominant historical renderings of the period. As told by many U.S. officials and conservative commentators, the history of this episode is a clear-cut story of good and evil. Internal instability resulted mainly from the havoc wrought by Soviet-sponsored "professional guerrilla movements." These legions established a "Communist reign of terror" in Nicaragua, and sought to sow violence throughout Latin America as part of a "sinister" program to "destabilize the entire region."[24] Their dastardly plan was thwarted, not by the hand-wringing of "human-rights activists" on the Left, but by Reagan's steadfast resistance to communist encroachment and his unwavering advocacy of political and economic freedom. Reagan's policies stemmed the communist tide, constituted a "spectacularly successful fight to introduce and sustain Western political norms in the region," and above all, placed the United States "on the right side of history."[25] In this telling, the course of Latin America's Cold War affirms the efficacy and morality of American power.

Many leading scholars agree that Latin America's Cold War had a profound moral significance, but take a far darker view of what that meaning was. For historians like Greg Grandin, Steve Stern, Daniela Spenser, and others, the Cold War was a period of immense carnage, one in which conservative elites joined forces with the United States and reactionary elements of their own societies to destroy revolutionary movements and the prospects for democracy. This era thus saw not the triumph of the good over the malign, but of the malign over the good. "Master architects of 'radical evil'" successfully conducted a "savage crusade" to eradicate popular movements and impoverish the masses.[26] It was "Cold War terror—either executed, patronized, or excused by the United States," argues Grandin, that "fortified illiberal forces, militarized societies," and cast a pall over Latin American politics.[27] Accordingly, Spenser writes, recent scholarship rightly avoids "detached narrative and analysis of the Latin American Cold War," instead showing "moral outrage" at the destructive consequences of that conflict.[28]

The conclusions presented above suggest that both of these interpretations need rethinking. It is hardly necessary to argue that ethical calculations have no place in the writing of history to recognize that the moral certitude prominent in the appraisals of both the triumphalists and their critics has tended to occlude fundamental characteristics of Latin America's Cold War.[29] The former view is almost laughably simplistic. It ignores the reality that U.S. power repeatedly contributed to Cold War repression, glosses over the diverse grievances that informed guerrilla movements, and exaggerates the benefits of democratization and reform in the 1980s while minimizing the impact of the authoritarianism of earlier decades. Above all, it obscures the fact that for those who lived it, Latin America's Cold War could be a brutal, terrifying, and often deadly experience. This simple reality gives the lie to the glib assertions of those who view this conflict as a testament to the virtues of intervention and democracy promotion.[30]

Yet the latter view is also problematic. Its emphasis on the malignancy of the Right and its foreign allies is not necessarily incorrect, but it is certainly incomplete. Left–Right polarization and violence, foreign intervention, U.S.–Latin American relations, and the ultimate failure of the revolutionaries were thoroughly complicated and multisided phenomena; this considerably less simple reality undermines the claims of those who reduce the history of the era to a narrative of Right repression, U.S. complicity, and popular victimization.

The traumas that plagued postwar Latin America stemmed not solely from the malevolence of any one set of actors, but from the complex and self-reinforcing nature of Latin America's Cold War. Extremism fostered extremism, intervention induced intervention, and one layer of instability exacerbated another. The cumulative effects of these processes were all too frequently devastating. In sum, recognition of complexity and intricacy is central to understanding the intensity and outcomes of Latin America's Cold War. To lose sight of these characteristics is to risk distorting essential dynamics of the period.

The literature on Latin America's Cold War will continue to grow in the coming decades, as new archives open and our perceptions of this period evolve.[31] As this occurs, scholars should not be blind to the moral implications of their subject, nor should they be blinded by them. The morality-play feel that often characterizes interpretations of Latin America's Cold War obscures as much as it reveals, and does a disservice to the tangled causality of that conflict. To grapple with Latin America's Cold War in its full richness, nuance, and indeed, tragedy, perhaps detached narrative and analysis are in order after all.

Notes

Selected Abbreviations

AGCA	Archivo General de Centroamérica
AGNARG	Archivo General de la Nación de Argentina
AGNCOL	Archivo General de la Nación de Colombia
AGNMEX	Archivo General de la Nación de México
AGNNIC	Archivo General de la Nación de Nicaragua
AHGE	Archivo Histórico Genaro Estrada
ANH	Archivo Nacional Histórico (Chile)
APDH	Archivo de la Asamblea Permanente de Derechos Humanos
APP	American Presidency Project
ARB	Archivo Rómulo Betancourt
CDSP	*Contemporary Digest of the Soviet Press*
CDYA	Centro de Documentación y Archivo (Paraguay)
CELS	Archivo del Centro de Estudios Legales y Sociales
CIA	Central Intelligence Agency
CIRMA	Centro de Investigaciones Regionales y Mesoamericanas
CISPES	Committee in Solidarity with the People of El Salvador
CONADEP	National Commission on the Disappearance of Persons
CSD	Castro Speech Database

CUC	Campesino Unity Committee
CWIHP	Cold War International History Project Virtual Archive
DDRS	*Declassified Documents Reference System*
DIPBA	Archivo de la ex-Dirección de Inteligencia de la Policía de Buenos Aires
DPI	Dirección de Política International
EBB	Electronic Briefing Book
EBD	Executive Board Documents
EBM	Executive Board Meeting
ECLA	Economic Commission for Latin America
EEUU	United States *(Estados Unidos)*
EG	Ernesto Geisel Collection
EGP	Guerrilla Army of the Poor
ERP	People's Revolutionary Army
FBIS	Foreign Broadcast Information Service
FGV	Getulio Vargas Foundation
FRUS	*Foreign Relations of the United States*
GFL	Gerald Ford Presidential Library
HAK	Henry A. Kissinger
IHNCA	Instituto de la Historia de Nicaragua y Centroamérica
IMF	International Monetary Fund
INR	State Department Bureau of Intelligence and Research
IPS	Dirección General de Investigaciones Políticas y Sociales
JCL	Jimmy Carter Library
JFKL	John F. Kennedy Library
KDMP	Kremlin Decision-Making Project
LAASF	Latin American Affairs Staff Files
LAC	Library and Archives Canada
LACRO	Latin America and the Caribbean Regional Office (World Bank)
LBJL	Lyndon Baines Johnson Library
LOC	Library of Congress

MemCon	Memorandum of Conversation
MRE	Ministry of Foreign Relations
MRECHILE	Archivo del Ministerio de Relaciones Exteriores de Chile
MREGUAT	Archivo del Ministerio de Relaciones Exteriores de Guatemala
MREURU	Archivo del Ministerio de Relaciones Exteriores de Uruguay
MREVEN	Archivo Central del Ministerio de Relaciones Exteriores de Venezuela
NARA	U.S. National Archives and Records Administration
NIE	National Intelligence Estimates
NPM	Nixon Presidential Materials Project
NSA	National Security Archive
NSC	National Security Council
NSDD	National Security Decision Directive
NSF	National Security File
NSSM	National Security Study Memorandum
OAS/OEA	Organization of American States (Organizción de Estados Americanos)
PCFLA	President's Country Files for Latin America
PRC	Policy Review Committee
RG	Record Group
RRL	Ronald Reagan Library
SAPMO	Stiftung Archiv der Parteien und Massenorgenisationen der DDR im Bundesarchiv
SCC	Special Coordination Committee
SDN	Secretaría de la Defensa Nacional
SERPAJ	Servicio de Paz y Justicia Uruguay
SNF	Subject Numeric File
SNI	National Intelligence Service (Brazil)
SRE	Secretariado de Relaciones Exteriores
WBA	World Bank Archives
WHCF	White House Counsel Files
ZBDM	Zbigniew Brzezinski Donated Material

Introduction

1. John Lewis Gaddis, *The Long Peace: Inquiries into the History of the Cold War* (New York, 1987).
2. I use the terms "Third World" and "global south" interchangeably, to connote underdevelopment rather than nonalignment.
3. There is no good way to deal with geographical terminology in discussing Latin America and the United States. Referring to people from the United States as "Americans" risks offending those from elsewhere in the Americas. Given that people from the United States call themselves "Americans," referring to them as "North Americans" seems equally inappropriate (and equally offensive to Canadians and Mexicans). For lack of a better alternative, I have chosen the following approach. People from the United States are "Americans," people from the countries to the south are "Latin Americans." "The Americas" refers to North, South, and Central America.
4. For examples of this literature, see the sources cited in later chapters.
5. Piero Gleijeses, *Conflicting Missions: Havana, Washington, and Africa, 1959–1976* (Chapel Hill, NC, 2002); Timothy Naftali and Aleksandr Fursenko, *"One Hell of a Gamble": Khrushchev, Castro, and Kennedy, 1958–1964* (New York, 1997); Christopher Andrew and Vasili Mitrokhin, *The World Was Going Our Way: The KGB and the Battle for the Third World* (New York, 2005); Jorge Castañeda, *Compañero: The Life and Death of Che Guevara* (New York, 1997); Greg Grandin, *The Last Colonial Massacre: Latin America and the Cold War* (Chicago, 2004); Gilbert Joseph and Daniela Spenser, eds., *In from the Cold: Latin America's New Encounter with the Cold War* (Durham, NC, 2008).
6. Jonathan Haslam, *The Nixon Administration and the Death of Allende's Chile: A Case of Assisted Suicide* (London, 2005); Grandin, *Last Colonial Massacre;* Tanya Harmer, "The Rules of the Game: Allende's Chile, the United States and Cuba, 1970–1973" (Ph.D. Dissertation, London School of Economics, 2008); Odd Arne Westad, *The Global Cold War: Third-World Interventions and the Making of Our Times* (New York, 2005); William Robinson, *Transnational Conflicts: Central America, Social Change, and Globalization* (New York, 2003); John Dinges, *The Condor Years: How Pinochet and His Allies Brought Terrorism to Three Continents* (New York, 2004).
7. See Walter LaFeber, *Inevitable Revolutions: The United States in Central America* (New York, 1983).
8. This viewpoint is characterized in Greg Grandin, *Empire's Workshop: Latin America, the United States, and the Rise of the New Imperialism* (New York, 2006), 223–226. As an example, see Rich Lowry, "Smearing Negroponte," *National Review Online,* February 22, 2005, www.nationalreview.com.
9. Grandin, *Last Colonial Massacre,* xiv; also Daniela Spenser, "Standing Conventional Cold War History on Its Head," in Joseph and Spenser, eds.,

In from the Cold, 394; Steve Stern, "Between Tragedy and Promise: The Politics of Writing Latin American History in the Late Twentieth Century," in Gilbert Joseph, ed., *Reclaiming the Political in Latin American History* (Durham, NC, 2001), 55.

1. Convergent Conflicts

1. For instance, Steve Stern, ed., *Resistance, Rebellion, and Consciousness in the Andean World, 18th to 20th Century* (Madison, WI, 1988).

2. David Healy, *Drive to Hegemony: The United States in the Caribbean, 1898–1917* (Madison, WI, 1988).

3. John Lewis Gaddis, *Surprise, Security, and the American Experience* (Cambridge, MA, 2004), 22–28; Michael Lind, *The American Way of Strategy: U.S. Foreign Policy and the American Way of Life* (New York, 2006), 48–50.

4. Thomas O'Brien, *The Revolutionary Mission: American Enterprise in Latin America, 1900–1945* (New York, 1996).

5. Eileen Findlay, "Love in the Tropics: Marriage, Divorce, and the Construction of Benevolent Colonialism in Puerto Rico, 1898–1910," in Gilbert Joseph, Catherine Legrand, and Ricardo Salvatore, eds., *Close Encounters of Empire: Writing the Cultural History of U.S.–Latin American Relations* (Durham, NC, 1998), 139–172; Elizabeth Cobbs Hoffman, *The Rich Neighbor Policy: Rockefeller and Kaiser in Brazil* (New Haven, 1992).

6. Cited in Thomas G. Paterson et al., *American Foreign Relations since 1895: A History* (Boston, 2005), 153. See also C. Neale Ronning, *Intervention in Latin America* (New York, 1972), 42–49.

7. Norman Long and Bryan Roberts, "The Agrarian Structures of Latin America, 1930–1990," in Leslie Bethell, ed., *The Cambridge History of Latin America,* Vol. 6, Part 1 (New York, 1995), 329.

8. Jorge Nef, "Democratization and Democratic Transition in Latin America," in Sandor Halbesky et al., eds., *Capital, Power, and Inequality in Latin America* (Boulder, CO, 1995), 84–86; Rudiger Bornbusch and Sebastian Edwards, *The Macroeconomics of Populism in Latin America* (Chicago, 1991), 19–22.

9. Greg Grandin, "Your Americanism and Mine: Americanism and Anti-Americanism in the Americas," *American Historical Review* 111 (2006): 1048–1051.

10. Quoted in Steven Schwartzberg, "Rómulo Betancourt: From a Communist Anti-Imperialist to a Social Democrat with U.S. Support," *Journal of Latin American Studies* 29 (1997): 626.

11. Interpretations of Roosevelt's policies include Lloyd Gardner, *Economic Aspects of New Deal Diplomacy* (Boston, 1971); Gerald Haines, "Under the Eagle's Wing: The Franklin Roosevelt Administration Forges an American Hemisphere," *Diplomatic History* 1 (1977): 373–388; Peter Smith, *Talons of the Eagle: Dynamics of U.S.–Latin American Relations* (New York, 2000), chapter 3.

12. Eric Roorda, *The Dictator Next Door: The Good Neighbor Policy and the Trujillo Regime in the Dominican Republic, 1930–1945* (Durham, NC, 1998); Max Paul Friedman, *Nazis and Good Neighbors: The United States Campaign against the Germans of Latin America in World War II* (New York, 2003).

13. Piero Gleijeses, *Shattered Hope: The Guatemalan Revolution and the United States, 1944–1954* (Princeton, 1991), 22–24; Melvyn Leffler, *A Preponderance of Power: National Security, the Truman Administration, and the Cold War* (Stanford, 1992), 172–173.

14. See Elizabeth Borgwardt, *A New Deal for the World: America's Vision for Human Rights* (Cambridge, MA, 2006).

15. Frederick Stirton Weaver, *Inside the Volcano: The History and Political Economy of Central America* (Boulder, CO, 1994), 135; Thomas Leonard and John Bratzel, *Latin America during World War II* (New York, 2006), 49.

16. Manuel Caballero, *Latin America and the Comintern, 1919–1943* (New York, 1986), 121–148.

17. Leslie Bethell and Ian Roxborough, "Latin America between the Second World War and the Cold War: Some Reflections on the 1945–48 Conjuncture," *Journal of Latin American Studies* 20 (1988): 167–189.

18. Grandin, *Last Colonial Massacre,* 4–5, 8–10; Victor Bulmer-Thomas, *The Political Economy of Central America since 1920* (Cambridge, UK, 1987), 133–148.

19. A recent account is Mary Riordan, *Blood and Fire: La Violencia in Antioquia, Colombia, 1946–1953* (Durham, NC, 2002).

20. Stephen G. Rabe, *Eisenhower and Latin America: The Foreign Policy of Anti-Communism* (Chapel Hill, NC, 1989), 39, 87. See also José Gilberto Quintero Torres, *Venezuela-USA: Estrategia y seguridad en lo regional y en lo bilateral, 1952–1958* (Caracas, 2000).

21. Bethell and Roxborough, "Latin America between the Second World War and the Cold War," esp. 183–187. See also Rabe, *Eisenhower and Latin America,* chapter 1; Steven Schwartzberg, *Democracy and U.S. Policy in Latin America during the Truman Years* (Gainesville, FL, 2003), passim.

22. On the Bogotazo, see Jorge Osterling, *Democracy in Colombia: Clientelist Politics and Guerrilla Warfare* (New Brunswick, NJ, 1989), 88–89.

23. Robert Alexander, *Bolivia: Past, Present, and Future of Its Politics* (New York, 1982), 80–81; Cole Blasier, "The United States and the Revolution," in James Malloy and Richard Thorn, eds., *Beyond the Revolution: Bolivia since 1952* (Pittsburgh, 1971), 100.

24. Gleijeses, *Shattered Hope;* Nick Cullather, *Secret History: The CIA's Classified Account of Its Operations in Guatemala, 1952–1954* (Stanford, 1999).

25. On the post-coup period, see Stephen Streeter, *Managing the Counterrevolution: The United States and Guatemala, 1954–1961* (Athens, OH, 2000).

26. Greg Grandin, *The Blood of Guatemala: A History of Race and Nation* (Durham, NC, 2000), 209–218; Jennifer Schirmer, *The Guatemalan Military Project: A Violence Called Democracy* (Philadelphia, 1998), 13–14.

27. Cullather, *Secret History,* 95–96.

28. Mark Hove, "The Arbenz Factor: Salvador Allende, U.S.-Chilean Relations, and the 1954 U.S. Intervention in Guatemala," *Diplomatic History* 31 (2007): 623.

29. Grandin, *Empire's Workshop,* 54; "Manifestaciones de sentimientos anti-norteamericanos en algunos puntos de Latinoamérica," 12 de noviembre de 1959, Dirección de Política Internacional (DPI), Estados Unidos, Expediente (Exp.) 12, Archivo Central del Ministerio de Relaciones Exteriores de Venezuela (MREVEN).

30. National Security Council Report on U.S. Policy toward Latin America, May 21, 1958, *Declassified Documents Reference System (DDRS);* Alan McPherson, *Yankee No! Anti-Americanism in U.S.-Latin American Relations* (Cambridge, MA, 2003), esp. chapter 3.

31. Ernesto Guevara, *The Motorcycle Diaries: Notes on a Latin American Journey* (New York, 2004), 168; Richard Immerman, *The CIA in Guatemala: The Foreign Policy of Intervention* (Austin, TX, 1982), 188; Westad, *The Global Cold War,* 149.

32. Ulises Casas, *Origen y desarrollo del movimiento revolucionario colombiano* (Bogota, 1980), 77–78.

33. Clara Aldrighi, *La izquierda armada: Ideología, ética e identidad en el MLN-Tupamaros* (Montevideo, 2001).

34. H. W. Brands, *The Specter of Neutralism: The United States and the Emergence of the Third World* (New York, 1990), 323–328.

35. See Mexico City to State, September 2, 1961, Box 141, Country File, National Security File (NSF), John F. Kennedy Library (JFKL); Central Intelligence Agency (CIA), "Survey of Latin America," April 1, 1964, Box 1, Latin America Country File, NSF, Lyndon Baines Johnson Library (LBJL).

36. Jonathan Hartlyn and Arturo Valenzuela, "Democracy in Latin America since 1930," in Leslie Bethell, ed., *The Cambridge History of Latin America,* Vol. 6, Part 2 (New York, 1995), 160.

37. Quoted in "Reunião do Conselho de Ministros Realizada em 11 de Janeiro de 1962," EG pr 1961.09.14, Arquivo Ernesto Geisel, Getulio Vargas Foundation (FGV); "United States Policy toward Latin America," July 3, 1961, *Foreign Relations of the United States, 1961–1963,* Vol. 12, Document #15. Hereafter, documents from the *Foreign Relations* series are cited as *FRUS* followed by year, volume, and document number.

38. Quoted in Embajada en Buenos Aires al Secretario de Relaciones Exteriores, septiembre de 1962, Exp. 1, Legajo (Leg.) 68, Archivo Histórico Genaro Estrada (AHGE); also Daniel James, *Resistance and Integration:*

Peronism and the Argentine Working Class, 1946–1976 (New York, 1988), chapters 1–4.

39. Luigi Einaudi, *Changing Contexts of Revolution in Latin America* (Santa Monica, 1966).

40. Margaret Champion, *Peru and Peruvians in the Twentieth Century: Politics and Prospects* (New York, 2006), 182.

41. Daniel Hellinger, *Venezuela: Tarnished Democracy* (Boulder, CO, 1991), 94–95; Gastón Carvallo, *Clase dominante y democracia representativa en Venezula* (Caracas, 1995), 73–76; Christopher Abel and Marco Palacios, "Colombia since 1958," in Leslie Bethell, ed., *The Cambridge History of Latin America*, Vol. 8 (New York, 1992), 634–636.

42. Economic Commission for Latin America (ECLA), *Economic Survey of Latin America, 1958* (Mexico City, 1959), 3–6, 57, 73; Victor Bulmer-Thomas, *The Economic History of Latin America since Independence* (Cambridge, UK, 1994), 309–312; Rosemary Thorp, *Progress, Poverty and Exclusion: An Economic History of Latin America in the 20th Century* (Baltimore, 1998), 178–180; ECLA, *Economic Survey of Latin America, 1963* (New York, 1965), 159–163.

43. Leon G. Campbell, "The Historiography of the Peruvian Guerrilla Movement, 1960–1965," *Latin American Research Review* (1974): 45.

44. Chester Bowles, "Cry for Land in Latin America," *New York Times*, November 22, 1959.

45. Daniel Levy, *Higher Education and the State in Latin America: Private Challenges to Public Dominance* (Chicago, 1986), 41–43; Bryan Roberts and Orlandina de Oliveira, "Urban Growth and Urban Social Structure in Latin America, 1930–1990," in Bethell, ed., *The Cambridge History of Latin America*, Vol. 6, Part 1, 256; Victor Alba, *Politics and the Labor Movement in Latin America* (Stanford, 1968), 211; Ian Roxborough, "The Urban Working Class and Labour Movement in Latin America since 1930," in Bethell, ed., *The Cambridge History of Latin America*, Vol. 6, Part 2, 348.

46. German G. Rama and Juan Carlos Tedesco, "Education and Development in Latin America (1950–1975)," *International Review of Education* 25 (1979): 207; Daniel Levine, *Conflict and Political Change in Venezuela* (Princeton, 1973), 148.

47. Jeremi Suri, *Power and Protest: Global Revolution and the Rise of Détente* (Cambridge, MA 2003), chapter 1; Westad, *Global Cold War*, chapters 1–2; Melvyn Leffler, *For the Soul of Mankind: The United States, the Soviet Union, and the Cold War* (New York, 2007), 82–83, 171–176.

48. Westad, *Global Cold War*, 93.

49. Andrew and Mitrokhin, *The World Was Going Our Way*, 9–10. See also "Minutes of the Meeting of the CPSU CC Plenum on the State of Soviet Foreign Policy," June 24, 1957, Cold War International History Project Virtual Archive (CWIHP).

50. Khrushchev in Alvin Rubinstein, ed., *The Foreign Policy of the Soviet Union* (New York, 1972), 266–269; Andrew and Mitrokhin, *The World Was Going Our Way.*

51. "USSR Economic and Technical Aid to Developing Countries, as of Nov. 1, 1967," translation from *Vneshnaya Torgovlya* 9 (1967): 4, Box 11, Henry Shapiro Papers, Library of Congress (LOC); John Lewis Gaddis, *We Now Know: Rethinking Cold War History* (New York, 1997), 156–167, 181–183; Timothy Naftali and Aleksandr Fursenko, *Khrushchev's Cold War: The Inside Story of an American Adversary* (New York, 2007), 80–82.

52. Quoted in Michael Beschloss, *The Crisis Years: Kennedy and Khrushchev, 1960–1963* (New York, 1991), 60; also William Taubman, *Khrushchev: The Man and His Era* (New York, 2004), 348.

53. "Address to the Congress on Urgent National Needs," May 25, 1961, American Presidency Project (APP).

54. Westad, *Global Cold War,* chapter 4.

55. The literature on the Cuban revolution is enormous. Recent contributions include Samuel Farber, *The Origins of the Cuban Revolution Reconsidered* (Chapel Hill, NC, 2006); Jon Lee Anderson, *Che Guevara: A Revolutionary Life* (New York, 1997); Castañeda, *Compañero;* Julia Sweig, *Inside the Cuban Revolution: Fidel Castro and the Urban Underground* (Cambridge, MA, 2003).

56. Dispatch from the Embassy in Guatemala, March 3, 1959, Box 1, Roland Ebel Collection, Tulane University Latin American Library; Rio de Janeiro to Ottawa, October 30, 1960, Vol. 5047, File 2348–40, Library and Archives Canada (LAC); Bureau of Intelligence and Research (INR), "The Outlook for Brazil," April 7, 1961, Box WH-40A, Schlesinger Papers, JFKL.

57. Thomas Wright, *Latin America in the Era of the Cuban Revolution* (New York, 2003), 49–51.

58. Campbell, "Historiography of the Peruvian Guerrilla Movement," 51–54; Wilfredo Kapsoli, *Los Movimientos Campesinos en el Perú, 1879–1965* (Lima, 1977), 124–143.

59. "Cuba: Ejemplo de los anhelos de América Latina," *Combate* (Havana), 3 de agosto de 1960; also Embamex la Habana a SRE, 4 de agosto de 1960, Topográfica III-1987–13, Archivo de Concentraciones, Ministerio de Relaciones Exteriores, México; and "Informationsbulletin Nr. 5," undated (1960–61), DY 24/6826, Stiftung Archiv der Parteien und Massenorgenisationen im Bundesarchiv (SAPMO).

60. INR, "The Impact of Castro on Latin America and the Caribbean Area," February 28, 1961, Box WH-40A, Schlesinger Files, JFKL; INR, "Latin American Reaction to the U.S. Break with Cuba," January 23, 1961, ibid.; "Bericht über die Reise der Delegation des Buros des Zentralrats nach Chile," undated (1960), DY 24/6826, SAPMO.

61. CIA Information Telegram, May 26, 1962, Electronic Briefing Book (EBB) 124, National Security Archive (NSA); "Acto conmemorativo del asalto al

Cuartel Moncada de Cuba," 20 de julio de 1966, Caja 456, Dirección General de Investigaciones Políticas y Sociales (IPS), Archivo General de la Nación de México (AGNMEX); "Manifestación mitin de grupos de Izquierda, celebrada hoy," 26 de julio de 1966, ibid.

62. "Declaración conjunta emitida en la Habana, Cuba, por la CNED y la Organización Latinoamericana de Estudiantes," 4 de julio de 1967, Caja 464, IPS, AGNMEX; "Homenaje a Davíd Aguilar Mora en la Escuela Nacional de Economía UNAM," 20 de julio de 1966, Caja 456, ibid.

63. Mexico to State, August 31, 1961, EBB 124, NSA.

64. Editorial in *Excélsior,* quoted in "Caso Cubano: Medio Político en México," *El Bien Público,* 26 de abril de 1961; Díaz Ordaz a Alberto T. Casella, Lázaro Cárdenas, Domingo Velasco, y Olga Poblete, 22 de marzo de 1961, Caja 1465A, IPS, AGNMEX.

65. Habana a SRE, 4 de agosto de 1960, Topográfica III-1987–13, Archivo de Concentraciones.

66. San Salvador to State, November 3, 1960, 716.00(W)/11–360, Record Group (RG) 59, U.S. National Archives and Records Administration (NARA); see also Michael J. Francis, "Revolutionary Labor in Latin America," *Journal of Inter-American Studies* 10 (1968), 597–616.

67. Einaudi, *Changing Contexts of Revolution in Latin America.*

68. Levine, *Conflict and Political Change in Venezuela,* 48, 155.

69. Héctor Béjar, *Peru 1965: Notes on a Guerrilla Experience,* trans. William Rose (New York, 1969), 47; also Casas, *Origen y desarrollo del movimiento revolucionario colombiano,* 89–93.

70. FULNA, "Proclama al Pueblo Paraguayo," febrero de 1959, DNAT-C-53, Centro de Documentación y Archivo (CDYA), Corte Suprema de la Justicia, Asunción.

71. Jefe Sección de Información a varios Ministerios, 23 de marzo de 1961, Caja 16, Despacho Ministro, Ministerio de Gobierno, Archivo General de la Nación de Colombia (AGNCOL); Embamex Managua, "Informe sobre la situación política de Nicaragua," 25 de marzo de 1961, Caja 4547, AHGE; INR, "The Impact of Castro on Latin America and the Caribbean Area," February 28, 1961, Box WH-40A, Schlesinger Papers, JFKL; INR, "The Situation in Honduras," January 6, 1961, ibid.; Richard Gott, *Las Guerrillas en América Latina* (Santiago, 1971), 21.

72. Quoted in Hugh Thomas, *Cuba: The Pursuit of Freedom* (New York, 1971), 1293; see also Anderson, *Che Guevara,* 419; "Lista de individuos que formaron parte del grupo revolucionario que invadió el territorio de Nicaragua, conocido como 'Grupo del Chaparral,'" 25 de octubre de 1960, LSD 002, Instituto de la Historia de Nicaragua y Centroamérica (IHNCA); Frente Unitario Nicaraguense, "Manifiesto al Pueblo de Nicaragua," febrero de 1960, JGRN 0010, IHNCA.

73. Ydígoras to Kennedy, March 16, 1961, Guatemala Collection, NSA. See also "El PNR '44 Se Solidariza con la Revolución Cubana," *La Picota,* 30 de marzo de 1960, Hemeroteca, Archivo General de Centroamérica (AGCA).

74. "Informe diplomático-político," octubre de 1959, Caja 176, Transferencia 8, Ministerio de Relaciones Exteriores (MRE), AGNCOL; Aide-Memoire de Alejandro Montiel Arguello a Embajada de los Estados Unidos, 26 de marzo de 1960, Caja 44, Sección Relaciones Exteriores, Fondo Presidencial, Archivo General de la Nación de Nicaragua (AGNNIC).

75. "Somocistas Disparan Contra Estudiantes," *El Cronista* (Tegucigalpa), 24 de julio de 1959; Ramiro Sacasa Guerrero a MRE, 28 de octubre de 1959, Caja 42, Sección Ministro, Colección Relaciones Exteriores, Fondo Presidencial, AGNNIC.

76. Alfred Stepan, "The New Professionalism of Internal Warfare and Military Role Expansion," in Abraham Lowenthal, ed., *Armies and Politics in Latin America* (New York, 1976), 247–250; Daniel Masterson, "Caudillismo and Institutional Change: Manuel Odría and the Peruvian Armed Forces, 1948–1956," *Americas* 40 (1984): 486.

77. Pedro J. Prokupchuk a Stroessner, 3 de marzo de 1961, DNAT-C-98, CDYA; also Nota No. 49/Ex., 20 de abril de 1961, ibid.

78. Golbery do Couto e Silva, *Conjuntura Política Nacional o Poder Executivo e Geopolítica do Brasil* (Rio de Janeiro, 1981), 24; also idem, *Geopolítica do Brasil* (Rio de Janeiro, 1967), 198–199.

79. "Text of Dr. Fidel Castro's TV Appearance on September 17, 1959," Castro Speech Database (CSD), University of Texas; R. Hart Phillips, *The Cuban Dilemma* (New York, 1962), 28.

80. McPherson, *Yankee No,* 52.

81. Quotes from "Castro Delivers Speech at Presidential Palace," January 17, 1959; and "Castro Interviewed on 'Meet the Press,'" February 24, 1959, CSD.

82. Fidel Castro, *My Life: A Spoken Autobiography* (New York, 2008), 609; also undated interview with Fidel Castro, Box 15, Cuban Revolution Collection, Yale University Manuscripts and Archives.

83. "Summary of Speeches Made at October 26, 1959 Mass Demonstration," CSD.

84. Fidel Castro, *Obras Escogidas de Fidel Castro, Tomo I* (Madrid, 1976), 99.

85. "Cuba: Ejemplo de los anhelos de América Latina," *Combate* (Havana), 3 de agosto de 1960; Rodney Arismendi, *Problemas de una revolución continental* (Montevideo, 1962), 20; Embamex la Habana a SRE, 4 de agosto de 1960, Topográfica III-1987–13, Archivo de Concentraciones.

86. San Salvador to State, August 16, 1962, 716.00/8–1660, RG 59, NARA.

87. CIA Intelligence Memorandum, July 25, 1963, Box 60, Country File, NSF, JFKL.

88. *Avante: Por la Democracia del Pueblo y el Socialismo,* marzo de 1961, 11, Caja 1465A, IPS, AGNMEX.

89. Eric Zolov, *"¡Cuba sí, Yanquis no!* The Sacking of the Instituto Cultural México-Norteamericano in Morelia, Michoacán, 1961," in Joseph and Spenser, eds., *In from the Cold,* 223–224.

90; Alan McPherson, "Courts of World Opinion: Trying the Panama Flag Riots of 1964," *Diplomatic History* 28 (2004), 83–112, esp. 85–87; "Fanned Flames," *Time,* December 7, 1959; Embamex la Habana a SRE, 17 de enero de 1966, Topográfica III-5758–1, Archivo de Concentraciones; National Intelligence Estimate (NIE), 85–67, "Key Issues and Prospects for Castro's Cuba," March 2, 1967, Box 9, National Intelligence Estimates, NSF, LBJL.

91. "Memorandum para información del C. Representante de México en el Consejo de la Organización de los Estados Americanos," 25 de febrero de 1961, Exp. 2, Leg. 1, Embamex Costa Rica, AHGE; see also Telegram from José Chiriboga Villagómez to Tello, 23 de enero de 1961, Topográfica III-5607–1, Archivo de Concentraciones.

92. INR, "The Outlook for Brazil," April 7, 1961, Box WH-40A, Schlesinger Papers, JFKL; "Em Havana," *Estado de São Paulo,* 1 de fevereiro de 1961. On Quadros's attempts to forge a more independent foreign policy, see James Hershberg, "'High-Spirited Confusion': Brazil, the 1961 Belgrade Non-Aligned Conference, and the Limits of an 'Independent' Foreign Policy during the High Cold War," *Cold War History* 7 (2007): 373–388.

93. Tello a Dorticós, 18 de julio de 1960, Topográfica SPR-329–17, Archivo de Concentraciones; "Discurso del señor Presidente López Mateos al recibir al de Cuba, Dr. Dorticós," undated, Topográfica SPR-407–3, Archivo de Concentraciones; Gilberto Bosques, *Historia Oral de la Diplomacia Mexicana,* 140, Oral History Number 2, AHGE.

94. Memorandum of Conference with President Kennedy, January 25, 1961, *FRUS 1961–1963,* X: Document #26.

95. Naftali and Fursenko, *Khrushchev's Cold War,* 295.

96. Anderson, *Che Guevara,* 174, 415; Naftali and Fursenko, *One Hell of a Gamble,* 11–14.

97. Anderson, *Che Guevara,* 443.

98. The best discussions of the Soviet–Cuban alliance are Naftali and Fursenko, *One Hell of a Gamble;* idem, *Khrushchev's Cold War,* chapters 12 and 17; also Yuri Pavlov, *Soviet-Cuban Alliance, 1959–1961* (Coral Gables, FL, 1994).

99. Dean Rusk, *As I Saw It* (London, 1991), 245; also Vladislav Zubok, *A Failed Empire: The Soviet Union in the Cold War from Stalin to Gorbachev* (Chapel Hill, NC, 2007), 182; Taubman, *Khrushchev,* 534–535.

100. Nikita Khrushchev, *Khrushchev Remembers,* trans. Strobe Talbott (Boston, 1970), 492.

101. Pavlov Interview, http://www.gwu.edu/~nsarchiv/coldwar/interviews/episode-18/pavlov1.html (accessed 6/23/07); also Memorandum of Conversation between Castro and Mikoyan, November 4, 1962, CWIHP.

102. The deterioration of U.S.–Cuban relations is described in Thomas G. Paterson, *Contesting Castro: The United States and the Triumph of the Cuban Revolution* (New York, 1994); and Richard Welch, *Response to Revolution: The United States and the Cuban Revolution* (Chapel Hill, NC, 1985). On Mikoyan's visit, see Embamex la Habana a SRE, 19 de febrero de 1960, Topográfica III-1987–13, Archivo de Concentraciones; and Ernesto Madero al Secretario, 18 de febrero de 1960, Exp. 11, Leg. 19, Embamex Moscú, AHGE.

103. Farber, *Origins of the Cuban Revolution Reconsidered*, 75–84.

104. Quoted in "Radio-Television Interview with Rafael Rodríguez," October 15, 1960, CSD; see also Embajada de Colombia en la Habana, "Informe político," enero de 1961, Caja 176, Transferencia 8, MRE, AGNCOL; "Bericht über die Teilnahme am 4. Kongress der Sozialistischen Jugend Kubas," 13 Mai 1960, DY 24/6826, SAPMO.

105. State Department, "Principal Soviet Public Statements of Defense of Cuba," undated, Cuban Missile Crisis Collection, NSA; Gaddis, *We Now Know*, 183.

106. Andrew and Mitrokhin, *The World Was Going Our Way*, 40.

107. Memorandum from the Joint Chiefs of Staff to Secretary of Defense McNamara, January 27, 1961, *FRUS 1961–1963*, X: Document #28; CIA, "Cuba," February 17, 1961, *FRUS 1961–1963*, X: Document #46; Memorandum of Conversation, June 30, 1963, *FRUS 1961–1963*, XII: Document #295.

108. I. Zarco, "Problemas y Soluciones," *Prensa Libre*, 5 de enero de 1961, Hemeroteca, AGCA; see also "El Peligro de la Infiltración Totalitaria," *El Plata* (Montevideo), 14 de enero de 1961; Mensaje Transcribido en Memorandum para Ramiro Sacasa Guerrero, 22 de febrero de 1960, Caja 44, Sección Relaciones Exteriores, Fondo Presidencial, AGNNIC.

109. "Boletím SEI," Nos. 447 y 484, agosto y noviembre de 1960, DNAT-C-75, CDYA; also Luís Somoza a Ydígoras, 16 de marzo de 1960, Caja grande 9 (Caja pequeña 522), Secretaría Privada, Fondo Presidencial, AGNNIC.

110. CIA, "Prospects for Political Stability in the Caribbean in 1960 with Particular Reference to Cuba, Panama, and Guatemala," December 29, 1959, *DDRS*.

111. Somoza a Ydígoras, 16 de marzo de 1960, Caja granda 9 (Caja pequeña 522), Secretaría Privada, Fondo Presidencial, AGNNIC; also undated message from Somoza, ibid.; Ydígoras a MRE, 22 de agosto de 1960, Paquete 1, 1960, Dirección de Asuntos Bilaterales, Archivo del Ministerio de Relaciones Exteriores de Guatemala (MREGUAT); Memorandum para el Señor Presidente de la República, 4 de mayo de 1960, ibid.; Ydígoras to Kennedy, March 16, 1961, Guatemala Collection, NSA.

112. "Telegram from the Embassy in the Soviet Union to the Department of State," April 18, 1961, *FRUS 1961–1963*, VI: Document #9; Trumbull Higgins, *Perfect Failure: Kennedy, Eisenhower, and the CIA at the Bay of Pigs* (New York, 1987), passim.

113. Ministro de Educación Nacional al Ministro de Gobierno, 12 de mayo de 1961, Caja 16, Despacho Ministro, Ministerio de Gobierno, AGNCOL.

114. Embajada en Santiago, "Informe político-diplomático," abril de 1961, Caja 202, Transferencia 8, MRE, AGNCOL; Colonia a SRE, 18 de mayo de 1961, Topográfica III-5607–1, Archivo de Concentraciones; Caracas a SRE, 18 de abril de 1961, ibid.; Embassy Dispatch, April 20, 1961, Box 1, Ebel Collection, Tulane.

115. "Information über eine Aussprache mit dem Generalsekretär der Sozialist-ischen Volkspartei Kubas, Blas Roca, am 13.6.61," DY 24/6826, SAPMO.

116. Untitled photograph, Print 96, Book VII, Folder 539, Box 5, Cuban Revolution Collection, Yale; Memorandum, 17 de mayo de 1961, Topográ-fica III-5664–1, Archivo de Concentraciones.

117. "Conversation with Comandante Ernesto Guevara of Cuba," August 22, 1961, Cuban Missile Crisis Collection, NSA.

118. "Talking Points on the Vienna Conversations," June 12, 1961, Box 300, Bowles Papers, Yale; Taubman, *Khrushchev*, 497; CIA, "Chronology of Significant Events since 20 January 1961," Box WH-31, Schlesinger Papers, JFKL; "BCP Politburo Secret Resolution on Arms Delivery to Cuba," December 2, 1961, CWIHP.

119. "Mikoyan's Meeting with Cuban Leaders," November 5, 1962, CWIHP.

120. "Memorandum estrictamente confidencial para el Señor Presidente de la República," 19 de mayo de 1961, Topográfica SPR-400–9, Archivo de Concentraciones.

2. Intervention and the Limits of Power

1. Memorandum of Conversation between Castro and Mikoyan, November 4, 1962, CWIHP.

2. Memorandum of Conversation, June 30, 1963, *FRUS 1961–1963*, XII: Document #295.

3. FULNA, "Proclama al Pueblo Paraguayo," febrero de 1959, DNAT-C-53, CDYA; Aníbal Miranda, *Lucha armada en Paraguay* (Asunción, 1992); Declaración Indagatoria No. 97, 12 de diciembre de 1959, DI-L-L14, CDYA.

4. Cooke a Perón, 24 de julio de 1961, Juan Domingo Perón and John William Cooke, *Correspondencia Perón-Cooke*, Vol. 2 (Buenos Aires, 1973), 203; also Carlos Acuña, *Por amor al odio: La tragedia de la subversión en la Argentina* (Buenos Aires, 2000), 276–298.

5. "Muertos por la Violencia en Departamento de Tolima durante los años de 1958, 1959 y 1960"; "Relación de los muertos habidos en el Departamento

del Tolimo en el Año de 1958," 24 de enero de 1961, Caja 3, Despacho Ministro, Ministerio de Gobierno, AGNCOL.

6. "Instrumentos de Defensa Política," undated, Caja 182, Transferencia 3, MRE, AGNCOL.

7. Kennedy to McNamara, October 4, 1963, *DDRS*.

8. General de Brigada J.M. Castro-León a Betancourt, 13 de noviembre de 1959, Complemento E, Tomo 35, Archivo Rómulo Betancourt (ARB).

9. Telegrama de Base Militar Puerto Barrios al Señor Presidente de la República, 13 de noviembre de 1960, Box 1, Miguel Ydígoras Fuentes Materials, Tulane.

10. INR, "The Impact of Castro on Latin America and the Caribbean Area," February 28, 1961, Box WH-40A, Schlesinger Files, JFKL.

11. *World Bank Development Report, 1983* (Washington, DC, 1984), 192; *World Bank Development Report, 1979* (Washington, DC, 1980), 166–167; Stephen G. Rabe, *The Most Dangerous Area in the World: John F. Kennedy Confronts Communist Revolution in Latin America* (Chapel Hill, NC, 1999), 22–24; Tony Smith, *America's Mission: The United States and the Worldwide Struggle for Democracy in the Twentieth Century* (Princeton, 1994), 218; South America Department, Report WH-210a, "Current Economic Position and Prospects of Brazil," November 30, 1971, World Bank Archives (WBA).

12. Óscar Pinochet de la Barra, ed., *El Pensamiento de Eduardo Frei* (Santiago, 1982), 61.

13. USIA Research Report, July 10, 1963, Box 216, Regional Security File, NSF, JFKL.

14. CIA, "Instability in Latin America," May 19, 1965, Box 2, Latin America Country File, NSF, LBJL; "Mikoyan's Meeting with Cuban Leaders," November 5, 1962, CWIHP; also Naftali and Fursenko, *"One Hell of a Gamble,"* 172.

15. Ernesto Guevara, *Episodes of the Cuban Revolutionary War, 1956–1958* (New York, 1996), 338–339; idem, *Ernesto Che Guevara: Escritos y Discursos,* Vol. 4 (Havana, 1977), 169–170.

16. Carlos Franqui, *Diary of the Cuban Revolution* (New York, 1980), 294; Castro, *My Life,* 609.

17. Memorandum para Acuerdo Presidencial, 25 de febrero de 1961, Topográfica III-5607–1, Archivo de Concentraciones.

18. "Review of Continued Sino-Soviet Intervention in This Hemisphere," undated (1963), Box 60, Country File, NSF, JFKL; Gleijeses, *Conflicting Missions,* 21. The motives of Cuban interventionism are discussed in Gleijeses, "Las motivaciones de la política exterior cubana," in Daniela Spenser, ed., *Espejos de la guerra fría* (Mexico City, 2004), 151–173.

19. Naftali and Fursenko, *"One Hell of a Gamble,"* 49–50; idem, *Khrushchev's Cold War,* 305, 428.

20. Zubok, *Failed Empire,* 182–183; Mitrohkin and Andrew, *The World Was Going Our Way,* 40.

21. Memorandum of Conversation between Castro and Mikoyan, November 4, 1962, CWIHP; Nikita Khrushchev, *Khrushchev Remembers: The Last Testament,* trans. Strobe Talbott (Boston, 1974), 510.

22. Memorandum of Conversation between Castro and Mikoyan, November 4, 1962, CWIHP.

23. CIA, "Chronology of Significant Events since 20 January 1961," Box WH-31, Schlesinger Files, JFKL; NIE 85–64, "Situation and Prospects in Cuba," Box 9, NIE, NSF, LBJL.

24. Guevara, "The Tactics and Strategy of the Latin American Revolution," *Juventud Rebelde,* October 2, 1968, translated as "Guevara Discusses Latin American Revolution," *DDRS;* Jorge Domínguez, *To Make a World Safe for Revolution: Cuba's Foreign Policy* (Cambridge, MA, 1989), 64.

25. "Declaraciones en la prensa cubana dadas por German Lairet, Jefe de la Misión de las FALN," undated; and "Lista de Comunistas Venezolanos en Cuba," 27 de mayo de 1965, in Luis Vera Gómez, ed., *La subversión armada 1964–1967 en sus documentos* (Caracas, 2005), 250–251, 270–272.

26. BCP Politburo Secret Resolution on Arms Delivery to Cuba, December 2, 1961, CWIHP.

27. See "Antecedentes," 18 de junio de 1976, DI-B-1051, CDYA; CIA Intelligence Memorandum, July 25, 1963, Box 60, Country File, NSF, JFKL; Benigno (Daniel Alarcón Ramirez), *Memorias de un soldado cubano: Vida y muerte de la revolución* (Barcelona, 1997), 48–52; "Boletín para la Junta de Inteligencia Nacional," 21 de noviembre de 1967, Caja 83, Despacho Ministro, Ministerio del Interior, AGNCOL; "Rendición de aportes entregados en 1966," 26 de diciembre de 1966, and "Aprobación de aportes para 1970," 28 de diciembre de 1969, in "Chile en los archivos de la URSS," *Estudios Públicos* 72 (1998): 398–400; Daniela Spenser, "The Caribbean Crisis: Catalyst for Soviet Projection in Latin America," Joseph and Spenser, eds., *In from the Cold,* 99–100.

28. "Actividades del PCM con motivo del XIII Aniversario de la revolución cubana," 13 de julio de 1966, Caja 456, IPS, AGNMEX; CIA, "The Situation in Cuba," January 2, 1962, Box WH-40A, Schlesinger Files, JFKL; Carta de R. Iglesias Patiño a Alejando Hidrovo Rosales, 9 de marzo de 1965," in Vera Gómez, ed., *La subversión armada,* 251–252.

29. CIA Current Intelligence Memorandum, January 19, 1963, Box 51, Country File, NSF, JFKL; Westad, *Global Cold War,* 176.

30. "Cooperation between the Czechoslovak and Cuban Intelligence Services," January 11, 1967, CWIHP; "Complaint by Brazil Regarding Czechoslovak Transport of Guerrilla Fighters from Cuba to Latin America," undated, CWIHP; INR, "Cuba and Africa," January 5, 1965, Box 2, Country File, NSF, LBJL; Agustín Blanco Muñoz, ed., *La Lucha Armada: Hablan Seis*

Comandantes (Caracas, 1981), 51–52; Secretario General del Ministerio del Interior a Don Antonio Campos Alum, 17 de junio de 1969, DNAT-C-2A, CDYA; Benigno, *Memorias de un soldado cubano*, 47.

31. Informe de Dirección de Asuntos Confidenciales, 2 de octubre de 1963, DI-L-E2, CDYA; Informe Confidencial No. 350, 14 de agosto de 1963, ibid.; "Boletín para la junta de inteligencia nacional," 7 de noviembre de 1967, Caja 83, Despacho Ministro, Ministerio del Interior, AGNCOL; Acuña, *Por amor al odio*, 34–37.

32. "Declaraciones en la prensa cubana dadas por German Lairet," undated, in Vera Gómez, ed., *La subversión armada*, 270–272; "Review of Continued Sino-Soviet Intervention in This Hemisphere," undated (1963), Box 60, Country File, NSF, JFKL; CIA Intelligence Memorandum, July 25, 1963, ibid.; Benigno, *Memorias de un soldado cubano*, 48.

33. Westad, *Global Cold War*, 177.

34. Ernesto Guevara, *Guerrilla Warfare* (New York, 1961), 15; Michael Lowy, *The Marxism of Che Guevara* (New York, 1973), 91–93.

35. Guevara, *Guerrilla Warfare*, 75; Guevara, *Episodes of the Cuban Revolutionary War*, 397–398; Guevara, "Tactics and Strategy of the Latin American Revolution."

36. "Speech by Prime Minister Fidel Castro at Closing Ceremony of First LASO Conference," August 11, 1967, CSD.

37. Guevara, *Guerrilla Warfare*, 15; Blanco Muñoz, ed., *La Lucha Armada*, 349.

38. "Second Declaration of Havana," February 4, 1962, *Cuban Foreign Policy, 1950–62*, Reel 1; Special Memorandum 1–67, "Latin American Insurgencies Revisited," February 17, 1967, Box 3, Latin America Country File, NSF, LBJL.

39. "Address at a White House Reception for Members of Congress and for the Diplomatic Corps of the Latin American Republics," March 13, 1961, APP.

40. "Report from the Task Force on Immediate Latin American Problems to President-elect Kennedy," January 4, 1961, *FRUS 1961–1963*, XII: Document #2; "Report to the President on Latin American Mission," March 10, 1961, Box WH-40, Schlesinger Files, JFKL; "Address on the First Anniversary of the Alliance for Progress," March 13, 1962, APP.

41. Betancourt a Kennedy, 25 de octubre de 1961, Complemento B, Tomo 38, ARB; "Report to the President on Latin American Mission."

42. McPherson, *Yankee No*, 73.

43. "Betancourt Viewpoint," *Christian Science Monitor*, April 12, 1962; also Betancourt a Kennedy, 10 de noviembre de 1960, Complemento D, Tomo 37, ARB.

44. "U.S. Overseas Internal Defense Policy," August 1, 1962, Box 319, Meetings and Memoranda, NSF, JFKL; Michael Latham, *Modernization as Ideology: American Social Science and "Nation Building" in the Kennedy Era* (Chapel Hill, NC, 2000), 45.

45. "Report to the President on Latin American Mission"; "Summary Minutes of Meeting," November 29, 1961, *FRUS 1961–1963,* XII: Document #35.

46. "Selling a Revolution to Latin America," *New York Times,* December 17, 1961. On the outlines of the Alliance, see Jeffrey Taffet, *Foreign Aid as Foreign Policy: The Alliance for Progress in Latin America* (New York, 2007), chapters 2–3; Ronald L. Scheman, *The Alliance for Progress: A Retrospective* (New York, 1988).

47. Arthur Schlesinger, Jr., *A Thousand Days: John F. Kennedy in the White House* (New York, 2002), 774; Gordon to the Undersecretary, November 16, 1966, Box 2, Latin America Country File, NSF, LBJL.

48. "U.S. Overseas Internal Defense Policy," August 1, 1962, Box 319, Meetings and Memoranda, NSF, JFKL.

49. Ibid.

50. "A Summary of U.S. Military Counterinsurgency Accomplishments since 1 January 1961," Box 319, Meetings and Memoranda, NSF, JFKL; Robert Holden, "Securing Central America against Communism: The United States and the Modernization of Surveillance in the Cold War," *Journal of Interamerican Studies and World Affairs* 41 (1999): 1–30; Michael Gambone, *Capturing the Revolution: The United States, Central America, and Nicaragua, 1961–1972* (Westport, CT, 2001), chapter 2.

51. Thomas Wright, *State Terrorism in Latin America: Chile, Argentina and International Human Rights* (New York, 2007), 23–24; Michael McClintock, *The American Connection,* Vols. 1–2 (Toronto, 1985); Grandin, *Empire's Workshop,* 96–99.

52. Marie-Monique Robin, *Escadrons de la mort, l'école française* (Paris, 2004); Gustavo Moraes Rego Reis Oral History, 44, Oral Histories, FGV; Depoimento de Antônio Carlos Murici, 29, Oral Histories, FGV.

53. Golbery, *Geopolítica do Brasil* [1967 edition], 198–199; "Boletím SEI," No. 447, agosto de 1960, DNAT-C-75, CDYA.

54. Guatemala to State, September 26, 1961, Guatemala Collection, NSA; Communique de la Secretaría de Información de Guatemala, 26 de diciembre de 1962, Caja 42, Sección Ministro, Colección Relaciones Exteriores, Fondo Presidencial, AGNNIC.

55. Brian Loveman, *For la Patria: Politics and the Armed Forces in Latin America* (New York, 1999), 254.

56. Remarks by Alexis Johnson, in Inter-American Defense College, "Graduation Ceremonies," June 10, 1966, OAS Archives; "Military Actions for Latin America," November 1961, Box 333, Meetings and Memoranda, NSF, JFKL.

57. Thomas Dodd to Rusk and Dulles, July 18, 1961, Box WH-27, Schlesinger Files, JFKL; Telegram from the Department of State to the Embassy in the United Kingdom, February 19, 1962, *FRUS 1961–1963,* XII: Document #264.

58. Memorandum of Conversation, June 30, 1963, *FRUS 1961–1963*, XII: Document #295; "Selections from a Press Conference on January 16, 1965," Box 8, Chase Files, NSF, LBJL.

59. Kennedy to McNamara, October 4, 1963, *DDRS*; NSC Meeting, March 13, 1963, Box 314, Meetings and Memoranda, NSF, JFKL; "Address in Miami before the Inter-American Press Association," November 18, 1963, APP; "Radio and Television Report to the American People on the Situation in the Dominican Republic," May 2, 1965, ibid.

60. Paper Prepared for the National Security Council by an Interagency Task Force on Cuba, May 4, 1961, *FRUS 1961–1963*, X: Document #202; Mark J. White, ed., *The Kennedys and Cuba: The Declassified Documentary History* (Chicago, 1999), 74; "The Cuba Project," February 20, 1962, Box 319, Meetings and Memoranda, NSF, JFKL.

61. Clara Nieto, *Masters of War: Latin America and United States Aggression from the Cuban Revolution through the Clinton Years*, trans. Chris Brandt (New York, 2003), 103; Don Bohning, *The Castro Obsession: U.S. Covert Operations in Cuba, 1959–1965* (Washington, DC, 2005).

62. Alekseev to Moscow, September 7, 1962, CWIHP; also Sergo Mikoyan Oral History Interview, October 13, 1987, Cuban Missile Crisis Collection, NSA. For similar statements by Cuban officials, see Alekseev to Moscow, September 11, 1962, CWIHP.

63. Nikita Khrushchev, *Khrushchev Remembers: The Glasnost Tapes*, trans. Jerrold Schecter and Vyacheslav Luchkov (Boston, 1990), 170.

64. Minutes 32A, May 21, 1962, Kremlin Decision-Making Project (KDMP), Miller Center for Public Affairs, University of Virginia.

65. Notes of NSC Meeting, October 20, 1962, Box 313, Meetings and Memoranda, NSF, JFKL.

66. Minutes 60A, October 22, 1962; Minutes 61C, October 25, 1962, KDMP. The literature on the missile crisis is extensive. See Naftali and Fursenko, *Khruschev's Cold War*, 428–492; Sheldon Stern, *Averting "The Final Failure": John F. Kennedy and the Secret Cuban Missile Crisis Meetings* (Stanford, 2003).

67. Minutes 71A, December 3, 1962, KDMP.

68. Pinochet de la Barra, ed., *Pensamiento de Eduardo Frei*, 61.

69. López Mateos a Kennedy, 29 de octubre de 1962; and SRE a Bosques, 23 de octubre de 1962, Topográfica III-5664–1, Archivo de Concentraciones; Domínguez, *To Make a World Safe for Revolution*, 28.

70. "Memorandum sobre Cuba," undated; and Memorandum No. 2, "Sobre procedimiento para adelantar una Reunión de Consulta sobre el caso de Cuba," undated, Caja 184, Transferencia 8, MRE, AGNCOL.

71. "Memorandum: Universidad Autónoma de México," 18 de septiembre de 1964, Topográfica A-636–2, Archivo de Concentraciones; Rusk to Johnson, February 18, 1964, EBB 83, NSA; Embassy in Mexico City to State, June 28, 1967, ibid.; Christopher White, *Creating a Third World: Mexico, Cuba,*

and the United States during the Castro Era (Albuquerque, NM, 2007), chapters 4–5.

72. "Cuba: Resumen de la Situación," 13 de enero de 1963, Topográfica III-2671–1, Archivo de Concentraciones; CIA Current Intelligence Weekly Summary, February 1, 1963, Box WH-32, Schlesinger Files, JFKL; Joseph Hart, *Che: The Life, Death, and Afterlife of a Revolutionary* (New York, 2003), 238–240.

73. Robert Packenham, "Capitalist Dependency and Socialist Dependency: The Case of Cuba," *Journal of Interamerican Studies and World Affairs* 28 (1986): 59–92.

74. "Notes of Conversation between A. I. Mikoyan and Fidel Castro," November 3, 1962, CWIHP; Gleijeses, *Conflicting Missions,* 19.

75. "Mikoyan's Meeting with Cuban Leaders," November 5, 1962, CWIHP.

76. FBIS Transcript of Khrushchev's speech, May 23, 1963, Box 46, Country File, NSF, JFKL; "Speech by Prime Minister Fidel Castro at Havana's Plaza de la Revolución," May 1, 1966, CSD; INR, "Implications of Cuba's Renewed Campaign of Incitation to Violent Revolution in Latin America," November 12, 1963, Box 39, Country File, NSF, JFKL.

77. "Polish Record of Conversation," June 24, 1967, CWIHP; CIA, "Bolsheviks and Heroes," November 21, 1967, EBB 67, NSA.

78. Cole Blasier, *The Giant's Rival: The USSR and Latin America* (Pittsburgh, 1983), 105–107; James Blight and Philip Brenner, *Sad and Luminous Days: Cuba's Struggle with the Superpowers after the Missile Crisis* (New York, 2002), 121–127.

79. *Pravda,* July 30, 1967, in *Contemporary Digest of the Soviet Press (CDSP)* XIX, No. 30: 19.

80. Ministerio de Relaciones Interiores, "Confidencial No. 1," 25 de mayo de 1964, in Vera Gómez, ed., *La subversión armada,* 22. See "Fidel Castro 13 March Anniversary Speech," March 13, 1967, CSD; John Martz, "Doctrine and Dilemmas of the Latin American 'New Left,'" *World Politics* 51 (1970): 190–192.

81. "Fidel Castro Speech at LASO Closing Session," August 11, 1967, CSD; "Respuesta del Partido Comunista a Fidel Castro," *El Nacional* (Caracas), 17 de marzo de 1967.

82. "The Position of the Bolivian Communist Party on the Armed Struggle," January 11, 1967, Reel 4, *The United States and Castro's Cuba, 1950–1970;* Carlos Soria Galvarro, ed., *El Che en Bolivia: Documentos y Testimonios,* Vol. 5 (La Paz, 1992), 70–72, 83.

83. Quoted in J. Posadas, "La función de la guerrilla en la lucha por el poder obrero," 12 de febrero de 1966, Notebook 9, Guevara and the Bolivian Guerrillas Collection, Tulane; see also "Unidad popular y antiimperialista," octubre de 1964, Notebook 5, ibid.; "En torno a la situación política," *Liberación* (edición clandestina), junio de 1967, Notebook 1, ibid.

84. Embajada la Habana a SRE, 17 de enero de 1966, Topográfica III-5758–1, Archivo de Concentraciones.

85. U.S. Department of the Army, "The Latin American Solidarity Organization Conference and Its Aftermath," October 17, 1967, Caja 1, Estados Unidos, Archivo del Ministerio de Relaciones Exteriores de Uruguay (MREURU); "Fidel Castro Speech at LASO Closing Session," August 11, 1967, CSD.

86. "Statement of Communist Parties of Seven Latin American Countries," *Pravda*, June 19, 1967, *CDSP* XIX, No. 25: 22; also CIA, "Latin American Solidarity Organization Conference," September 22, 1967, Box 3, Latin America Country File, NSF, LBJL.

87. "Boletín de la Junta de Inteligencia Nacional," 10 de octubre de 1967, 21 de noviembre de 1967, y 12 de diciembre de 1967, Caja 83, Despacho Ministro, Ministerio del Interior, AGNCOL.

88. "La unidad de las fuerzas revolucionarias," undated (1971), Colección Documentos, Centro de Investigaciones Regionales y Mesoamericanas (CIRMA); Deborah Levenson-Estrada, *Trade Unionists against Terror: Guatemala City, 1954–1985* (Chapel Hill, NC, 1994), 43–46.

89. "Carta de Arauca (Francisco Prada), Primer Comandante del Frente Guerrillero de los Llanos, a los Combatientes del Mismo," junio de 1966; and "Carta de Suárez, del MIR, a Florent (Fabricio Ojeda)," 4 de octubre de 1966, in Vera Gómez, ed., *La subversión armada*, 453–576, 595–596.

90. "Informe de Actividades de Carácter Sindical por el Movimiento Demócrata Cristiano de Nuestro País," 5 de agosto de 1964, DI-L-P57, CDYA; "Convocatoria a la Conferencia Nacional Preparatoria del III Congreso del PCP," 16 de diciembre de 1966, DI-L-C11, CDYA; "Transcripción de un informe," 11 de noviembre de 1965, DI-L-E6, CDYA.

91. Matt D. Childs, "An Historical Critique of the Emergence and Evolution of Ernesto Che Guevara's Foco Theory," *Journal of Latin American Studies* 27 (1995): 595–624; Harry Vanden, "Marxism and the Peasantry in Latin America: Marginalization or Mobilization?" *Latin American Perspectives* 9 (1982): 88.

92. Timothy Wickham-Crowley, *Guerrillas and Revolution in Latin America: A Comparative Study of Insurgents and Regimes since 1956* (Princeton, 1992), 104–108, 115–116; Béjar, *Peru 1965*, 38; Francisco Leal Buitrago, *Estado y política en Colombia* (Bogota, 1984), 213–220; Jesús Antonio Bejarano, "Campesinado y luchas agrarias en Colombia," in Pablo González Casanova, ed., *Historia política de los campesinos latinoamericanos*, Vol. 3 (Mexico City, 1985), esp. 59–61; Paul Lewis, "Paraguay since 1930," in Bethell, ed., *The Cambridge History of Latin America*, Vol. 8, 256.

93. Béjar, *Peru 1965*, 86; Timothy Wickham-Crowley, "Elites, Elite Settlements, and Revolutionary Movements in Latin America, 1950–1980," *Social*

Science History 18 (1994): 554; idem, "The Rise (and Sometimes Fall) of Guerrilla Governments in Latin America," *Sociological Forum* 2 (1987): 481; Richard Maullin, *Soldiers, Guerrillas, and Politics in Colombia* (Toronto, 1973), 69–79; Jean Lartéguy, *The Guerrillas* (New York, 1970), 137; Carvallo, *Clase dominante y democracia representativa,* 64.

94. For instance, Francois Bourricaud, *Power and Society in Contemporary Peru,* trans. Paul Stevenson (London, 1970), 222.

95. Rachel May, "'Surviving All Changes Is Your Destiny': Violence and Popular Movements in Guatemala," *Latin American Perspectives* 26 (1999): 72; Jim Handy, *Gift of the Devil* (Boston, 1984), 161.

96. Levine, *Conflict and Political Change in Venezuela,* 162.

97. EGP, "Guerra Popular," No. 3, noviembre de 1975, Colección Documentos, CIRMA; also FAR, "La unidad de las fuerzas revolucionarias," ibid.

98. "Guevara Discusses Latin American Revolution," *DDRS.*

99. Schirmer, *Guatemalan Military Project,* 16; Richard Weitz, "Insurgency and Counterinsurgency in Latin America, 1960–1980," *Political Science Quarterly* 101 (1986): 401.

100. Guatemalan Army Intelligence Report, early 1960, attached to letter from M. Ydígoras-Laparra to Roland Ebel, February 25, 2002, Box 1, Miguel Ydígoras Fuentes Materials, Tulane.

101. Dirk Kruijt, *Revolution by Decree: Peru, 1968–1975* (Amsterdam, 1994), 55; also George Philip, *The Rise and Fall of the Peruvian Military Radicals, 1968–1976* (London, 1978), 56–57; Lima to State, August 26, 1965, *DDRS.*

102. "Fragmentos del informe político discutido por el Secretario Nacional del MIR realizado en enero de 1964," Complemento A, Tomo 41, ARB.

103. Organization of American States, Economic and Social Council, *Latin America's Development and the Alliance for Progress* (Washington, DC, 1973), 205–217; Organization of American States, *Synthesis of Economic Performance in Latin America* (Washington, DC, 1979), 16.

104. "The Potential for Revolution in Latin America," March 28, 1968, Box 8, NIE File, NSF, LBJL; Draft Memorandum for the President, undated, Box 12, NSC Histories File, NSF, LBJL.

105. Quoted in TelCon between Johnson and Mann, November 18, 1964, PNO3, WH6411.23, LBJL. See also Steven Bachelor, "Miracle on Ice: Industrial Workers and the Promise of Americanization in Cold War Mexico," in Joseph and Spenser, eds., *In from the Cold,* 253–272; "Alliance for Progress," State Department Administrative History on Inter-American Relations, Box 1, Administrative Histories, LBJL.

106. "A Review of Small Farmer Credit in Bolivia," *AID Spring Review of Small Farmer Credit* III (February 1973): 1–2; "Small Farmer Credit in Costa Rica," *AID Spring Review of Small Farmer Credit* II (Spring 1973): 49.

107. CIA, "Survey of Latin America," April 1, 1964, Box 1, Latin America Country File, NSF, LBJL. The classic work on modernization and instabil-

ity is Samuel Huntington, *Political Order in Changing Societies* (New Haven, 1968).

108. State to Lima, July 23, 1962, Box 151, Country File, NSF, JFKL.

109. Airgram from the Consulate in the Dominican Republic to the Department of State, March 22, 1961, *FRUS 1961–63*, XII: Document #304; "Notes on Crisis Involving the Dominican Republic," June 3, 1961, Box 392, Bowles Papers, Yale; Stephen G. Rabe, "The Caribbean Triangle: Betancourt, Castro, and Trujillo and U.S. Foreign Policy, 1958–1963," *Diplomatic History* 20 (1996): 65–71.

110. Smith, *America's Mission*, 230.

111. Santo Domingo to State, September 22, 1963, Box 66, Country File, NSF, JFKL; and William Brubeck to Bundy, June 4, 1963, ibid.

112. TelCon with Thomas Mann, April 30, 1965, PNO 12, WH6504.08, LBJL; TelCon with Richard Russell, June 2, 1966, PNO 4, WH6606.01, LBJL.

113. Schlesinger to Kennedy, February 11, 1961, Box WH-31, Schlesinger Files, JFKL.

114. Goodwin to Bundy, June 8, 1961, Box 66, Country File, NSF, JFKL.

115. Ruth Leacock, *Requiem for Revolution: The United States and Brazil, 1961–1969* (Kent, OH, 1990); Riordan Roett, *The Politics of Foreign Aid in the Brazilian Northeast* (Nashville, TN, 1974), chapter 9; Howard Wiarda, *Dictatorship, Development, and Disintegration: Politics and Social Change in the Dominican Republic* (Ann Arbor, MI, 1975), chapters 11–19.

116. Leslie Gill, *The School of the Americas: Military Training and Political Violence in the Americas* (Durham, NC, 2004), 59–80; Rabe, *Most Dangerous Area in the World*, 130.

117. Comisión Permanente del CONDECA, Boletín Informativo No. 1, 9 de julio de 1965; Ministro de la Defensa a Schick, 6 de octubre de 1965, Caja 13, Sección Guerra, Marina y Aviación, Fondo Presidencial, AGNNIC.

118. Memorandum from Director of Central Intelligence Helms to President Johnson, October 11, 1967, *FRUS 1964–1968*, XXXI: 171.

119. Longan to Engle, January 4, 1966; and CIA Cable, March 1966, in EBB 11, NSA; Grandin, *Last Colonial Massacre*, 95–100.

120. Guatemala to State, April 3, 1963, Box 101, Country File, NSF, JFKL; "Conversation with Defense Minister's Brother on Plan to Overthrow President Ydígoras," March 12, 1963, ibid.

121. Stephen G. Rabe, *U.S. Intervention in British Guiana: A Cold War Story* (Chapel Hill, NC, 2005).

122. TelCon with Mann, November 18, 1964, PNO3, WH6411.23, LBJL. On Costa Rica, see Rielly to Humphrey, September 14, 1965, *FRUS 1964–1968*, XXXI: Document #79; Bowdler to Bundy, November 18, 1965, Document #81, ibid. On Chile, see, most recently, Margaret Power, "The Engendering of Anticommunism and Fear in Chile's 1964 Presidential Election," *Diplomatic History* 32 (2008): 931–953.

123. Komer to Bundy, July 7, 1965, *DDRS.*

124. Teniente General Tomás Sánchez de Bustamante, "La Guerra Revolucionaria," in Alicia S. Garcia, ed., *Doctrina de la Seguridad Nacional* (Buenos Aires, 1991), I: 67.

125. Michael McClintock, *Instruments of Statecraft: U.S. Guerrilla Warfare, Counterinsurgency, and Counter Terrorism, 1940–1990* (New York, 1992), 222; Grandin, *Empire's Workshop*, 96; "Report of Visit to Colombia, South America, by a Team from Special Warfare Center," March 12, 1962, Box 319, Meetings and Memoranda, NSF, JFKL. See also Martha Huggins, *Political Policing: The United States and Latin America* (London, 1998).

126. Undated message from Luís Somoza, Caja grande 9 (Caja pequeña 522), Secretaría Privada, Fondo Presidencial, AGNNIC; Jeffrey Gould, *To Lead as Equals: Rural Protest and Political Consciousness in Chinandega, Nicaragua, 1912–1979* (Chapel Hill, NC, 1990), 107.

127. Guatemala to Ottawa, June 9, 1967, Vol. 8954, 20-GMA-1–4, LAC.

128. Grandin, *Last Colonial Massacre,* 99; McClintock, *American Connection,* Vols. 1–2.

129. Rabe, *Most Dangerous Area in the World,* 116.

130. Lima to State, July 18, 1962, Box 151, Country File, NSF, JFKL.

131. Betancourt a López Mateos, 23 de julio de 1962, Complemento B, Tomo 39, ARB; Arinos in "Notas taquigráficas da reunião do conselho de ministros," 14 de agosto de 1962, EG apr 1961.09.14, FGV.

132. Lima to State, July 24, 1962, Box 151, Country File, NSF, JFKL; State to All Posts, October 5, 1963, Box 216, Regional Security File, NSF, JFKL.

133. "Cut to Aid in Ecuador Revealed," *New York Times,* April 15, 1967; Robert Smetherman and Bobbie Smetherman, "The Alliance for Progress: Promises Unfulfilled," *American Journal of Economics and Sociology* 31 (1972): 83–84.

134. Quoted in Béjar, *Peru 1965,* 86. On Venezuela and Peru, see the sources cited above. On Chile, see Julio Faúndez, *Marxism and Democracy in Chile: From 1932 to the Fall of Allende* (New Haven, 1988), 144, 254; Andrew Kirkendall, "Paulo Freire, Eduardo Frei, Literacy Training and the Politics of Consciousness Raising in Chile, 1964 to 1970," *Journal of Latin American Studies* 36 (2004): 687–717; Luis Moulián and Gloria Guerrero, *Eduardo Frei M. (1911–1982): Biografía de un estadista utópico* (Santiago, 2000), esp. 161–165.

135. Bowles to Rusk, October 20, 1961, Schlesinger Papers, Box WH-2, JFKL; also T. Lynn Smith, "Land Reform in Brazil," *Luso-Brazilian Review* 1 (1964): 4.

136. Howard Blutstein et al., *Area Handbook for El Salvador* (Washington, DC, 1971), 159–160; Edelberto Torres-Rivas, "Central America since 1930," in Leslie Bethell, ed., *The Cambridge History of Latin America,* Vol. 7 (New York, 1990), 182–184; LaFeber, *Inevitable Revolutions,* 164.

137. Laura Enríquez, *Harvesting Change: Labor and Agrarian Reform in Nicaragua, 1979–1990* (Chapel Hill, NC, 1991), 8–9, 41–48; Bulmer-Thomas, *Political Economy of Central America since 1920*, chapters 8–9; Robert Williams, *Export Agriculture and the Crisis in Central America* (Chapel Hill, NC, 1986), 28–73, 134–150; Victor Antonio Orellana, *El Salvador: Crisis and Structural Change* (Miami, 1985), 6–7; Santiago Ruíz Granadino, "Modernización agrícola en El Salvador," *Estudios sociales centroamericanos* 22 (1979): 71–100.

138. World Bank Report 4195-GU, "Guatemala: Country Economic Memorandum," May 31, 1983; and World Bank Report 2945-ES, "El Salvador: An Inquiry into Urban Poverty," November 5, 1980, Latin America and the Caribbean Regional Office (LACRO), WBA.

139. Declaración Indagatoria de Canuto Villasboa Salinas, 27 de diciembre 1976, DI-B-128, CDYA.

140. Sol Linowitz Oral History, 61, Oral Histories, LBJL.

141. Ernest Feder, "When Is a Land Reform a Land Reform? The Colombian Case," *American Journal of Economics and Sociology* 24 (1965): 122; idem, "Land Reform under the Alliance for Progress," *Journal of Farm Economics* 47 (1965): 654.

142. Interview with Juan José Arévalo, July 14, 1963, Folder 2, deLesseps Story Morrison Collection, Tulane.

143. Rabe, *Most Dangerous Area in the World*, 171.

144. Cristóbal Kay, "Reflections on Rural Violence in Latin America," *Third World Quarterly* 22 (2001): 746; Katherine Hite, *When the Romance Ended: Leaders of the Chilean Left, 1968–1998* (New York, 2000), 172; Joseph Tulchin, "The United States and Latin America in the 1960s," *Journal of Interamerican Studies and World Affairs* 30 (1988): 19.

145. "Reunião do Conselho de Ministros Realizada em 23 de Maio de 1962," EG apr 1961.09.14, FGV.

146. "Background on Current Situation in Brazil," undated, Box 13, Country File, NSF, JFKL; MemCon with Goulart, April 4, 1962, Box WH-26, Schlesinger Files, JFKL; INR Research Memorandum, October 2, 1962, ibid.; Andrew Kirkendall, "Entering History: Paulo Freire and the Politics of the Brazilian Northeast, 1958–1964," *Luso-Brazilian Review* 41 (2004): 172–173.

147. Ata Conselho de Ministros, 1a. Reunião, 14 de Setembro de 1961, EG apr 1961.09.14, FGV; "Reunião do Conselho de Ministros Realizada em 11 de Janeiro de 1962," ibid.

148. Roberto de Oliveira Campos Oral History Interview, May 29, 1964, Oral Histories, JFKL, 34; Phyllis Parker, *Brazil and the Quiet Intervention, 1964* (Austin, TX, 1978), 49.

149. Andrew Kirkendall, "Kennedy Men and the Fate of the Alliance for Progress in LBJ Era Brazil and Chile," *Diplomacy and Statecraft* 84 (2007):

753, referencing John W. F. Dulles, *Castelo Branco: The Making of a Brazilian President* (College Station, TX, 1978), 18.

150. Rio to State, October 26, 1962, Country File, NSF, JFKL.

151. Leacock, *Requiem for Revolution*, 135–144.

152. Juan Bosch, *The Unfinished Experiment: Democracy in the Dominican Republic* (London, 1966), 154–155.

153. Rómulo Betancourt, *Venezuela: Oil and Politics* (Boston, 1978), 389.

154. Harold Trinkunas, *Crafting Civilian Control of the Military in Venezuela: A Comparative Perspective* (Chapel Hill, NC, 2005), 115–135; Wickham-Crowley, "Elites, Elite Settlements, and Revolutionary Movements," 554.

155. Leacock, *Requiem for Revolution*, 213–214; Federico Gil and Charles Parrish, *The Chilean Presidential Election of September 4, 1964* (Washington, DC, 1965).

156. TelCon with Abe Fortas, April 30, 1965, PNO 1, WH6504.08, LBJL; Piero Gleijeses, *The Dominican Crisis: The 1965 Constitutionalist Revolt and American Intervention* (Baltimore, 1978).

157. TelCon with Michael Mannsfield, April 30, 1965, PNO 7, WH6504.08, LBJL.

158. Ibid.

159. Tomic a MRE, 11 de mayo de 1965, EmbaChile EEUU, Oficios Reservados, Archivo del Ministerio de Relaciones Exteriores de Chile (MRE-CHILE); "Instrumentos de Defensa Política," undated (1965), Caja 182, Transferencia 3, MRE, AGNCOL.

160. Quoted in Juan de Onís, "Latin-American View," *New York Times*, January 19, 1964; Júlio César Borges Duarte, "Panamá Debe Ser Soberana en la Zona del Canal," *El Tiempo* (Bogota), 12 de enero de 1964; McPherson, "Courts of World Opinion."

161. "Uruguay Se Opone a la 'Doctrina Johnson,'" *El Tiempo* (Bogota), 5 de mayo de 1965; "Venezuela Condena los Desembarcos," *La Prensa* (Buenos Aires), 5 de mayo de 1965; "Estudiantes Invaden la Embajada de los EE. UU.," *El Tiempo*, 8 de mayo de 1965.

162. Handwritten Notes of NSC Meeting, July 9, 1969, Box H-121, Minutes of Meetings, NSC Institutional Files, Nixon Presidential Materials Project (NPM).

3. From Crisis to Crisis

1. NIE 80/90–68, "The Potential for Revolution in Latin America," March 28, 1968, Box 8, NIE, NSF, LBJL.

2. TelCons between Kissinger and Nixon, October 24 and 31, 1969, Box 2, HAK TelCons, NPM.

3. Guillermo O'Donnell, "Modernization and Military Coups: Theory, Comparisons, and the Argentine Case," in Abraham Lowenthal, ed.,

Armies and Politics in Latin America (New York, 1976), 208; Deborah Norden, *Military Rebellion in Argentina: Between Coups and Consolidation* (Lincoln, NE, 1996), 20–27; Daniel Masterson, *Militarism and Politics in Latin America: Peru from Sánchez Cerro to Sendero Luminoso* (Westport, CT, 1991), esp. 46; Peter Klaren, *Peru: Society and Nationhood in the Andes* (New York, 2000), chapters 9–10.

4. Antônio Carlos da Silva Murici, *Palavras de um soldado* (Rio de Janeiro, 1971), 81; Informe Confidencial, 6 de febrero de 1966, DI-L-C11, CDYA.

5. Army Intelligence Report, early 1960, Box 1, Ydígoras Materials, Tulane; Communique de la Secretaría de Información de Guatemala, 26 de diciembre de 1962, Caja 42, Sección Ministro, Colección Relaciones Exteriores, Fondo Presidencial, AGNNIC.

6. João Paulo Moreira Burnier Oral History, 75, Oral Histories, FGV; Daniel Krieger, *Desde as Missões . . . Saudades, Lutas, Esperanças* (Rio de Janeiro, 1976), 157.

7. "Discurso pronunciado en la Escuela Superior de Guerra," *La Nación*, 3 de octubre de 1961.

8. Harry Schlaudeman to Kissinger, August 3, 1976, EBB 124, NSA; Pedro J. Prokopchuk a Stroessner, 3 de marzo de 1961, DNAT-C-98, CDYA; also Nota No. 49/Ex., 20 de abril de 1961, ibid.; "Informe (D2)," 14 de junio de 1976, DI-B-47, CDYA.

9. Golbery do Couto e Silva, *Conjuntura Política Nacional*, 24; Mayor Edgardo Bautista Matute, "Eficaz respuesta al castro-comunismo," *Revista de la Escuela Superior de Guerra*, mayo–agosto de 1967, 111–112.

10. David Pion-Berlin, "Theories on Political Repression in Latin America: Conventional Wisdom and an Alternative," *PS* 19 (1986): 51; Eduardo Galeano, *Memoria del fuego, vol. III: El siglo del viento* (Buenos Aires, 1986), 109.

11. Teniente General Tomás Sánchez de Bustamante, "La Guerra Revoluciona-ria," in *Doctrina de la Seguridad Nacional*, I: 67.

12. Wright, *State Terrorism in Latin America*, 25.

13. Klaus Dodds and David Atkinson, *Geopolitical Traditions: A Century of Geopolitical Thought* (New York, 2000), 163–175; Stepan, "The New Professionalism of Internal Warfare," 247–250; Masterson, "Caudillismo and Institutional Change," 486.

14. Craig Arceneaux, *Bounded Missions: Military Regimes and Democratization in the Southern Cone and Brazil* (University Park, PA, 2001), 49–50; William C. Smith, *Authoritarianism and the Crisis of the Argentine Political Economy* (Stanford, 1991), 133–138.

15. Kruijt, *Revolution by Decree*, 42.

16. James Petras and Henry Veltmeyer, *Cardoso's Brazil: A Land for Sale* (New York, 2003), 7–8; Naomi Klein, *The Shock Doctrine: The Rise of Disaster Capitalism* (New York, 2007), 125.

17. "Onganía no Brasil Desde Ontem Para Ver Como Agir: Urugai," *Jornal da Bahia*, 19 de agosto de 1965.

18. CIA Information Cable, April 23, 1964, *DDRS;* "Confidencial AAA/520.1(22)," undated, Caja CIE-VII-1, MREURU; Ministro de Relaciones Exteriores a Buenos Aires, 6 de septiembre de 1965, Caja 1, Telegramas Cifrados Recibidos, Fondo 2.2, MREURU; "Brasil pretendería intervenção militar no Urugai," *La Tribuna*, 18 de maio de 1965.

19. Montevideo to Thomas Hughes, June 7, 1965, *DDRS*.

20. Buenos Aires a MRE, 4 de abril de 1967, Caja 1 (Confidenciales), Fondo 2.2, MREURU; "VI Conferencia de Ejércitos Americanos," 18 de noviembre de 1965, Caja 2, Fondo 2.2, MREURU; "Acuerdo Bilateral de Inteligencia FF.AA.Paraguay/Ejército Argentino," 12 de septiembre de 1972, DNAT-C-2a, CDYA.

21. Emanuel de Kadt, *Catholic Radicals in Brazil* (New York, 1970), 191; Michael Burdick, *For God and the Fatherland: Religion and Politics in Argentina* (Albany, NY, 1995), 222–227.

22. Mark Osiel, "Constructing Subversion in Argentina's Dirty War," *Representations* 75 (2001): 134–136.

23. Bautista Matute, "Eficaz respuesta al castro-comunismo," 111–112. Similar ideas can be found in Ernesto Geisel, "Trecho do Discurso na Convenção da ARENA, em Brasília, a 15 de Setembro de 1973," EG pr 1978.00.00, FGV.

24. João Paulo Moreira Burnier Oral History, 60, FGV.

25. News clipping, "Presidente Goulart será deposto em breve," undated (1961), JG pr 1961.09.00, Arquivo João Goulart, FGV; Entrevista do Antônio Carlos Murici, February 2, 1981–May 20, 1981, Depoimentos, FGV; João Paulo Moreira Burnier Oral History, 96, FGV; Gustavo Moraes Rego Reis Oral History, 60, FGV.

26. Announcement for "Concentração popular dia 13 de março na Central do Brasil," undated, JG pr 1964.02.19, Arquivo João Goulart, FGV; Krieger, *Desde as Missões*, 167; Joseph Comblin, *A Ideologia da Segurança Nacional: O Poder Militar na América Latina* (Rio de Janeiro, 1980), 77, cited in Shawn Smallman, "The Professionalization of Military Terror in Brazil, 1945–1964," *Luso-Brazilian Review* 37 (2000): 123.

27. Murici, *Palavras de um Soldado*, 212.

28. Thomas Skidmore, *The Politics of Military Rule in Brazil, 1964–1985* (New York, 1988), 1–67; Youssef Cohen, "Democracy from Above: The Political Origins of Military Dictatorship in Brazil," *World Politics* 40 (1987): 30–54; Alfred Stepan, *Rethinking Military Politics: Brazil and the Southern Cone* (Princeton, 1988), 1–26.

29. Carta de la Directiva para el Planamiento y Desarrollo de la Acción de Gobierno al Excelentísimo Señor Presidente de la Nación, 22 de agosto de 1967, Caja 3 (1968), Fondo 2.2, MREURU; Ronaldo Munck, "The

'Modern' Military Dictatorship in Latin America: The Case of Argentina (1976–1982)," *Latin American Perspectives* 12 (1985): 52–53; O'Donnell, "Modernization and Military Coups," esp. 207–209.

30. See Alejandro Lanusse's speech, 12 de abril de 1967, *Doctrina de la seguridad nacional,* I: 106.

31. A concise summary is David Rock, *Authoritarian Argentina: The Nationalist Movement, Its History and Its Impact* (Berkeley, CA, 1995), 195–205.

32. Miles D. Wolpin, "Military Radicalism in Latin America," *Journal of Interamerican Studies and World Affairs* 23 (1981): 411; Guillermo Thorndike, *No, mi General* (Lima, 1976), 43–45.

33. Julio Cotler, "Peru since 1960," in Bethell, ed., *The Cambridge History of Latin America,* Vol. 8, 457; Juan Martín Sánchez, *La revolución peruana: Ideología y práctica política de un gobierno militar* (Sevilla, 2002), 58.

34. Sánchez, "El comité de asuntos civiles: Nexo civil-militar," *Revista de la Escuela Superior de Guerra,* octubre–diciembre 1963, 44, in Frederick Nunn, "Professional Militarism in Twentieth-Century Peru: Historical and Theoretical Background to the *Golpe de Estado* of 1968," *Hispanic American Historical Review* 59 (1979): 398.

35. Luigi Einaudi, "Revolution from Within? Military Rule in Peru since 1968," in David Chaplin, ed., *Peruvian Nationalism: A Corporatist Revolution* (New Brunswick, NJ, 1976), 409–414.

36. Lima to State, October 5, 1968, *DDRS;* Abraham Lowenthal, "Six Weeks in Peru: Some First Impressions," August 29, 1969, Folder 2, Thompson Collection of Reports on Latin America, Tulane.

37. Deborah Yashar, *Contesting Citizenship in Latin America: The Rise of Indigenous Movements and the Postliberal Challenge* (New York, 2005), 241–245; Jo-Marie Burt, "Contesting the Terrain of Politics: State–Society Relations in Urban Peru, 1950–2000," in Paul Drake and Eric Hershberg, eds., *State and Society in Conflict: Comparative Perspectives on Andean Crises* (Pittsburgh, 2006), 227–230.

38. Frederick Nunn, *The Time of the Generals: Latin American Professional Military in World Perspective* (Lincoln, NE, 1992), 217.

39. Memorandum of Conversation, January 20, 1970, Box 2662, SNF 70–73, RG 59, NARA.

40. J. Patrice McSherry, *Incomplete Transition: Military Power and Democracy in Argentina* (New York, 1997), 52; Schirmer, *Guatemalan Military Project,* 237; Gill, *School of the Americas,* 61; Kenneth Duane Lehman, *Bolivia and the United States: A Limited Partnership* (Athens, GA, 1999), 150.

41. Wright, *State Terrorism in Latin America,* 23.

42. Carlos Alberto da Fontoura Interview, 7, Oral Histories, FGV; Depoimento de Antônio Carlos Murici, 29, Oral Histories, FGV; Patricia Marchak, ed., *God's Assassins: State Terrorism in Argentina in the 1970s* (Montreal, 1999), 279.

43. Golbery, *Geopolítica do Brasil,* 198–199.

44. Juan Gasparini, *Montoneros: Final de cuentas* (Buenos Aires, 1988), 93, in Paul Lewis, *Guerrillas and Generals: The "Dirty War" in Argentina* (Westport, CT, 2001), 136.

45. John Baines, "U.S. Military Assistance to Latin America: An Assessment," *Journal of Interamerican Studies and World Affairs* 14 (1972): 477; also David Feldman, "Argentina, 1945–1971: Military Assistance, Military Spending, and the Political Activity of the Armed Forces," *Journal of Interamerican Studies and World Affairs* 24 (1982): esp. 328–331.

46. Cotler, "Peru since 1960," 456.

47. "Manifiesto del Gobierno Revolucionario," *Peruvian Political Party Documents,* Folder 6, Reel 1; Enrique León Velarde, *¿El Chino y yo jodimos al Perú? Confesiones de Enrique León Velarde* (Lima, 2000), 138.

48. Brasilia to State, August 28, 1970, Box 2134, SNF, RG 59, NARA; Rio de Janeiro to State, August 4, 1967, *FRUS 1964–1968,* XXXI: Document #230; Sonny Davis, *A Brotherhood of Arms: Brazil–United States Military Relations, 1945–1977* (Niwot, CO, 1996), 101–102, 119.

49. "Notes from NSC Meeting, October 15, 1969," Box 89, Papers of Eliot Richardson, LOC.

50. "Boletím SEI," No. 447, agosto de 1960, DNAT-C-75, CDYA.

51. Pedro J. Prokopchuk a Stroessner, 3 de marzo de 1961, DNAT-C-98, CDYA.

52. Gustavo Moraes Rego Reis Interview, 60, Oral Histories, FGV; Somoza a Ydígoras, 16 de marzo de 1960, Caja grande 9 (Caja pequeña 522), Secretaría Privada, Fondo Presidencial, AGNNIC; Guatemala City to Ottawa, April 13, 1964, Vol. 8954, 20-GMA-1–4, LAC; "Meeting with Latin American Foreign Ministers," October 2, 1962, Box 247, Trips and Conferences, NSF, JFKL.

53. Max Paul Friedman, "Retiring the Puppets, Bringing Latin America Back In: Recent Scholarship on United States–Latin American Relations," *Diplomatic History* 27 (2003): 621. For books and articles that buck this trend, see those cited in Friedman's article.

54. Jorge Castañeda, *Utopia Unarmed: The Latin American Left after the Cold War* (New York, 1994), 191–192.

55. Quoted in Nancy Gina Bermeo, *Ordinary People in Extraordinary Times: The Citizenry and the Breakdown of Democracy* (Princeton, 2003), 110; James Miller, "Urban Terrorism in Uruguay: The Tupamaros," in Bard O'Neill, William Heaton, and Donald Alberts, eds., *Insurgency in the Modern World* (Boulder, CO, 1980), 139–140.

56. "Uruguay—Part II, 1965 Article XIV Consultations," October 22, 1965, SM/65/89, Executive Board Documents, International Monetary Fund (IMF) Archives; Robert Dix, "Why Revolutions Succeed and Fail," *Polity* 16 (1984): 430; Instituto de Economía, *El Proceso Económico de Uruguay*

(Montevideo, 1969), 274, 330; Aldrighi, *La izquierda armada,* 15–17; Martin Weinstein, *Uruguay: The Politics of Failure* (Westport, CT, 1975), 119–120.

57. James Brennan, *The Labor Wars in Córdoba: Ideology, Work, and Labor Politics in an Argentine Industrial City* (Cambridge, UK, 1994), chapters 4–5.

58. Raúl Burgos and Carlos Pérez, "Gramscian Intervention in the Theoretical and Political Production of the Latin American Left," *Latin American Perspectives* 29 (2002): 10; Lewis, *Guerrillas and Generals,* 22–23.

59. Julia Preston and Samuel Dillon, *Opening Mexico: The Making of a Democracy* (New York, 2004), 67; also CIA Report, "Mexico: The Problems of Progress," October 20, 1967, Box 60, Country File, NSF, LBJL; Eric Zolov, *Refried Elvis: The Rise of the Mexican Counterculture* (Berkeley, CA, 1999), 1–4, 127.

60. Mark J. van Aken, "The Radicalization of the Uruguayan Student Movement," *The Americas* 33 (1976): 126; Lewis, *Guerrillas and Generals,* 29.

61. "Resoluciones del I Congreso Nacional de Estudiantes Revolucionarios," octubre de 1967, Caja 9, Secretaría de la Defensa Nacional (SDN), AGNMEX.

62. MOEC, "Con Cuba hasta la muerte," 18 de abril de 1961, Caja 16, Despacho Ministro, Ministerio de Gobierno, AGNCOL; Embajada en Santiago, "Informe político-diplomático," abril de 1961, Caja 202, Transferencia 8, MRE, AGNCOL.

63. "Estudiantes Invaden la Embajada de los EE.UU.," *El Tiempo,* 8 de mayo de 1965; "500 Estudiantes en Manifestación de Cartagena," ibid., 7 de mayo de 1965; "Manifestación mitin de grupos de Izquierda, celebrada hoy," 26 de julio de 1966, Caja 456, IPS, AGNMEX.

64. "Report of the Student Unrest Study Group," January 17, 1969, *DDRS;* Suri, *Power and Protest,* 1–2.

65. "Homenaje a David Aguilar Mora en la Escuela Nacional de Economía UNAM," 20 de julio de 1966, Caja 456, IPS, AGNMEX; also "Declaración conjunta emitida en la Habana, Cuba, por la CNED y la Organización Continental Latinoamericana de Estudiantes," 4 de julio de 1967, Caja 464, IPS, AGNMEX; "Actividades del Comité de Solidaridad 'Pro-Cuba y Vietnam," 13 de julio de 1966, Caja 456, ibid.

66. San José a SRE, 17 de enero de 1967, Exp. 12, Leg. 3, Embamex Costa Rica, AHGE.

67. Marchak, ed., *God's Assassins,* 181; Roberto Cirilo Perdía, *La otra historia: Testimonio de un jefe montonero* (Buenos Aires, 1997), 70–71; Directorate of Intelligence, "Argentina's Students and the University System," December 10, 1968, Box 6, Country File, NSF, LBJL.

68. "Sea Patriota, defienda a México," undated (1968); and Memorandum del Director Federal de Seguridad, "Propaganda contra la actitud estudiantil," 8 de noviembre de 1968, Caja 1465A, IPS, AGNMEX.

69. Comité de Lucha ENCR, "Al Pueblo de México," 19 de noviembre de 1968, Caja 8, SDN, AGNMEX.

70. Preston and Dillon, *Opening Mexico,* 67.

71. Charles D. Brockett, *Land, Power, and Poverty: Agrarian Transformation and Political Conflict in Central America* (Boston, 1988), 71; Carol A. Smith, "The Militarization of Civil Society in Guatemala: Economic Reorganization as a Continuation of War," *Latin American Perspectives* 17 (1990): 9–10.

72. Bulmer-Thomas, *Political Economy of Central America,* 178; Enríquez, *Harvesting Change,* 40–50.

73. Declaración Indagatoria de Serafín Flores, 1 de octubre de 1976, DI-L-L98–100, CDYA.

74. Christian Smith, *The Emergence of Liberation Theology: Radical Religion and Social Movement Theory* (Chicago, 1991), 18.

75. Gustavo Gutiérrez, *A Theology of Liberation* (Maryknoll, NY, 1973), 138; John Gerassi, ed., *Revolutionary Priest: The Complete Writings and Messages of Camilo Torres* (New York, 1971), 368.

76. Kenneth Westhues, "The Established Church as an Agent of Change," *Sociological Analysis* 34 (1973): 106–123; Smith, *Emergence of Liberation Theology,* 79, 93.

77. Declaración Indagatoria de Eulogia Falcón Escobar, 16 de agosto de 1976, DI-L-E32, CDYA.

78. Beatriz Sarlo, *La batalla de las ideas (1943–1973)* [Buenos Aires, 2001], 167–168; Aldrighi, *La izquierda armada,* 81.

79. "Intervención del Clero en el Problema Suscitado entre los Alumnos del Instituto Tecnológico y de Estudios Superiores de Monterrey y su Alianza con las Izquierdas, de Acuerdo con la Nueva Línea Mesiánica de la 'Justa Violencia,'" 30 de enero de 1969, Caja 2032, IPS, AGNMEX.

80. Clipping attached to Memorandum para Señor Don Guillermo Lang, 10 de diciembre de 1960, Caja 44, Sección Relaciones Exteriores, Fondo Presidencial, AGNNIC; also Mann to State, March 4, 1963, EBB 124, NSA.

81. See Torres-Rivas, "Central America since 1930"; James Dunkerley, "El Salvador since 1930"; Victor Bulmer-Thomas, "Nicaragua since 1930," in Bethell, ed., *The Cambridge History of Latin America,* Vol. 7, 190–194, 260–265, 342–346.

82. Brocket, *Land, Power, and Poverty,* 150; Carlota McAllister, "Rural Markets, Revolutionary Souls, and Rebellious Women in Cold War Guatemala," in Joseph and Spenser, eds., *In from the Cold,* 358–365; Michael Dodson, "The Politics of Religion in Revolutionary Nicaragua," *Annals of the American Academy of Political and Social Science* 483 (1986): 39–40; Gabriel Aguilera Peralta and John Beverly, "Terror and Violence as Weapons of Counterinsurgency in Guatemala," *Latin American Perspectives* 7 (1980): 107.

83. Guatemala City to Ottawa, June 9, 1967, Vol. 8954, 20-GMA-1-4, LAC.

84. "Informe sobre los sucesos en Jejui-Ybybe-[illegible]," undated (1975), DI-L-P57, CDYA; Declaración de Juan Félix Martínez, 26 de abril de 1976, DCA-C-4, CDYA; José Luis Simón, *Testimonio de la represión política en Paraguay, 1954–1974* (Asunción, 1991), 34.

85. Consulate in Tijuana to State, September 24, 1962, Box 1510, File 712.00, RG 59, NA; also "Encuentro entre campesinos y soldados del Municipio de Uruapan," 13 de julio de 1967, Caja 464, IPS, AGNMEX.

86. Skidmore, *Politics of Military Rule in Brazil*, 88–89.

87. Quoted in Martin Needler, *Mexican Politics: The Containment of Conflict* (London, 1995), 18; also MemCon between Rusk and Antonio Carrillo Flores, September 18, 1962, Box 141, Country File, NSF, JFKL; Bosques, *Historia Oral de la Diplomacia Mexicana*, 140–141.

88. Zolov, *Refried Elvis*, 120.

89. "Mexico City Sitrep," September 26, 1968, EBB 99, NSA. The classic work on Tlatelolco is Elena Poniatowska, *La Noche de Tlatelolco* (Mexico City, 2001).

90. Rafael Montaño Anaya, "Doscientos Detenidos por Relaciones con Guerrillas," *La Prensa*, 25 de abril de 1971; "Documentos Capturados al MAR," undated (early 1970s), Caja 23, SDN, AGNMEX; INR, "Mexico: Terrorism Still on the Rise," November 29, 1972, EBB 105, NSA.

91. "Problema estudiantil," 27 de noviembre de 1968, Caja 1465A, IPS, AGNMEX; "Mitin estudiantil organizado en la Ciudad Universitaria," 31 de octubre de 1968, Caja 1465A, IPS, AGNMEX; Gilbert Joseph, Anne Rubenstein, and Eric Zolov, "Assembling the Fragments: Writing a Cultural History of Mexico since 1940," in Joseph, Rubenstein, and Zolov, eds., *Fragments of a Golden Age: The Politics of Culture in Mexico Since 1940* (Durham, NC, 2001), 11–12.

92. MRE a Buenos Aires, 6 de septiembre de 1971, Caja Roja No. 2, Fondo 2.2, MREURU.

93. The quotes are from "Proclama del Ejército Revolucionario del Pueblo en la Ciudad de Avellaneda," 28 de julio de 1972, attached to "Intimidación Pública en Avellaneda," 28 de julio de 1972, Leg. 434, Mesa D(s), Archivo de la ex-Dirección de Inteligencia de la Policía de Buenos Aires (DIPBA); José María Moyano, *Argentina's Lost Patrol: Armed Struggle, 1969–1979* (New Haven, 1995), 145.

94. "Meets Socialist Priests," November 30, 1971, Castro Speech Database; Declaración Indagatoria de Diego Abente Brun, 26 de mayo de 1976, DI-B-128, CDYA.

95. Quoted in "Declaración Indagatoria de Francisco Humberlino Delgado Candia," 6 de octubre de 1976, DI-L-L98–100, CDYA; also "Declaración Indagatoria de Pedro López Estigarribia," 10 de septiembre de 1976, ibid.; Aguilera Peralta and Beverly, "Terror and Violence as Weapons of Counter-insurgency," 101; Manus Midlarsky and Kenneth Roberts, "Class, State and

Revolution in Central America: Nicaragua and El Salvador Compared,"
Journal of Conflict Resolution 29 (1985): 177–178.

96. "Acuerdo Bilateral de Inteligencia FF.AA.Paraguay/Ejército Argentino," 12
de septiembre de 1972, DNAT-C-2A, CDYA; also "Anexo A," attached to
ibid.

97. "Situación Base Jurisdicción de la Br. I VII," undated, attached to ibid.

98. Early expressions of dependency analysis include Fernando Henrique
Cardoso and Enzo Faletto, *Dependencia y desarrollo en América Latina*
(Lima, 1967); Celso Furtado, *Economic Development of Latin America:
Historical Background and Contemporary Problems* (New York, 1970); Andre
Gunder Frank, *Latin America: Underdevelopment of Revolution: Essays on the
Development of Underdevelopment and the Immediate Enemy* (London, 1970).
For more recent assessments, see Cristóbal Kay, *Latin American Theories of
Development and Underdevelopment* (New York, 1989); Stephen Haber,
"Economic Growth and Latin American Economic Historiography," in
Haber, ed., *How Latin America Fell Behind: Essays on the Economic Histories
of Brazil and Mexico, 1800–1914* (Stanford, 1997), 1–19.

99. Westad, *Global Cold War,* 91.

100. "Joint Declaration of the Seventy-Seven Developing Countries Made at
the Conclusion of the United Nations Conference on Trade and Development," June 15, 1964, http://www.g77.org/doc/Joint%20Declaration.html
(accessed 9/21/2007).

101. Rafael Caldera, *El Bloque Latinoamericano* (Santiago, 1961); "Carta a los
Señores Prebisch, Mayobre, Herrera, y Santa María," 6 de enero de 1965,
in Óscar Pinochet de la Barra, *Eduardo Frei, Obras Escogidas, 1931–1982*
(Santiago, 1993), 316.

102. Quoted in Michael Dodson, "Liberation Theology and Christian Radicalism in Contemporary Latin America," *Journal of Latin American Studies* 11
(1979): 208.

103. "Alliance for Progress," State Department Administrative History on
Inter-American Relations, Box 1, Administrative Histories File, LBJL;
Paul Sigmund, *Multinationals in Latin America: The Politics of Nationaliza-
tion* (Madison, WI, 1980), 35; Norma Stoltz Chinchilla, "Class Struggle in
Central America: Background and Overview," *Latin American Perspectives* 7
(1980): 4; Donald E. Schulz and Deborah Sundloff Schulz, *The United
States, Honduras, and the Crisis in Central America* (Boulder, CO, 1994), 34.

104. Robinson, *Transnational Conflicts,* esp. 66–71.

105. Covey Oliver, "Foreign and Human Relations with Latin America," *Foreign
Affairs* 48 (1969): 525–526; Abraham Lowenthal, "Alliance Rhetoric versus
Latin American Reality," *Foreign Affairs* 49 (1970): 501; Furtado quoted in
Oswaldo Sunkel, "Big Business and 'Dependencia': A Latin American
View," *Foreign Affairs* 51 (1972): 527

106. Quoted in Dodson, "Liberation Theology and Christian Radicalism," 208.

107. "Nicaraguan Youths Riot on Rockefeller," *Los Angeles Times,* May 17, 1969; Jon Kofas, *The Sword of Damocles: U.S. Financial Hegemony in Colombia and Chile, 1950–1970* (Westport, CT, 2002), 84.

108. *Venezuela y México: Visita del Presidente de los Estados Unidos de México, Licenciado Luís Echeverría Alvarez a Venezuela* (Caracas, 1974), 23.

109. ECLA, *Economic Survey of Latin America, 1971* (Santiago, 1972), 23; David Lehmann, *Democracy and Development in Latin America: Economics, Politics, and Religion in the Post-war Period* (Philadelphia, 1992), 48–51.

110. "Exposición del Doctor Alfredo Vázquez Carrizosa," November 2, 1966, OEA/Ser G. VII/CE/CP-URC-13, OAS Archives; "Progress toward Economic Integration in Latin America," August 25, 1967, Box 3, Country File, NSF, LBJL.

111. Juan Velasco Alvarado, *La voz de la Revolución* (Lima, 1972), 320–322; "Memorandum Confidencial," 24 de agosto de 1971, "Memoran-dums: Dirección de Relaciones Internacionales, 1964–1971," MRECHILE.

112. A. D. Horne, "21 Latin Countries Present Manifesto on Links to U.S.," *Washington Post,* June 12, 1969.

113. Domingo Santa María, "Memoria de la Embajada de Chile en Washing-ton," 1 de noviembre de 1970, "Memoria entre años 1968–1970," EmbaChile EEUU, MRECHILE.

114. Untitled transcript of speech to the General Assembly, 8 de octubre de 1974, Vol. 40, Parte I: 78, Archivo Alfonso García Robles, AHGE.

115. Mercado, *Ensayos,* 91, 217; "Es caso especial expropriación del complejo IPC," *La Prensa,* February 1, 1969; "What Peru Wants," *Christian Science Monitor,* September 18, 1969.

116. The geological metaphors are borrowed from Gaddis, "Living in Candle-stick Park," *The Atlantic* 283 (April 1999): 65–74.

4. The Third World War

1. Formally, the National Liberation Movement (MLN)-Tupamaros.

2. "Statement of the Ambassador of Uruguay, Dr. Héctor Luisi," August 1970, Caja 10, Fondo 2.6, MREURU.

3. "Statement from the Embassy of Uruguay," August 1970, ibid.

4. Pamphlet appended to "Registro de Hechos Subversivos," 24 de septiembre de 1973, Leg. 1112, Mesa D(s), DIPBA.

5. This criticism was common among Southern Cone guerrilla groups. See ERP, "Bolivia, Uruguay, Chile, Argentina: La lucha es la misma en América Latina," undated, Leg. 1112, Mesa D(s), DIPBA; "Tupamaros y Gobierno: Dos Poderes," *Granma,* 8 de octubre de 1970. On Marighella, see Frei Betto, *Batismo de sangue: Os dominicanos e a morte de Carlos Marighela* (Rio de Janeiro, 1982).

6. "El Llanto del Enemigo," *Cristianismo y revolución,* abril de 1971, 70–73, quoted in Richard Gillespie, *Soldiers of Perón: Argentina's Montoneros* (New York, 1982), 102; Acuña, *Por amor al odio,* 276–298.

7. Oficina Central de Información, "Uruguay: Los Tupamaros," enero de 1971, Exp. 1–71 (Uruguay 1971), DPI, MREVEN. On Sendic, see Samuel Blixen, *Sendic* (Montevideo, 2000).

8. Lindsay DuBois, *The Politics of the Past in an Argentine Working-Class Neighborhood* (Toronto, 2005), 58; Eric Stener Carlson, *I Remember Julia: Voices of the Disappeared* (Philadelphia, 1996), 98.

9. Quote from "Documento 1," in Movimiento de Liberación Nacional, *Documentación Propia* (Heverlee-Louvain, Belgium, 1973), 37; also Miller, "Urban Terrorism in Uruguay," 139–140; "Economic Memorandum on Argentina," Report 1282-AR, September 8, 1976, p. ii, LACRO, WBA; E. Fernández Huidobro, *Historia de los tupamaros: Los orígenes* (Montevideo, 1986), esp. 132; Luís Costa Bonino, *Crisis de los partidos tradicionales y movimiento revolucionario en el Uruguay* (Montevideo, 1985).

10. Roberto Baschetti, ed., *Documentos de la Resistencia Peronista, 1955–1970* (La Plata, 1997), 615; Sarlo, *La batalla de las ideas,* 167–168; Aldrighi, *La izquierda armada,* 81.

11. Quoted in "Montoneros—Comunicado No. 5," 5 de junio de 1970, www .galeon.com/elortiba/memoria1.html (accessed 10/15/09); Gillespie, *Soldiers of Perón,* 52–58; Cirilo Perdía, *La Otra Historia,* 67.

12. Abraham Guillén, *Philosophy of the Urban Guerrilla: The Revolutionary Writings of Abraham Guillén,* trans. Donald C. Hodges (New York, 1973), 92, 134–135.

13. "El Llanto del Enemigo," *Cristianismo y revolución,* abril de 1971, 70–73, quoted in Gillespie, *Soldiers of Peron,* 102.

14. Marchak, ed., *God's Assassins,* 115, 124; Aldrighi, *La izquierda armada,* 81.

15. Quoted in Peter Ranis, "Peronismo without Perón Ten Years after the Fall (1955–1965)," *Journal of Inter-American Studies* 8 (1966): 115.

16. James Brennan, "Clasismo and the Workers: The Ideological-Cultural Context of 'Sindicalismo de Liberación' in the Cordoban Automobile Industry, 1970–1975," *Bulletin of Latin American Research* 15 (1996): 293–308; James Brennan and Mónica B. Gordillo, "Class Protest, Popular Revolt, and Urban Insurrection in Argentina: The 1969 'Cordobazo,'" *Journal of Social History* 27 (1994): 477–498; Gordillo, "Movimientos sociales e identidades colectivas: Repensando el ciclo de protesta obrera cordobés de 1969–1971," *Desarrollo económico* 39 (1999): 385–408.

17. Baschetti, ed., *Documentos de la Resistencia Peronista,* 585, 594, 731; Gillespie, *Soldiers of Perón,* 61–62; James Kohl and John Lott, eds., *Urban Guerrilla Warfare in Latin America* (Cambridge, MA, 1974), 385.

18. "Nuevo comunicado de los Tupamaros denuncia penetración yanqui en Uruguay," *Granma,* 14 de agosto de 1970.

19. "Dan a conocer los Tupamaros su comunicado número diez," *Granma*, 12 de agosto de 1970; Coronel Sergio Luís d'Oliveira, *El Uruguay y Los Tupamaros* (Montevideo, 1996), 85; Howard Handelman, "Labor-Industrial Conflict and the Collapse of Uruguayan Democracy," *Journal of Interamerican Studies and World Affairs* 23 (1981): 377–378; van Aken, "Radicalization of the Uruguay Student Movement," 126.

20. Guillén, *Philosophy of the Urban Guerrilla*, 237.

21. Carlos Marighella, *Manual of the Urban Guerrilla* (Chapel Hill, NC, 1985), 63.

22. Kohl and Litt, eds., *Urban Guerrilla Warfare in Latin America*, 286.

23. "Proclama del Ejército Revolucionario del Pueblo en la Ciudad de Avellaneda," 28 de julio de 1972, attached to "Intimidación Pública en Avellaneda," 28 de julio de 1972, Leg. 434, Mesa D(s), DIPBA.

24. "Tupamaros: Documento No. 5," *Cuestión*, 28 de agosto de 1971, in MLN, *Documentación Propia*, 73; see also Organización Primero de Marzo, "El Pueblo Vencerá en Su Justa Lucha," undated, DI-B-126, CDYA.

25. A. J. Langguth, *Hidden Terrors* (New York, 1978), 229.

26. Gaetano Pellegrini Giampietro, *Nada Personal: Setenta y tres días en manos de los Tupamaros* (Montevideo, 1996), 115; Alain Labrousse, *The Tupamaros: Urban Guerrillas in Uruguay*, trans. Dinah Livingstone (Middlesex, UK, 1973), 36–37.

27. MRE a Buenos Aires, 23 de septiembre de 1970, Caja 2 (1970), Fondo 2.2, MREURU; see also "FAU-ROB-OPR 33," undated, DI-B-246, CDYA.

28. "Proclama del Ejército Revolucionario del Pueblo en la Ciudad de Avellaneda," 28 de julio de 1972, attached to "Intimidación Pública en Avellaneda," 28 de julio de 1972, Leg. 434, Mesa D(s), DIPBA.

29. Volante del ERP, undated, Leg. 417, Mesa D(s), DIPBA.

30. Guillén, *Philosophy of the Urban Guerrilla*, 21.

31. Marchak, ed., *God's Assassins*, 181.

32. Guillén, *Philosophy of the Urban Guerrilla*, 242; "Report from Brazil: What the Left Is Saying," *New York Times*, December 7, 1969. A recent account disputes these estimates of early Montonero strength. See Lucas Lanusse, *Montoneros: El mito de sus 12 fundadores* (Buenos Aires, 2005).

33. See "Toma del establecimiento textil Lanera San Blas en Bahía Blanca por ERP," 24 de mayo de 1973, Leg. 783, Mesa D(s) DIPBA; "Registro de Hechos Subversivos," 6 de septiembre de 1973, Leg. 908, ibid.; Jorge Domínguez, "Insurgency in Latin America and the Common Defense," *Political Science Quarterly* 101 (1986): 812–813.

34. ERP, "A Los Vecinos del Barrio Lujo," en "Distribución de productos lácteos por el ERP en Campana el 17/10/73," Leg. 1120, Mesa D(s), DIPBA; untitled memorandum, 4 de abril de 1975, Leg. 3402, ibid.; "Actividades del ERP en Campana y Zárate Durante el Mes de Marzo,"

ibid.; "Robo de Arma al Cabo Ernesto Maidana por Integrantes del 'ERP,' 29 de noviembre de 1975," ibid.

35. Mario Firmenich y Norma Arrostito, "Cómo murió Aramburu," *La Causa Peronista*, reprinted in www.elortiba.org/memoria1.html (accessed 10/15/2009); Robert Crassweller, *Perón and the Enigmas of Argentina* (New York, 1988), 337–338.

36. D'Oliveira, *El Uruguay y los Tupamaros*, 127; also MRE a Buenos Aires, 6 de septiembre de 1971, Exp. A6–1, Caja Roja No. 2, Fondo 2.2, MREURU.

37. See the estimates in Lewis, *Guerrillas and Generals*, 46–47. Brazilian intelligence supported the estimate of 30,000 guerrillas. SNI, Apreciação Sumária No. 01/74, 5 de maio de 1974, EG pr 1974.03.00/1, FGV.

38. Guillermo O'Donnell, "Democracia en la Argentina, Micro y Macro," in Oscar Oszlak, ed., *"Proceso," crisis y transición democrática*, vol. 1 (Buenos Aires, 1984), 23, cited in Wolfgang S. Heinz and Hugo Fruhling. *Determinants of Gross Human Rights Violations by State and State-Sponsored Actors in Brazil, Uruguay, Chile, and Argentina* (The Hague, 1999), 622; also Jaime E. Malamud-Goti, *Game without End: State Terror and the Politics of Justice* (Norman, OK, 1996), 30–33; Moyano, *Argentina's Lost Patrol*, 27–28.

39. "Primera Reunión de Inteligencia Nacional," 29 de octubre de 1975, DI-B-246, CDYA.

40. Martin Edwin Andersen, *Dossier Secreto: Argentina's Desaparecidos and the Myth of the "Dirty War"* (Boulder, CO, 1993); Wright, *State Terrorism in Latin America*.

41. "Documento 1," junio de 1967, MLN, *Documentación Propia*, 35–36; Guillén, *Philosophy of the Urban Guerrilla*, 254.

42. Memorando del MRE y Culto al Subsecretario de Defensa Nacional, 24 de diciembre de 1960, Caja 141, Secretos, Confidenciales y Reservados, Ministerio del Interior, Archivo General de la Nación de Argentina (AGNARG); Memorandum al Señor Ministro de Gobierno de la Provincia de Formosa, 31 de enero de 1961, ibid.; "Antecedentes de las personas mencionadas en la nómina remitida por la Comisión de Derechos Humanos y sus implicancias en actividades subversivas contra la paz y seguridad de la Nación," undated, DNAT-C-25, CDYA.

43. FF.AA. de Argentina, "Situación Base Jurisdicción de la Br. I VII," 12 de septiembre de 1972, DNAT-C-2A, CDYA; Guillén, *Philosophy of the Urban Guerrilla*, 264.

44. Ministerio del Interior, Nota No. 84, 17 de junio de 1969, DNAT-C-2A, CDYA; Memorandum, Policía de la Capital, 4 de septiembre de 1972, DI-L-C11, CDYA.

45. Miguel Ángel Bestard a Don Antonio Campos Alum, 17 de junio de 1969, DNAT-C-2A, CDYA.

46. "Soviet–Cuban Relations," March 1, 1972, Vol. 8906, 20-Cuba-1–3-USSR, LAC; Guillén, *Philosophy of the Urban Guerrilla*, 92.

47. Havana to Ottawa, May 13, 1975, Vol. 10847, 20-Cuba-1–3, LAC.

48. James Blight, Bruce Allyn, and David Welch, eds., *Cuba on the Brink: Castro, the Missile Crisis, and the Soviet Collapse* (New York, 2002), 298.

49. Policía de la Capital, Informe, 29 de diciembre de 1975, DI-B-1051, CDYA. On Goiburú, see also Informe (D-3), 26 de noviembre de 1974, DI-(B)-245, ibid.; "Antecedentes," 18 de junio ed 1976, DI-B-1051, CDYA.

50. "Nómina de personas que viajaron a la Habana (Cuba)," 10 de abril de 1975, DI-B-143, CDYA; Informe 89/76, 20 de octubre de 1976, DI-B-245, CDYA; Ministerio del Interior, Nota No. 84, 17 de junio de 1969, DNAT-C-2A, CDYA; "Procedimiento contrasubversivo vinculado a la Junta Coordinadora Revolucionaria," undated, Leg. 3010, Mesa D(s), DIPBA; Gillespie, *Soldiers of Peron*, 83.

51. D'Oliveira, *El Uruguay y Los Tupamaros*, 31; Tanya Harmer, "The Rules of the Game: Allende's Chile, the United States and Cuba, 1970–1973" (Ph.D. Dissertation, London School of Economics, 2008), 178.

52. Kirkendall, "Kennedy Men and the Fate of the Alliance for Progress," 747; NIE 80/90–67, "Economic Trends and Prospects in Latin America," July 20, 1967, Box 8, NIE Files, NSF, LBJL.

53. Arturo Valenzuela, *The Breakdown of Democratic Regimes: Chile* (Baltimore, 1978), 3–39; Barbara Stallings, *Class Conflict and Economic Development in Chile, 1958–1973* (Stanford, 1978), 42–43.

54. Oficio No. 237, de Ramón Maturana Gutiérrez, Servicio Nacional de Salud, 21 de septiembre de 1965, Vol. 1677, Ministerio de Agricultura; also "Programa de Crédito Agricola del Instituto de Desarrollo Agropecuario," undated, Vol. 1675, Ministerio de Agricultura, Archivo Nacional de la Administración (ANA) de Chile. On the Revolution in Liberty, see Albert Michaels, "The Alliance for Progress and Chile's 'Revolution in Liberty,' 1964–1970," *Journal of Interamerican Studies and World Affairs* 18 (1976): 74–99.

55. Davíd Gómez, "Gobierno: Una política económica de fracaso en fracaso," *Principios*, marzo–junio de 1969, 8.

56. Eduardo Frei Montalvo, "The Alliance That Lost Its Way," *Foreign Affairs* 46 (1967): 441–443; Hite, *When the Romance Ended*, 172.

57. Julio César Jobet, *El Partido Socialista de Chile* (Santiago, 1971), 130–133.

58. Regis Debray, *Conversations with Allende: Socialism in Chile* (London, 1971), 74; Transcript of a Speech by Allende in Guadalajara, 2 de diciembre de 1972, Topográfica 5988–5, Archivo de Concentraciones.

59. Valenzuela, *Breakdown of Democratic Regimes*, 39–40.

60. Jorge Edwards a MRE, 10 de diciembre de 1970, "1970 Cuba," MRE-CHILE; see also "Conversación del Embajador N. B. Alekseev con Volodia Teitelboim," 14 de octubre de 1970, in "Chile en los Archivos," 412.

61. Comunicado 118, 6 de mayo de 1972, MLN, *Documentación propia,* 139–140; also Arturo Porzecanski, *Uruguay's Tupamaros: The Urban Guerrilla* (New York, 1973), 22.

62. Comunicado 118, 6 de mayo de 1972, MLN, *Documentación Propia,* 139–140; "Documento de la JCR en publicación Che Guevara, N. 2, Febrero de 1975," in Presidencia de la República de Uruguay, *Investigación Histórica sobre Detenidos Desaparecidos,* Vol. 1 (Montevideo, 2007), 263; Harmer, "Rules of the Game," 131–132.

63. "Asunto: JCR," undated (1975), DI-B-245, CDYA.

64. "Documento de la JCR en publicación Che Guevara," 263; Departamento Central de Informaciones a SIPBA, 11 de julio de 1974, Leg. 1908, Mesa D(s), DIPBA; Dinges, *Condor Years,* 51–52.

65. "Asunto: JCR," undated (1975), DI-B-245, CDYA.

66. Declaración Indagatoria de María Felicita Jiménez de Carrillo, 4 de diciembre de 1976, DI-B-128; Informe 023/77, 31 de marzo de 1977, DI-B-246; "Informaciones Generales," abril de 1975, DI-B-245; Informe 64, 20 de octubre de 1975, DI-B-245, CDYA.

67. "Procedimiento contrasubversivo vinculado a la Junta Coordinadora Revolucionaria," undated, Leg. 3010, Mesa D(s), DIPBA; Jefe de Policía, Informe (Esmagenfa), 29 de agosto de 1975, DI-B-246, CDYA; Pedido de Busqueda 28/76, 5 de agosto de 1976, DI-B-245, CDYA; Declaración Indagatoria de Diego Abente Brun, 26 de mayo de 1976, DI-B-128; Declaración Indagatoria de Gladis María Fariña Insfran, 17 de noviembre de 1976, ibid.

68. ERP, "Recuperando algo de lo mucho que ESSO roba al pueblo," undated, en "Material de propaganda del ERP, que circula en la ciudad de Tucumán," 24 de marzo de 1975, Leg. 3235, Mesa D(s), DIPBA; "Procedimiento contrasubversivo vinculado a la Junta Coordinadora Revolucionaria," undated, Leg. 3010, Mesa D(s), DIPBA.

69. Carlos Alberto da Fontoura Oral History, 96, Oral Histories, FGV; Skidmore, *Politics of Military Rule in Brazil,* 125.

70. SNI, Apreciaçâo Sumária No. 01/74, 5 de maio de 1974, EG pr 1974.03.00/1, FGV; also SNI, Untitled report, March 1974, ibid.

71. Mexico City to State, April 19, 1974, EBB 105, NSA. On the Mexican guerrillas, see Jaime López, *10 años de guerrillas en Mexico, 1964–1974* (Mexico City, 1974); José de Jesús Morales Hernández, *Memorias de un guerrillero: La guerra sucia del México de los 70's* (Zapopan, Jalisco, 2006).

72. "El Pueblo Vencerá en Su Justa Lucha," undated, DI-B-126, CDYA; "Declaración Indagatoria de Daniel Campos Ruíz Díaz," en Pastor Coronel a Jefe de Policía de la Capital, 25 de abril de 1978, DI-B-126; Alfredo Boccia Paz, *La década inconclusa: Historia real de la OPM* (Asuncion, 1997), 105–124.

73. Kohl and Litt, *Urban Guerrilla Warfare,* 272. On Mitrione, see Jeffrey Ryan, "Turning on Their Masters: State Terrorism and Unlearning Democracy in

Uruguay," in Cecilia Menjívar and Néstor Rodriguez, eds., *When States Kill: Latin America, the U.S., and Technologies of Terror* (Austin, TX, 2005), 280–287.

74. Montevideo to State, September 9, 1971, Box 2662, SNF 70–73, RG 59, NARA; Handelman, "Labor-Industrial Conflict," 377–378.

75. Aldrighi, *La izquierda armada*, 43.

76. "Statement from the Embassy of Uruguay," August 1970, Caja 10, Fondo 2.6, MREURU; "Preliminary Analysis and Strategy Paper—Uruguay," August 25, 1971, EBB 71, NSA; Robert Kaufman, "Industrial Change and Authoritarian Rule in Latin America: A Concrete Review of the Bureaucratic-Authoritarian Model," in David Collier, ed., *The New Authoritarianism in Latin America* (Princeton, 1979), 191.

77. Buenos Aires to State, July 16, 1971, Box 2085, SNF 70–73, RG 59, NARA.

78. Liliana de Riz, *Retorno y derrumbe: El último gobierno peronista* (Mexico City, 1981), 63.

79. Guido Di Tella, *Perón-Perón 1973–1976* (Buenos Aires, 1983), 55; also ERP, "Bolivia, Uruguay, Chile, Argentina: La lucha es la misma en America Latina," in "Registro de Hechos Subversivos," 24 de septiembre de 1973, San Martín, Mesa D(s), Leg. 1112, DIPBA.

80. "Porque el ERP no dejará de combatir," en "Panfletos del ERP Hallados en La Plata," enero de 1973, Leg. 638, Mesa D(s); also Acuña, *Por amor al odio*, 643–652; Alicia Ziccardi, "El tercer gobierno peronista y las villas miseria de la ciudad de Buenos Aires (1973–1976)," *Revista Mexicana de Sociología* 46 (1984): 145–172.

81. Michael Reid, *Forgotten Continent: The Battle for Latin America's Soul* (New Haven, 2008), 114.

82. "Material de propaganda del ERP, que circula en la ciudad de Tucumán," 24 de marzo de 1975, Leg. 3235, Mesa D(s), DIPBA; "Informe Relacionado a Las Actividades de la OPM-PRT-ERP, en la Zona de la Localidad de Campana, Procedente del Comando General del Ejército Jefatura II," 23 de mayo de 1975, Leg. 3369, Mesa D(s), DIPBA; "Actividades del ERP en Campana y Zárate Durante el Mes de Marzo," 2 de abril de 1975, Leg. 3402, Mesa D(s), DIPBA.

83. SNI, Apreciação Sumário No. 02.74, 16 de maio de 1974, EG pr 1974.03.00/1, FGV; ERP, "La verdad sobre Tucumán," early 1975, Leg. 3232, Mesa D(s), DIPBA.

84. "Comunicado del Comando Jorge Ulia Clarisa Lea Place del ERP," 1973, Leg. 2421, Mesa D(s), DIPBA; LACRO, "Economic Memorandum on Argentina," Report 1282-AR, September 8, 1976, WBA.

85. Miguel González Pino and Arturo Fontaine Talavera, eds., *Los mil días de Allende,* Vol. 1 (Santiago, 1997), 64; "Somos una organización marxista," *La Nación* (Santiago), 16 de noviembre de 1970.

86. Santiago to Ottawa, February 22, 1972, Vol. 8633, 20–1–2-Chile, LAC; Haslam, *Nixon Administration and the Death of Allende's Chile*, 181; Faúndez, *Marxism and Democracy in Chile*, 216.

87. Pamela Constable and Arturo Venezuela, *A Nation of Enemies: Chile under Pinochet* (New York, 1991), 28–29; Harmer, "Rules of the Game."

88. The former school is represented by Dinges, *Condor Years;* the latter is represented by Andersen, *Dossier Secreto;* Wright, *State Terrorism in Latin America;* Cecilia Menjívar and Nestor Rodríguez, *When States Kill: Latin America, the U.S., and Technologies of Terror* (Austin, TX, 2005).

89. William Columbus Davis, *Warnings from the Far South: Dictatorship versus Democracy in Uruguay, Argentina, and Chile* (Westport, CT, 1995), 45; also Alexandra Barahona de Brito, *Human Rights and Democratization in Latin America: Uruguay and Chile* (London, 1997), esp. 36.

90. Kohl and Litt, eds., *Urban Guerrilla Warfare*, 227.

91. Ernesto F. Betancourt, *Revolutionary Strategy: A Handbook for Practitioners* (New Brunswick, NJ, 1991), 131–132; also Charles Gillespie, *Negotiating Democracy: Politicians and Generals in Uruguay* (Cambridge, UK, 1991), 25–26.

92. Lawrence Weschler, *A Miracle, A Universe: Settling Accounts with Torturers* (Chicago, 1998), 108.

93. Davis, *Warnings from the Far South*, 45.

94. Department of State Information Memorandum, "The Uruguayan Elections," November 26, 1971, EBB 71, NSA; Gillespie, *Negotiating Democracy*, 24–32, 41.

95. Kohl and Litt, *Urban Guerrlla Warfare*, 233; D'Oliveira, *El Uruguay y los Tupamaros*, 85.

96. Edy Kaufman, *Uruguay in Transition: From Civilian to Military Rule* (New Brunswick, NJ, 1978), 35.

97. MRE a Buenos Aires, 13 de septiembre de 1971, Caja Roja No. 2, Carpeta A6–1, Fondo 2.2, MREURU; MRE a Buenos Aires, Boletín Número 5, 15 de abril de 1972, Caja Roja No. 1, Carpeta A6–1, Fondo 2.2, MREURU. The statistics are in MRE a Buenos Aires, 1 de julio de 1972, "Caja Roja 1," 1972, Fondo 2.2, MREURU.

98. Memorandum of Conversation, April 10, 1973, Box 2662, SNF, RG 59, NARA.

99. Quoted in Montevideo to State, November 3, 1973, Box 2660, SNF, RG 59, NARA; Montevideo to State, February 12, 1973, Box 2662, ibid.

100. Norden, *Military Rebellion in Argentina*, 43; James McGuire, *Peronism without Perón: Unions, Parties, and Democracy in Argentina* (Stanford, 1997), 158.

101. Ysabel Trujillo, "Peron Calls His Left Wing 'Stupid,'" *Chicago Tribune*, May 2, 1974; Moyano, *Argentina's Lost Patrol*, 41.

102. "Testimonio del Inspector . . . Rodolfo Peregrino Fernández, sobre la estructura de la represión ilegítima en la Argentina," 8 de marzo de 1983,

Caja "Represores," Colección Testimonios, Archivo de la Asamblea Permanente de Derechos Humanos (APDH).

103. Volante de la Alianza Anticomunista Argentina, 9 de julio de 1975, DI-B-234, CDYA; Ministerio de Gobierno de la Provincia, "Campaña de acción psicológica del ERP: Presunta lista de víctimas de la organización A-A-A," 27 de abril de 1975, Leg. 3384, Mesa D(s), DIPBA.

104. Oscar Britos al Ministerio del Interior, 12 de enero de 1974, Caja 26, Expedientes Generales, Ministerio del Interior, AGNARG.

105. Shlaudeman to Kissinger, August 3, 1976, EBB 125, NSA; Testimonio de Luís Alberto Martínez, Caja 1.90–1.121, Colección Centros Clandestinos de Detención, APDH.

106. SRE a Buenos Aires, 18 de octubre de 1977, Topográfica III-3317–1, Archivo de Concentraciones.

107. Buenos Aires to State, March 16, 1976, EBB 125, NSA; "Testimonio del Vicealmirante (RE) Luis María Mendía," *El Diario del Juicio,* 27 de mayo de 1985, Colección Testimonios, Archivo del Centro de Estudios Legales y Sociales (CELS).

108. "Testimono del Doctor Italo Luder," *El Diario del Juicio,* 27 de mayo de 1985, Colección Testimonios, CELS.

109. "Situación Base Jurisdicción de la Br. I VII," undated, attached to "Acuerdo Bilateral de Inteligencia FF.AA.Paraguay/Ejército Argentino," 12 de septiembre de 1972, DNAT-C-2A, CDYA.

110. Buenos Aires to State, September 21, 1976, EBB 125, NSA.

111. Buenos Aires to State, February 16, 1976, EBB 125, NSA; Ramón Genaro Díaz Bessone, *Guerra Revolucionaria en la Argentina (1959–1978)* (Buenos Aires, 1986), 258.

112. "Discurso pronunciado en la Sala de Representantes de la Ciudad de Buenos Aires," 30 de junio de 1975, *Doctrina de la seguridad nacional,* I: 175.

113. Buenos Aires to State, March 29, 1976, EBB 125, NSA; Marchak, *God's Assassins,* 212; also Roque González Salazar a SRE, 5 de abril de 1976, Topográfica III-6105–8, Archivo de Concentraciones.

114. Faúndez, *Marxism and Democracy in Chile,* 203–204.

115. "Statement by Mr. Massad on Chile—Executive Board Meeting 74/5/," January 30, 1974, EBD 74/6, IMF.

116. "Medidas que podríamos adopotar para establecer algún 'modus-vivendi' con Estados Unidos," 5 de septiembre de 1972, Caja 2, Archivo Orlando Letelier, Archivo Nacional Histórico (ANH); Faúndez, *Marxism and Democracy in Chile,* 235–248; Haslam, *Nixon Administration and the Death of Allende's Chile,* 107–128.

117. Richard Helms, "Notes on Meeting with the President on Chile," September 15, 1970, EBB 8, NSA. U.S.–Chilean relations under Allende are discussed in greater detail in Chapter 5. Perspectives on this subject include

Haslam, *Nixon Administration and the Death of Allende's Chile;* William F. Sater, *Chile and the United States: Empires in Conflict* (Athens, GA, 1991), 171–184; Peter Kornbluh, *The Pinochet File: A Declassified Dossier on Atrocity and Accountability* (New York, 2004).

118. "Chile Debt Meeting," March 29–30, 1972, Box 52, WHDAI Country Files (Chile), Western Hemisphere Department Fonds, IMF; Ernest Sturc and Jorge Del Canto to the Managing Director, February 10, 1972, ibid.

119. Jussi Hanhimaki, *Flawed Architect: Henry Kissinger and American Foreign Policy* (New York, 2004), 104.

120. Robert S. McNamara Oral History Interview, May 10, 1991, Oral Histories, WBA.

121. "Memorandum: Conversaciones Sostenidas Entre Delegaciones de Chile y Estados Unidos," 24 de marzo de 1973, in "Memorandums: Dirección General de Política Exterior, 1961–1979," MRECHILE; "Chilean Debt Meeting," July 12–13, 1973, Box 52, WHDAI Country Files (Chile), Western Hemisphere Department Fonds, IMF.

122. John Irwin II to Kissinger, December 22, 1971, Box 1, Pinochet/Chile Project File, Gerald Ford Presidential Library (GFL).

123. González Pino and Fontaine Talavera, *Los mil días,* 66–67, quoted in Haslam, *Nixon Administration and the Death of Allende's Chile,* 94. See also Peter Winn, *Weavers of Revolution: The Yarur Workers and Chile's Road to Socialism* (New York, 1989), chapters 13–18.

124. Constable and Venezuela, *Nation of Enemies,* 28–29.

125. Cirilo Perdía, *La Otra Historia,* 197.

126. Constable and Valenzuela, *Nation of Enemies,* 29; Fernando Mires, *La rebelión permanente: Las revoluciones sociales en América Latina* (Mexico City, 1989), 359.

127. Genaro Arriagada Herrera, *Pinochet: The Politics of Power* (New York, 1988), 9; Wright, *State Terrorism in Latin America,* 57.

128. CIA Report, August 11, 1973, Box 1, Pinochet Collection, NPM.

129. Castro to Allende, July 29, 1973, quoted in "Speech by Major Fidel Castro," Reel 41, *Politics in Chile,* Princeton University Latin American Pamphlet Collection.

130. Raúl Silva Henríquez, *Memorias,* Vol. 2 (Santiago, 1991), 258.

131. Memorandum Confidencial, 6 de enero de 1972, "Memorandums: Dirección de Relaciones Internacionales, 1974–1978," MRECHILE.

132. CIA Intelligence Information Cable, September 6, 1973, Box 1, Pinochet Collection, NPM.

133. "Comunicado de Eaton Fundaciones ICSA," 8 de noviembre de 1973, Leg. 1209, Mesa D(s), DIPBA.

134. C. L. Arceneaux, "Institutional Design, Military Rule, and Regime Transition in Argentina (1976–1983): An Extension of the Remmer Thesis,"

Bulletin of Latin American Research 16 (1997): 333. The preceding two paragraphs draw on Santiago a MRE, 9 de enero de 1976, Caja 9, Chile, MREURU; Gillespie, *Negotiating Democracy*, 33–47; Norden, *Military Rebellion in Argentina*, 42–45; Patricio Silva, "Collective Memories, Fears and Consensus: The Political Psychology of the Chilean Democratic Transition," in Peter Winn, ed., *Victims of the Chilean Miracle: Workers and Neoliberalism in the Pinochet Era, 1973–2002* (Durham, NC, 2004), 171–174; Handelman, "Labor-Industrial Conflict," 377–378.

135. Arriagada Herrera, *Pinochet*, 12; "La acusación," *Diario del Juicio*, 8 de octubre de 1985, Colección Testimonios, CELS.

136. George Lawson, *Negotiated Revolutions: The Czech Republic, South Africa, and Chile* (London, 2005), 182; Monte Real and J. Y. Smith, "A Chilean Dictator's Dark Legacy," *Washington Post*, December 11, 2006.

137. The estimate of 9,000 given by the National Commission on the Disappearance of Persons (CONADEP) is certainly low; human rights groups' estimates of 30,000 deaths are perhaps slightly high. The real number probably lies somewhere between this upper boundary and the military's internal estimate of 22,000.

138. "Reestructuración de jurisdicciones y adecuación orgánica para intensificar las operaciones contra la subversión," mayo de 1976, *Diario del Juicio*, 16 de julio de 1985, Colección Testimonios, CELS; Memorandum for the Files, August 21, 1980, EBB 73, NSA.

139. CONADEP, *Nunca Más*, www.nuncamas.org (accessed 9/12/07).

140. See Chapter 3; also Peter Winn, "The Pinochet Era," in Winn, ed., *Victims of the Chilean Miracle*, 17.

141. Adolfo Canitrot, "La disciplina como objetivo de la política económica: Un ensayo sobre el programa económico del gobierno argentino desde 1976," *Desarrollo económico* 19 (1980): 453–475; Pablo Pozzi, "Argentina 1976–1982: Labour Leadership and Military Government," *Journal of Latin American Studies* 20 (1988): esp. 114–116; Paul Buchanan, "The Varied Faces of Domination: State Terror, Economic Policy, and Social Rupture during the Argentine 'Proceso,' 1976–1981," *American Journal of Political Science* 31 (1987): 336–382; Constable and Valenzuela, *Nation of Enemies*, 168–198.

142. Declaración Indagatoria de Miguel Ángel Ignacio López Perito, 6 de julio de 1976, DI-L-E32, CDYA.

143. "Puntos de vista del Jefe de Policía con relación a la Subversión," undated, DI-B-47, CDYA.

144. Quoted in Erwin Kohmann a Francisco José, 23 de febrero de 1975, DI-L-P57, CDYA; "Informe de los Trabajos Realizados Zona-Jejuí-San Pedro-Lima, Tacuatí, Santani y Sus Alrededores," undated, DI-L-P57, CDYA; "Nomina de Detenidos Recluidos en el Dpto. de Investigaciones," 1 de septiembre de 1975, DI-L-BP1, CDYA.

145. See "Lista de personas detenidas en la Colonia Nueva Esperanza," 9 de abril de 1980, DCA-C-4, CDYA; "Integrantes de la Organización Político Militar 'OPM' Sector Capital," 7 de noviembre de 1980, DI-L-F13.

146. "Testimonio del Brigadier Mayor (RE) Aquilino Guerra," *Diario del Juicio*, 27 de mayo de 1985, Colección Testimonios, CELS.

147. "Testimonio del Inspector . . . Rodolfo Peregrino Fernández, sobre la estructura de la represión ilegítima en la Argentina," 8 de marzo de 1983, Caja "Represores," Colección Testimonios, APDH; "Consideraciones Sobre la Juventud y la Vigencia del Art. 3 de la DUDH," undated, Caja B7.130, ibid.; Thomas Klubock, "Class, Community, and Neoliberalism in Chile: Copper Workers and the Labor Movement during the Military Dictatorship and Restoration of Democracy," in Winn, ed., *Victims of the Chilean Miracle*, 210–214.

148. McGuire, *Peronism without Perón*, 170.

149. "Establecimiento Militar de Reclusión Número 2," undated, Archivo de Impunidad, Servicio de Paz y Justicia Uruguay (SERPAJ). For similar statements from Argentine officials, see "Placintara: El Plan Secreto de la Marina," *Diario del Juicio,* 19 de noviembre de 1985; "Reestructuración de jurisdicciones y adecuación orgánica para intensificar las operaciones contra la subversión," *El Diario del Juicio,* 16 de julio de 1985, Colección Testimonios, CELS.

150. "Testimonio del señor Alberto Felipe Maly," *Diario del Juicio,* 11 de junio de 1985, Coleccion Testimonios, CELS; "Escuelita de Famaillá," Caja 1.1–89, Colección Centros Clandestinos de Detención, APDH; "Ingenio Nueva Baviera," ibid.; CONADEP, *Nunca Más.*

151. "Discurso del General de División Santiago Omar Riveros el 24 de enero de 1980 en la Junta Interamericana de Defensa," Caja B7.124, APDH.

152. Daniel Rey Piuma, *Los crímenes del Río de la Plata* (Cordoba, 1984), 80.

153. "Testimonio del Inspector . . . Rodolfo Peregrino Fernández, sobre la estructura de la represión ilegítima en la Argentina," 8 de marzo de 1983, Caja "Represores," Colección Testimonios, APDH.

154. See "Establecimiento Militar de Reclusión Número 2," undated; "El Penal de Punta de Rieles: Experiencia de una detenida durante 5 años," undated; "El Penal de Libertad: Testimonio," undated, Carpeta Centros de Reclusión, Archivo de Impunidad, Servicio Paz y Justicia Uruguay.

155. Arriagada Herrera, *Pinochet,* 18; Hugh O'Shaughnessy, *Pinochet: The Politics of Torture* (New York, 2000), 65; Jeffrey Sluka, *Death Squad: The Anthropology of State Terror* (Philadelphia, 1999), 94.

156. Pinochet Speech, September 11, 1975, Roll 1, "Chilean Government Pamphlets, 1973–1976," Sterling Memorial Library Microfilm Collection, Yale University.

157. MemCon between Carter and Pinochet, September 6, 1977, Box 9, North-South Files, NSA File, Jimmy Carter Library (JCL); Pinochet a Carter, 14 de octubre de 1977, Embachile EEUU, Oficios Secretos Enviados, MRECHILE.

158. "Minuta de la reunión de los Presidentes Pinochet y Carter," 6 de septiembre de 1977, Embachile EEUU, Oficios Secretos Recibidos, MRECHILE; Santiago to State, April 11, 1988, *DDRS*.

159. "Statement by Mr. Gavaldá on Chile," Executive Board Meeting 76/81, June 4, 1976, IMF; "Statement by Mr. Massad on Chile—Executive Board Meeting 74/5," January 30, 1974, EBD 74/6, IMF; Marcelo Pollack, *The New Right in Chile, 1973–1997* (New York, 1999), 39–72; Marcus Kurtz, "Chile's Neo-Liberal Revolution: Incremental Decisions and Structural Transformation, 1973–89," *Journal of Latin American Studies* 31 (1999): 399–427; Eugenio Tironi, *Los silencios de la revolución* (Santiago, 1988), 92.

160. Report 1282-AR, "Economic Memorandum on Argentina," September 8, 1976, LACRO, WB; Report 4513-AR, "Argentina: 1983 Economic Memorandum," LACRO, WB; "Uruguay—Staff Report and Proposed Decision for the 1976 Article XIV Consultation," July 21, 1976, SM/76/166, Executive Board Documents, IMF; Gillespie, *Negotiating Democracy*, 52–65; Pion-Berlin, "The Armed Forces and Politics," 147–155.

161. Charles Gillespie, "Uruguay's Return to Democracy," *Bulletin of Latin American Research* 4 (1985): 99–101.

162. Quoted in "Impresionantes declaraciones del General Camps, publican en Madrid," *Razón*, 4 de noviembre de 1983, APDH; also "Los Niños Desaparecidos" and "Affidavit de Eduardo Otilio Corro," 24 de septiembre de 1984, caja "Niños Desaparecidos," Archivo de los Familiares de los Detenidos-Desaparecidos (Uruguay).

163. LACRO, "Argentina: 1983 Economic Memorandum," Report 4513-AR, May 23, 1983, WBA.

164. Quoted in Robert Pastor to Brzezinski, May 23, 1977, Box 4, Country File, NSA Files, Jimmy Carter Presidential Library (JCL). On economic policy, see Henry Finch, "Democratisation in Uruguay," *Third World Quarterly* 7 (1985): 595–597; Canitrot, "La disciplina como objetivo de la política económica," 453–475; Pozzi, "Argentina 1976–1982," 111–138; "Uruguay—Staff Report and Proposed Decision for the 1973 Article XIV Consultation," February 15, 1974, SM/74/33, Executive Board Documents, IMF.

165. Steve Stern, *Remembering Pinochet's Chile: On the Eve of London 1998* (Durham, NC, 2004).

166. Aside from the studies cited above, see Guillermo O'Donnell, *Modernization and Bureaucratic Authoritarianism: Studies in South American Politics* (Berkeley, CA, 1973); Wright, *State Terrorism in Latin America*; Jorge Nef, "The Politics of Repression: The Social Pathology of the Chilean Military,"

Latin American Perspectives 1 (1974): 58–77; Kornbluh, *The Pinochet File;*
Klein, *Shock Doctrine.*

167. Stern, "Between Tragedy and Promise," 55.

168. It should be pointed out that the Uruguayan, Argentinian, and Brazilian
juntas scrupulously avoided personalistic rule. There is also a lively debate
about whether this description is appropriate in Pinochet's case. See
Robert Barros, "Personalización y controles institucionales: Pinochet, la
Junta Militar y la Constitución de 1980," *Desarrollo económico* 41 (2001):
17–35.

169. Osiel, "Constructing Subversion in Argentina's Dirty War," 131.

170. Ibid.

5. The Latin American Diplomatic Challenge

1. "Latin American Press on Aid Cuts," undated (late 1968), Box 5, Country
File, NSF, LBJL; "Informe Anual 1968," Tomo 2, Anexos Confidenciales,
EmbaChile EEUU, MRECHILE; Embaven EEUU a MRE, 28 de marzo
de 1968, Exp. 1 (1968), Dirección General, MREVEN.

2. MemCon, December 17, 1974, Box 7, Robinson Papers, RG 59, NARA.

3. "Castro Outlines Support for Other Revolutions," August 5, 1971, CSD;
Allende Speech to UNCTAD, April 13, 1972, in Víctor Farías, ed., *La
izquierda chilena (1969–1973): Documentos para el estudio de su línea estratégica*
(Berlin, 2001–2004), III: 2143.

4. "Memoria de la Embajada de Chile en Washington," 1 de noviembre de
1970, "Memoria Entre Años 1968–1970," EmbaChile EEUU, MRE-
CHILE. For similar statements, see *Perú: Documentos fundamentales del
proceso revolucionario* (Buenos Aires, 1973), 55; Interagency Intelligence
Memorandum, "Latin American Perceptions of the United States," April
26, 1976, Box 2, President's Country Files for Latin America (PCFLA),
GFL; Alfredo Vázquez Carrizosa a MRE, 24 de agosto de 1966, Caja 212,
Transferencia 3, MRE, AGNCOL.

5. Debray, *Conversations with Allende,* 126; Kruijt, *Revolution by Decree,* 104;
MRE a Letelier, 24 de julio de 1971, Caja 2, Archivo Letelier, ANH.

6. Castro quoted in Habana a MRE, 13 de agosto de 1971, "Oficios R,"
EmbaChile Cuba, MRECHILE.

7. "Último día em Viet Nam," *O Globo* (Rio de Janeiro), March 30, 1973, in
Brasilia to State, March 30, 1973, NARA Archival Database; DIA
Analysis, "Brazil's View of Changes in US Relationship," April 16, 1976,
Box 2, PCFLA, GFL; Dinges, *Condor Years,* 11.

8. "El Pacto Andino es la vía más segura para llegar al desarrollo económico,"
El Comercio, 20 de junio de 1972; "Castro Interviewed in Ecuador,"
December 5, 1971, CSD; also Pablo Valdés a MRE, 9 de noviembre de
1971, Caja 6, Archivo Letelier, ANH.

9. "Algunos Aspectos de Estado Actual de las Relaciones de Chile con Estados Unidos," 3 de noviembre de 1971, Caja 2, Archivo Letelier, ANH.

10. *Entrevista de los presidentes de la Argentina y Brasil* (Buenos Aires, 1972), 14; Emílio Garrastazu Médici, *Nosso Caminho* (Brasilia, 1972), 7. Subsequent Brazilian governments affirmed this judgment. See "Secreto: Política Externa Americana," undated (1974), EG 1974.03.00/2, FGV.

11. Pérez to Gerald Ford, 19 de septiembre de 1974, DPI, Exp. 2-B-74, Interior, MREVEN.

12. "Memorandum Interno: Integración, Desarrollo y Política," 8 de enero de 1975, DPI, Exp. 2-A-74, Interior, MREVEN; also Dirección de Política Internacional al Gabinete del Ministro, noviembre de 1974, ibid.

13. Mexico became a net exporter after the discovery of additional reserves in 1975–1976.

14. ECLA, *Economic Survey of Latin America, 1975* (Santiago, 1976), 14–20.

15. Carlos Andrés Pérez, *Manos a la obra: Textos de mensajes, discursos y declaraciones del Presidente de la República, Tomo I* (Caracas, 1975), 147; ECLA, *Economic Survey of Latin America, 1973* (Santiago, 1974), 2, 3, 9.

16. Speech to the Congress, February 21, 1973, *Una Voz del Tercer Mundo* (Mexico City, 1974), 15; Carlos Andrés Pérez, *Primer mensaje del Ciudadano Presidente de la República Carlos Andrés Pérez al Congreso Nacional, 12 de marzo 1975* (Caracas, 1975), 417.

17. *Voz del Tercer Mundo*, 14.

18. *Primer mensaje del Ciudadano Presidente de la República*, 417; Edgardo Mercado Jarrín, *Ensayos* (Lima, 1974), 212; idem, *Seguridad, Política, Estrategia* (Lima, 1974), 174.

19. "Informe," 9 de julio de 1970, Caja 9, SDN, AGNMEX.

20. Mexico City to State, May 28, 1971, EBB 91, NSA.

21. Mexico City to State, May 28, 1971, EBB 91, NSA; see also Mexico City to State, January 6, May 28, June 11, and June 25, 1971, EBB 91, NSA.

22. Mexico City to State, January 5, 1975, Box 5, PCFLA, GFL; also Yoram Shapira, "Mexico's Foreign Policy under Echeverría: A Retrospect," *Inter-American Economic Affairs* 31 (1978): 34–43.

23. "Manifiesto del Gobierno Revolucionario," *Peruvian Political Party Documents*, Folder 6, Reel 1.

24. Rosario Arias Quincot and Rosa María Santistevan de Noriega, *Voces y ecos: Conversando con la generación de los 70* (Lima, 2002), 31–32, 75; María del Pilar Tello, ed., *¿Golpe o revolución? Hablan los militares del 68* (Lima, 1983), 292.

25. See Airgram from Brasilia, September 17, 1971, Box 2131, SNF, RG 59, NARA; Rio to State, October 26, 1970, Box 2129, ibid.; Cintia Vieira Souto, *A Diplomacia do Interesse Nacional: A Política Externa do Governo Médici* (Porto Alegre, 2003), 14–20, 68–72.

26. Memorandum of Conversation, April 17, 1971, Box 2085, SNF, RG 59, NARA; Alejandro Lanusse, *Mi testimonio* (Buenos Aires, 1977), 240–242.

27. "Unidad Popular: Programa básico de gobierno," in Farías, ed., *Izquierda Chilena*, I: 115, 131; Víctor Pey, Joan E. Garcés, and Gonzalo Martínez, eds., *Salvador Allende, 1908–1973: Obras Escogidas* (Madrid, 1992), 565; Sater, *Chile and the United States*, 165–172; Mark Falcoff, *Modern Chile, 1970–1989: A Critical History* (London, 1989), 25–43.

28. María Teresa Romero, *Política exterior venezolana (El proyecto democrático, 1959–1999)* [Caracas, 2002], esp. 69–70.

29. Policía de la Capital, "Informe Confidencial," 4 de septiembre de 1972, DI-L-C11, CDYA.

30. "Memorandum" del MRE, 22 de octubre de 1968, Exp. 1–4 (1968), Peru, DPI, MREVEN; Javier de Belaúnde Ruiz de Somocurcio, *Político por vocación: Testimonio y memorias* (Lima, 1996), 523–524.

31. "Peruvians and Soviet Sign Their First Trade Accord," *New York Times*, February 18, 1969; also Moscú a MRE, 3 de mayo de 1972, Oficios Confidenciales D, EmbaChile Moscú, MRECHILE; Ruben Berrios and Cole Blasier, "Peru and the Soviet-Union (1969–1989): Distant Partners," *Journal of Latin American Studies* 23 (1991): esp. 365–375.

32. Pilar Tello, ed., *Hablan los militares*, 61; Lima to State, December 5, 1973, NARA Archival Database; SNI, Apreciação Sumária No. 02/74, 16 de maio de 1974, EG pr. 1974.03.00/1, FGV.

33. Velasco Alvarado, *La voz de la Revolución*, 78; Kruijt, *Revolution by Decree*, 102–104; also Mercado Jarrín, *Ensayos*, 217; idem, *Seguridad, Política, Estrategia*, 174.

34. Mercado in *Financial Times*, February 25, 1969.

35. Lima a SRE, 28 de febrero de 1969, Topográfica III-5902–4, Archivo de Concetraciones; Tegucigalpa a SRE, 18 de marzo de 1969, ibid.; Dirección General del Servicio Diplomático a Lic. Jesús Reyes Heroles, 8 de marzo de 1969, Topográfica III-5947–11, ibid.

36. Editorial Note, *FRUS 1969–1972*, IV: Document #148; NSC Summary of Memos Leading to NSDM 21, April 11–July 22, 1969, *DDRS;* Nixon comment recalled in Lima to State, September 28, 1971, Box 2543, SNF, RG 59, NARA.

37. Haig to Nixon, June 23, 1972, Box 854, VIP Visits, NSC Files, NPM; NSSM 158, August 13, 1972, Presidential Directives, NSA; Lima to State, January 11, 1974, Central Foreign Policy Files, RG 59, NARA Archival Database; "Peru y EU firman hoy convenio sobre situación de inversions de ese país," *El Comercio*, February 19, 1974.

38. Santa María, "Memoria de la Embajada de Chile en Washington," 1 de noviembre de 1970, "Memoria Entre Años 1968–1970," EmbaChile EEUU, MRECHILE.

39. "Medidas que podríamos adoptar para establecer algún 'modus-vivendi' con Estados Unidos," 5 de septiembre de 1972, Caja 2, Archivo Letelier, ANH.

40. Telex Cifrado No. 792, 7 de diciembre de 1971; Letelier a Almeyda, 9 de mayo de 1972, Caja 2, Archivo Letelier, ANH.

41. Letelier a MRE, 10 de agosto de 1971, Oficios Confidenciales Recibidos, EmbaChile EEUU, MRECHILE.

42. Memorandum of Conversation, February 19, 1971, Box 2201, SNF, RG 59, NARA; "El futuro de la revolución chilena," 1 de mayo de 1971, in Patricio Quiroga, ed., *Salvador Allende: Obras escogidas, 1970–1973* (Barcelona, 1989), 70.

43. Oficio Confidencial No. 212/25, 3 de marzo de 1972, Oficios Confidenciales Recibidos, EmbaChile Cuba, MRECHILE.

44. Memorandum Confidencial, 6 de enero de 1972, "Memorandums: Dirección de Relaciones Internacionales, 1974–1978," MRECHILE; Sater, *Chile and the United States,* 168–169.

45. Oficina de Planificación Nacional, "El Gobiernio Popular y una Nueva Estrategia Económica Latinoamericana," septiembre de 1971, *Politics in Chile,* Reel 45; Speech at UNCTAD, April 4, 1972, in Farías, ed., *Izquierda Chilena,* III: 2141.

46. Moscú a MRE, 20 de agosto de 1971, Aerogramas Recibidos, EmbaChile Moscú, MRECHILE; "Conversación del ministro consejero de la embajada soviética con Director del Departamento Económico del Ministerio de Relaciones Exteriores de Chile," January 25, 1972; and "Informe de delegación soviética," November 27, 1970, in "Chile en los Archivos," 414, 422.

47. Jorge Edwards a MRE, 10 de diciembre de 1970, Telex Enviados, EmbaChile Cuba, MRECHILE.

48. Havana to Ottawa, June 17, 1969, Vol. 8906, 20-Cuba-1-3-USSR, LAC.

49. Moscow to Ottawa, May 17, 1969, ibid.

50. Habana a SRE, 22 de agosto de 1968, Topográfica SPR-566-5, Archivo de Concentraciones; "Castro Comments on Czechoslovak Crisis," August 24, 1968, CSD; Blight and Brenner, eds., *Sad and Luminous Days,* 122.

51. Moscow to Ottawa, July 5, 1971, Vol. 8906, 20-Cuba-1-3-USSR, LAC.

52. Jorge Edwards a MRE, 10 de diciembre de 1970, "1970 Cuba," MRECHILE; Habana a MRE, 20 de marzo de 1973, Oficios Confidenciales Recibos, EmbaChile Habana, ibid. See also "Kommuniqué über den Besuch der Partei und Regierungsdelegation der Republik Kuba in der Deutschen Demokratischen Republik," 19 Juni 1972, DY 30/2461, SAPMO.

53. Sergio Del Valle to Ángel Solakov, April 14, 1971, CWIHP; Domínguez, *To Make a World Safe for Revolution,* 222–226.

54. MemCon, August 15, 1974, Kissinger Transcripts, NSA; "Cuba Policy," August 15, 1975, Box 2, PCFLA, GFL; *Department of State Bulletin,* January 20, 1975, 67.

55. Memorandum of Conversation, June 4, 1970, Box 943, VIP Visits, NSC Files, NPM; *Primer mensaje del Ciudadano Presidente de la República,* 417. On the background to the nationalization, see Stephen G. Rabe, *The Road to OPEC: United States Relations with Venezuela, 1919–1976* (Austin, TX, 1982), 169–190; Tomás Polanco Alcántara, Simón Alberto Consalvi, and Edgardo Mondolfi Gadat, *Venezuela y Estados Unidos a través de 2 siglos* (Caracas, 2000), 375–432.

56. Pérez a Houari Boumediene, 7 de noviembre de 1974, Exp. 1–6-C-74, Interior, MREVEN; Judith Ewell, *Venezuela and the United States: From Monroe's Hemisphere to Petroleum's Empire* (Athens, GA, 1996), 205–207.

57. DPI, "Memorandum Interno," 14 de junio de 1974, Exp. 2–1–1–74, Interior, DPI, MREVEN; Fondo de Inversiones de Venezuela, *Memoria y Cuenta, 1974* (Caracas, 1975), 13–22; idem, *Memoria y Cuenta 1975* (Caracas, 1976), 89.

58. Júlio Chocano Becerra a Molina Orantes, 26 de noviembre de 1974, Exp. AM-24 PE-3.13, Paquete 1 (1985), Bilaterales, MREGUAT.

59. Fernando Coronil, *The Magical State: Nature, Money, and Modernity in Venezuela* (Chicago, 1997), 10, 237.

60. *Voz del tercer mundo,* 76.

61. Ibid., 339–340; Transcript of Echeverría's Speech to the OAS, June 16, 1972, Caja 4545, Embamex Nicaragua, AHGE.

62. Bogotá a SRE, 9 de mayo de 1975, Topográfica III-6063–1, Archivo de Concentraciones; "Mexico's President Calls Castro a Hero of History," *Los Angeles Times,* August 19, 1975.

63. Mexico City to State, December 31, 1974, and January 5, 1975, Box 5, PCFLA, GFL.

64. Jorge Eduardo Navarrete a SRE, 21 de mayo de 1974, Topográfica III-4978-I, Archivo de Concentraciones; "Memorandum para Información del C. Embajador Manuel Tello," 20 de febrero de 1975, Topográfica III-6063-I, ibid.; "Declaración Conjunta de los Presidentes de los Estados Unidos Mexicanos y de la República de Venezuela," 29 de julio de 1974, Topográfica III-4978-I, ibid.

65. Transcript of the Secretary's Staff Meeting, November 5, 1975, Kissinger Transcripts, NSA.

66. Artur da Costa e Silva, *Mensagem ao Congresso Nacional* (Brasilia, 1969), 109; Emílio Garrastazu Médici, *Mensagem ao Congresso Nacional* (Brasilia, 1970), 72; Rio de Janeiro to State, April 23, 1970, Box 2129, SNF, RG 59, NARA; Brasilia to State, August 28, 1970, Box 2134, ibid.; William Lowrance, "Nuclear Futures for Sale: To Brazil from West Germany, 1975," *International Security* 1 (1976): 147–166.

67. Lecture Delivered by Antônio F. Azeredo da Silveira, March 4, 1975, 20-BRA-1–3, LAC.

68. Recife to State, January 14, 1973, Box 2129, Subject Numeric File, RG 59, NARA; and Rio de Janeiro to State, October 26, 1970, ibid.; also Vieira Souto, *A Diplomacia do Interesse Nacional,* esp. 41–83, 99–110.

69. Ana María Treviño al Embajador, 24 de febrero y 19 de marzo de 1976, Topográfica III-3295–2, Archivo de Concentraciones; Brasilia to Ottawa, November 25, 1975, 20-BRA-1–3, LAC; INR Intelligence Note, December 11, 1972, Box 2130, SNF, RG 59, NARA.

70. Lecture Delivered by Silveira, March 4, 1975, 20-BRA-1–3, LAC. The best treatment of Silveira's diplomacy is Matias Spektor, "Equivocal Engagement: Kissinger, Silveira and the Politics of U.S.-Brazil Relations (1969–1983)" (D.Phil., Oxford University, 2006).

71. Lima a MRE, 25 de octubre de 1975, Exp. Folder AM-23 PE-2.17, Paquete 2 (1985), Bilaterales, MREGUAT.

72. INR, "Intelligence Summary," September 17, 1975, Box 1, Dale Van Atta Papers, GFL; San Jose to State, September 16, 1977, Butler Chief of Staff Files, JCL.

73. NSC Minutes, July 23, 1975, NSC Meeting Minutes, GFL; MemCon, May 24, 1976, Kissinger Transcripts, NSA; Walter LaFeber, *The Panama Canal: The Crisis in Historical Perspective* (New York, 1989), 140–144.

74. Felipe Herrera, *Nacionalismo, regionalismo, internacionalismo: América Latina en el contexto internacional* (Buenos Aires, 1970), 164; "Texto del discurso del Canciller de la Flor pronunciado en la OEA," *El Comercio,* 13 de abril de 1972; Kubisch to the Acting Secretary, August 28, 1973, Box 2545, SNF, RG 59, NARA.

75. Secretary's Staff Meeting, April 10, 1974, Box 3, Transcripts of Kissinger's Staff Meetings, RG 59, NARA.

76. Lehmann, *Democracy and Development in Latin America,* 48–51.

77. Sigmund, *Multinationals in Latin America,* 37–38; CIA, "Trends and Implications of Prime Minister Burnham Nationalizing Guyana's Bauxite Industry," April 1, 1971, *DDRS;* Maurice Stens to Nixon, August 27, 1971, Presidential Directives Collection, NSA.

78. OAS, General Assembly, *Actas y documentos, tomo I* (Washington, DC, 1972), 36; Stephen Kobrin, "Expropriation as an Attempt to Control Foreign Firms in LDCs: Trends from 1960 to 1979," *International Studies Quarterly* 28 (1984): 329–348.

79. *Entrevista de los Presidentes de la Argentina y Perú* (Buenos Aires, 1971), 30; *Entrevista de los Presidentes de la Argentina y Colombia* (Buenos Aires, 1972), 13, 18.

80. "Memorandum Interno: Integración, Desarrollo y Política," 8 de enero de 1975, Exp. 2-A-74, Interior, DPI, MREVEN; Rafael Caldera, *La solidaridad pluralística de América Latina* (Caracas, 1973), 81; DPI al Gabinete del Ministro, noviembre de 1974, Exp. 2-A-74, Interior, DPI, MREVEN.

81. Bulmer-Thomas, *Economic History of Latin America since Independence,* 289.

82. *Entrevista de los presidentes de la Argentina y Brasil,* 11. On Brazilian views of the Third World, see Ministerio das Relações Exteriores, "Reunião Entre os Assessores de Planejamento do Ministério das Relações Exteriores e do Departamento de Estado Americano," 21 de janeiro de 1975, EG pr 1973.03.00/2, FGV.

83. Secretary's Staff Meeting, February 15, 1974, Kissinger Transcripts, NSA.

84. *Entrevista de los presidentes de la Argentina y Brasil,* 31; CIA Directorate of Intelligence, "Latin America Looks to Eastern Europe," March 29, 1969, Box 3, Country File, NSF, LBJL; "Eastern Europe and Latin America," December 1972, Vol. 8677, 20-LATAM-1–3, LAC.

85. Estudo Sucinto No. 053/1a.SC/74, 17 de julho de 1974, EG pr 1974.03.—/2, FGV.

86. *Isvestia,* July 10, 1966, in *CDSP* XVIII, No. 28, 9; Blasier, *The Giant's Rival,* 105–107.

87. "Foreign Policy Memorandum," January 13, 1967, in Anatoly Dobrynin, *In Confidence: Moscow's Ambassador to Six Cold War Presidents* (New York, 1995), 649–652.

88. *Pravda,* December 15, 1967, *CDSP* XIX, No. 50, 15; also Alexandr Sizonenko, "Los Principios Leninistas de la Política Exterior de las Relaciones de la URSS con los Países de América Latina," *América Latina,* 1970, in Moscú a MRE, 26 de noviembre de 1970, Oficios Confidenciales Recibidos, EmbaChile Moscú, MRECHILE.

89. Santiago to Ottawa, November 27, 1964, Vol. 8848, 20-Chile-1–3, LAC; "Acordo de Comércio e Pagamentos entre os Estados Unidos do Brasil e a União das Repúblicas Socialistas Soviéticas," abril de 1963, Caja 104, Transferencia 8, MRE, AGNCOL; Robert K. Evanson, "Soviet Political Uses of Trade with Latin America," *Journal of Interamerican Studies and World Affairs* 27 (1985): 100–105.

90. "Transcripción de la comunicación de Señor Guillermo Lang," 25 de junio de 1969, Caja 44, Sección Relaciones Exteriores, Fondo Presidencial, AGNNIC.

91. Transcript of Speech to the United Nations, September 26, 1978, Exp. 13, Leg. 32, Embamex Grecia, AHGE.

92. John Lewis Gaddis, *Strategies of Containment: A Critical Appraisal of American National Security Policy during the Cold War* (New York, 2005), 297.

93. Memorandum enclosed in J. Wesley Jones to Irwin, April 3, 1969, *DDRS.*

94. Treasury Department Position Paper, July 13, 1971, *FRUS 1969–1972,* IV: Document #156; Benjamin Welles, "We Don't Have Any Friends Anyway," *New York Times,* August 15, 1971; also Connally to Nixon, June 11, 1971, *FRUS 1969–1972,* IV: Document #154; Hal Brands, "Richard Nixon and

Economic Nationalism in Latin America: The Problem of Expropriations, 1969–1974," *Diplomacy and Statecraft* 18 (2007): 215–235.

95. "Secreto: Política Externa Americana," undated (1974), EG 1974.03.00/2, FGV.

96. Kissinger to Nixon, November 5, 1970, Box H-029, Meetings File, NSC Institutional File, NPM.

97. NSC Meeting, November 5, 1970, ibid.; also Vernon Walters to Kissinger, November 5, 1970, ibid.

98. MRE, "Algunos Aspectos del Estado Actual de las Relaciones de Chile con Estados Unidos," 3 de noviembre de 1971, Caja 2, Archivo Letelier, ANH; also MRE a Letelier, 24 de julio de 1971, ibid.

99. Almeyda a Washington, undated (marzo de 1972), Telex Enviados, EmbaChile EEUU, MRECHILE; also Letelier a Almeyda, 23 de marzo de 1972, Caja 2, Archivo Letelier, ANH.

100. "De la entrevista al periódico mexicano *Excélsior*," September 6, 1971, in Farías, ed., *Izquierda Chilena*, II: 1054–1055; MemCon, November 13, 1973, Kissinger Transcripts, NSA.

101. See, for instance, "Aufzeichnung des Ministerialdirektors Lahn," 3 Dezember 1975, *Akten zur Auswärtigen Politik der Bundesrepublik Deutschland, 1975*, Volume 2 (München: Oldenbourg, 2006), Document #363.

102. MRE, "Memorandum," 23 de noviembre de 1972, Caja 2, Archivo Letelier, ANH.

103. Washington a MRE, 9 de octubre de 1970, Telex Recibidos, EmbaChile EEUU, MRECHILE; also Moscú a MRE, 31 de mayo de 1972, Oficios Confidenciales D, MRECHILE.

104. "Informe de delegación soviética," 27 de noviembre de 1970; and "Informe sobre la situación chilena elaborado por el Instituto de América Latina de la Academia de Ciencias de la URSS," undated," in "Chile en los Archivos," 414, 440; see also Moscow to Ottawa, October 5, 1970, Vol. 8848, 20-Chile-1-3, LAC.

105. Moscú a MRE, 29 de mayo de 1971, Telex Recibidos, EmbaChile Moscú, MRECHILE; on East European aid, see "Anregungen für die Aussprache mit Vertretern der NFG aus Lateinamerika," March 23, 1973, DY 13/2059, SAPMO.

106. Moscú a MRE, 20 de noviembre de 1970, Oficios Confidenciales Recibidos, EmbaChile Moscú, MRECHILE.

107. "Medidas que podríamos adoptar para establecer algún 'modus-vivendi' con Estados Unidos," 5 de septiembre de 1972, Caja 2, Archivo Letelier, ANH; also MRE, "Memorandum," 3 de noviembre de 1971, ibid.

108. MemCon, February 16, 1971, Box 1000, Haig Special File, NSC Files, NPM; Raymond Garthoff, *Détente and Confrontation: American–Soviet Relations from Nixon to Reagan* (Washington, DC, 1985), 76–83; "Rendición

de Aportes Entregados en 1966," 26 de diciembre de 1966; "Aprobación de
Aportes para 1970," 28 de diciembre de 1969; and "Rendición de Aportes
Entregados en 1973," 17 de diciembre de 1973, in "Chile en los archivos,"
398–402.

109. IMF, "A Facility to Assist Members in Meeting the Initial Impact of the
Increase in Oil Prices," February 19, 1974, Box B66, Arthur Burns File,
GFL; United Nations, *World Economic Survey: Fluctuations and Developments in the World Economy* (New York, 1975), Part 1, 16–17; ECLA,
Statistical Yearbook for Latin America, 1976 (New York, 1977), 53.

110. *United Nations World Economic Survey, 1974* (New York, 1975), Part 1, 25,
72; Inter-American Development Bank, *External Debt and Economic
Development in Latin America* (Washington, DC, 1984), 21; ECLA,
Economic Survey of Latin America, 1977 (Santiago, 1978), 12–15; Bulmer-
Thomas, *Economic History of Latin America since Independence,* 313–326.

111. See Ministério do Trabalho, "Repercussões sobre o nível de emprego
provocadas pelas medidas de política monetária e de alteração nos investimentos públicos . . . nos programas e projectos para o exercício de 1,977,"
undated, EG pr 1974.04.10/2, FGV.

112. Bulmer-Thomas, *Economic History of Latin America since Independence,*
chapters 9–10.

113. William Clark Oral History, October 5, 1983, Oral Histories, WB.

114. MemCon, October 21, 1974, Box 13, LAASF, NSA, GFL.

115. IMF, "A Facility to Assist Members in Meeting the Initial Impact of the
Increase in Oil Prices," February 19, 1974, Box B66, Burns Files, GFL.

116. "Relations between Developed and Developing Countries," undated, Box
B62, Burns Files, GFL.

117. Ibid.

118. Harold James, *International Monetary Cooperation since Bretton Woods* (New
York, 1996), 269–341; *IMF Annual Report, 1978* (Washington, DC, 1979),
10–14; Eric Helleiner, *States and the Reemergence of Global Finance: From
Bretton Woods to the 1990s* (Ithaca, NY, 1994), 123–168.

119. "Mexico—Use of Fund Resources," September 23, 1976, EBS/76/424,
IMF; "Mexico: Discussion with President-Elect," December 2, 1976, Box 6,
Country Files, Central Files, IMF; Miguel D. Ramirez, "Mexico's
Development Experience, 1950–85: Lessons and Future Prospects," *Journal
of Interamerican Studies and World Affairs* 28 (1986): 39–65; Jorge del Canto
to the Managing Director, November 13, 1974, Box 6, Country Files,
Central Files, IMF.

120. MemCon between Ford and López Portillo, September 24, 1976, Box 15,
LAASF, NSA, GFL; "Mexico: Discussion with President-Elect," December 2, 1976, Box 6, Country Files, Central Files, IMF.

121. CIA Intelligence Cable, October 27, 1976, Box B80, Burns Files,
GFL; George Grayson, *Oil and Mexican Foreign Policy* (Pittsburgh, 1988), 25.

122. "Financial Situation and Prospects of Peru," November 27, 1975, Box 10, Country Files, Central Files, IMF; "Peru: Relations with the Fund," July 29, 1976, ibid.

123. Karen de Young, "Peru Appears on the Verge of Defaulting on Foreign Loans," *Washington Post,* March 14, 1978.

124. Sigmund, *Multinationals in Latin America,* 217; Stephen Gorman, "The Peruvian Revolution in Historical Perspective," in Gorman, ed., *Post-Revolutionary Peru: The Politics of Transformation* (Westview, CO, 1982), 24–29.

125. Linda M. Koenig to the Managing Director, "Mission to Peru," December 14, 1976, Box 10, Country Files, Central Files, IMF; Walter Robichek to the Managing Director, April 3, 1978, ibid.; Daniel M. Schydlowsky and Juan Wicht, *Anatomía de un fracaso económico: Perú, 1968–1978* (Lima, 1982), 97–106; Óscar Ugarteche, *Teoría y práctica de la deuda externa en el Perú* (Lima, 1980), 47–48.

126. ECLA, *Economic Survey of Latin America, 1975,* 6.

127. James, *International Monetary Cooperation since Bretton Woods,* 341.

128. Sao Paulo to State, January 18, 1971, Box 2129, SNF, RG 59, NARA; see also SNI, "Anexo No. 2 ao estudo sobre o problema da subversão no Brasil: Súmula da atuação do movimento comunista internacional no âmbito mundial e continental," undated, EG pr 1974.03.00/1, FGV.

129. MemCon between Samuel Eaton and Héctor Luisi, December 17, 1970, Box 2662, SNF, RG 59, NARA.

130. MemCon between Kissinger and Mercado, September 29, 1971, Box 2544, SNF, RG 59, NARA; Lima to State, April 30, 1971, Box 2543, ibid.; Memorandum for Mr. Kissinger, January 21, 1972, Box 2544, ibid.

131. CONADEP, *Nunca Más.*

132. "Normalización de relaciones diplomáticas entre Cuba y los Estados Unidos," 31 de enero de 1974, in "Memorandums: Dirección de Relaciones Internacionales, 1974–1978," MRECHILE; "Memorandum estrictamente confidencial," 8 de enero de 1974, ibid.; MemCon, June 8, 1976, Kissinger Transcripts, NSA.

133. MemCon, June 8, 1976, Kissinger Transcripts, NSA; MemCon, February 7, 1974, Box 1028, Presidential/HAK MemCons, NSC Files, NPM.

134. *Department of State Bulletin,* December 8, 1969, 505; Westad, *Global Cold War,* 197.

135. MemCon, October 5, 1973, Kissinger Transcripts, NSA; MemCon, August 29, 1974, Box 12, LAASF, NSA, GFL; Nixon in Transcript of Conversation, June 15, 1972, EBB 95, NSA.

136. Kissinger's disdain for Latin America is covered in Alan McPherson, *Intimate Ties, Bitter Struggles: The United States and Latin America since 1945* (Washington, DC, 2006), 74.

137. Secretary's Staff Meetings, November 11, 1974, and November 5, 1975; and Meeting with Secretary Simon, October 13, 1975, Kissinger Transcripts, NSA.

138. MemCon, December 8, 1971, Box 911, VIP Visits, NSC Files, NPM.

139. Sao Paulo to State, January 18, 1971, Box 2129, SNF, RG 59, NARA.

140. Carlos Alberto da Fontoura Oral History, FGV; Canberra to State, June 17, 1972, Box 954, VIP Visits, NSC Files, NPM.

141. Buenos Aires a MRE, 29 de octubre de 1971, Caja 2, Fondo 2.2, MRE-URU; "Conversation between President Richard Nixon and Secretary of State William Rogers," December 7, 1971, EBB 71, NSA.

142. "Conversation between President Richard Nixon and Secretary of State William Rogers," December 7, 1971, EBB 71, NSA.

143. "Secreto: Política Externa Americana," undated (1974), EG 1974.03.00/2, FGV.

144. *Visita do Presidente Emílio Garrastazu Médici*, 11.

145. "Lecture Delivered by Antônio F. Azeredo da Silveira," March 3, 1975, 20-BRA-1-13, LAC; Ministerio das Relações Exteriores, "Reunião entre os assessores de planejamento do Ministério das Relações Exteriores e do Departamento de Estado Americano," 21 de janeiro de 1975, EG pr 1974.03.00/2, FGV.

146. Quoted in "Memorandum Confidencial: Formación de un Frente Anti-marxista Continental," 8 de marzo de 1974, "Memorandums: Dirección de Relaciones Internacionales, 1974–1978," MRECHILE; also "Memorandum Confidencial: Entrevista entre el Ministro de Relaciones Exteriores y el Embajador de Guatemala," 30 de enero de 1974, ibid.; and "Memorandum: Acción Conjunta Chileno-Uruguaya," 9 de julio de 1974, ibid.

147. Alejandro Fretes Davalos a Gral. de División Francisco Britez, 27 de abril de 1976, DI-B-246, CDYA.

148. Invitación de Manuel Contreras Sepúlveda a Don Francisco Britez, octubre de 1975, ibid.; "Primera Reunión de Inteligencia Nacional," 29 de octubre de 1975, ibid.

149. J. Patrice McSherry, *Predatory States: Operation Condor and Covert War in Latin America* (New York, 2005), discusses U.S. complicity.

150. The covert transport of prisoners between Argentina and Uruguay is described in an unsigned letter to Julio César Strassera, julio de 1985, Caja "Represores," Testimonios, APDH; Testimonio de Armanda Víctor Luchina, 30 de mayo de 1985, Caja 1.90–1.121, CCD, APDH; "Informe de la entrevista de Marta Castilla de Zaffaroni con el Militar Argentino que hizo las declaraciones al 'Estado de São Paulo,'" undated, Archivo de los Familiares de los Detenidos-Desaparecidos (Uruguay).

151. Testimonio de Andrés Francisco Valdés, 6 de junio de 1984, Caja "Represores," Testimonios, APDH; Testimonio de Luís Alberto Martínez, Caja 1.90–1.121, CCD, APDH.

152. Scowcroft to Ford, July 19, 1976, *DDRS*.

153. Memorandum for Jack Watson, undated (late 1976), Box 9, Cyrus Vance Papers, Yale; Joseph Smith, *The United States and Latin America: A History of American Diplomacy, 1776–2000* (New York, 2005), 143.

154. Kathryn Sikkink, *Mixed Signals: U.S. Human Rights Policy and Latin America* (Ithaca, NY, 2004), 121–147.

155. See Robert Burr, *By Reason or Force: Chile and the Balancing of Power in South America* (Berkeley, CA, 1965); Gary Frank, *Struggle for Hegemony in South America: Argentina, Brazil, and the United States during the Second World War* (Coral Gables, FL, 1979).

156. The former interpretation is represented by Samuel Flagg Bemis, *The Latin American Policy of the United States: An Historical Interpretation* (New York, 1943); the latter is assessed in Gilderhus, "An Emerging Synthesis?"

6. The Revolution in Context

1. See LaFeber, *Inevitable Revolutions*.

2. Enríquez, *Harvesting Change*, 48–49.

3. "General Anastasio Somoza Debayle's Address to the Convention of the Nationalist Liberal Party on the Occasion of his Nomination as Candidate for the Presidency of the Republic," undated, Caja grande 9 (Caja pequeña 523), Secretaría Privada, Fondo Presidencial, AGNNIC.

4. Midlarsky and Roberts, "Class, State and Revolution in Central America," 163–193; Dodson, "The Politics of Religion in Revolutionary Nicaragua," 36–49.

5. Undated message from Luís Somoza, Caja grande 9 (Caja pequeña 522), Secretaría Privada, Fondo Presidencial, AGNNIC.

6. Jefe del Estado Mayor GN a Jefe Supremo de la Guardia Nacional, 12 de mayo de 1972, "Movimientos de protesta con motivo del alza de la gasolina y la leche," ASD-069, IHNCA; Gould, *To Lead as Equals*.

7. "Information Memorandum from the Director of the Office of Central American Affairs to the Assistant Secretary of State for Inter-American Affairs," January 10, 1967, *FRUS 1964–1968*, XXXI: Document #91.

8. Managua to State, February 10, 1967, *FRUS 1964–1968*, XXXI: Document #95.

9. "El Gral. Anastasio Somoza está descalificado para ser Candidato o Presidente Constitucional," 29 de agosto de 1974, ASD-023, IHNCA.

10. The literature on *somicismo*'s demise is enormous. Consult Thomas Walker, *Revolution and Counter-Revolution in Nicaragua* (Boulder, CO, 1991); Edelberto Torres-Rivas, "El estado contra la sociedad: Las raíces de la revolución Sandinista," *Estudios sociales centroamericanos* 27 (1980): 79–96; John Booth, "Celebrating the Demise of *Somocismo:* Fifty Recent Sources on the Nicaraguan Revolution," *Latin American Research Review* 17 (1982): 173–189; Julio López and Serres Chamorro, *La caída del Somocismo y la lucha Sandinista en Nicaragua* (San José, 1979); and Rose Spalding, ed., *The Political Economy of Revolutionary Nicaragua* (Boston, 1987), as well as the sources cited in this chapter.

11. Wickham-Crowley, *Guerrillas and Revolution in Latin America*, 271.

12. Managua to State, September 9, 1978, Nicaragua Collection, NSA.

13. *Latin America Weekly Review,* January 19, 1978, Nicaragua Collection, NSA; Robert Kagan, *A Twilight Struggle: American Power and Nicaragua, 1977–1990* (New York, 1996), 43–48. Though Somoza's regime was widely considered to have been behind the murder, there is no conclusive proof as to who ordered Chamorro's killing.

14. "Algunos aspectos del trabajo entre las masas," 1971, JGRN 0029, IHNCA.

15. "Informe de la Guardia Nacional de Nicaragua referente a situación político militar," undated (1978), ASD-038, IHNCA.

16. "Acontecimientos en Nicaragua," 15 de junio de 1979, Caja RC.XVII.1, Reuniones Cancilleres, MREURU.

17. Matilde Zimmerman, *Sandinista: Carlos Fonseca and the Nicaraguan Revolution* (Durham, NC, 2000), 171; also Harry Vanden and Gary Prevost, *Democracy and Socialism in Sandinista Nicaragua* (Boulder, CO, 1996), 39–40. Certain FSLN commanders later denied ever having been attracted to *foquismo.* See Tomás Borge, *Carlos, the Dawn Is No Longer beyond Our Reach* (Vancouver, 1984), esp. 42–43.

18. Zimmerman, *Sandinista,* 171; Roger Miranda and William E. Ratliff, *Civil War in Nicaragua: Inside the Sandinistas* (New Brunswick, NJ, 1993), 31; Donald Clark Hodges, *Intellectual Foundations of the Nicaraguan Revolution* (Austin, TX, 1986), 217–219.

19. "Algunos aspectos del trabajo entre las masas."

20. Zimmerman, *Sandinista,* 191; María Terese Blandón, "The Coalición Nacional de Mujeres"; and Ilja Luciak, "Gender Equality, Democratization, and the Revolutionary Left in Central America," both in Victoria González and Karen Kampwirth, eds., *Radical Women in Latin America* (University Park, PA, 2001), 112, 189; Norma Stoltz Chinchilla, "Revolutionary Popular Feminism in Nicaragua," *Gender and Society* 4 (1990): 370–397.

21. Gould, *To Lead as Equals,* 283–284.

22. "Algunos aspectos del trabajo entre las masas"; Brockett, *Land, Power, and Poverty,* 168; Gould, *To Lead as Equals,* chapter 12.

23. "Manifiesto del Frente Sandinista de Liberación Nacional a Todas Las Fuerzas Democráticas, Progresistas, Patrióticas y Anti-Imperialistas del Mundo," enero de 1977, GRV 001, IHNCA; Thomas Walker, *Nicaragua without Illusions: Regime Transition and Structural Adjustment in the 1980s* (Wilmington, DE, 1997), 150–151.

24. Phil Ryan, *The Fall and Rise of the Market in Sandinista Nicaragua* (Montreal, 1995), 46; Comunicado de la Dirección Nacional Conjunta, undated, JGRN 0024, IHNCA.

25. Humberto Ortega al Estado Mayor del Frente Norte "Carlos Fonseca Amador," 7 de enero de 1979, JGRN 0057, IHNCA.

26. Ibid.

27. "Declaraciones de un miembro de la Dirección Nacional del FSLN al periodista Vegard Bye," 24 de febrero de 1979, JGRN 0056, IHNCA.

28. Ortega al Estado Mayor, 7 de enero de 1979.

29. "Manifiesto del Frente Sandinista de Liberación Nacional a todas las fuerzas democráticas, progresistas, patrióticas y anti-imperialistas del mundo," enero de 1977, GRV 001, IHNCA.

30. The quotes are from "Aspectos básicos de los Acuerdos de Unidad del Frente Sandinista de Liberación Nacional," 7 de marzo de 1979, JGRN 0058, IHNCA; "Manifiesto del Frente Sandinista de Liberación Nacional a todas las fuerzas democráticas, progresistas, patrióticas y anti-imperialistas del mundo," enero de 1977, GRV 001, IHNCA.

31. Interview with Víctor Tirado, August 31, 2007, Managua.

32. Ortega al Estado Mayor, 7 de enero de 1979.

33. FSLN-Proletarian Tendency, "No al diálogo burgués, derrocar a la dictadura es la tarea," in Gabriel García Márquez, *Los Sandinistas* (Bogota, 1979), 183; Humberto Ortega, *Sobre la insurrección* (Havana, 1981), 38, 40, cited in Ryan, *Rise and Fall*, 46.

34. Zimmerman, *Sandinista*, 217. Other estimates can be found in CIA, "Situation in Nicaragua," undated (1978), NLC-6–56–7–31–3, JCL; James DeFronzo, *Revolutions and Revolutionary Movements* (Boulder, CO, 1996), 217.

35. Zimmerman, *Sandinista*, 217. For examples of cooperation with the National Guard, see G-2, "Apreciación de inteligencia," 26 de noviembre de 1978, ASD 076, IHNCA; Cptn. Hugo E. Briceño H. a Sr. Jefe del Estado Mayor, 31 de octubre de 1978, ASD 063, ibid.; Raúl Gutiérrez a Jefe de la Oficina de Seguridad Nacional, 12 de diciembre de 1978, ASD 063, ibid.

36. "Informe de la Guardia Nacional de Nicaragua referente a situación político-militar," 1978, ASD 038, IHNCA.

37. Managua to State, February 6, 1978, Nicaragua Collection, NSA; John Booth, *The End and the Beginning: The Nicaraguan Revolution* (Boulder, CO, 1985), 145–163.

38. Managua to State, February 6, 1978, NSA; PRC Meeting, January 26, 1979, Box 25, Subject File, Zbigniew Brzezinski Donated Material (ZBDM), JCL.

39. Managua a SRE, 29 de noviembre de 1978, Caja 4550, Embamex Nicaragua, AHGE; Managua to State, September 9, 1978, Nicaragua Collection, NSA; Mauricio Solaún, *U.S. Intervention and Regime Change in Nicaragua* (Lincoln, NE, 2005), 97–131. In addition to Solaún's book, the most detailed studies of U.S. policy toward Somoza are Robert Pastor, *Condemned to Repetition: The United States and Nicaragua* (Princeton, 1987); Anthony Lake, *Somoza Falling: A Case Study of Washington at Work* (Amherst, MA, 1989); and Morris Morley, *Washington, Somoza and the Sandinistas: Stage and Regime in U.S. Policy toward Nicaragua, 1969–1981* (New York, 2002).

40. Anthony Lake to Vance, January 16, 1978, Box HU-1, White House Counsel Files (WHCF), JCL.

41. "PRM/NSC-28: Human Rights," July 7, 1977, Box 19, WHCF, JCL.

42. David Schmitz and Vanessa Walker, "Jimmy Carter and the Foreign Policy of Human Rights: Toward the Development of a Post–Cold War Foreign Policy," *Diplomatic History* 28 (2004): 113–143.

43. Transcript of Brzezinski Remarks, December 20, 1978, Box 139, Hedrick Smith Papers, LOC.

44. Mike Bowker and Phil Williams, *Superpower Détente: A Reappraisal* (New York, 1988), 171; also "Foreign Policy Report," March 2, 1978, Anthony Lake Papers, LC. On Carter's attempt to revamp U.S. foreign policy, see Gaddis Smith, *Morality, Reason, and Power: American Diplomacy in the Carter Years* (New York, 1987); Douglas Brinkley, "The Rising Stock of Jimmy Carter: The 'Hands on' Legacy of Our Thirty-Ninth President," *Diplomatic History* 20 (1996): 505–529.

45. PRC Meeting, March 24, 1977, Box 24, Subject File, ZBDM, JCL; Carter, "Address at Commencement Exercises at the University of Notre Dame," May 22, 1977, APP.

46. Carter, "Address at Commencement Exercises at the University of Notre Dame."

47. Lipshutz to Carter, December 7, 1977, Box 18, WHCF, JCL; Brzezinski speech draft, May 1976, Box 17, 1976 Presidential Campaign Files, JCL.

48. David Schmitz, "Senator Frank Church, the Ford Administration, and the Challenges of Post-Vietnam Foreign Policy," *Peace and Change* 21 (1996): 438–463; Council on Hemispheric Affairs, "National Leaders Speak Out on Chile," February 26, 1977, Topográfica III-6010–1, Archivo de Concentraciones; Sikkink, *Mixed Signals,* 48–77; Robert David Johnson, *Congress and the Cold War* (New York, 2006), chapter 6.

49. Quoted in Carter Address to Chicago Council on Foreign Relations, March 15, 1976, Box 17, 1976 Presidential Campaign Files, JCL; also Brzezinski to Carter, December 3, 1977, Box 18, WHCF, JCL; "PRM/NSC-28: Human Rights, July 7, 1977," Box 19, WHCF, JCL.

50. Ministerio das Relações Exteriores, "O Brasil e os EUA," undated, EG pr 1974.03.00/2, FGV; Centro de Informações do Exército, "Relatório Periódico de Informações No. 08/77," agosto de 1977, EG pr 1974.03.25/3.

51. Brzezinski to Carter, September 20, 1977, NLC-1–3–7–13–6, JCL; Rick Inderfurth to Brzezinski, December 1, 1978, NLC-11–3–7–10–8, JCL; "Human Rights Progress in Latin America," August 19, 1977, Box 101, Butler File, Chief of Staff Files, JCL.

52. Pastor to Jerry Doolittle, February 9, 1978, Box 14, Subject Files, Speechwriter Files, JCL; "PRM/NSC-28: Human Rights," July 7, 1977, Box 19, WHCF, JCL.

53. Cauas a MRE, 27 de junio de 1977, Telex Recibidos, EmbaChile EEUU, MRECHILE; Cauas a MRE, 18 de marzo de 1977, Aerogramas Reservados Recibidos, EmbaChile EEUU, MRECHILE.

54. Cauas a MRE, 24 de febrero de 1978, Oficios Secretos Recibidos, EmbaChile EEUU, MRECHILE; Washington a MRE, 16 de agosto de 1977, Oficios Reservados Recibidos, EmbaChile EEUU, MRECHILE.

55. Robert Hunter to Brzezinski, November 29, 1978, Box 45, Country File, NSA File, JCL; Memorandum de Embajada en Washington a MRE, noviembre de 1977, Caja 21, EEUU, MREURU.

56. Ministerio das Relações Exteriores, "Relações Brasil–Estados Unidos da América," undated, EG pr 1974.03.00/2, FGV; also letter from Geisel to Carter, undated, EG pr 1974.06.07, FGV.

57. La Paz to State, April 25, 1979, Box 27, Country File, NSA File, JCL.

58. Pinochet a Gustavo Leigh Guzmán, 26 de diciembre de 1977, in Cauas a MRE, 15 de febrero de 1978, Oficios Secretos Recibidos, EmbaChile EEUU, MRECHILE; "Minuta de la Reunión de los Presidentes Pinochet y Carter," 6 de septiembre de 1977, Oficios Secretos Recibidos, EmbaChile EEUU, MRECHILE; Cauas a MRE, 24 de febrero de 1978, Oficios Secretos Recibidos, EmbaChile EEUU, MRECHILE.

59. "Human Rights Policy Impact: Latin America," May 11, 1977, Box HU-1, WHCF, JCL; CIA, "Impact of the U.S. Stand on Human Rights," June 7, 1977, ibid.; Jorge Domínguez, "Democratic Transitions in Central America and Panama," in Domínguez and Marc Lindenberg, eds., *Democratic Transitions in Central America* (Gainesville, FL, 1997), 8; Alison Brysk, *The Politics of Human Rights in Argentina: Protest, Change, and Democratization* (Stanford, 1994), 53.

60. Managua to State, February 6, 1978; also Managua to State, March 13, 1978, Nicaragua Collection, NSA.

61. Anastasio Somoza Debayle, *Nicaragua Betrayed* (Boston, 1980), 105; quoted in Misagha Parsa, *States, Ideologies, and Social Revolutions* (New York, 2000), 91; also Brzezinski to Pastor, June 12, 1978, Box 33, North–South Files, NSA File, JCL.

62. Managua to State, February 6, 1978, Nicaragua Collection, NSA; Managua to State, March 13, 1978, ibid.

63. Managua a SRE, 29 de noviembre de 1978, Caja 4550, Embamex Nicaragua, AHGE.

64. Smith, *America's Mission,* 250; Pastor, *Condemned to Repetition,* 19; Lake, *Somoza Falling.*

65. Pastor to Brzezinski, June 8, 1979, Box 25, Subject File, ZBDM, JCL; Joe Aragon to Pastor, September 13, 1978, Box 33, North–South Files, NSA File, JCL.

66. Brzezinski to Carter, June 20, 1979, Box 30, Subject File, ZBDM, JCL.

67. Acta-Minuta de la 2ª Sesión PLN-FAO, 16 de diciembre de 1978, JGRN 0062, IHNCA; "Somoza histérico sólo promete sangre," *La Prensa,* 6 de noviembre de 1978; CIA, "Situation in Nicaragua," undated (1978), NLC-6–56–7–31–3, JCL; Robert Pastor, *Not Condemned to Repetition: The United States and Nicaragua* (Boulder, CO, 2002), 55–57.

68. Quoted in Managua to State, September 1, 1978, Box 33, North-South Files, NSA File, JCL; also Bruce E. Wright, "Pluralism and Vanguardism in the Nicaraguan Revolution," *Latin American Perspectives* 17 (1990): 38–44; Midlarsky and Roberts, "Class, State and Revolution in Central America," 178–179.

69. Comisión de Alternativa del FAO, "Breve crítica al análisis [illegible]," late 1978, FAO 001, IHNCA; PRC Meeting, June 11, 1979, Box 25, Subject Files, ZBDM, JCL.

70. "Memorandum of Todor Zhivkov–Fidel Castro Conversation, Havana," April 9, 1979, CWIHP. On early Cuban–FSLN ties, see Oficina de Seguridad Nacional, "Consolidado de declaraciones individuales," 7 de marzo de 1962, LSD 010, IHNCA.

71. "Text of Interview with Barbara Walters and Castro," June 21, 1977, Box 3, Bonsal Papers, LOC; CIA, "The Nonaligned Movement at the Havana Summit," August 1979, NLC-24–58–8–1–3, JCL.

72. Memorandum of Conversation, June 15, 1978, Box 10, Geographic File, ZBDM, JCL.

73. "Speech by Major Fidel Castro," *Politics in Chile,* Reel 41, Frame 94, Princeton University Latin American Pamphlet Collection.

74. Havana to Ottawa, May 13, 1975, Vol. 10847, 20-Cuba-1–3, LAC.

75. "Conversation between Carlos Rafael Rodríguez, the Vice President of Cuba and Thomas L. Hughes, President of the Carnegie Endowment for International Peace," March 16, 1978, Box 10, Geographic File, ZBDM, JCL; "Information über die Teilnahme einer Delegation des Zentralrates der FDJ am III. Kongress der Union Junger Kommunisten Kubas (UJC) vom 31.3.-4.4.1977 in Havana," DY 24/11215, SAPMO.

76. "Memorandum of Todor Zhivkov–Fidel Castro Conversation, Havana," April 9, 1979, CWIHP.

77. See "Bericht über die Teilnahme einer Delegation des Zentralrates der FDJ am 1. Kongreß des Verbandes der Universitätsstudenten Kubas und am 6. Kongreß der Studenten Lateinamerikas in der Zeit von 11. bis 17.3.1979," DY 24/11332, SAPMO.

78. Pastor to Brzezinski, June 21, 1979, Box 57, Country File, NSA File, JCL; CIA, "Situation in Nicaragua," undated (1978), NLC-6–56–7–31–3, JCL; CIA, "The Opposition in Nicaragua," November 1978, NLC-24–34–2–1–5, JCL.

79. Welch et al., eds., *Cuba on the Brink,* 233.

80. Carlos Andrés Pérez to Carter, September 20, 1978, Box 21, President's Correspondence with Foreign Leaders File, NSA File, JCL; CIA, "Situa-

tion in Nicaragua," undated (1978), NLC-6–56–7–31–3, JCL; Pastor to Brzezinski, January 19, 1979, Box 57, Country File, NSA File, JCL; Pastor, *Not Condemned to Repetition*, 56–58.

81. Managua a SRE, 2 de enero de 1979, Caja 4550, Embamex Nicaragua, AHGE; Edward Williams, "Mexico's Central American Policy: Apologies, Motivations, and Principles," *Bulletin of Latin American Research* 2 (1982): 25–26, 33.

82. "Memorandum para información del C. Presidente de la República," 27 de noviembre de 1978, Caja 4550, Embamex Nicaragua, AHGE.

83. Chris Carvounis, *United States Trade and Investment in Latin America: Opportunities for Business in the 1990s* (Westport, CT, 1992), 87.

84. "Memorandum para información"; Managua a SRE, 17 de septiembre de 1978, Caja 4550, Embamex Nicaragua, AHGE.

85. Jorge Castañeda, "Don't Corner Mexico!" *Foreign Policy* 60 (1985): 76.

86. Pastor, *Not Condemned to Repetition*, 54.

87. Pastor to Brzezinski, January 19, 1979, Box 57, Country File, NSA File, JCL; G-2, Guardia Nacional, "Apreciación de inteligencia," 26 de noviembre de 1978, ASD 076, IHNCA; Stansfield Turner, "Communist Intervention Comparison," August 15, 1979, NLC-24–13–7–1–3, JCL.

88. "Informe de la Guardia Nacional de Nicaragua referente a situación político militar," undated (1978), ASD 038, IHNCA; "Actividades subversivas desarrolladas por elementos del Frente Sandinista de Liberación Nacional y mercenarios internacionales," undated, ASD 067, IHNCA.

89. See Estado Mayor GN, "Cronológico de actividades desarrolladas por elementos de la brigada internacional comunista a lo largo de la frontera sur límite internacional con Costa Rica, desde el 1.ro de enero hasta la fecha," 13 de febrero de 1969, ASD-067, IHNCA.

90. "Acta de 1a Sesión Extraordinaria celebrada el 28 de diciembre de 1978," Caja RC.XVII.1, Reuniones Cancilleres, MREURU; David Mares, "Mexico's Foreign Policy as a Middle Power: The Nicaragua Connection, 1884–1986," *Latin American Research Review* 23 (1988): 95–96; Embajada de Chile en Montevideo a MRE, 13 de junio de 1979, Caja RC.XVII.1, Reuniones Cancilleres, MREURU.

91. Pastor to Brzezinski, January 18, 1981, Box 34, Subject File, ZBDM, JCL.

92. See, for instance, MRE a Washington, 22 de agosto de 1979, Oficios Secretos Enviados, EmbaChile EEUU, MRECHILE; Washington a MRE, 20 de junio de 1979, Caja RC.XVII.1, Reuniones Cancilleres, MREURU. Somoza did obtain military and technical support from the Argentine junta. Ariel Armony, *Argentina, the United States, and the Anti-Communist Crusade in Central America, 1977–1984* (Athens, OH, 1997), 77.

93. "Record of Conference with First Secretary of the Central Committee of the Communist Party of Cuba and Chairman of the State Council and Council of Ministers of the Republic of Cuba, Comrade Fidel Castro Ruz," June 25, 1979, CWHIP; Pastor to Brzezinski, July 19, 1979, Box 30,

Subject File, ZBDM, JCL; see also Ralph Pezzullo and Lawrence Pezzullo, *At the Fall of Somoza* (Pittsburgh, 1994), esp. 71.

94. William LeoGrande, *Our Own Backyard: The United States in Central America, 1977–1992* (Chapel Hill, NC, 1998), 30; John Soares, "Strategy, Ideology, and Human Rights: Jimmy Carter Confronts the Left in Central America, 1979–1981," *Journal of Cold War Studies* 8 (2006): 63–71.

95. Managua a SRE, 30 de octubre de 1981, Topográfica III-3490–1, Archivo de Concentraciones; Ryan, *Fall and Rise,* 46.

96. "CIA Talking Points—Nicaragua," February 21, 1980, NLC-24–37–6–8–1, JCL.

97. Charles Krause, "Sandinistas Indicate They Will Keep Power," *Washington Post,* August 1, 1979; Memorandum for Brzezinski, December 16, 1979, NLC-1–13–6–7–3, JCL.

98. Memorandum of Conversation with Raúl Castro, September 1, 1979, CWIHP; Stephen Gorman, "Power and Consolidation in the Nicaraguan Revolution," *Journal of Latin American Studies* 13 (1981): 138–139; Jaime Wheelock Román, "Revolution and Democratic Transition in Nicaragua," in Jorge Domínguez and Marc Lindenberg, eds., *Democratic Transitions in Central America* (Gainesville, FL, 1997), 73–75.

99. "Informe interno de la Revolución Administrativa," 17 de noviembre de 1979, JGRN 0064, IHNCA.

100. Gorman, "Power and Consolidation," 133.

7. Maelstrom

1. Westad, *Global Cold War,* 347.

2. William H. Durham, *Scarcity and Survival in Central America: Ecological Origins of the Soccer War* (Stanford, 1979), 21–51; John Booth, "Socioeconomic and Political Roots of National Revolts in Central America," *Latin American Research Review* 26 (1991): 40, 46–47; Tommie Sue Montgomery, *Revolution in El Salvador: Origins and Evolution* (Boulder, CO, 1982), 94–95; James Dunkerley, *Power in the Isthmus: A Political History of Modern Central America* (New York, 1988).

3. Arias Foundation for Peace and Human Progress, *Demobilization, Reintegration and Pacification in El Salvador* (San José, 1997), 11; LACRO, "El Salvador: An Inquiry into Urban Poverty," November 5, 1980, Report 2945-ES, WBA; LACRO, "El Salvador: Demographic Issues and Prospects," undated (1975–76), El Salvador–PM Files, WBA.

4. PGT, "Algunos rasgos del momento actual y nuestras tareas inmediatas," 30 de marzo de 1977, Box 1, PGT Papers, Tulane; Bulmer-Thomas, *Political Economy of Central America since 1920,* 219.

5. Shelton Davis, "Sowing the Seeds of Violence," in Robert Carmack, ed., *Harvest of Violence: The Maya Indians and the Guatemala Crisis* (Norman,

OK, 1988), 21; "Guatemalan Indians Form First Political Party," *Times of the Americas,* July 20, 1977.

6. CUC Flyer, "Los Trabajadores Debemos Luchar por Establecer un Gobierno Revolucionario, Popular, y Democrático," 1 de mayo de 1980, Folder "Derechos Humanos," Paquete 2, 1980, MREGUAT.

7. Romero to Carter, February 17, 1980, Box 20, Country File, NSA, JCL; "U.S. Catholic Leader Deplores Killing of Archbishop Romero," March 25, 1980, attached to Stephen Aiello to David Aaron et al., March 25, 1980, Box 177, Office of the Staff Secretary File, JCL. On Romero, see Marie Dennis, Renny Golden, and Scott Wright, *Óscar Romero: Reflections on His Life and Writings* (Maryknoll, NY, 2000).

8. Robert Armstrong and Janet Shenk, *El Salvador: The Face of Revolution* (Boston, 1982), 86–87; May, "'Surviving All Changes Is Your Destiny,'" 74–75; Ralph Lee Woodward, *Central America: A Nation Divided* (New York, 1999), 262.

9. Aguilera Peralta and Beverly, "Terror and Violence as Weapons of Counterinsurgency," 106.

10. Guatemala City to Ottawa, July 31, 1970, Vol. 8954, 20-GMA-1–4, LAC.

11. Inter-American Commission on Human Rights, *Report on the Situation of Human Rights in El Salvador,* November 17, 1978 (Washington, DC, 1978), 51, OEA/Ser.L/V/II.46, OAS; Anna Lisa Peterson, *Martyrdom and the Politics of Religion: Progressive Catholicism in El Salvador's Civil War* (Albany, NY, 1997), 63; Sikkink, *Mixed Signals,* 140.

12. Robert Carmack, "The Story of Santa Cruz Quiché," in Carmack, ed., *Harvest of Violence,* 53.

13. T. David Mason and Dale Krane, "The Political Economy of Death Squads: Toward a Theory of the Impact of State-Sanctioned Terror," *International Studies Quarterly* 33 (1989): 177–180; Cynthia McClintock, *Revolutionary Movements in Latin America: El Salvador's FMLN and Peru's Shining Path* (Washington, DC, 1998), 251–260; Daniel Adler and Thomas Long, "El Salvador: Tales of the Struggle," *NACLA Report on the Americas* 26 (1992): 25–31, esp. 26; Booth, "Socioeconomic and Political Roots," 55–57.

14. Fontaine to Allen, May 19, 1981, RAC Box 8, Fontaine Files, Ronald Reagan Library (RRL); Jack Donnelly, *International Human Rights* (Boulder, CO, 1998), 92; McClintock, *Revolutionary Movements in Latin America,* 251–259.

15. Midlarsky and Roberts, "Class, State, and Revolution in Central America." A dissent from this conclusion is McClintock, *Revolutionary Movements in Latin America.*

16. "Entrevista con el Capitán Rodolfo Muños Piloña," 17 de abril de 1986, Colección Documentos, CIRMA; Arias Foundation, *Demobilization, Reintegration and Pacification in El Salvador,* 67.

17. EGP, "Guerra Popular," No. 3, noviembre de 1975, Colección Documentos, CIRMA; William Bolinger, "'Learn from Others, Think for Ourselves': Central American Revolutionary Strategy in the 1980s," *Review of African Political Economy* 32 (1985): 56–63; José Ángel Moroni Bracamonte and David Spencer, *Strategy and Tactics of the Salvadoran FMLN Guerrillas: Last Battle of the Cold War, Blueprint for Future Conflicts* (London, 1995), 15.

18. "Entrevista con Silvia Solórzano Foppa del EGP," 1981, Colección Luis Pedro Taracena, CIRMA; EGP, "Materiales de Formación Política: Nivel I," julio de 1979, 18, Colección Payeras-Colom, CIRMA.

19. Norma Vazquéz, "Motherhood and Sexuality in Times of War: The Case of Women Militants of the FMLN in El Salvador," *Reproductive Health Matters* 5 (1997): 139–146; "Guatemala: Women in the Revolution," *Latin American Perspectives* 10 (1983): 106.

20. "Entrevista con el Sacerdote Rutilio Sánchez," marzo de 1988, in "Radio Farabundo Martí" transcript, Box 3, El Salvador Collection, Hoover Institution; EGP, "Materiales de Formación Política: Nivel I" julio de 1979, Colección Payeras-Colom, CIRMA; also FAR, "Guerrillero No. 1," mayo de 1973, Colección Luís Pedro Taracena, CIRMA.

21. Michael Richards, "Cosmopolitan World View and Counterinsurgency in Guatemala," *Anthropological Quarterly* 58 (1985): 93; Richard Wilson, *Maya Resurgence in Guatemala: Q'Eqchi' Experiences* (Norman, OK, 1999), 208–209; John Booth and Thomas Walker, *Understanding Central America* (Boulder, CO, 1993), 111; Jeffrey Ryan, "The Impact of Democratization on Revolutionary Movements," *Comparative Politics* 27 (1994): 38; Joaquin Villalobos, "Popular Insurrection: Desire or Reality?" *Latin American Perspectives* 16 (1989): 5–37.

22. The various estimates come from Daniel Premo, "Political Assassination in Guatemala: A Case of Institutionalized Terror," *Journal of Interamerican Studies and World Affairs* 23 (1981): 438; U.S. Senate, Committee on Foreign Affairs, *El Salvador at the Crossroads: Peace or Another Decade of War?* (Washington, DC, 1990), 43; Wickham-Crowley, *Guerrillas and Revolution*, 289–291; R. L. Leiken, "The Salvadoran Left," in Leiken, ed., *Central America: Anatomy of Conflict* (Elmsford, NY, 1984), 118; Benjamin C. Schwarz, *American Counterinsurgency Doctrine and El Salvador: The Frustrations of Reform and the Illusions of Nation Building* (Santa Monica, CA, 1991), 78.

23. Grandin, *Last Colonial Massacre*, 151–154.

24. "Comunicado Interno," junio de 1978, Box 1, PGT Papers, Tulane; June Carolyn Erlick, *Disappeared: A Journalist Silenced* (New York, 2004), 221–222.

25. Carlos Figueroa Ibarra and John F. Uggen, "Shipwreck and Survival: The Left in Central America," *Latin American Perspectives* 24 (1997): 117; EGP, "El Ejército Guerrillero de Los Pobres, EGP, Golpea a Los Enemigos del

Pueblo, de Sus Luchas y de la Revolución," abril de 1980, Colección Luís Pedro Taracena, CIRMA; "Paros estudiantes contra la represión," *7 días en la USAC,* 10 de septiembre de 1978; "Comunicado Interno," 21 de agosto de 1978, Box 1, PGT Papers, Tulane.

26. "Proclama Unitaria de las Organizaciones Revolucionarias EGP, FAR, ORPA y PGT al Pueblo de Guatemala," undated, Colección Documentos, CIRMA; David Stoll, *Rigoberta Menchú and the Story of All Poor Guatemalans* (Boulder, CO, 2000), 101–102.

27. EGP, "El Ejército Guerrillero de Los Pobres, EGP, Golpea a Los Enemigos del Pueblo, de Sus Luchas y de la Revolución," abril de 1980, Colección Luís Pedro Taracena, CIRMA.

28. Marginal notation in "Lineamientos estratégicos y tácticos para la región central en la fase actual," mayo de 1982, Box 1, PGT Papers, Tulane; EGP Comunicado, 18 de febrero de 1982, Colección Documentos, CIRMA. On U.S.–Guatemalan ties, see "Datos para el Mensaje Presidencial Política Exterior," 6 de abril de 1981, Paquete 2, 1979, MREGUAT; Memorandum of Conversation between Rafael Castillo Valdéz, Vance, and Brzezinski, undated (May 1979), ibid.

29. "Summary of the President's Meeting with the Special Presidential Mission to El Salvador," December 11, 1980, Box 33, Subject File, ZBDM, JCL.

30. SCC Meeting, February 15, 1980, Box 32, Subject File, ZBDM, JCL.

31. "One Shot from 50 Feet Killed El Salvador Prelate," *Atlanta Journal-Constitution,* March 26, 1980.

32. "Incertidumbre y Temor Tras El Asesinato del Arzobispo," *El Imparcial,* 25 de marzo de 1980; Stephen Aiello to David Aaron et al., March 25, 1980, Box 177, Office of the Staff Secretary File, JCL.

33. Thomas P. Anderson, *Politics in Central America* (New York, 1988), 100; Brenda Uekert, *Rivers of Blood: A Comparative Study of Government Massacres* (Westport, CT, 1995), 155–156; David Spencer, *From Vietnam to El Salvador: The Saga of the FMLN Sappers and Other Guerrilla Special Forces* (Westport, CT, 1996), 44, 73.

34. Brzezinski to the President, January 29, 1980, Box 32, Subject File, ZBDM, JCL.

35. "Record of Conference with . . . Comrade Fidel Castro Ruz," June 25, 1979, CWIHP.

36. Bishop to Castro, undated (early 1981), Box 3, Grenada Documents Collection, Special Collections, Georgetown University.

37. "Notas sobre la conversación sostenida entre el Secretario General y el Presidente Fidel Castro," 28 de mayo de 1985, Box 35, Javier Pérez de Cuellar Papers, Yale; Brzezinski to Carter, March 13, 1979, NLC-1-10-1–5-3, JCL. See also "Stenografische Niederschrift der offiziellen Gespräche des Generalsekretärs des Zentralkomitees der Sozialistischen Einheitspartei Deutschlands und Vorsitzenden des Staatsrates der Deutschen De-

mokratischen Republik, Genossen Erick Honekcer, mit dem Ersten Sekretaär des Zentralkomitees der Kommunistischen Partei Kubas, dem Vorsitzenden des Staatsrates und des Ministerrates der Republik Kuba, Fidel Castro Ruz," 28 Mai 1980, DY 30/2462, SAPMO.

38. Constantine Menges, *The Twilight Struggle: The Soviet Union v. The United States Today* (Washington, DC, 1990), 29; Garthoff, *Détente and Confrontation: American–Soviet Relations from Nixon to Reagan* (Washington, DC, 1994), 750–751.

39. "Meeting between Chiefs of General Staff of Soviet Armed Forces and People's Revolutionary Armed Forces of Grenada," March 10, 1983, Box 90931, Crisis Management Center, NSC Files, RRL; Record of Meeting between Bishop and Gromyko, April 15, 1983, Box 3, Grenada Documents Collection, Georgetown; Pavlov Interview, www.gwu.edu/~nsarchiv/coldwar/interviews/episode-18/pavlov3.html, accessed January 15, 2008; Raymond Duncan, "Soviet Interests in Latin America: New Opportunities and Old Constraints," *Journal of Interamerican Studies and World Affairs* 26 (1984): 167.

40. Richard H. Schultz, *Soviet Union and Revolutionary Warfare: Principles, Practices, and Regional Comparisons* (Stanford, 1988), 161; Ilya Prizel, *Latin America through Soviet Eyes: The Evolution of Soviet Perceptions during the Brezhnev Era, 1964–1982* (Cambridge, UK, 1990), 34.

41. For instance, LeoGrande, *Our Own Backyard;* Paterson et al., *A History of American Foreign Relations,* 444.

42. "Algunos aspectos del trabajo entre las masas," 1971, JGRN 0029, IHNCA; "Discurso de Cmdte. de la Rev. Víctor Tirado López," 11 de marzo de 1983, JGRN 0093, IHNCA; "Declaraciones de un miembro de la Dirección Nacional del FSLN al periodista Vegard Bye," 24 de febrero de 1979, JGRN 0056, IHNCA.

43. Ortega Interview, www.cnn.com/SPECIALS/cold.war/episodes/18/interviews/ortega/ (accessed 1/8/08); Comunicado del FSLN Proletario a "El Pueblo de Nicaragua," enero de 1979, JGRN 0022, IHNCA.

44. Gary Prevost, "Cuba and Nicaragua: A Special Relationship?" *Latin American Perspectives* 17 (1990): 125–130; Mary Desjeans and Peter Clement, "Soviet Policy toward Central America," *Proceedings of the Academy of Political Sciences* 36 (1987): 226–227; Theodore Schwab and Harold Sims, "Relations with the Communist States," in Thomas Walker, ed., *Nicaragua: The First Five Years* (New York, 1985), 448.

45. Protocol #213/39, May 29, 1980, CWIHP; CPSU CC Decree, May 1980, ibid.

46. Pavlov Interview; Edmé Domínguez Reyes, "Soviet Relations with Central America, the Caribbean, and Members of the Contadora Group," *Annals of the American Academy of Political and Social Science* 481 (1985): 148–151; Westad, *Global Cold War,* 369–371; Prizel, *Latin America through Soviet*

Eyes, 34–37; Desjeans and Clement, "Soviet Policy toward Central America," 225.

47. Elihu Lauterpacht and C. J. Greenwood, *International Law Reports* 76 (1988): 750, 828; also Discurso del Comandante Jaime Wheelock, 28 de enero de 1981, JGRN 0084, IHNCA; Kagan, *A Twilight Struggle*, 160–162.

48. "El Salvador Pictured as Apex of Revolutionary Struggle in Latin America," *Soviet World Outlook*, February 15, 1981, in Box 26, Jack Matlock Files, RRL; Managua to State, February 19, 1983, Box 32, NSC Executive Secretariat File, RRL.

49. Schultz, *Soviet Union and Revolutionary Warfare*, 169–185; Richard Allen to NSPG, March 24, 1981, Box 91305, NSC Executive Secretariat File, RRL; "El Salvador: International Support for the Insurgency," February 5, 1981, Box 29, ibid.; Allen to Reagan, February 6, 1981, Box 32, ibid.; Prizel, *Latin America through Soviet Eyes*, 37, 147; Kagan, *A Twilight Struggle*, 160–162; CIA Report, "El Salvador: Military Prospects," January 2, 1981, Box 24, Subject Files, ZBDM, JCL; "Cuba Directs Salvador Insurgency, Former Salvadoran Guerrilla Says," *New York Times*, July 28, 1983.

50. "Niederschrift über ein Gespräch des Genossen Erich Honecker, Generalsekretär des ZK der SED und Vorsitzender des Staatsrates der DDR, mit Genossen Daniel Ortega, Koordinator der Regierungsjunta der Nationalen Erneuerung Nikaraguas, am 14.2.1984 in Moskau," DY 30/2473, SAPMO.

51. Douglas Brinkely, ed., *The Reagan Diaries* (New York, 2007), 24; "Address before a Joint Session of the Congress on Central America," April 27, 1983, APP.

52. "Address to the Nation on United States Policy in Central America," May 9, 1984, APP; NSDD 32, "U.S. National Security Strategy," May 20, 1982, Box 1, NSDD Files, NSC Executive Secretariat Files, RRL.

53. "Address before a Joint Session of the Congress on Central America," April 27, 1983, APP; "Radio Address to the Nation on Central America," March 24, 1984, ibid.; also Lars Schoultz, *National Security and United States Policy toward Latin America* (Princeton, 1987), 310.

54. Kiron Skinner and Annelise Graebner Anderson, *Reagan, in His Own Hand: The Writings of Ronald Reagan that Reveal His Revolutionary Vision for America* (New York, 2001), 479.

55. Reagan, "Address before a Joint Session of the Congress on Central America," April 27, 1983, APP.

56. "Remarks of Nestor D. Sanchez," December 11, 1981, Box 5, Latin America Subject Collection, Hoover Institution.

57. "Remarks at the Annual Convention of the Congressional Medal of Honor Society," December 12, 1983, APP; William LeoGrande, "A Splendid Little War: Drawing the Line in El Salvador," *International Security* 6 (1981): 27.

58. LeoGrande, *Our Own Backyard*, xii; Cheryl Rubenberg, "Israeli Foreign Policy in Central America," *Third World Quarterly* 8 (1986): 896–915.

59. Interview with Bud McFarlane, March 20, 1986, Box 48, Hedrick Smith Papers, LOC; Richard Reeves, *President Reagan: The Triumph of Imagination* (New York, 2005), 30.

60. Even fervent anticommunists opposed Haig on this issue. Envoy Vernon Walters dismissed the idea of "military adventures" in Central America. See "Reunión con General Vernon Walters, Enviado Especial del Presidente de los Estados Unidos de América," 26 de febrero de 1981, Oficios Secretos Recibidos, EmbaChile EEUU, MRECHILE.

61. Richard Allen to Reagan, April 16, 1981, Box 29, NSC Executive Secretariat Files, RRL.

62. Comptroller General, "U.S. Military Aid to El Salvador and Honduras," August 22, 1985, 2–20, Box 2, North Files, RRL.

63. Armony, *Argentina, the United States, and the Anti-Communist Crusade*, 77–89, 120–130.

64. Brinkley, ed., *Reagan Diaries*, 52. The *contras* preferred to be called *comandos* or "the resistance."

65. Quoted in Managua to State, September 3, 1981; see also Managua to State, February 17, 1981; Managua to State, August 13, 1981; and Managua to State, April 27, 1982, Box 32, NSC Executive Secretariat File, RRL.

66. Reagan, "Address before a Joint Session"; Bob Woodward, *Veil: The Secret Wars of the CIA* (New York, 1987), 281.

67. LeoGrande, *Our Own Backyard*, 69; SCC Minutes, January 12, 1981, Box 33, Subject Files, ZBDM, JCL.

68. Comptroller General, "U.S. Military Aid to El Salvador and Honduras," 1–3.

69. Quoted in Pamphlet produced by the Committee in Solidarity with the People of El Salvador, undated, Folder 1, CISPES Political Ephemera, Tulane; see also Schwarz, *American Counterinsurgency Doctrine and El Salvador*, 19–20, 36–40; San Salvador to State, June 24, 1981, Box 29, NSC Executive Secretariat Files, RRL; Knut Walter and Philip Williams, "The Military and Democratization in El Salvador," *Journal of Interamerican Studies and World Affairs* 35 (1993): 63; Mark Danner, *The Massacre at El Mozote: A Parable of the Cold War* (New York, 2005).

70. LeoGrande, *Our Own Backyard*, 127–128.

71. Bremer to Clark, February 5, 1983, Box 29a, NSC Executive Secretariat Files, RRL; CIA, "El Salvador: Controlling Rightwing Terrorism," February 1985, Box 132, North Files, RRL.

72. Thomas Carothers, *In the Name of Democracy: U.S. Policy toward Latin America in the Reagan Years* (Berkeley, CA, 1991), 23.

73. San Salvador to State, April 13, 1982, Box 29, NSC Executive Secretariat Files, RRL; Margarita Flores, "El Salvador: trayectoria de la

reforma agraria, 1980–1998," *Revista Mexicana de Sociología* 60 (1998): 136–137.

74. William Schneider, "Public Still Rejects Reagan's 'Vital Interest' Argument on El Salvador," *National Journal*, May 21, 1983, 1082–1083; San Salvador to State, December 7, 1982, Box 29, NSC Executive Secretariat Files, RRL; Christian Smith, *Resisting Reagan: The U.S. Central America Peace Movement* (Chicago, 1996), 93.

75. Westad, *Global Cold War*, 345.

76. "Niederschrift über ein Gespräch des Genossen Erich Honecker, Generalsekretär des ZK der SED und Vorsitzender des Staatsrates der DDR, mit Genossen Daniel Ortega, Koordinator der Regierungsjunta der Nationalen Erneuerung Nikaraguas, am 14.2.1984 in Moskau," DY 30/2473, SAPMO.

77. "Notas sobre la conversación sostenida entre el Secretario General y el Presidente Fidel Castro," 28 de mayo de 1985, Box 35, Pérez de Cuellar Papers, Yale; "Information Provided by Salvadoran Insurgent Commander Alejandro Montenegro," undated, late 1982, Box 32, NSC Executive Secretariat File, RRL; Moroni Bracamonte and Spencer, *Strategy and Tactics of the Salvadoran FMLN Guerrillas*, 128–132, 136; Robert Pastor, "The Bush Administration and Latin America: The Pragmatic Style and the Regionalist Option," *Journal of Interamerican Studies and World Affairs* 33 (1991): 4; Desjeans and Clement, "Soviet Policy toward Central America," 230–231.

78. "Declaraciones de Roger Miranda," 15 de diciembre de 1987, Box 7, Nicaragua Subject Collection, Hoover Institution; CIA Assessment, "El Salvador: Performance on Certification Issues," July 1983, Box 102, North Files, RRL.

79. Anderson, *Politics in Central America*, 107; Booth and Walker, *Understanding Central America*, 156.

80. San Salvador to State, December 7, 1982, Box 29, NSC Executive Secretariat Files, RRL; LeoGrande, *Our Own Backyard*, 179.

81. CIA Assessment, "El Salvador: Performance on Certification Issues," July 1983, Box 102, North Files, RRL; Brockett, *Land, Power, and Poverty*, 141; Flores, "El Salvador," 139; Mitchell Seligson, "Thirty Years of Transformation in the Agrarian Structure of El Salvador, 1961–1991," *Latin American Research Review* 30 (1995): 65.

82. Schwarz, *American Counterinsurgency Doctrine and El Salvador*, 7, 51–52.

83. Quoted in CIA, "El Salvador: Performance on Certification Issues," July 1983, Box 102, North Files, RRL; also State Department, "Report on the Situation in El Salvador," July 12, 1984, ibid.; Richard Stahler-Sholk, "El Salvador's Negotiated Transition: From Low-Intensity Conflict to Low-Intensity Democracy," *Journal of Interamerican Studies and World Affairs* 36 (1994): 2–6; Montgomery, *Revolution in El Salvador*, 186.

84. Midlarsky and Roberts, "Class, State and Revolution in Central America."

85. CIA, "El Salvador—Pressure on the Left," May 31, 1984, Box 29a, NSC Executive Secretariat Files, RRL; Wickham-Crowley, *Guerrillas and Revolution*, 282; Michael Foley, "Laying the Groundwork: The Struggle for Civil Society in El Salvador," *Journal of Interamerican Studies and World Affairs* 38 (1996): 71.

86. San Salvador to State, July 9, 1986, Box 1, North Files, RRL.

87. Shultz to Reagan, undated, Box 91284, NSC Executive Secretariat Files, RRL; LACRO, "El Salvador: Country Economic Memorandum," April 15, 1986, Report 5939-ES, WBA.

88. Phillip Berryman, *The Religious Roots of Rebellion: Christians in Central American Revolutions* (Maryknoll, NY, 1984), 81; Brockett, *Land, Power, and Poverty*, 141.

89. Brockett, *Land, Power, and Poverty*, 141; Moroni Bracamonte and Spencer, *Strategy and Tactics of the Salvadoran FMLN Guerillas*, 185; Wickham-Crowley, "The Rise (and Sometimes Fall) of Guerrilla Governments," 493.

90. Jeff Goodwin, *No Other Way Out: States and Revolutionary Movements, 1945–1991* (New York, 2001), 205; McClintock, *Revolutionary Movements in Latin America*, 73–74.

91. Montgomery, *Revolution in El Salvador*, 199; Moroni Bracamonte and Spencer, *Strategy and Tactics of the Salvadoran FMLN Guerrillas*, 136, 180; Mario Lungo Uclés, *El Salvador in the Eighties: Counterinsurgency and Revolution* (Philadelphia, 1996), 177.

92. EGP, "Los factores internos: El Golpe de Estado del 23 de marzo," undated, Colección Payeras-Colom, CIRMA.

93. Guatemala to State, July 1, 1982, Box 91368, NSC Executive Secretariat Files, RRL; "Guatemalan Vows to Aid Democracy," *New York Times*, December 6, 1982.

94. McClintock, *American Connection*, 230; Beatriz Manz and Aryeh Neier, *Paradise in Ashes: A Guatemalan Journey of Courage, Terror, and Hope* (Berkeley, CA, 2004), 118.

95. "Entrevista con el Capitán Rodolfo Muños Piloña," 17 de abril de 1986, Colección Documentos, CIRMA; Susanne Jonas, *Of Centaurs and Doves: Guatemala's Peace Process* (Boulder, CO, 2000), 24.

96. Richards, "Cosmopolitan World View and Counterinsurgency," 101.

97. Carmack, "The Story of Santa Cruz Quiché," 57; Davis, "Sowing the Seeds of Violence," 24; Susanne Jonas, *The Battle for Guatemala: Rebels, Death Squads, and U.S. Power* (Boulder, CO, 1991), 155.

98. "Características de las acciones militares al iniciarse la insurrección," undated, Box 1, PGT Papers, Tulane; "El movimiento revolucionario es la

primera línea de lucha contra la intervención: Entrevista con el Comandante Rolando Morán," *Compañero,* No. 7, noviembre de 1983, 8.

99. "Informe Balance del Comité Sesional," noviembre de 1983, Box 1, PGT Papers, Tulane; EGP, "Circular de la Comisión Ejecutiva de la DN a todos los miembros del EGP sobre el trabajo unitario," marzo de 1983, Colección Payeras-Colóm, CIRMA; URNG, "Comunicado internacional urgente," 4 de mayo de 1982, Colección Luís Pedro Taracena, ibid.

100. Piero Gleijeses, "Grappling with Guatemala's Horror," *Latin American Research Review* 32 (1997): 231.

101. Jonas, *Battle for Guatemala,* 152; INR, "Guatemala's Guerillas Retreating in the Face of Government Pressure," March 3, 1983, Box 62, North Files, RRL.

102. Davis, "Sowing the Seeds of Violence," 28. On the economic effects of the PACs, see Smith, "Militarization of Civil Society in Guatemala," 12–13.

103. EGP Comunicado, 18 de febrero de 1982, Colección Documentos, CIRMA; EGP Parte de Guerra, abril de 1982, Colección Luís Pedro Taracena, CIRMA.

104. Berryman, *Religious Roots of Rebellion,* 115–120; Defense Intelligence Agency, "Guerrilla Division of Labor," August 23, 1984, Box 90509, Latin American Affairs Directorate Files, RRL.

105. Guatemala a SRE, 29 de octubre de 1979, Exp. 9, Leg. 127, Embamex Guatemala, AHGE; Manz and Neier, *Paradise in Ashes,* 112–113.

106. Davis, "Sowing the Seeds of Violence," 26.

107. Ibid.; Manz and Neier, *Paradise in Ashes,* 113–116; EGP Comunicado, 16 de abril de 1980, Colección Documentos, CIRMA; FAR, "Síntesis del accionar de las FAR: 1981," undated, Colección Luís Pedro Taracena, CIRMA.

108. See David Stoll, *Between Two Armies in the Ixil Towns of Guatemala* (New York, 1993); Yvon Le Bot, *La guerra en tierras mayas: Comunidad, violencia y modernidad en Guatemala (1970–1992)* (Mexico City, 1995). See also Stoll, *Rigoberta Menchú and the Story of all Poor Guatemalas,* and the responses in the November 1999 issue of *Latin American Perspectives.*

109. David Stoll, "Evangelicals, Guerrillas, and the Army: The Ixil Triangle under Ríos Montt," in Carmack, ed., *Harvest of Violence,* 105.

110. INR, "Guatemala's Guerrillas Retreating in the Face of Government Pressure," March 3, 1983, Box 62, North Files, RRL; "Discurso del Ministro de Defensa Héctor Alejandro Gramajo Morales," 30 de junio de 1987, Colección Documentos, CIRMA.

111. "Participant Cites Objective of 23 Mar. 82 Coup," FBIS Transcript, March 22, 1982, Colección Documentos, CIRMA; Jennifer Schirmer, "The Guatemalan Politico-Military Project: Whose Ship of State?" in Kees Koonings and Dirk Kruijt, eds., *Political Armies: The Military and Nation*

Building in the Age of Democracy (London, 2002), 64–67; Jonas, *Of Centaurs and Doves,* 26.

112. Jonas, *Battle for Guatemala,* 146–163.

113. PGT, "Algunos Elementos Sobre la Situación Nacional," junio de 1987, Box 1, PGT Papers, Tulane; also "Carta de los cuadros, militantes y combatientes que rompen con la DN del EGP, a la DN y a los compañeros de esa organización. . ," 12 de febrero de 1984, Colección Luís Pedro Taracena, CIRMA.

114. Jonas, *Of Centaurs and Doves,* 30–37.

115. Thomas Walker, *Reagan versus the Sandinistas: The Undeclared War on Nicaragua* (Boulder, CO, 1987).

116. "Information und Schlussfolgerungen über den Freundschaftsbesuch einer Delegation des Zentralrats der Freien Deutschen Jugend unter Leitung von Egon Krenz in Nikaragua und Mexico in der Zeit vom 7. bis 17. Oktober 1981," DY 24/11.215, SAPMO; Vanden and Prevost, *Democracy and Socialism in Sandinista Nicaragua,* 50–52; Dennis Gilbert, *Sandinistas* (New York, 1991), 31–33.

117. Managua to State, February 19, 1983, Box 32, NSC Executive Secretariat File, RRL; Inter-American Commission on Human Rights, *Report on the Situation of Human Rights in the Republic of Nicaragua, June 30, 1981* (Washington, DC, 1981), 135; Janusz Bugajski, *Sandinista Communism and Rural Nicaragua* (New York, 1990), 18.

118. Anderson, *Politics in Central America,* 196; Westad, *Global Cold War,* 347.

119. Miranda and Ratliff, *Inside the Sandinistas,* 235.

120. Enríquez, *Harvesting Change,* 88; Tegucigalpa to State, March 2, 1982, Box 90501, Jacqueline Tillman Files, RRL; CIA, "Nicaragua: Repression of the Miskito Indians," March 1982, ibid.; Philip Dennis, "The Costeños and the Revolution in Nicaragua," *Journal of Interamerican Studies and World Affairs* 23 (1981): 290.

121. Brooklyn Rivera, "The Indian Conflict and Negotiations with Nicaragua," March 25, 1985, Box 7, Nicaragua Subject Collection, Hoover Institution.

122. Timothy Charles Brown, *The Real Contra War: Highland Peasant Resistance in Nicaragua* (Norman, OK, 2001), 6; Lynn Horton, *Peasants in Arms: War and Peace in the Mountains of Nicaragua* (Athens, OH, 1998); Michael Radu, "The Origins and Evolution of the Nicaraguan Insurgencies, 1979–1985," *Orbis* 29 (1986): 89; Miranda and Ratliff, *Inside the Sandinistas,* 235.

123. Miranda and Ratliff, *Inside the Sandinistas,* 237.

124. Managua to State, November 20, 1981, Box 90501, Jacqueline Tillman Files, RRL.

125. Álvaro Taboada, "Carta de Renuncia a Toda Ulterior Colaboración con el Gobierno Sandinista," 22 de noviembre de 1982, Folder 8, CISPES Political Ephemera, Tulane.

126. Armony, *Argentina, the United States, and the Anti-Communist Crusade,* 141.

127. Undated notes of telephone conversations with Edgardo Chamorro, Box 148, Hedrick Smith Papers, LOC.

128. Ronald Reagan, "Address to the Nation on United States Policy in Central America," May 9, 1984, APP; Undated notes of telephone conversations with Edgardo Chamorro, Box 148, Hedrick Smith Papers, LOC; Robert Pastor, *Exiting the Whirlpool: U.S. Foreign Policy toward Latin America and the Caribbean* (Boulder, CO, 2001), 73.

129. Richard Sobel, "Contra Aid Fundamentals: Exploring the Intricacies and the Issues," *Political Science Quarterly* 110 (1995): 289, 303. This relative stinginess also encouraged the *contras* to become active in the drug trade, a practice generally ignored by Reagan.

130. Stockholm to State, January 18, 1984, Box 36, Matlock Files, RRL; Desjeans and Clement, "Soviet Policy toward Central America," 225; Miranda and Ratliff, *Inside the Sandinistas,* 242; Schulz and Schulz, *United States, Honduras, and the Crisis in Central America,* 173; LeoGrande, *Our Own Backyard,* 440. On Cuban pilots, see "Memorandum para información superior," 10 de diciembre de 1985, Topográfica III-3966–1, Archivo de Concentraciones.

131. Department of State Telegram, July 20, 1983, NSC Executive Secretariat File, RRL; James Baker, *The Politics of Diplomacy: Revolution, War, and Peace, 1989–1992* (New York, 1995), 48; Author's interview with Cresencio Arcos, June 13, 2007.

132. "Minutes of Executive Board Meeting," March 5, 1984, EBM 84/36, IMF; William LeoGrande, "Making the Economy Scream: U.S. Economic Sanctions against Sandinista Nicaragua," *Third World Quarterly* 17 (1996): 329–348; Pastorino, "Outline of Strategy for Peace and Democracy in Central America," undated, Box 92348, Pastorino Files, RRL.

133. Ortega to Honecker, 3 Juli 1986, DY 30/2473, SAPMO; Vanden and Prevost, *Democracy and Socialism in Sandinista Nicaragua,* 140; "Minutes of Executive Board Meeting 86/83," May 16, 1986, EBM 86/83, IMF. See also Erin Canin, "'Work, a Roof, and Bread for the Poor': Managua's Christian Base Communities in the Nicaraguan 'Revolution from Below,'" *Latin American Perspectives* 24 (1997): 82; Roger Lancaster, *Life Is Hard: Machismo, Danger, and the Intimacy of Power in Nicaragua* (Berkeley, CA, 1994).

134. Richard Stahler-Sholk, "Sandinista Economic and Social Policy: The Mixed Blessings of Hindsight," *Latin American Research Review* 30 (1995): 240; Carlos Vilas, "La contribución de la política económica y la negociación internacional a la caída del gobierno Sandinista," *Revista Mexicana de Sociología* 52 (1990): 332–335.

135. Department of State Cable, "Comandante Ruiz on Economic Situation," undated, Box 148, Hedrick Smith Papers, LC; Author's interview with Víctor Tirado, August 31, 2007.

136. Ortega to Honecker, April 2, 1985, DY 30/2473, SAPMO.

137. Quoted in "Entrevista de Playboy" (Spanish translation of an interview printed in *Playboy* magazine in September 1983), JGRN, IHNCA; and Wheelock, "Revolution and Democratic Transition in Nicaragua," 83. See also DeFronzo, *Revolutions and Revolutionary Movements,* 259–261.

138. Ministerio de Educacion, "Parte de Guerra," 23 de agosto de 1980, CNA 0028, IHNCA; Fernando Cardenal a Lenin Cerna, 26 de mayo de 1980, CNA 0004, IHNCA; Author's Interview with Bosco Matamoros, June 14, 2007.

139. "Meeting with NDR Directorate," undated, Box 1, Handwriting File, Presidential Meetings File, RRL.

140. Quoted in "Protócolo 1740: Sesión Extraordinario No. 47," undated (1987), Box 4, Robert Claxton Collection on Allende's Chile, Tulane; Radu, "Origins and Evolution of the Nicaraguan Insurgencies," 91–96; Mayra Gómez, *Human Rights in Cuba, El Salvador, and Nicaragua: A Sociological Perspective on Human Rights Abuses* (New York, 2003), 170; Michael J. Waller, "Tropical Chekists: The Sandinista Secret Policy Legacy in Nicaragua," *Demokratizatsiya* 12 (2004): 427–449.

141. Miranda and Ratliff, *Inside the Sandinistas,* 243; Horton, *Peasants in Arms,* 261.

142. "Vermerk über das Gespräch des Genossen Erich Honecker, General-sekretär des ZK der SED und Vorsitzender des Staatsrates der DDR, mit Genossen Bayardo Arce, Stellvertretender Koordinator der Executivkom-mission der Nationalleitung der FSLN Nikaraguas, am 4. Maerz 1988 im Hause des Zentralkomitees," SAPMO.

143. Quoted in Baker, *Politics of Diplomacy,* 47. On these issues, see "Nota sobre la reunión de Álvaro de Soto con el Presidente de Honduras, Sr. Rafael Leonardo Callejes," 28 de enero de 1990, Box 36, Pérez de Cuellar Papers, Yale; William LeoGrande, "From Reagan to Bush: The Transition in U.S. Policy towards Central America," *Journal of Latin American Studies* 22 (1990): 608–609.

144. Quoted in Odom to the Secretary of the Army, May 11, 1984, Box 14, William Odom Papers, LOC; Peter Shearman, "Gorbachev and the Restructuring of Soviet–Cuban Relations," in Richard Gillespie, ed., *Cuba after Thirty Years: Rectification and the Revolution* (New York, 1989), 71; Margot Light, "Soviet Policy in the Third World," *International Affairs* 67 (1991): 266–270.

145. FBIS Special Memorandum, "Gorbachev: Selected Statements on Inter-national Affairs," May 30, 1985, Box 26, Matlock Files, RRL; Westad, *Global Cold War,* 370; also Celeste Wallander, "Third World Conflict in Soviet Military Thought: Does the 'New Thinking' Grow Prematurely Grey?" *World Politics* 42 (1989): 31–63.

146. Gorbachev to Reagan, April 2, 1986, Box 214, Donald Regan Papers, LOC.

147. Quoted in Note to the File, December 14, 1989, Box 36, Pérez de Cuellar Papers, Yale; also "Vermerk über das Gespräch des Genossen Erich Honecker, Generalsekretaär des ZK der SED und Vorsitzender des Staatsrates der DDR, mit Genossen Jorge Risquet, Mitglied des Politbüros und Sekretär des ZK der KP Kubas, am 17.4.1989," DY 30/2462, SAPMO.

148. Jan S. Adams, *A Foreign Policy in Transition: Moscow's Retreat from Central America and the Caribbean, 1985–1992* (Durham, NC, 1992), 77; "Protócolo 1740: Sesión Extraordinario No. 47," undated (1987), Box 4, Robert Claxton Collection on Allende's Chile, Tulane.

149. Janette Habel and Jon Barnes, *Cuba: The Revolution in Peril* (London, 1991), 126–128; Habana a SRE, 8 de mayo de 1985, Topográfica III-3963–1, Archivo de Concentraciones.

150. "Niederschrift von dem Gespräch des Genossen Erich Honecker, Generalsekretär des ZK der SED und Vorsitzender des Staatsrates der DDR, mit Genossen Fidel Castro, Erster Sekretär des ZK der KP Kubas und Vorsitzender des Staatsund Ministerrates der Republik Kuba, am 3.3.1986," DY 30/2462, SAPMO.

151. Francesc Vendrell, "Note for the Secretary-General," August 28, 1989, Box 35, Pérez de Cuellar Papers, Yale; see also Havana to Berlin, July 27, 1987, DY 30/2462, SAPMO.

152. Adams, *A Foreign Policy in Transition*, 85–90; Habel and Barnes, *Cuba*, 128.

153. Ortega quoted in "Vermerk über ein Gespräch des Stellvertreters des Vorsitzenden des Staatsrates der DDR und Vorsitzenden der National-Demokratischen Partei Deutschlands, Prof. Dr. Heinrich Homann, mit dem Koordinator des Regierungsrates der Nationalen Erneurung der Republik Nikaragua, Cmdte. Daniel Ortega, am 11.12.1983," DY 30/2473, SAPMO. On the peace process, see Bruce Michael Bagley, "Contadora: The Failure of Diplomacy," *Journal of Interamerican Studies and World Affairs* 28 (1986): 1–32; Jack Child, *The Central American Peace Process, 1983–1991: Sheathing Swords, Building Confidence* (Boulder, CO, 1992).

154. LeoGrande, "From Reagan to Bush," 608–611; Guido Fernández, *El Desafío de la Paz en Centroamérica* (San José, 1989), 139–141; Laura O'Shaughnessy and Michael Dodson, "Political Bargaining and Democratic Transitions: A Comparison of Nicaragua and El Salvador," *Journal of Latin American Studies* 31 (1999): 102.

155. Gaddis Smith, *The Last Years of the Monroe Doctrine* (New York, 1994), 207–208; "Memorandum de Conversación," 23 de abril de 1985, Topográfica III-3962–1, Archivo de Concentraciones; "Protócolo 1740: Sesión

Extraordinario No. 47," undated (1987), Box 4, Robert Claxton Collection on Allende's Chile, Tulane.

156. Smith, *Last Years of the Monroe Doctrine,* 207–208; Richard Stone to Powell, undated, Box 92476, Powell Files, RRL.

157. Note for the File, October 26, 1989, Box 32, Pérez de Cuellar Papers, Yale.

158. "Protócolo 1740: Sesión Extraordinario No. 47," undated (1987), Box 4, Robert Claxton Collection on Allende's Chile, Tulane. See also "Vermerk über das Gespräch des Genossen Erich Honecker, Generalsekretär des ZK der SED und Vorsitzender des Staatsrates der DDR, mit Genossen Bayardo Arce, Stellvertretender Koordinator der Executivkommission der National-leitung der FSLN Nikaraguas, am 4 Maerz 1988 im Hause des Zentr-alkomitees," SAPMO.

159. David Close, *Nicaragua: The Chamorro Years* (Boulder, CO, 1999), 40–44.

160. Carothers, *In the Name of Democracy,* x; Author's interview with Arcos.

161. Stahler-Sholk, "El Salvador's Negotiated Transition."

162. John Lewis Gaddis, *The Cold War: A New History* (New York, 2005), chapter 7.

8. The End of History?

1. "Question-and-Answer Session with Reporters on the President's Trip to Latin America," December 4, 1982, APP.

2. The best discussion of democratization is Peter Smith, *Democracy in Latin America: Political Change in Comparative Perspective* (New York, 2005). For a comparative study, see Samuel Huntington, *The Third Wave: Demo-cratization in the Late Twentieth Century* (Norman, OK, 1993).

3. Castañeda, *Utopia Unarmed,* 3.

4. "Fiscal Policy and Economic Reconstruction in Latin America," November 2, 1989, WP/89/94, IMF.

5. Schydlowsky and Wicht, *Anatomía de un fracaso económico,* 97–106; "Finan-cial Situation and Prospects of Peru," November 27, 1975, Box 10, Country Files, Central Files, IMF; "Peru: Relations with the Fund," July 29, 1976, ibid.

6. SNI, Apreciação Sumario No. 08/74, 15 de julho de 1974, EG pr 1974.03.00/1, FGV.

7. *World Bank Development Report, 1985* (Washington, DC, 1986), 63; "Mission to Venezuela," June 27, 1979, Box 183, WHDAI Country Files, Western Hemisphere Department, IMF; *World Bank Development Report, 1981* (Washington, DC, 1982), 52.

8. Howard Handelman and Werner Baer, "The Economic and Political Costs of Austerity," in Handelman and Baer, eds., *Paying the Costs of Austerity in Latin America* (Boulder, CO, 1989), 2.

9. *World Bank Development Report, 1981,* 3; LACRO, "Country Economic Memorandum: Brazil," August 22, 1982, Report 4674-BR, WBA.

10. *World Bank Development Report, 1983* (Washington, DC, 1984), 2; Riordan Roett, "The Debt Crisis and Economic Development," in Michael LaRosa and Frank Mora, eds., *Neighborly Adversaries: Readings in U.S.-Latin American Relations* (New York, 2006), 206–209.

11. Indeed, "neoliberals" deny that there is anything "neo" about them, and often prefer to be known as "liberals." I use these terms interchangeably. This terminology should not be confused with the way the terms "liberal" and "conservative" are often used to describe political affiliation, as many "neoliberals" were political conservatives.

12. A good critique of ISI is Bulmer-Thomas, *Economic History of Latin America since Independence,* chapters 9–10.

13. Quoted in Winn, "The Pinochet Era," 26–27; also Glen Biglaiser, "The Internationalization of Chicago's Economics in Latin America," *Economic Development and Cultural Change* 50 (2002): 269, 276–279; Juan Gabriel Valdés, *Pinochet's Economists: The Chicago School in Chile* (New York, 1995); Pollack, *New Right in Chile,* 39–42.

14. Robinson, *Transnational Conflicts*; Blanca Heredia, "Mexican Business and the State: The Political Economy of a Muddled Transition," in Ernest Bartell and Leigh Payne, eds., *Business and Democracy in Latin America* (Pittsburgh, 1995), 189–192; Rosario Espinal, "The Right and the New Right in Latin America," in Jonathan Hartlyn, Lars Schoultz, and Augusto Varas, eds., *The United States and Latin America in the 1990s: Beyond the Cold War* (Chapel Hill, NC, 1993), 92–96; James Dunkerley, *Political Suicide in Latin America and Other Essays* (London, 1992), 207–208.

15. Kurtz, "Chile's Neo-Liberal Revolution," 405–409; Constable and Valenzuela, *Nation of Enemies,* 171–173.

16. NSC Meeting, November 18, 1986, Box 91304, Meetings File, NSC Executive Secretariat File, RRL.

17. Arceneaux, "Institutional Design, Military Rule, and Regime Transition," 340–341.

18. LACRO, "Country Economic Memorandum: Brazil," August 22, 1982, Report 4674-BR, WBA; Skidmore, *Politics of Military Rule in Brazil,* 201; John Markoff and Silvio R. Duncan Baretta, "Brazil's Abertura: A Transition from What to What?" in James Malloy and Mitchell Seligson, eds., *Authoritarians and Democrats: Regime Transition in Latin America* (Pittsburgh, 1987), 46–47.

19. Quoted in Norman Bailey to Roger Robinson, August 18, 1983, Box 42, Subject File, NSC Executive Secretariat File, RRL; also Regan Statement to Senate Committee on Banking, Housing, and Urban Affairs, February 14, 1982, Box 152, Regan Papers, LOC; *World Bank Development Report,*

1981, 111–112; Treasury Department Briefing Book, February 14, 1983, Box 152, Regan Papers, LOC.

20. "The Chairman's Remarks at the Conclusion of the Discussion on Adjustment Programs," February 8, 1980, Box 47, WHDAI Economic Subject File, Western Hemisphere Department, IMF.

21. "Statement at the First Plenary Session of the International Meeting on Cooperation and Development in Cancun, Mexico," October 22, 1981, APP.

22. "Address to a Joint Session of Parliament in Ottawa, Canada," April 6, 1987, APP; "Address to the 42nd Session of the United Nations General Assembly," September 21, 1987, APP; Barbara Stallings, *Global Change, Regional Response: The New International Context of Development* (New York, 1995), 182–183.

23. William Clark Oral History, October 5, 1983, Oral Histories, WBA.

24. Draft of an Address to a Joint Meeting of the World Bank and the International Monetary Fund, September 24, 1987, OA 18965, Robert Schmidt Files, RRL; see also Cabinet Council on Economic Affairs, Minutes, September 23, 1981, OA9946, Meese Files, RRL.

25. On the links between the Reagan administration and the international banks, see Caiola to Sanson, January 19, 1981, Box 52, WHDAI Economic Files, Western Hemisphere Department, IMF; "Meeting with Representatives of the Reagan Transition Team," December 17, 1980, Box 2, President's Council Minutes, Fonds 03–04, WBA.

26. "President's Council Meeting," February 4, 1980, Box 2, President's Council Minutes, Fonds 03–04, WBA; "Clausen's Debut," *Time,* July 13, 1981; Kendall Stiles, *Negotiating Debt: The IMF Lending Process* (Boulder, CO, 1991), 117; Helen Hughes, *Achieving Industrialization in East Asia* (New York, 1988), 106.

27. James Boughton, "From Suez to Tequila: The IMF as Crisis Manager," *Economic Journal* 110 (2000): 285–286; Ernest Oliveri, *Latin American Debt and the Politics of International Finance* (Westport, CT, 1992), chapter 4; Tom Barry and Deb Preusch, *The Soft War: The Uses and Abuses of U.S. Economic Aid in Central America* (New York, 1988), 186–189.

28. "Fiscal Policy and Economic Reconstruction in Latin America," November 2, 1989, WP/89/94, IMF; *World Bank Development Report, 1990* (Washington, DC, 1991), 218–223.

29. SRE a Bogotá, 22 de mayo de 1984, Exp. 7, Leg. 1, Embamex Colombia, AHGE; Jesús Silva-Herzog, "Why the Baker Plan Isn't Enough," *Institutional Investor,* March 1986, 25; Riordan Roett, "The Debt Crisis and Economic Development in Latin America," in Schoultz, Hartlyn, and Varas, eds., *The United States and Latin America in the 1990s,* 139–140.

30. "Declaración de Quito: Plan de Acción," 13 de enero de 1984, Vol. 59: III, Archivo Alfonso García Robles, AHGE.

31. Norman Bailey to Roger Robinson, August 18, 1983, Box 42, Subject File, NSC Executive Secretariat File, RRL; "Niederschrift über ein Gespräch des Generalsekretärs des ZK der SED und Vorsitzenden des Staatsrates der DDR, Genossen Erich Honecker, mit dem 2. Sekretär des ZK der KP Kubas, 1. Stellvertreter des Staats- und Ministerrates und Minister der Revolutionären Streitkräfte Kubas, Genossen Raul Castro Ruz, em 8. April 1985 in Hause des ZK," DY 30/2462, SAPMO.

32. Belgrade a SRE, 17 de marzo de 1980, Topográfica III-6274-I, Archivo de Concentraciones; see also "Documentos sobre la reunión del Buro de Coordinación de Países No Alineados," 15 de mayo de 1986, Vol. 64A: II, Archivo Alfonso García Robles, AHGE.

33. Silva-Herzog, "Why the Baker Plan Isn't Enough," 25; also Needler, *Mexican Politics*, 93.

34. *World Bank Development Report, 1985*, iii; also Minutes of Executive Board Meeting, June 6, 1984, EBM/84/87, IMF.

35. "Mexico—Discussion with President-Elect," December 2, 1976, Box 6, Country Files, Central Files, IMF; see also "The Chairman's Summing Up," Executive Board Meeting, November 28, 1983, Box 10, Country Files, Central Files, IMF; James Boughton, *Silent Revolution: The International Monetary Fund, 1979–1989* (Washington, DC, 2001), 331–332.

36. William Chislett, "IMF Monetarism Raises Mexican Passions," *Financial Times*, September 24, 1982; Sepúlveda a Bogotá, 27 de mayo de 1984, Exp. 7, Leg. 1, Embamex Colombia, AHGE.

37. "The Chairman's Summing Up," Executive Board Meeting, November 28, 1983, Box 10, Country Files, Central Files, IMF; S. T. Beza to the Managing Director, May 16 and July 28, 1983, Box 183, WHDAI Country Files, Western Hemisphere Department, IMF; Kenneth Roberts, "Economic Crisis and the Demise of the Legal Left in Peru," *Comparative Politics* 29 (1996): 78; Duncan Green, "Latin America: Neoliberal Failure and the Search for Alternatives," *Third World Quarterly* 17 (1996): 112–113.

38. *World Bank Development Report, 1990*, 160; "Fiscal Policy and Economic Reconstruction in Latin America," November 2, 1989, WP/89/94, IMF; Green, "Neoliberal Failure," 113; "Mexico—Restructuring of External Debt," September 10, 1984, EBS/84/194, IMF.

39. "Fiscal Policy and Economic Reconstruction in Latin America," November 2, 1989, WP/89/94, IMF; Victor Bulmer-Thomas, "Globalization and the New Economic Model in Latin America," in Victor Bulmer-Thomas, John Coatsworth, and Roberto Cortés Conde, eds., *The Cambridge Economic History of Latin America* (New York, 2006), 145–146.

40. Robinson, *Transnational Conflicts*, 97.

41. El Poder Ejecutivo Nacional, Decreto 2284, 31 de octubre de 1991, "Antecedentes, Legislación, Privatizaciones," AGNARG; Deborah Norden and Roberto Russell, *The United States and Argentina: Changing Relations in a Changing World* (New York, 2002), 71; Ravi Ravamurti, "The Impact of Privatization on the Latin American Debt Problem," *Journal of Interamerican Studies and World Affairs* 34 (1992): 97–98; Pablo Gerchunoff and Juan Carlos Torre, "La política de liberalización económica en la administración de Menem," *Desarrollo económico* 36 (1996): 735–738.

42. Address to the World Economic Forum, February 1, 1990, RDA-7–1, AHGE; Manuel Pastor and Carol Wise, "State Policy, Distribution and Neoliberal Reform in Mexico," *Journal of Latin American Studies* 29 (1997): 419–456, esp. 421–434.

43. "Remarks by Secretary Brady Before the Bretton Woods Committee," July 12, 1991, EBD/91/215, IMF.

44. Thomas Skidmore and Peter Smith, *Modern Latin America* (New York, 2001), 60–61, 135; "The Restoration of Latin America's Access to Voluntary Capital Market Financing—Developments and Prospects," August 1991, WP/91/74, IMF; Forrest Colburn, *Latin America at the End of Politics* (Princeton, 2002), 36.

45. See Gary Springer and Jorge Molina, "The Mexican Financial Crisis: Genesis, Impact, and Implications," *Journal of Interamerican Studies and World Affairs* 37 (1995): 57–81.

46. LACRO, "Poverty in Latin America: The Impact of Depression," August 6, 1986, Report 6369, WBA.

47. Ibid.; *World Bank Development Report, 1990,* 36; Dirección Federal de Seguridad, "Panorama General del Estado de Michoacán," 11 de julio de 1984, Caja 465, SDN, AGNMEX.

48. *World Bank Development Report, 1990,* iii; also Robert Devlin, *Debt and Crisis in Latin America: The Supply Side of the Equation* (Princeton, 1989), 23.

49. Quoted in Eugene Black Oral History, August 6, 1961, 40, WBA; E. Patrick Coady Oral History, April 19, 1993, 15–16, WBA; Author's interview with Cresencio Arcos, June 14, 2007. See also "President's Council Meeting," February 4, 1980, Box 2, President's Council Minutes, Fonds 03–04, WBA.

50. Michel Chossudovsky, "Under the Tutelage of IMF: The Case of Peru," *Economic and Political Weekly* 27 (1992): 340–346; *World Bank Development Report, 1990,* 103; Philip Oxhorn, "Is the Century of Corporatism Over? Neoliberalism and the Rise of Neopluralism," in Oxhorn and Graciela Ducatenzeiler, eds., *What Kind of Democracy? What Kind of Market? Latin America in the Age of Neoliberalism* (University Park, PA, 1998), 199–211; also Tironi, *Los silencios de la revolución,* 92.

51. "Message for Dr. K, from Minister Leitaõ de Abreu," October 3, 1983, Box 104, Regan Papers, LOC; Mercedes González de la Rocha, "Economic Crisis, Domestic Reorganization and Women's Work in Guadalajara, Mexico," *Bulletin of Latin American Research* 7 (1988): 207–223.

52. Colburn, *Latin America at the End of Politics,* 120–121; Juan Gabriel Tokatlian, "Colombia en guerra: Las diplomacias por la paz," *Desarrollo Económico* 39 (1999): 339–344.

53. Steve Ellner, *Venezuelan Politics in the Chávez Era: Class, Polarization, and Conflict* (Boulder, CO, 2004), 31; Dan La Botz, *Democracy in Mexico: Peasant Rebellion and Political Reform* (Boston, 1996), 25; Steve Stern, ed., *Shining and Other Paths: War and Society in Peru, 1980–1995* (Durham, NC, 1998); Nikolas Kozloff, *Hugo Chavez: Oil, Politics, and the Challenge to the U.S.* (New York, 2007), 171.

54. Gillespie, "Uruguay's Return to Democracy," 100; Michael Wallerstein, "The Collapse of Democracy in Brazil: Its Economic Determinants," *Latin American Research Review* 15 (1980): 5; LACRO, "Economic Position and Prospects of Brazil," June 20, 1974, Report 355a-BR, WBA; LACRO, "Country Economic Memorandum: Brazil," August 22, 1982, Report 4674-BR, ibid.; Colburn, *Latin America at the End of Politics,* 36.

55. Skidmore, *Politics of Military Rule in Brazil,* 201; Carlos Acuña, "Business Interests, Dictatorship, and Democracy in Argentina," in Ernest Bartell and Leigh Payne, eds., *Business and Democracy in Latin America* (Pittsburgh, 1995), 106–108; Eva Bellin, "Contingent Democrats: Industrialists, Labor, and Democratization in Late-Developing Countries," *World Politics* 52 (2000): 193–195.

56. Huntington, *Third Wave,* 67; Scott Mainwaring, "The Transition to Democracy in Brazil," *Journal of Interamerican Studies and World Affairs* 28 (1996): 152.

57. Ata da Quinquagésima Terceira Sessão do Conselho de Segurança Nacional, 23 de junho de 1978, EG pr 1975.05.02, FGV; Duncan Baretta and Markoff, "Brazil's Abertura," 43–55; also Aspasia Camargo and Walder de Góes, *Meio Século de Combate: Diálogo com Cordeiro de Farias* (Rio de Janeiro, 1981).

58. Ata da Quinquagésima Segunda Sessão do Conselho de Segurança Nacional, 1 de abril de 1977, EG pr 1975.05.02, FGV.

59. Helio Contreras, *Militares Confissões: Histórias Secretas do Brasil* (Rio de Janeiro, 1998), 101.

60. "Trecho do discurso feito aos dirigentes da ARENA, no Palácio da Alvorada em 29 de agosto de 1974," EG pr 1978.00.00, FGV; "Trecho do discurso na primeira reunião ministerial em Brasilia, a 19 de março de 1974," EG pr 1978.00.00, FGV; see also "Trecho do discurso na convenção da ARENA, em Brasília, a 15 de setembro de 1973," ibid.

61. Marshak, ed., *God's Assassins,* 72.

62. Mark Ensalaco, *Chile under Pinochet: Recovering the Truth* (Philadelphia, 1999), 135–136; CIA, "Prospects for Chile," September 2, 1983, Box 28, Country File, NSC Executive Secretariat File, RRL.

63. INR, "Chile: Political Revival and Party Realignment," May 24, 1983, Box 62, North Files, RRL; Silva, "Collective Memories, Fears and Consensus," 181; Cathy Lise Schneider, *Shantytown Protest in Pinochet's Chile* (Philadelphia, 1995), 13–14.

64. The literature on the Falklands War is immense. As a start, see Daniel Gibran, *The Falklands War: Britain versus the Past in the South Atlantic* (New York, 1998).

65. S. T. Beza, "Peru—Visit of Peruvian Delegation," August 4, 1977, Box 10, Country Files, Central Files, IMF; Robichek to the Managing Director, July 27, 1978, ibid.; Koenig to Acting Managing Director, August 14, 1979, ibid.; Roberts, "Economic Crisis and the Demise of the Legal Left in Peru," 73.

66. "Extracto de la información," 9 de agosto y 4 de noviembre de 1976, Caja 1536A, Dirección General, IPS, AGNMEX; "Décimo Sexto Congreso de la Federación CCI," 3 de julio de 1977, Caja 1583A, ibid.; Joe Foweraker, *Popular Mobilization in Mexico: The Teachers' Movement, 1977–1987* (New York, 1993), 36–39.

67. "Activistas del CLESE se presentaron en el CCH Vallejo, solicitando ayuda económica y apoyo en su movimiento," 10 de febrero de 1978, Caja 1571B, Dirección General, IPS, AGNMEX; also "Todos los Mexicanos Demebos Luchar Contra la Liberación de Precios: PC," *El Día*, 13 de febrero de 1978.

68. Quoted in S-2 Inteligencia, "Panorama General," Caja 113, 9 de enero de 1984, Caja 113, SDN, AGNMEX; also Preston and Dillon, *Opening Mexico*, 136; Dirección Federal de Seguridad, "Panorama General del Estado de Michoacán," 11 de julio de 1984, Caja 465, SDN, AGNMEX; "Para informar a la superioridad," 13 de enero de 1984, ibid.

69. "Posición del Partido Revolucionario Institucional Frente a la Reforma Política," 3 de agosto de 1977, Caja 1583A, Dirección General, IPS, AGNMEX; also "Palabras Pronunciadas por el Lic. Carlos Sansores Pérez, Presidente del CEN del PRI, en el Consejo Nacional Celebrado en el Auditorio 'Plutarco Elías Calles,'" 25 de noviembre de 1977, ibid.; Luis Rubio and Roberto Blum, "Recent Scholarship on the Mexican Political and Economic System," *Latin American Research Review* 25 (1990): 182.

70. "Mexico: Ruling Party Escalates Campaign against the Right," undated (1984), Box 90509, Latin American Affairs Directorate Files, NSC Files, RRL.

71. Mexico City to State, July 18, 1986, Box 91063, Latin American Affairs Directorate, NSC Files, RRL; INR Analysis, August 12, 1986, ibid.; Isabel

Rueda Peiro, *México: Crisis, reestructuración económica, social y política* (Mexico City, 1996), 77–81.

72. "Highlights: Secretary's Seminar on Mexico," October 15, 1988, Box 92350, Pastorino Files, RRL.

73. Albert Hirschman, "The Political Economy of Latin American Development: Seven Exercises in Retrospection," *Latin American Research Review* 22 (1987): 29; Karen Remmer, "Democracy and Economic Crisis: The Latin American Experience," *World Politics* 42 (1990): 318–321.

74. Leigh Payne, "Brazilian Business and the Democratic Transition," in Ernest Bartell and Leigh Payne, eds., *Business and Democracy in Latin America* (Pittsburgh, 1995), 231–232.

75. Quoted in Michael Coppedge, "Venezuelan Parties and the Representation of Elite Interests," in Kevin J. Middlebrook, *Conservative Parties, the Right, and Democracy in Latin America* (Baltimore, 2000), 110; Kurt Weyland, "Neoliberalism and Democracy in Latin America: A Mixed Record," *Latin American Politics and Society* 46 (2004): 141–144.

76. "Issues and Objectives for the President's Visit to Brazil, Colombia, and Costa Rica," November 1982, Box 91284, Meetings File, NSC Executive Secretariat File, RRL.

77. Townsend Friedman, "Memorandum for the Files," September 11, 1979, EBB 85, NSA.

78. George Weigel, "Catholicism and Democracy: The Other Twentieth-Century Revolution," in Brad Roberts, ed., *The New Democracies: Global Change and U.S. Policy* (Cambridge, MA, 1990), 33; also Payne, "Brazilian Business and the Democratic Transition," 231–232; Juan Linz and Alfred Stepan, "Political Crafting of Democratic Consolidation or Destruction: European and South American Comparisons," in Robert Pastor, ed., *Democracy in the Americas: Stopping the Pendulum* (New York, 1989), 47.

79. Directorate of Intelligence, "The Chilean Communist Party and Its Allies: Intentions, Capabilities, and Prospects," May 1986, Box 91703, Ludlow Flower Files, RRL.

80. Brysk, *Politics of Human Rights in Argentina,* 57–58; also MemCon between Kissinger and Guzzetti, October 7, 1976, EBB 104, NSA.

81. Schlaudeman to Kissinger, August 3, 1976, EBB 125, NSA.

82. Townsend Friedman, "Memorandum for the Files," September 11, 1979, EBB 85, NSA; also Buenos Aires to State, March 21, 1984, EBB 73, NSA.

83. Townsend Friedman, "Memorandum for the Files," August 18, 1980, EBB 73, NSA.

84. MemCon with "Jorge Contreras," August 7, 1979, EBB 73, NSA. On the persistence of human rights violations, see CELS, "Informe sobre la situación de los Derechos Humanos en Argentina," octubre de 1979–octubre de 1980, Archivo, CELS; idem, "Informe sobre la

situación de los Derechos Humanos en Argentina," noviembre de
1980–febrero de 1982, ibid.

85. SNI, "Apreciação Semanal No. 01/10/AC/79," 6 de janeiro de 1979, EG pr
1974.03.00/1, FGV; SNI, "Aspectos conjuturais da atualidade," agosto de
1977, ibid.

86. Centro de Informações do Exército, "Relatório periódico de informações
No. 08/77," agosto de 1977, EG pr 1974.03.25/3, FGV; see also SNI,
"Anexo No. 2 ao estudo sobre o problema da subversão no Brasil: Súmula da
atuação do movimento comunista internacional no âmbito mundial e
continental," undated, EG pr 1974.03.00/1, FGV.

87. Jose Resende-Santos, "The Origins of Security Cooperation in the Southern
Cone," *Latin American Politics and Society* 44 (2002): 107–108.

88. Brysk, *Human Rights,* 59–60; Cynthia Bejarano, "Las Super Madres de
Latino América: Transforming Motherhood by Challenging Violence in
Mexico, Argentina, and El Salvador," *Frontiers: A Journal of Women Studies*
23 (2002): 132–136.

89. Kenneth Serbin, "The Anatomy of a Death: Repression, Human Rights,
and the Case of Alexandre Vannucchi Leme in Authoritarian Brazil,"
Journal of Latin American Studies 30 (1998): 18.

90. INR, "Chile: Political Revival and Party Realignment," May 24, 1983, Box
62, North Files, RRL; Paul Sondrol, "1984 Revisited? A Re-Examination
of Uruguay's Military Dictatorship," *Bulletin of Latin American Research* 11
(1992): 191–193; Kent Eaton, "Risky Business: Decentralization from Above
in Chile and Uruguay," *Comparative Politics* 37 (2004): 7; Philip Oxhorn,
"Where Did All the Protestors Go? Popular Mobilization and the Transition
to Democracy in Chile," *Latin American Perspectives* 21 (1994): 49–68.

91. Payne, "Brazilian Business and the Democratic Transition," 231–232; Peter
Smith, "Crisis and Democracy in Latin America," *World Politics* 43 (1991):
622.

92. Quoted in INR, "Chile: Political Revival and Party Realignment," May 24,
1983, Box 62, North Files, RRL.

93. Huntington, *Third Wave,* 86.

94. Dominique Fournier, "The Alfonsín Administration and the Promotion of
Democratic Values in the Southern Cone and the Andes," *Journal of Latin
American Studies* 31 (1999): 39–74.

95. Huntington, *Third Wave,* 96; Brzezinski to Carter, September 20, 1977,
NLC-1-3-7-13-6, JCL; Brysk, *Politics of Human Rights in Argentina,*
52–55.

96. "Address Before a Joint Session of the Congress on the State of the Union,"
February 6, 1985, APP.

97. MRE a Washington, 7 de septiembre de 1981, Oficios Secretos Enviados,
EmbaChile EEUU, MRECHILE; also "Visita a Chile de la Representante
Permanente de los Estados Unidos de América, Señora Embajador Jeanne

Kirkpatrick," agosto de 1981, ibid.; "Entrevista con el General Vernon Walters," 16 de noviembre de 1981, EmbaChile EEUU, ibid.

98. Carothers, *In the Name of Democracy*, 103–104, 129; James Malloy and Eduardo Gamarra, *Revolution and Reaction: Bolivia, 1964–1985* (New Brunswick, NJ, 1988), 176; Smith, *America's Mission*, 300–301.

99. "Meeting with NDR Directorate," undated (1987–88), Box 1, Handwriting File, Presidential Meetings, RRL.

100. Quoted in Hal Brands, *From Berlin to Baghdad: America's Search for Purpose in the Post–Cold War World* (Lexington, KY, 2008), 44; William Webster Oral History Interview, August 21, 2002, Miller Center, University of Virginia; Michael Conniff, *Panama and the United States: The Forced Alliance* (Athens, GA, 1992), 161.

101. Tillman to Poindexter, November 17, 1986, Box 91304, Meetings File, NSC Executive Secretariat File, RRL.

102. "Talking Points," undated (1982–83), Box 1, Handwriting File, Presidential Meetings, RRL; Abrams to the Acting Secretary, October 15, 1987, *DDRS*.

103. Smith, *America's Mission*, 292.

104. "Transcript of Speech at Westminster," June 8, 1982, OA 85, Subject File, Records of the Assistant to the President's Special Assistant, RRL. On Reagan's Wilsonianism, see Henry Kissinger, *Diplomacy* (New York, 1994), 772–773.

105. "U.S. Policy toward Chile," February 1985, Box 91713, Latin American Affairs Directorate, NSC Files, RRL.

106. Carothers, *In the Name of Democracy*, 54.

107. "Radio Address to the Nation on Central America," March 24, 1984, APP; "Talking Points," undated (1982–83), Box 1, Handwriting File, Presidential Meetings, RRL.

108. In private, Reagan did push the Guatemalan generals to hold elections and respect human rights. See Reagan to Mejía, October 30, 1985, Box 91176, Latin American Affairs Directorate Files, NSA Files, RRL.

109. Odom to Meyer, June 8, 1982, Box 13, Odom Papers, LC; also "Falklands Rountable," May 16, 2003, 26–41, Oral Histories, Miller Center.

110. Gabriel Marcella, "Latin American Military, Low Intensity Conflict, and Democracy," *Journal of Interamerican Studies and World Affairs* 32 (1990): 47–48; Malloy and Gamarra, *Revolution and Reaction*, 176; Huntington, *Third Wave*, 95.

111. Kirk Bowman, "Taming the Tiger: Militarization and Democracy in Latin America," *Journal of Peace Research* 33 (1996): 301; Thomas Leonard, "Central America, U.S. Policy, and the Crisis of the 1980s: Recent Interpretations," *Latin American Research Review* 31 (1996): 198.

112. MemCon between Bush and Cerezo, January 14, 1986, Box 91176, LA Affairs Directorate, NSC Files, RRL.

113. "Chile," undated (1973–74), Box 40, Series I, Pre-Presidential File, RRL.

114. Santiago to State, March 11, 1982, Box 28, Country File, NSC Executive Secretariat Files, RRL.

115. NSC Meeting, November 18, 1986, Box 91304, Meetings File, NSC Executive Secretariat File, RRL.

116. Ibid. For Pinochet's speech, see "Pinochet Visits Talcahuano, Concepción," July 10, 1986, Latin American Affairs Directorate, NSC Files, RRL.

117. Notes for Address to the Council on Foreign Relations, February 18, 1987, Box 1, Papers of Harry G. Barnes, LOC.

118. "Audiencia concedida por el Sr. Ministro al Subsecretario de Estado Adjunto Sr. Robert Gelbard," 20 de agosto de 1987, Oficios Secretos Enviados, EmbaChile EEUU, MRECHILE; State Department Cable, November 9, 1987, *DDRS;* State to Various Posts, February 25, 1988, *DDRS;* Jose Sorzano to Colin Powell, March 9, 1988, *DDRS;* "Summary Notes," May 27, 1988, Box 1, Papers of Harry Barnes, LOC; Paul Sigmund, *The United States and Democracy in Chile* (Baltimore, 1993), 169–174.

119. José Luis Simón, "Aislamiento político y desonconcertación: El Paraguay de Stroessner de espaldas a América Latina," *Revista Paraguaya de Sociología* 25 (1988): 185–243; Stroessner quoted in Frederick Nunn, "The South American Military and (Re) Democratization: Professional Thought and Self-Perception," *Journal of Interamerican Studies and World Affairs* 37 (1995): 15.

120. Andrew Nickson, "The Overthrow of the Stroessner Regime: Re-Establishing the Status Quo," *Bulletin of Latin American Research* 8 (1989): 198–205; Diego Abente, *Paraguay en Transición* (Caracas, 1993).

121. Mark Amstutz, *The Healing of Nations: The Promise and Limits of Political Forgiveness* (New York, 2004), 149.

122. Reid, *Forgotten Continent,* 159–160; Kozloff, *Hugo Chávez,* 106; Javier Corrales, "Latin America's Neocaudillismo: Ex-Presidents and Newcomers Running for President . . . and Winning," *Latin American Politics and Society* 50 (2008): 22–26.

123. Francis Fukuyama, "The End of History?" *National Interest* 16 (1989): 3–18.

124. Abe Lowenthal to Warren Christopher, August 7, 1992, Box 14, Anthony Lake Papers, LOC; "Remarks by Secretary Brady Before the Bretton Woods Committee," July 12, 1991, EBD/91/215, IMF.

Conclusion

1. Smith, "Crisis and Democracy in Latin America," 629.

2. For the best of this new literature, see Dinges, *Condor Years;* Jurgen Buchenau, *In the Shadow of the Giant: The Making of Mexico's Central America Policy, 1876–1930* (Tuscaloosa, AL, 1996); Vieira Souto, *A Diplomacia do*

Interesse Nacional; Romero, *Política exterior venezolana*; Harmer, "Rules of the Game"; as well as the examples discussed in Friedman, "Retiring the Puppets." See also Pastor, *Exiting the Whirlpool*.

3. Friedman, "Retiring the Puppets," 624; The "puppets" theme is reiterated explicitly in Lars Schoultz, *Beneath the United States: A History of U.S. Policy toward Latin America* (Cambridge, MA, 1998); also Víctor Grimaldi, *Golpe y revolución: El derrocamiento de Juan Bosch y la intervención norteamericana* (Santo Domingo, 2000); Luís Fernando Ayerbe, *Estados Unidos e América Latina: A construção da soberania* (São Paulo, 2001).

4. Armony, *Argentina, the United States, and the Anti-Communist Crusade*.

5. For an early explication of this dynamic, see Robert Pastor, "Explaining U.S. Policy toward the Caribbean Basin: Fixed and Emerging Images," *World Politics* 38 (1986): 483–515.

6. Tony Smith, "New Bottles for New Wine: A Pericentric Framework for the Study of the Cold War," *Diplomatic History* 24 (2000): 567–591; Hope Harrison, *Driving the Soviets up the Wall: Soviet–East German Relations, 1953–1961* (Princeton, 2003).

7. The animal metaphor comes from Kyle Longley, *The Sparrow and the Hawk: Costa Rica and the United States during the Rise of José Figueres* (Tuscaloosa, AL, 1997), 156.

8. Examples include Grandin, *Last Colonial Massacre*, xiv; Menjívar and Rodríguez, eds., *When States Kill*; Wright, *State Terrorism in Latin America*; Schoultz, *Beneath the United States*; McClintock, *American Connection*, vols. 1–2; Grandin, *Empire's Workshop*, 96–99; McClintock, *Instruments of Statecraft*; Huggins, *Political Policing*.

9. "Latin American state terror," write two analysts, is "a derivative of a U.S.-dominated regional system." Menjívar and Rodríguez, "State Terror in the U.S.-Latin American Interstate Regime," in Menjívar and Rodríguez, eds., *When States Kill*, 4.

10. The need for a comprehensive study of U.S. democracy promotion programs in Latin America, identified by Abraham Lowenthal nearly twenty years ago, remains unfilled. Lowenthal, "Preface and Acknowledgements," in Lowenthal, ed., *Exporting Democracy: The United States and Latin America* (Baltimore, 1991), vii.

11. Pedro Prokopchuk a Stroessner, 3 de marzo de 1961, DNAT-C-98, CDYA; Smith, *Talons of the Eagle*, 237; Rabe, *Most Dangeous Area in the World*, 59–60. Exceptions include Domínguez, *To Make a World Safe for Revolution*, as well as the sources cited in chapters 2 and 7.

12. Grandin, *Last Colonial Massacre*, xiv.

13. The exception being Peru, where the Shining Path insurgency may have claimed more lives than the government. The debate on body counts in Peru is covered in McClintock, *Revolutionary Movements in Latin America*, 311; Eric Selbin, "Resistance, Rebellion, and Revolution in Latin America and

the Caribbean at the Millenium," *Latin American Research Review* 36 (2001): 172–183.

14. Frei, "Alliance That Lost Its Way," 441–443.

15. Wickham-Crowley, *Guerrillas and Revolution in Latin America,* 316; James Petras, "Revolution and Guerrilla Movements in Latin America: Venezuela, Colombia, Guatemala and Peru," in Petras and Maurice Zeitlin, eds., *Latin America, Reform or Revolution: A Reader* (New York, 1968), 353, quoted in ibid.

16. As former Assistant Secretary of State William Rogers has sought to do. See William Rogers, "Fleeing the Chilean: Coup: The Debate over U.S. Complicity," *Foreign Affairs* 83 (2004): 160–165.

17. Richard Gott, *Rural Guerrillas in Latin America* (New York, 1973), 573.

18. The Guevarist legacy is strongly critiqued in Stoll, *Rigoberta Menchú and the Story of All Poor Guatemalans.*

19. Robinson, *Transnational Conflicts,* 72; idem, *A Faustian Bargain: U.S. Intervention in the Nicaraguan Elections and American Foreign Policy in the Post–Cold War Era* (Boulder, CO, 1992); also Lancaster, *Life Is Hard.* Other scholars have cited U.S. power as the primary factor in frustrating nationalist revolutions throughout the Third World. See Michael Hunt, *American Ascendancy: How the United States Gained and Wielded Global Dominance* (Chapel Hill, NC, 2007), 188–223, for a measured argument.

20. Author's interview with Víctor Tirado, August 31, 2007.

21. Castañeda, *Utopia Unarmed,* 243; James Petras with Todd Cavaluzzi, Morris Morley, and Steve Vieux, *The Left Strikes Back: Class Conflict in Latin America in the Age of Neoliberalism* (Boulder, CO, 1999), 45–46.

22. Peter Hakim, "Is Washington Losing Latin America?" *Foreign Affairs* 85 (2006): 39; Kim Holmes, *Liberty's Best Hope: American Leadership for the 21st Century* (Washington, DC, 2008), 56.

23. Gaddis, *Cold War,* ix.

24. Reagan, "Address to the Nation on United States Policy in Central America," May 9, 1984, APP; "Address before a Joint Session of the Congress on Central America," April 27, 1983, ibid.

25. Rich Lowry, "Smearing Negroponte," *National Review Online,* February 22, 2005, http://old.nationalreview.com/lowry/lowry200502220746.asp, accessed March 7, 2008. This viewpoint is summarized in Grandin, *Empire's Workshop,* 223–225.

26. Grandin, *Last Colonial Massacre,* xiv; Stern, "Between Tragedy and Promise," 55. Similar accounts include Nieto, *Masters of War;* Menjívar and Rodríguez, eds., *When States Kill;* McClintock, *American Connection,* vols. 1–2; as well as many others.

27. Grandin, *Last Colonial Massacre,* xiv.

28. Spenser, "Standing Conventional Cold War History on its Head," 394.

29. On moral relativism and the Cold War, see John Lewis Gaddis, "On Moral Equivalency and Cold War History," *Ethics and International*

Affairs 10 (1996): 131–148; Michael Hogan, "State of the Art: An Introduction," in Michael Hogan, ed., *America in the World: The Historiography of American Foreign Relations since 1941* (New York, 1995), esp. 4–9.

30. For perceptive critiques of Cold War triumphalism, see Richard Ned Lebow and Janice Gross Stein, *We All Lost the Cold War* (Princeton, 1994); David Schmitz, *Thank God They're on Our Side: The United States and Right-Wing Dictatorships, 1921–1965* (Chapel Hill, NC, 1999).

31. See Thomas Blanton, "Recovering the Memory of the Cold War: Forensic History and Latin America," in Joseph and Spenser, eds., *In from the Cold;* also "The Guatemalan Police Archives," EBB 170, NSA.

Archives and Other Sources

In researching this volume I consulted documents drawn from roughly forty archives in thirteen countries, materials held by the Cold War International History Project and the Kremlin Decision-Making Project, and various compendiums and databases of government records. A complete list of these collections is available below.

Discussing the particulars of these collections—and my reasons for visiting some archives and omitting others—would require a lengthy essay. What can be said briefly is that in conducting my archival research, I sought to assemble material on three broad subjects: Latin American governance and statecraft; social, political, and economic conditions in the region; and the role of foreign powers in Latin America. In each area the character and quality of the available records vary enormously. Nonetheless, in each case there is now a rich body of documentation.

With respect to the first category, it is now possible to examine a wide range of Latin American government records. Foreign ministry files are plentiful, especially in Mexico, Guatemala, Chile, Uruguay, Venezuela, and Colombia. Records of interior ministries, defense ministries, agricultural reform agencies, and other government offices are also available in several of these countries, though documents on some sensitive subjects—such as the Tlatelolco massacre—are conspicuous by their absence. Despite these lacunae, Latin America boasts several archives with excellent collections on internal security, intelligence, and repression. The best of these are located in Paraguay, Argentina, Nicaragua, and Guatemala; less complete collections can be found in Mexico, Colombia, Uruguay, and Brazil. Finally, a few collections of personal papers—such as those of Orlando Letelier in Chile, Rómulo Betancourt in Venezuela, and Ernesto Geisel in Brazil—shed considerable light on government policymaking.

Documentation regarding social, political, and economic conditions in Latin America is also plentiful. Privately funded archives in Nicaragua, Uruguay, Argentina, Guatemala, and other countries provide invaluable insight into both peaceful and violent political movements. Useful information on these subjects can also be found in the files of intelligence and security services in the countries listed above. Collections at the Hoover Institution and Tulane University, various U.S. government repositories, and the Canadian national archives contain detailed reporting on social movements and general conditions in Latin America. Finally, the best information on macroeconomic conditions (and, often, their microeconomic consequences) can be found at the World Bank and International Monetary Fund.

The role of foreign powers in Latin America is also heavily documented. Records in U.S. presidential libraries, the National Archives, the National Security Archive, and various private repositories provide excellent coverage of the American perspective. The OAS archive contains useful records on that body and institutions like the Inter-American Defense College. World Bank and IMF records shine considerable light on questions regarding finance and commerce.

Soviet and Cuban sources are somewhat harder to come by. The Cuban archives are still closed to most researchers, and because I do not speak or read Russian, I was unable to work in the archives of the former Soviet Union. Accordingly, I relied on documents obtained by the Cold War International History Project and the Kremlin Decision-Making Project, memoirs and open-source materials from these countries, and documents found in countries such as Allende's Chile, Ortega's Nicaragua, and the German Democratic Republic. The GDR archives are particularly valuable, and contain detailed records of conversations between East German officials and their counterparts in Cuba, the Soviet Union, and various Latin American countries. I also consulted U.S. and Latin American intelligence records on Soviet and Cuban activities in the region.

The list of archives I visited is by no means exhaustive. Due to logistical concerns and my own limitations, I skipped some countries entirely (though I tried to skip those countries where the archival pickings seemed slimmest).

Moreover, some very promising archives—such as a recently discovered police archive in Guatemala—are not yet open to researchers. Accordingly, my research should be viewed as an opening rather than a final attempt at an international history of Latin America's Cold War.

Argentina

Archivo de la Asamblea Permanente de Derechos Humanos (APDH)
Archivo de la ex-Dirección de Inteligencia de la Policía de Buenos Aires (DIPBA)
Archivo del Centro de Estudios Legales y Sociales (CELS)
Archivo General de la Nación (AGNARG)

Brazil

Centro de Pesquisa e Documentação de História Contemporânea do Brasil,
  Fundação Getulio Vargas (FGV)

Canada

Library and Archives Canada (LAC)

Chile

Archivo del Ministerio de Relaciones Exteriores de Chile (MRECHILE)
Archivo Nacional de la Administración (ANA)
Archivo Nacional de la Historia (ANH)

Colombia

Archivo General de la Nación (AGNCOL)

Germany

Stiftung Archiv der Parteien und Massenorgenisationen der DDR im Bundesarchiv
  (SAPMO)

Guatemala

Archivo Central del Ministerio de Relaciones Exteriores de Guatemala
  (MREGUAT)
Archivo General de Centroamérica (AGCA)
Centro de Investigaciones Regionales y Mesoamericanas (CIRMA)

Mexico

Archivo de Concentraciones, Ministerio de Relaciones Exteriores (Archivo de
    Concentraciones)
Archivo General de la Nación (AGNMEX)
Archivo Histórico Genaro Estrada, Ministerio de Relaciones Exteriores (AHGE)

Nicaragua

Archivo General de la Nación (AGNNIC)
Instituto de la Historia de Nicaragua y Centroamérica (IHNCA)

Paraguay

Centro de Documentación y Archivo, Corte Suprema de la Justicia (CDYA)

United States

Georgetown University Special Collections (Georgetown)
Gerald Ford Presidential Library (GFL)
Hoover Institution on War, Revolution, and Peace (Hoover)
International Monetary Fund Archives (IMF)
Jimmy Carter Presidential Library (JCL)
John F. Kennedy Presidential Library (JFKL)
Latin American Library, Tulane University (Tulane)
Library of Congress, Manuscripts Division (LOC)
Lyndon Baines Johnson Presidential Library (LBJL)
Miller Center for Public Affairs, University of Virginia
National Archives and Records Administration (NARA)
National Security Archive (NSA)
Nixon Presidential Materials Project (NPM)
Organization of American States Archives (OAS)
Ronald Reagan Presidential Library (RRL)
World Bank Archives (WBA)
Yale University, Manuscripts and Archives (Yale)

Uruguay

Archivo de la Impunidad, Servicio de Paz y Justicia Uruguay (SERPAJ)
Archivo de los Familiares de los Detenidos-Desaparecidos
Archivo del Ministerio de Relaciones Exteriores (MREURU)

Venezuela

Archivo Central del Ministerio de Relaciones Exteriores (MREVEN)
Archivo Rómulo Betancourt (ARB)

Databases, Collections of Published Documents, Microfilm

Akten zur Auswärtigen Politik der Bundesrepublik Deutschland
American Presidency Project, University of California at Santa Barbara (APP)
Castro Speech Database, University of Texas (CSD)
Chilean Government Pamphlets Microfilm Collection, Sterling Memorial Library, Yale University
Cold War International History Project Virtual Archive (CWIHP)
Cuban Foreign Policy, 1950–1962, Princeton University Library Microfilms
Declassified Documents Reference System (DDRS)
Foreign Relations of the United States (FRUS)
Kremlin Decision-Making Project, Miller Center for Public Affairs (KDMP)
NARA Archival Database
Peruvian Political Party Documents Microfilm Collection, Princeton University Library Microfilms
Politics in Chile, Princeton University Latin American Pamphlet Collection
The United States and Castro's Cuba, 1950–1970: The Paterson Collection, Yale University Microfilms

Acknowledgments

As with any book, there are too many people to thank individually. This goes for archivists especially. I could not have managed the research involved in producing this volume without the aid of archivists and librarians in dozens of repositories in the United States, Latin America, and Europe. Nor could this project have been completed without financial assistance from the Society for Historians of American Foreign Relations, the George Marshall Library and Foundation, the Macmillan Center at Yale University, and, above all, International Security Studies at Yale.

Scott Moyers and Andrew Wylie guided the manuscript that resulted to Harvard University Press, where Kathleen McDermott and her able staff took over. The editors of *Diplomatic History* granted me permission to adapt portions of my article "Third World Politics in an Age of Global Turmoil," which appeared in that journal in January 2008. Gil Joseph and Paul Kennedy at Yale offered incisive comments. Robert Pastor and Stephen Rabe were similarly generous with their insights. Finally, my foremost debt is to John Gaddis, a superb mentor and teacher.

Index